MODULA-2

MODULA-2

A SOFTWARE DEVELOPMENT
APPROACH

Gary Ford
Richard Wiener
University of Colorado at Colorado Springs

John Wiley & Sons
New York   Chichester   Brisbane   Toronto   Singapore

Library of Congress Cataloging in Publication Data:

Wiener, Richard, 1941–
    Modula-2: a software development approach.

    Includes index.
    1. Modula-2 (Computer program language)   2. Electronic
digital computers—Programming.   I. Ford, Gary.   II. Title.
III. Title: Modula-two.
QA76.73.M63F67   1985   001.64'24   84-21972
ISBN 0-471-87834-0

Printed in the United States of America

10 9 8 7 6 5 4 3

To our parents
Maxine and Walter
Mary and Irving

PREFACE

This is a book on advanced programming and software development using the important and new language Modula-2. The book is aimed at intermediate to advanced level undergraduate computer science students as well as practicing computer science and software development professionals. We assume that most readers have some programming experience in Pascal.

Modula-2, introduced by Niklaus Wirth in 1980, extends Pascal upward, away from the machine, and supports modern, object-oriented software engineering. Modula-2 also extends Pascal downward, toward the machine, with low level features similar to those in the C programming language. We explore both of these directions.

The two principal goals of this book are to present the entire Modula-2 language and to illustrate its use in the context of modern software development. By coupling the presentation of Modula-2 with the principles of modular software construction and object-oriented design, we believe that both the full benefits of this language and the process of software development may be better understood.

Abstraction plays a central role in problem solving and in software development. We focus on the use of abstract data types and information hiding in the software development process. We show how the frame of a software system can be specified, at the design stage, using Modula-2 as a program design language. The ability to separate the specification of an abstraction from its implementation is one of the key features of Modula-2 that supports a powerful approach to software development. We emphasize and illustrate this approach in many chapters.

The concept of process abstraction and methodologies for concurrent programming are becoming increasingly important in the science of programming and software development. Although Modula-2 does not fully support concurrent programming, it does support a set of powerful and important process abstractions based on coroutines. We discuss and illustrate the use of the process abstraction in software development.

In Part One (Chapters 1–10), we focus on the syntax of the Pascal-like features of Modula-2. Syntax charts provide a precise definition of the language. It will be seen that the simplicity inherent in Pascal is retained in Modula-2, while many fundamental deficiencies of Pascal are overcome.

In Part Two (Chapters 11–17), we introduce the high and low level advanced features of Modula-2 and demonstrate their use. Data abstraction and data structures are covered in detail, as is the object-oriented approach to software development.

We recommend that a programmer unfamiliar with Pascal read Part One carefully and in order. Most Pascal programmers may read the chapters in Part One in any order. Very experienced programmers may wish to scan Part One, focusing on Chapters 4, 7, 9, and 10, which present those features of Modula-2 which are most likely to be unfamiliar. Chapter 11 should be read carefully. The remaining chapters should be read in order.

We thank Carol Beasley, Computer Science Editor at Wiley, for her support at every stage of this project. Her suggestions and confidence in us have contributed greatly to making this book a reality. We also thank Brenda Griffing for her masterful job of copy editing.

We thank Joel McCormick and Winsor Brown from Volition Systems for their support and suggestions. We are also grateful to Volition Systems for outstanding Modula-2 software support. Many of the programs in this book were written and tested on a Sage IV using the Volition Systems compiler.

We thank Gary Thrower, from the Computer Center of the University of Colorado at Colorado Springs, for his continuing help in supporting our work with the University of Hamburg Modula-2 compiler for the VAX 11/780, which was used to develop many of the programs in this book.

We are grateful to Niklaus Wirth for providing the world with another outstanding language. For most people of lesser genius, the development of Pascal would be a lifetime's accomplishment, but not for Dr. Wirth.

CONTENTS

LIST OF PROGRAMS

PART ONE

Introduction to Modula-2

Because of the history of Modula-2, it is not surprising that much of the syntax of the language is very similar to Pascal. Part One presents the features of Modula-2 that are most like Pascal. An experienced Pascal programmer will find only a few new concepts, and these will be small steps beyond Pascal. For the reader not familiar with Pascal, Part One will serve as an introduction to Modula-2 syntax and semantics. Part Two presents the major new features of Modula-2 and demonstrates their usefulness in the development of software.

Since Modula-2 is a relatively new language, there does not exist a recognized standard describing it. Thus each implementation of the language defines what is and what is not Modula-2. The syntax in this book is based on Niklaus Wirth's original language definition. The language continues to evolve, and newer implementations are expected to differ somewhat from the original definition. Appendix 3 describes the current state of this evolution.

Throughout the book we use syntax charts to define formally the syntax of the language. All these charts are collected in Appendix 1 for easy reference. For readers new to syntax charts, we offer this brief guide. Each chart describes a single syntactic entity of the language, whose name appears in the upper left-hand corner of the chart. Such an entity may be constructed by following any path through the chart beginning at the arrow at the left and exiting at the right. Rectangular boxes represent other syntactic entities, each described in its own chart, and a path through such a box means a path through the corresponding chart. Boxes with rounded ends, including circular boxes, represent characters or words that must appear exactly as shown. For example, in this chart:

loop statement

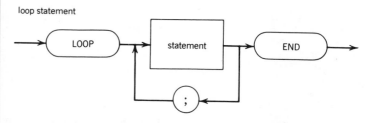

we find the name of the entity is "loop statement", and it consists of the word "LOOP", then a statement, then the word "END". The chart also provides an option; after a statement we may follow the arrow down to the semicolon box and back to the statement box again. Since the statement box is rectangular, it indicates another chart elsewhere. Anything defined by that other chart is acceptable here.

To simplify some of the charts, rounded boxes containing the words "letter", "digit", "octal digit", and "hex digit" appear. These indicate any character of that class may appear in that box. Letters include both upper- and lowercase, digits are 0 through 9, octal digits are 0 through 7, and hexadecimal digits are 0 through 9 and A through F.

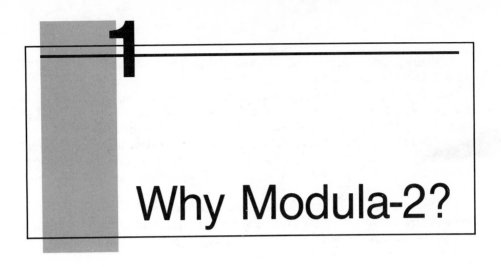

Why Modula-2?

Currently dozens of important high level programming languages are used extensively in the industry to support the development of software systems. Hundreds of additional programming languages have been developed and are sitting on shelves. Why another language? Why Modula-2?

In the past, an important reason for choosing a particular programming language was that a given computer would accept no other high level language. Today, however, many programming languages are available on most modern computer systems.

For the past fifteen years the cost of developing software systems has been steadily increasing while the cost of hardware systems has been decreasing. Because of the escalating costs of software systems and the reliability problems frequently associated with large software systems, a "software crisis" has been recognized by many computer scientists and software engineers.

It is becoming more and more common for large software systems to be delivered late, to run over budget, or to fail to meet specifications. The process of modification of the original software system (maintenance) has proved to be so difficult and expensive that many software organizations spend more than four-fifths of their budgets on software maintenance.

The discipline of software engineering has developed in response to this software crisis. A principal goal of software engineering is the systematization of the software development process, to lower the cost of software development and to improve software reliability.

Many great strides toward achieving this goal have already been made. In 1970 Niklaus Wirth introduced the language Pascal as a vehicle for teaching the principles and methodology of structured problem solving and programming. In recent years, Pascal has become the dominant language taught and used at many universities. In addition, various extensions to the original Pascal have gained widespread acceptance in industry and are finding many commercial applications. Associated with the increased use of Pascal is an increased awareness, on the part of software developers and programmers, of structured programming principles.

Pascal was never intended to be used for large-scale software development projects involving many programmers or programming teams. In Section 1.2 we examine some of Pascal's deficiencies and see why this language is ill suited to large-scale software systems.

As the discipline of software engineering has matured, it has become apparent that languages and software tools must be created to enhance software reliability, streamline the process of software development, and promote more efficient software maintenance. Early programming languages were designed with hardware compatibility as the overriding concern. The software practitioner was forced to accept many compromises. The more recent languages have been designed by, and for, software engineers.

In 1975 an international language design team was organized by the U.S. Department of Defense (DoD). Some of the world's best language designers were invited to join the effort. The goal of the group was to design a new software implementation language that would support efficient and reliable software development and would overcome the deficiencies observed in other languages. In 1983, after many years of work, an international competition among companies, and several language development iterations, the Ada programming language was born. This language has been mandated by the DoD to replace all existing DoD languages for future software development projects.

In 1980 Niklaus Wirth introduced Modula-2 as a sequel to Pascal and as a language much better suited to large-scale software development and system level programming. Modula-2 extends Pascal upward (with the module concept and concurrency) and downward (with low level machine access features).

Modula-2 introduces many important features and capabilities that parallel those found in Ada. Whereas Ada is a complex and somewhat ponderous language, Modula-2 retains the simplicity, clarity, and compactness of Pascal.

Modula-2 is not just another programming language and should not be studied as such. Modula-2 promotes a way of thinking about software development. It may be used at the design level. The architecture of a software system may be defined using Modula-2 as a program design language. The Modula-2 design may then serve as the frame that supports the final software implementation.

Modula-2 supports and encourages a much higher level of problem decomposition and abstraction than earlier languages such as Pascal and Fortran. This can lead to more efficient and reliable problem solving.

Decomposition is a process of reducing a large problem to a set of smaller, more manageable problems. Since software complexity increases with size, it is much easier, in principle, to develop 20 modules of 2000 lines each than to develop a single program with 40,000 lines of code.

Significant savings in the cost of software development and maintenance may be achieved by constructing a software system as a set of interrelated modules. The task of effectively merging a set of separately developed software modules into an integrated entity requires careful attention to sound human management and organization principles as well as to modular software design and implementation methodology. Many of the techniques that have proved successful in the development of hardware systems may be used to engineer software systems.

If we trace the development of computer languages from the mid-1940s to the present, we observe relatively few major jumps in the level of support for problem abstraction.

When the first digital computers were developed during World War II, all programming was done in machine language. Machine languages offer the system designer very little support for problem abstraction. All the entities and operations present in the problem domain must be mapped to a primitive set of machine instructions. As a consequence, the software development process is inefficient, and the product is often unreliable and expensive to maintain.

The advent of assemblers represented the first major step in abstraction by allowing both operations and addresses to be expressed with mnemonic names.

The next major step in the level of problem abstraction offered by computer languages occurred in the mid-1950s with the development of the first major high level languages, Fortran (FORmula TRANslation language) and Algol (ALGOrithmic Language). The predefined types and control structures defined in these languages provide the software developer much greater latitude in mapping the objects and operations of the problem domain to the software system.

Many additional high level languages have been developed and used since the introduction of Fortran and Algol. Indeed, thousands of high level language compilers have been written. But only a relatively small number of these languages have enjoyed extensive use and commercial success. Except for a few recent languages (including Modula-2 and Ada), only incremental improvements related to problem abstraction are evident in these numerous languages.

Another major step in the level of problem abstraction offered by computer languages occurred in the 1980s, with the development of Modula-2 and Ada. Features in Modula-2 and Ada such as the module and the package, data hiding, strong type checking across compilation boundaries, and concurrent processing provide perhaps the most significant improvement in support for problem abstraction and decomposition in the short history of language development. The powerful methodology of object-oriented design is now a reality because of Modula-2 and Ada. We will describe and illustrate this methodology in Chapter 17. We continue our discussion of abstraction in Section 1.3.

This book treats the Modula-2 language in the context of software development. Although we present and illustrate every feature of the Modula-2 language, this book is more than a language manual. We intend to present and illustrate the process of modern software development, and to integrate this presentation with an exposition of the Modula-2 language. After reading this book, we hope that programmers will be able to do more than "code" in Modula-2. We hope to influence the way they approach problem solving and software development. We are confident that they will be able to use Modula-2 to support the development of large software systems.

Part One of the book (Chapters 1–10) focuses on the Pascal-like features of Modula-2. Part Two (Chapters 11–17) concentrates on advanced features of the language and software development with Modula-2.

Since the purpose of this chapter is to present the motivation for Modula-2, we mention without detailed explanation many advanced features of the language. The reader may wish to reread this chapter after becoming familiar with these features.

1.1 Overview of Software Life Cycle

Many inexperienced software developers view the process of software development as two dimensional: write a program and test to see whether it works as desired. It is of course necessary that a program satisfy its specifications; but this is not sufficient. The manner in which the software is developed is as important as whether the program works. The ease with which changes can be made in the software (to upgrade performance, meet additional specifications, or rectify errors discovered later) is directly related to the quality of the software development process.

We present a brief overview of the major stages of the software development process.

1. Needs Analysis and Requirements. The customer works closely with the software development team to produce a problem definition. A set of requirements is established and approved by customer and software team. Often a prototype of the software system is rapidly developed to help bridge the gap between what the customer really desires and what the software vendor believes the customer desires.

2. Specifications. The analysis team develops a set of formal specifications that includes a detailed description of all functional entities, as well as operational constraints. The formal specifications often serve as a performance contract between the software developer and the customer. The development of machine-readable specifications and automatic program generation is an important area of recent research activity.

3. Design. A problem decomposition is performed, resulting in a set of subsystems or modules. The objects and operations identified in the problem domain are mapped into data, functional, and process abstractions in each of the modules. Algorithms for implementing the functional requirements are formulated in pseudo-code. Graphical procedures for representing the structure and architecture of the software system, such as SADT (Jackson, 1975) or modular design charts (Wiener and Sincovec, 1984), may be used.

4. *Implementation*. The modules, subprograms, and processes specified during the design phase must be implemented in a high level language that can be compiled and then executed on the target computer. Often, the code that implements the various module specifications is written by several programming teams and integrated into an overall program structure.

5. *Installation and Testing*. The completed software must be installed and tested on the target computer. Each software specification must be met by the finished software. Software components must be tested individually and as an integrated entity.

6. *Maintenance*. If errors are discovered, changes must be made to the original software. Additional requirements may be met later by again modifying the software. Improved algorithms may be substituted for their original counterparts to improve the performance of the system. If modular software design techniques have been employed, these maintenance changes will be highly localized and will produce negligible fallout effects in the rest of the software system. If good software construction procedures have not been followed, it may be cheaper to rebuild the software product from scratch than to maintain the existing product.

The software development process is iterative. During the design stage it may become necessary to modify the formal specifications (with the customer's approval), perhaps because it may not be possible to meet an operational constraint in the design process. Similarly, it may be necessary to rethink part of the design during the implementation stage because of unanticipated problems.

Boehm (1981) estimates that analysis, specification, and design account for 40% of development costs, implementation for 20%, and testing for 40%. However, the cost of maintenance is estimated to be between 4 and 50 times the cost of system development.

This book examines aspects of the design and implementation stages of the software development process using Modula-2.

1.2 Pascal Versus Modula-2: An Overview

In this section we briefly examine the history of Modula-2 and compare Pascal and Modula-2.

1.2.1 Brief History of Modula-2

Modula-2 is a descendant of Pascal and Modula. In 1975, less than a decade after designing Pascal, Niklaus Wirth developed the language Modula as a vehicle for investigating the programming problems associated with input/output devices and multiprocessing systems. Many of the low level features available in Modula-2 were spawned by Modula. In addition, the module construct was a central feature of the Modula language. Modula lacked Pascal's files, sets, and pointers.

Wirth discontinued his Modula language research after spending a year at Xerox Palo Alto Research Center. After using the Alto work station computer and Mesa programming language at Xerox, Wirth returned to Switzerland. In 1977 he embarked on a research project whose goal was to design a computer system coupled to a new computer language to support modern software engineering. The research on the computer (later called Lilith) and language (later called Modula-2) was conducted at the Institut für Informatik of ETH, Zurich. It is clear that the Mesa language greatly influenced Wirth's development of Modula-2.

The first implementation of Modula-2 was demonstrated on a PDP-11 computer in 1979. The language's definition was published as a technical report in March 1980. The first compiler was released a year later.

There is a growing list of Modula-2 vendors and complete Modula-2 software systems available for IBM Personal Computers, VAX, PDP-11, Sage, Apple, and other computer systems.

1.2.2 Standard Pascal Versus Modula-2

We begin our comparison of Pascal and Modula-2 by listing some of Pascal's shortcomings in Table 1.1 and Modula-2's remedies for these shortcomings in Table 1.2.

TABLE 1.1 Shortcomings of Standard Pascal

1. No facilities are provided for separate compilation, making problem decomposition and team programming very difficult. This deficiency alone disqualifies standard Pascal as a vehicle for large-scale software development.
2. No facilities are provided for data hiding. Subprograms are bound to a particular data representation. This limits the level of data abstraction that is possible.
3. No facilities for concurrent processing are provided.
4. Formal parameters of array types may be bound only to actual parameters of a single type. This makes it difficult to develop general-purpose procedure libraries.
5. Pascal does not provide static variables other than global variables (a static variable remains active for the duration of program execution). The need to use global variables as static variables in Pascal often forces a scope larger than desired.
6. The conditional evaluation (short-circuiting) of boolean expressions is not specified. This often requires the writing of cumbersome code.
7. No else clause is provided in the case statement. This causes the program to abort if the value of the case selector does not match any of the listed case constants.
8. The declaration order required for constants, types, variables, and subprograms inhibits the positioning of declarations near their point of application.
9. Type checking can never be suppressed.
10. The predefined file input/output facilities are extremely limited, allowing only sequential access. No extensions to the predefined set of input/output utilities are possible.
11. Low level access to the machine is not provided.

TABLE 1.2   Improved Features Present in Modula-2

1. Separate compilation with rigorous type checking across compilation boundaries is provided. This supports problem decomposition, decentralization, and team programming.
2. Data hiding is achieved through the module and the opaque type. Data hiding is central to object-oriented design.
3. Modula-2 provides support for coroutines.
4. Modula-2 supports one-dimensional open arrays.
5. Variables declared in a library module stay "alive for the duration of a program's existence. The scope of these variables can be carefully controlled.
6. Short-circuiting of the boolean operators is prescribed in the language. This leads to less cumbersome and more readable code.
7. Case statements can use an else clause for trapping unspecified case values. Subranges can be used in case constant lists, eliminating the need to list all case constant values individually.
8. The declaration order for data objects is relaxed, allowing the declaration of an object closer to its point of application.
9. Type checking may be suppressed by using the WORD type. This facilitates low level programming and allows generic procedures to be written.
10. The language has no input/output facilities. An implementation will provide a file system module that provides a rich set of file abstractions, usually including sequential and direct access. The set of input/output facilities supplied with the library may be expanded by creating customized library modules.
11. Low level programming facilities are provided for type transfer functions, pointer arithmetic, bit manipulation, and direct access to memory.

The most significant differences between standard Pascal and Modula-2 are separate compilation, data hiding, coroutines, and low level machine access.

The separate compilation features of Modula-2 (similar to those of Ada) are not shared by many languages. We describe and illustrate these in detail in Section 11.1. The lack of separate or independent compilation in standard Pascal imposes serious problems. Since the only Pascal compilation unit is a single program, any minute change made by the programmer requires recompilation of the entire program. This increases software development time, sometimes significantly. The complexity of a single large program becomes difficult to manage. This may lower software reliability. It is often difficult to test such a program systematically. Most important, it is very difficult to decentralize the programming effort when the structure of the software system is a single large program. For all these reasons, standard Pascal has not found extensive commercial application.

The three basic compilation units in Modula-2 are library module specifications (definition modules), library module implementations (implementation modules), and program modules. We describe each of these module types in detail in Chapter 11.

The data and functional abstractions used in the problem solution are specified in the definition modules of Modula-2. The architecture of the entire software system may be constructed using definition modules and program modules. Modula-2 may be used to great advantage at the design stage of software development as a program design language. We discuss this in detail in Chapter 17.

The implementation modules contain the "nuts and bolts" of the program. These modules may be modified at any time without recompiling any other modules in the system. All three module types may "import" entities (such as data types, objects, and subprograms) from other modules. A module version control system is supplied to ensure that if a definition module is recompiled, all its client modules (the set of modules that import entities from the recompiled module) are also recompiled before the system is allowed to run.

The three types of compilation unit in Modula-2 suggest an approach to problem solving and software development different from the approach used with standard Pascal. A high level of problem abstraction and decomposition is possible. Throughout this book we elaborate on this feature by discussing and illustrating the process of problem abstraction and decomposition using Modula-2. Indeed this is one of the principal goals of this book.

1.2.3   UCSD Pascal Versus Modula-2

An important and widely used extension to standard Pascal is UCSD(TM) Pascal, developed at the University of California, San Diego, in the mid-1970s. This dialect of Pascal is currently being used on many microprocessor-based computers as well as minicomputers. The language is being supported by Sof-Tech MicroSystems.

UCSD Pascal has important features not present in standard Pascal. We summarize some of those features in Table 1.3.

Perhaps the most significant feature of UCSD Pascal is the *unit*. This feature liberates UCSD Pascal from the fundamental shortcoming of standard Pascal, namely, lack of independent compilation.

In UCSD Pascal, the specification part of the compilation unit must be packaged with the implementation part. The only parts of the UCSD unit that are visible to the software system outside the unit are the parts contained in the specification part of the unit. In this regard, the UCSD Pascal unit is similar to a Modula-2 definition module. The similarities end here.

TABLE 1.3   UCSD Pascal Features not Present in Standard Pascal

1. Predefined static string type and associated operations.
2. Low level block read and block write operations.
3. Interactive file procedures. The end-of-file and end-of-line procedures differ from those of standard Pascal.
4. Direct access files.
5. Untyped files.
6. A limited form of separate compilation through *units*.
7. Exit statement.
8. Long integers.
9. A limited form of concurrent processing through semaphores.

The UCSD Pascal unit does not support data hiding such as is achieved in Modula-2 using opaque types. The unit does not allow implementation details to be changed without requiring recompilation of the entire unit. There is no counterpart in the unit for the sophisticated version control system present in Modula-2 that assures that client modules (modules in the software system that import one or more features from a given parent module) are recompiled whenever a parent module undergoes modification in its specifications.

Since the unit's procedures are bound to specific data structures, any change in implementation detail, such as new data structures, induces major changes in the entire software system. In Modula-2, definition module procedures do not have to be bound to any particular data representation. Indeed, the representational details may be totally hidden and made inaccessible from the rest of the software system. Thus, later changes in such details (e.g., one or more data structures) usually have no fallout effects on the rest of the software system.

To get around the data hiding problem in UCSD Pascal, many programmers create unit procedures that contain no parameters. Although technically this is a form of data hiding, only one instance of such a data type is permissible. This is a big price to pay for a limited form of data hiding. No such price is exacted by Modula-2.

UCSD Pascal does not support open array (conformant array) parameters (see Section 7.4.3), nor does it provide low level access to the machine.

UCSD Pascal resolves few of the deficiencies cited in Table 1.1. As an extension to standard Pascal it is important, yet it falls far short of the power available in Modula-2.

1.2.4   What About Ada?

Ada is a large and powerful programming language with an associated software support environment. Sponsored by the U.S. Department of Defense (DoD), Ada was developed for much the same reasons as Modula-2: to increase the reliability of software and lower the cost of development. When the Ada development effort was launched in the mid-1970s, there were estimated to be about 500 programming languages in use for government software development. It was believed that enormous savings could be achieved by replacing those languages with a single high level language.

The DoD formed the High Order Language Working Group (HOLWG) to specify the requirements of a common language. It soon became clear that no existing language met the requirements created by the HOLWG, and competitive designs for a new high level language were submitted by industrial and academic organizations. These designs were reviewed by specialists worldwide, and after extensive reviews the French company CII Honeywell–Bull won the competition. The Ada language was born, at least on paper.

After a lengthy compiler development effort, and several iterations and refinements, Ada received standardization by the American National Standards Institute (ANSI) in February 1983. To date, only a few compilers have been certified by the Ada Joint Program Office.

The Ada language reflects the fact that it was designed by a committee. Because of its many features, it would appear to be a language that is "all things to all people." The language is very large compared to Modula-2 or almost any other language. Comparing Ada and Modula-2 might be like comparing PL/I and Pascal.

Ada's size and complexity have been a cause of concern. Compilation speeds are generally quite slow. A fairly large memory capacity is required for compilers and run-time environments. It is not yet clear how expensive it will be to train the large numbers of software developers that will be required to develop Ada software in future years. When one properly learns Ada, one is really learning software engineering, as is the case with Modula-2.

All these problems notwithstanding, Ada is a magnificent language for software engineering and embedded computer applications. Its powerful floating-point features should make it very attractive for numerical applications. Its separate compilation features (similar to those of Modula-2) and support for data hiding and abstraction make it very well suited, like Modula-2, to developing large modular software systems.

Ada is superior to Modula-2 in the areas of floating-point support, exception handling, generics, concurrent processing, and embedded system applications. Some of Ada's advanced features such as generics may be partially or completely simulated in Modula-2. Each language contains unique features not to be found in earlier languages.

We refer the reader to recent books on Ada, such as Wiener and Sincovec (1983), Olsen and Whitehill (1983), and Downs and Goldsack (1982).

1.3 Abstraction

A major approach to problem solving is abstraction, which involves model building. Because people manage complexity by means of abstraction, abstractions provide a view of the essential components and processes that define a system.

Typically, abstractions deal with objects and operations on the objects. High level abstractions are not concerned with implementation details. For example, one may understand the concept of an automobile brake without caring whether it is a drum brake or disk brake. The abstraction (concept) of "braking" is independent of its implementation. Our ability to separate the high level abstractions that we use to view a system from the implementation details (lower level abstractions) allows us to understand complex systems.

As an example of problem abstraction, a queueing theorist might view the customer operations in a typical bank as a multiserver queueing process. Customers are assumed to enter the bank according to an arrival process (an abstraction). Once customers have entered, they either form one central waiting line feeding various tellers or are distributed among several waiting lines. A mechanism for choosing the appropriate waiting line is assumed (an abstraction of human organization). Each teller is assumed to follow a server process (another abstraction). The model for changing lines or leaving before service is another human organization abstraction. The server process may be linked to the time of day (allowing for fatigue) or to the length of the current line (another abstraction of human performance).

Using these process abstractions (the objects in the system being people; the operations involving arrival, choosing lines, changing lines, leaving lines, and service), the queueing theorist may estimate the performance of the system: the average length of each waiting line, the average delay per customer, the idle period of the servers, and so on.

Because software development is a form of problem solving, abstraction plays a central role, particularly at the design level. The specifications of a software system determine what a software system is to do. The design determines how it is to be done. It is here that a set of high level abstractions must be developed. These abstractions form our view of the system and provide the basis for later implementation. The interrelationships among the objects, operations, and processes that define the system must be identified. That is, the logical structure of the system must be represented.

What facilities do programming languages provide the software developer for problem abstraction? As we trace the brief history of programming languages and the software development methodologies associated with these languages, we see an evolution away from the machine.

As we indicated earlier in this chapter, the first programming languages, machine languages, require the software developer to think at the machine level. It is very difficult for the problem solver (software developer) to use high level abstractions in the problem-solving process when these abstractions must be translated by the programmer to the ones and zeros of the machine. Thus, a bottom-up, "worry about all the implementation details first" approach to software development was the methodology used by most early software developers.

Assembly languages were the first to provide software developers the facility of memory address abstraction. But in assembly languages, problem solving is still tied closely to a particular machine and processor.

The first high level languages (Fortran and Algol) provided the software developer with much better facilities to support problem abstraction than the original machine and assembly languages. Included among these new facilities were: name abstraction (variables), expression abstraction (operations that combine variables), control abstractions (iteration and conditional branching), data types (static and structured), and functional abstractions (subroutines).

These first high level languages enabled software developers to take a giant leap away from the machine. Now a problem could be translated into the expressions, loops, and conditional branch operations that have come to typify a whole era of programming. The age of the flowchart was born. Instead of linking a problem with a given machine, software developers linked a problem with the high level data and control constructs supported by their programming language. Software developers would "think" in a given language or class of languages and translate the attributes of a given problem to expressions, loops, and branch statements, perhaps using a flowchart.

Perhaps the most significant contribution of the Algol-like languages of the 1960s was the power and subtlety associated with scoping and visibility. Now software developers could seriously begin to face the challenge of partitioning a system into components at the subprogram level. Each subprogram would be targeted to perform a well-defined and, if possible, simple operation. Newer derivative languages like Pascal, introduced in the early 1970s, offered the software developer additional power in the form of richer data structures and control abstractions.

With the advent of Modula-2 and Ada in the early 1980s, the next giant step in language support for problem abstraction took place. Software engineers were liberated from tying their thinking to a particular language, at least at the design level. Instead of using a flowchart methodology at the design level (too much implementation detail too soon), the software engineer could invent data abstractions, object abstractions, and process abstractions to mirror directly the problem at hand.

Modula-2 and Ada allow a software developer to separate problem abstraction (conceptual definition) from implementation. For example, if a stack (a concept) is required in the solution, it can be specified without regard to its implementation. Its interrelationship with other abstractions that comprise the system (queues, trees, graphs, etc.) may be determined without regard to how these concepts will be implemented. Indeed Modula-2 and Ada allow a software developer to conceptualize and specify the architecture of an entire software system at a very high level of abstraction before writing a single line of implementation code.

We briefly introduce the notions of functional abstraction, data abstraction, and process abstraction.

1.3.1   Data and Functional Abstraction

Data abstraction requires the definition of a data type, which is a set of values and a set of operations defined on those values (see Chapter 4). It is imperative that the software developer be able to hide the type representation (implementation details) from users (perhaps other programmers). Representation hiding assures consistency in the use of the type and lowers maintenance costs if the representation is later changed. As long as the interface to the operations remains unchanged, program units that use the abstract data type will not have to be changed (or even recompiled, in the case of Modula-2).

Representation hiding for abstract data types creates a situation that is taken for granted by most programmers. As an example, a programmer is seldom concerned about the internal representation of an array. If this representation is changed (an upgraded compiler), the programs that use the array abstraction need only be recompiled (assuming that the interface to an array is unchanged). These changes in the low level implementation details do not affect the use of the array abstraction (the concept) in the problem solution.

The operations defined on an abstract data type constitute an important set of functional abstractions. Usually, each functional abstraction is implemented as a subprogram unit (procedure or function). As an example, the abstract data type of a stack is supported by the functional abstractions of push, pop, initialize, and empty. These operations "define" the notion of the stack abstraction and are usually implemented as procedures or functions.

1.3.2 Process Abstraction

A process is a program unit that works cooperatively and simultaneously (at least in concept) with other program units. Software design using processes requires abstractions of process initiation and termination, and interprocess synchronization and communication. Two major applications areas for process abstractions are interrupt handling and operating system design, but the applicability of these abstractions to other areas is being recognized. Numerical pipelining and distributed compilation are just two areas in which parallel activities are commonplace. As hardware support becomes more readily available to aid in the implementation of process abstraction, software developers must be encouraged to use this powerful form of abstraction in their software design.

With software developers learning to use Modula-2 or Ada as program design languages, it is hoped that significant improvements in software reliability will be achieved, as well as tremendous savings in software cost, particularly in maintenance.

As indicated earlier, a principal goal of this book is to describe and illustrate good software development methodology with Modula-2. We will focus on the use of data, functional, and process abstraction in Modula-2 in designing and implementing software systems.

1.4 A Few Comments About Programming Style

The physical layout of a program—its style—affects its readability and thus its maintainability. It is always important to pay close attention to program layout.

As authors and Modula-2 software developers, we are still experimenting with style. Although we have chosen to present a variety of program format styles, all our format decisions have been guided by some basic principles that should be familiar to experienced Pascal programmers. Rather than attempt a summary of program format rules, which we may occasionally break, we encourage you to take careful note of the range of format decisions evident in our code. You will probably wish to do your own experimentation before settling on a consistent style.

1.5 Summary

The cost of software systems has been steadily increasing, while the cost of hardware systems has been decreasing. The all too common occurrences of budget overruns in software development projects and poor reliability in the finished software product have led some observers to speak of a "software crisis." Among the important goals of software engineering are the reduction in the life cycle cost associated with software development and the improvement in software reliability.

It has become more and more apparent that programming languages and software tools must be created to support better the cost-effective development of reliable software systems. Some recent programming languages, most notably Modula-2 and Ada, have been created specifically to meet the two goals stated above.

Modula-2, released in the early 1980s, extends Pascal upward (away from the machine) with the module concept and coroutines, and downward (toward the machine) with facilities for low level machine access. The most significant differences between Pascal and Modula-2 are found in the areas of separate compilation, data hiding, coprocessing, and low level machine access.

Modula-2 promotes a powerful approach to problem solving and thinking about software development. When used as a program design language with object-oriented design, Modula-2 allows the essential concepts that underlie a software system to be established and the architectural frame of a software system to be created before the dominant concern becomes implementation details. Modula-2 allows a software developer to separate problem abstraction (conceptual definition) from implementation. This separation between the specification of a concept and its implementation may be used to localize and reduce the cost of maintainance, and to improve the reliability of a software system.

2

Lexical
Structure
of Modula-2

Modula-2 is like most modern languages in that it is expressed as a free-format character string. The lexical elements of the language include identifiers, literal constants, operators and delimiters, comments, and separators. Each of these is described in this chapter.

2.1 Identifiers

An *identifier* is a name chosen by the programmer to represent an entity in a program; such entities include variables, types, constants, procedures, and modules. An identifier is a sequence of characters, each of which is an upper- or lowercase alphabetic character or a digit character. An identifier must begin with an alphabetic character. Some compilers extend this definition to allow the underscore character in identifiers. Figure 2.1 shows the syntax of an identifier.

The following are all valid identifiers.

i	number	x1	ListOfEmployees
I	Number	X1	from1to100by2

The following are invalid identifiers, for the reasons given.

last-name	contains an illegal character
Ham&Eggs	contains an illegal character
7daysaweek	does not begin with a letter

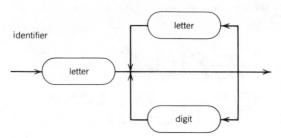

FIGURE 2.1   Syntax of an Identifier

In the original definition of Modula-2 (and in the ANSI Pascal standard), an identifier may be arbitrarily long, and all characters are significant. This definition notwithstanding, many implementations of both languages limit either the total length of identifiers, or the number of characters considered to be significant for purposes of distinguishing two identifiers. Thus, the identifiers

AccountsInArrears   AccountsInArea

sometimes are considered to be illegal (too long) or the same (not distinct within the first 8 or 12 characters). A programmer using an unfamiliar or new Modula-2 implementation should look for this kind of limitation on identifiers.

Modula-2 is unique among common languages in that it considers upper- and lowercase alphabetic characters to be distinct in identifiers. This is an area of controversy among language designers and software developers. Historically, early hardware provided uppercase-only card punches and printers, then uppercase-only terminals, and so early languages usually were limited to uppercase. Now that both cases are available on nearly all devices, it is possible to program in uppercase, lowercase, or mixed cases.

Modula-2's predecessors and competitors, including Pascal and Ada, allow mixed case, with upper- and lowercase considered indistinct except in character string literals. The main argument in favor of this approach is that it simplifies the human mental effort, since the entity represented by an identifier is stored mentally as a concept, not as a string of characters, and concepts do not have upper and lower cases. Also, there is some experimental evidence that programmers using all lowercase are more productive than those using all uppercase. We are not aware of any experimental evidence that demonstrates any advantage of mixed case; it clearly requires more keystrokes to enter a program. Programmers will have to decide for themselves how to use this capability of Modula-2 to their best advantage.

As we will see in Section 2.3, Modula-2 requires all reserved words to be in uppercase. Many predefined identifiers require uppercase or mixed case, and the case mixture exhibits no particular pattern; each must be memorized. To simplify the entry of programs into the computer, some programmers use all lowercase and preprocess the program before compilation. The preprocessor converts the reserved words and predefined identifiers into correct upper or mixed case. Such a preprocessor is given as an example in Section 17.5.

It is not always possible in Modula-2 to determine unambiguously the entity represented by an identifier. The Pascal programmer has seen this problem in specifying a field within a record object: the field name itself might refer to a field in several different records. Modula-2 introduces the concept of a *qualified identifier,* in which the potentially ambiguous identifier is preceded by a qualifying identifier and a period, as shown in Figure 2.2. The importance of this feature will be seen in Chapter 11.

2.2 Literal Constants

Data objects of several of the predefined data types can be represented by *literal constants*. The values of such objects are apparent from their representations. Literal constants exist for values of the integer, real, boolean, character, and string types.

An integer literal consists of a sequence of digit characters, optionally followed by a radix indicator. If that indicator is the character 'B', the number is interpreted as a base eight (octal) integer; if the indicator is the character 'H', the number is interpreted as a base-16 (hexadecimal) integer. A hexadecimal literal must begin with a decimal digit (0–9), not an extended hexadecimal digit (A–F), to allow the compiler to distinguish such a literal from an identifier. In some implementations, the radix indicator may be either upper- or lowercase. Figure 2.3 shows the syntax of an integer literal.

The following are correctly formed integer literals.

    0   1   177777B   0FFFFH   12345

The following are incorrectly formed integer literals, for the reasons given.

−1	sign not allowed
18B	illegal digit in octal notation
F000H	does not begin with decimal digit
77b	some implementations require uppercase B

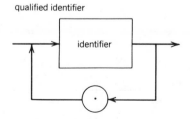

FIGURE 2.2 Syntax of a Qualified Identifier

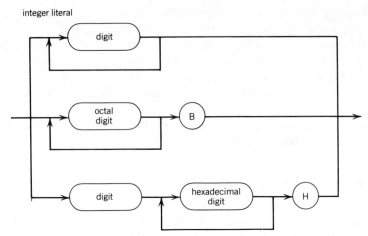

FIGURE 2.3   Syntax of an Integer Literal

Notice that no preceding sign is allowed in the definition. Both the plus and minus signs are considered to be operators (discussed in Sections 2.3 and 4.1.1), and a signed integer literal is considered to be an expression. This distinction is for syntactic purposes only; the programmer may use signed integers in the normal way.

Real literal constants consist of a sequence of digits representing the whole number part, a decimal point, an optional sequence of digits representing the fraction part, and an optional scale factor. The scale factor consists of the character 'E' (for "exponent"), an optional sign, and a sequence of digits; the meaning is "times 10 to the power of . . .". In some implementations, the exponent character may be either uppercase or lowercase. Figure 2.4 shows the syntax of a real literal.

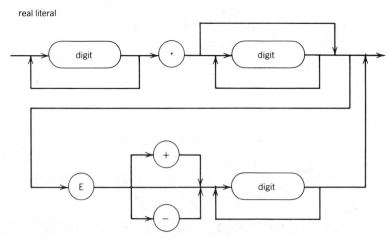

FIGURE 2.4   Syntax of a Real Literal

The following are all correctly formed real literals.

    0.   0.0   123.456   1.0E6   1.E−6

The following are all incorrectly formed real literals, for the reasons given.

.5	does not begin with a digit
−3.2	no sign allowed
6.023e23	some implementations require uppercase E

Notice that the syntax of reals in Modula-2 is different from Pascal, which requires at least one digit after the decimal point. Thus the Modula-2 real literals 3. and 3.E5 would have to be written 3.0 and 3.0E5 in Pascal.

The boolean literal constants are TRUE and FALSE. They must be expressed in uppercase letters and are not enclosed in apostrophes or quotation marks.

Single character literals and character string literals are enclosed either in apostrophes or quotation marks. Thus 'A' and "A" are equivalent character literals, and 'total' and "total" are equivalent character string literals.

Characters for which there does not exist a graphical representation, often called *control characters,* may be represented by their ordinal values expressed as octal literals followed by the letter 'C'. Some implementations may allow a lower case 'c'. Figure 2.5 shows the syntax of these literals.

The following are all correctly formed character and string literals.

    'A'   "A"   ' " '   " ' "   15C   127C
    "John's program"
    "string containing an apostrophe ' character"
    'string containing a quotation mark " character'
    '!@#$%ˆ&'

The following are incorrectly formed character and string literals, for the reasons given.

'John's program'	contains apostrophe
'John' 's program'	contains apostrophe
"He said, "Stop!""	contains quotation mark
19C	9 is not an octal digit
1234C	value too large for character set

Notice that a string enclosed in apostrophes may *not* contain an apostrophe, nor may strings enclosed in quotation marks contain a quotation mark. Therefore in Modula-2 it is impossible to construct a string literal that contains both an apostrophe and a quotation mark. The Pascal solution of doubling a contained apostrophe does not work in Modula-2.

Modula-2 allows the definition of set data types (see Section 4.2.3), including the predefined type BITSET. Set literals are expressed in familiar mathematical notation, as shown in Figure 2.6. The definition of a constant expression, given in Section 3.1, includes literal constants.

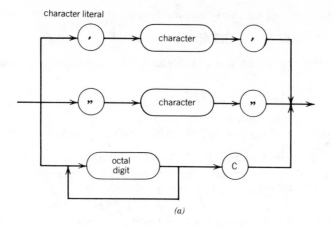

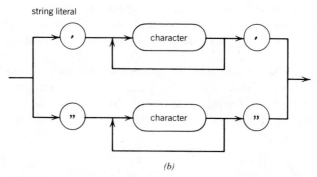

FIGURE 2.5 Syntax of (*a*) Character and (*b*) String Literals

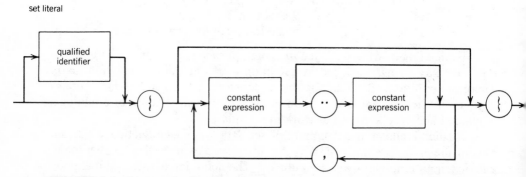

FIGURE 2.6 Syntax of a Set Literal

22

The following are examples of correctly formed set literals.

$$\{\ \}\qquad\{\ 1,\ 3,\ 5\ \}\qquad\{\ 1..5,\ 7..10\ \}$$

The following are examples of incorrectly formed set literals, for the reasons shown.

[1, 2, 3]	wrong delimiter characters
{ x, y, z }	elements are not constants

Pascal programmers will note that Modula-2 uses the brace or curly bracket characters to delimit sets, rather than the square brackets used in Pascal. Notice also that set literals contain only constant elements (however, see Appendix 3).

2.3   Operators and Delimiters

Operators in Modula-2 are lexical elements that denote that a particular action or operation is to be performed. Some operators are denoted by *reserved words,* which are sequences of alphabetic characters. These words, although meeting the definition of identifiers, may not be used as identifiers in a Modula-2 program (hence the adjective "reserved"). Other operators are denoted by one or two nonalphabetic characters.

Delimiters are lexical elements that denote the beginning or end of other entities. Again, some are denoted by reserved words, others by one or two nonalphabetic characters.

The reserved words in Modula-2 and the operators and delimiters denoted by nonalphabetic characters are shown in Tables 2.1 and 2.2, respectively.

2.4   Comments

A *comment* in Modula-2, as in most other common languages, is a sequence of characters that is (usually) ignored by the compiler. Comments are for the human reader and do not contribute anything to the semantics of the program. In Modula-2, comments are delimited by the two-character symbols (* and *). Pascal programmers should note that the curly braces { and }, which denote comments in Pascal, denote sets in Modula-2, not comments.

Comments may be nested. The construct

(* first and (* second *) comment *)

consists of two nested comments in Modula-2, whereas in Pascal the second occurrence of (* is insignificant, the first occurrence of *) terminates the comment, and the remaining characters would generate a compile-time error.

Comments are often used during software testing to exclude a section of a program from compilation and execution. Modula-2's nested comment capability allows such exclusions even when the program section contains comments.

TABLE 2.1   Reserved Words in Modula-2

AND	LOOP
ARRAY	MOD
BEGIN	MODULE
BY	NOT
CASE	OF
CONST	OR
DEFINITION	POINTER
DIV	PROCEDURE
DO	QUALIFIED
ELSE	RECORD
ELSIF	REPEAT
END	RETURN
EXIT	SET
EXPORT	THEN
FOR	TO
FROM	TYPE
IF	UNTIL
IMPLEMENTATION	VAR
IMPORT	WHILE
IN	WITH

TABLE 2.2   Operators and Delimiters in Modula-2

+	unary plus, addition, set union
−	unary minus, subtraction, set difference
*	multiplication, set intersection
/	real division, symmetric set difference
:=	assignment
&	boolean and
=	equal
<>	not equal
#	not equal
<	less than
>	greater than
<=	less than or equal to, subset
>=	greater than or equal to, superset
^	pointer dereference
( )	parentheses
[ ]	array index brackets, subrange brackets
{ }	set braces
(* *)	comment delimiters
..	subrange delimiter
.	period
,	comma
;	semicolon
:	colon
|	alternative delimiter

A similar attempt in Pascal would be interpreted incorrectly, as described above.

Developers of compilers and other language tools will recognize that the existence of nested comments makes it necessary for lexical analysis of Modula-2 programs to be based on the recognition of a context-free language, rather than a regular language.

In some implementations, comments may also be used to provide information to the compiler. Such directives or *pragmas* (as they are known in Ada) control such things as the compiler listing of the program, compilation of debugging, subscript checking, or range checking code into the program, or specification of a different programming language linkage convention for a procedure. The syntax of such directives varies from one implementation to another. One common form is exemplified by the comment (*$L+*), indicating that the directive called 'L' (may be the source code listing) is to be turned on ('+').

2.5 Separators

A Modula-2 programmer may insert spaces or start a new line wherever desired to make the program more readable for the human reader. In certain cases, separation of two lexical elements is mandatory to preserve the meaning of the program. For example, two consecutive identifiers or reserved words must be separated to prevent appearing as one longer identifier.

A *separator* in Modula-2 is white space (one or more blanks or, in some implementations, tabs), a new line, or a comment. None of the lexical elements described in this chapter may have embedded separators. We do not consider a blank in a character string literal or comment to be a separator; rather, it is a syntactically correct part of the entity. In the rest of this book it is understood that separators may appear on any arrow in a syntax chart. In a program, a separator may appear between any two lexical elements without affecting the meaning of the program. As indicated above, in a few cases a separator is required.

The tab character does not exist in the character sets of some computer systems, and where it does, operating systems and text editors may treat it in a variety of ways. Also, some Modula-2 implementations may not accept the tab as a separator.

3

Declarations

Five classes of entities must be declared in Modula-2 programs: constants, types, variables, procedures, and modules. This section discusses the first three of these classes; the others are covered in Chapters 7 and 11, respectively.

The experienced Pascal programmer will note the absence of label declarations. Modula-2 does not have labels, and thus no declarations of labels.

In contrast with Pascal, a block in Modula-2 (see Chapter 8) may contain any number of occurrences of constant, type, and variable declarations. They may occur in any order, provided that an object is declared before it is referenced. This often allows an object to be declared closer to its point of application.

Large programs may contain long lists of declarations. To make the declarations more easily readable, we recommend that programmers develop a style that presents declarations in tabular form, with names, definitions, and associated comments arranged in columns. This style is illustrated in many of the larger programming examples in Part Two of this book.

3.1 Constant Declarations

Constants are data objects whose values never change. We have already seen literal constants, whose values are apparent from their representations. Other constants may be defined that are represented by identifiers, and whose values are defined in a *constant declaration*. The syntax of a constant declaration section is shown in Figure 3.1.

Modula-2 extends the Pascal concept of constant declaration to include *constant expressions,* a feature not available in Pascal. Often two constants are related, and a change in one necessitates a change in the other. In Modula-2, such a relationship can be explicitly defined. Figures 3.2 through 3.5 show the syntax of constant expressions. Although not evident from the syntax chart, the qualified identifier in Figure 3.5 must be the identifier of a constant.

The following is a correct constant declaration section.

```
CONST
    terminator    = '$';
    upperlimit    = 9999;
    unknown       = NIL;
    pi            = 3.14159265;
    twopi         = 2.0 * pi;
    avogadro      = 6.023E23;
    debugging     = FALSE;
    queuesize     = 100;
    queuemax      = queuesize − 1;
    message       = "end of file encountered";
    prompt        = ">";
    squares       = { 0, 1, 4, 9 };
    nullset       = { };
```

constant declaration

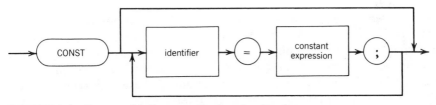

FIGURE 3.1   Syntax of a Constant Declaration Section

constant expression

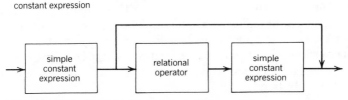

FIGURE 3.2   Syntax of a Constant Expression

simple constant expression

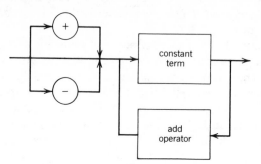

FIGURE 3.3   Syntax of a Simple Constant
Expression

constant term

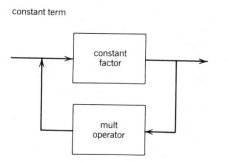

FIGURE 3.4   Syntax of a Constant Term

Constant expressions may be defined for several different, but not all,
data types. The examples illustrate constants of the scalar types integer, real,
character, boolean, and pointer, and of the structured types string and set.
Constant expressions do not exist for other structured types, such as arrays
and records. The next chapter presents details of these data types. Constant
expressions may not contain subprogram references.

Constants represented by appropriately chosen identifiers are beneficial
to the software developer in many ways. They can make a program more
readable, since a name like MaximumEmployees carries more meaning than a
literal constant like 100. When the value of such a constant must be changed
because of changing software requirements, only the definition of the constant
needs to be changed, not all occurrences. In large programs, finding all occurrences of literal constants that represent the same thing can be very difficult,
and missing even one can result in incorrect program behavior. Also, declaration of named constants often helps document software design decisions that
otherwise would not be evident.

constant factor

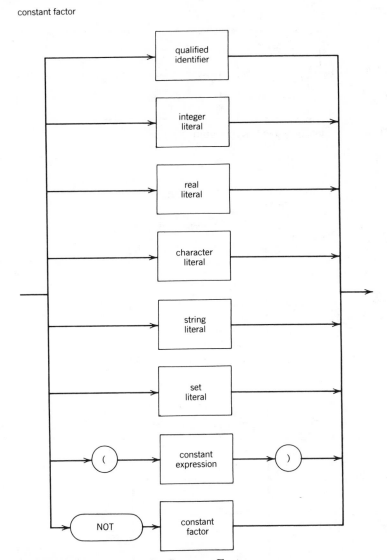

FIGURE 3.5   Syntax of a Constant Factor

3.2   Type Declarations

There are two different kinds of type declarations in Modula-2. The first is very similar to that of Pascal and is discussed here. The second is the declaration of abstract data types, which are represented in Modula-2 by modules; such declarations are described in depth in Chapters 11 and 12.

type declaration

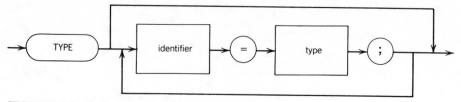

FIGURE 3.6   Syntax of a Type Declaration Section

type

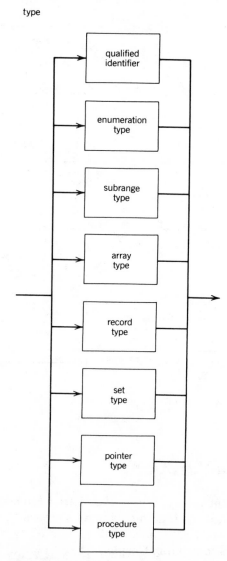

FIGURE 3.7   Syntax of a Type

The syntax of a type declaration section is identical to that of Pascal, and is shown in Figure 3.6.

There are several different categories of types that may be declared, as shown in Figure 3.7. These are discussed in detail in the next chapter. The following examples will look familiar to the Pascal programmer; for other readers, explanations are provided in the next chapter.

```
TYPE
    digit  = [ 0..9 ];
    color  = ( red, orange, yellow, green, blue, violet );
    list   = ARRAY [ 1..100 ] OF INTEGER;
    ptr    = POINTER TO node;
    node   = RECORD
                value : REAL;
                next : ptr
             END;
```

3.3 Variable Declarations

Variable declarations in Modula-2 are again identical to those of Pascal, as shown in Figure 3.8. The following are all correct variable declarations.

```
VAR
    number : INTEGER;
    letter  : CHAR;
    sum     : REAL;
```

The type required in a variable declaration may be either a single identifier or a type definition expression. For example, a variable named List may be declared in the following two equivalent ways.

variable declaration

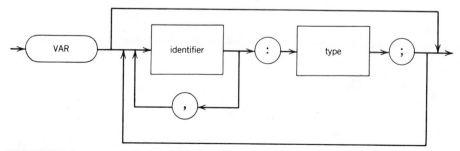

FIGURE 3.8 Syntax of a Variable Declaration Section

```
TYPE ClassList  = ARRAY [ 1..100 ] of StudentName;
VAR  List       : ClassList;

VAR  List       : ARRAY [ 1..100 ] of StudentName;
```

In the second example, List is said to be of an *anonymous type,* since the type does not have a name (identifier). Although List is structurally the same with either declaration, anonymous types sometimes can cause problems for the programmer (see Chapter 5 and Section 7.4).

4

Data Types and Expressions

A *data type* may be defined formally as a pair $<V, O>$, where

V is a set of *values*

O is a set of *operations* defined on those values

Like Pascal, the Modula-2 language includes several predefined or "standard" data types and provides for the definition of new data types by the programmer. In this chapter we consider the Modula-2 data types that are similar to those of Pascal; in Chapter 12 we will take a detailed look at the definition of *abstract data types*.

Modula-2 is a *strongly typed* language; that is, every constant, variable, and expression has associated with it a uniquely identifiable data type. Many features of the language are present solely to support this property, such as requiring variables to be declared before their use. For most programming situations, the value of strong typing is almost universally accepted, primarily because it allows what were subtle semantic errors ("logic" errors) in more primitive languages (such as Fortran) to be moved to the realm of simple semantic errors that can be detected by the compiler. In a few situations, however, the strong typing of languages like Pascal and Modula-2 is too restrictive, a disadvantage long lamented by Pascal programmers. Modula-2 addresses this problem by allowing formalized and controlled ways of circumventing the strong typing requirements (see Section 4.4.4).

33

The data types may be classified as *scalar* or *structured,* depending on whether the elements of the set of values of the data type are considered to be indivisible or atomic entities (scalar) or are made up of collections of still smaller entities (structured).

4.1 Scalar Data Types

There are six classes of scalar data types in Modula-2. Each is similar to the corresponding class in Pascal.

4.1.1 Integer and Cardinal

The *integer* data type, denoted INTEGER in Modula-2, is like that of Pascal. The set of values of the integer type is implementation dependent, usually determined by the hardware of the host machine. For example, on a machine that uses a 16-bit, two's-complement representation for integers, the set of values is $\{-2^{15}, \ldots, -1, 0, 1, \ldots, +2^{15} - 1\}$. Note that the integer type includes both positive and negative values.

The set of operations on the integer type includes addition, subtraction, multiplication, division, modulus or remainder, and negation. The symbols used in Modula-2 to represent these operations are as follows.

Operation	*Symbol*
addition	+
subtraction	−
multiplication	*
division	DIV
modulus	MOD
negation	−

The first three operations obey the normal mathematical definitions, but it is the responsibility of the programmer to ensure that the use of these operations does not produce a result that is too large or too small, or more precisely, is not a member of the set of values of the integer type. The result of integer *overflow* or *underflow* is implementation defined; some systems may ignore it and give erroneous results, while others may detect the error and abort the program.

The division operation always give an integer result, defined to be the mathematical quotient truncated to an integer. Thus 5 DIV 2 = 2, −5 DIV 2 = −2, and 5 DIV (−2) = −2. (Note the parentheses required in the third example; see Section 4.4 for the syntax of expressions.) It is not possible for division to produce overflow or underflow, but division by zero is not defined, and normally causes a program error.

The modulus or remainder operation differs from Pascal in that it is only defined for positive operands. The operation may be defined by:

$$\textbf{if } q = x \text{ DIV } y \textbf{ and } r = x \text{ MOD } y$$

then the following equation is satisfied:

$$x = q * y + r \textbf{ where } 0 \leq r < y$$

Both negation (sign inversion) and subtraction are represented by the minus sign. The operation that is intended is deduced from the context; negation requires a single operand, while subtraction requires two operands.

The *cardinal* data type, denoted CARDINAL in Modula-2, is similar to the integer data type; they share the same set of operations. The set of values of the cardinal type, however, includes only nonnegative integers $\{0, 1, 2, \ldots\}$. Having this type separate from the integer type affords the programmer many advantages.

First, on many computers, the set of values includes values beyond the maximum value of the integer set. For example, on a 16-bit, two's-complement machine, the maximum integer is $2^{15}-1$, while the maximum cardinal is $2^{16}-1$. Second, the machine instructions (especially multiply and divide) for unsigned integers are often faster than the corresponding signed integer instructions.

Third, and perhaps most important, because the cardinal data type allows the programmer to be more precise in stating what values a variable may have, the compiler can identify errors or potential errors in a program. For example, a variable used as a counter that ranges from a positive value down to zero may be declared to be of type cardinal rather than integer. If the programmer inadvertently allows the value to become negative, the error would be detected as a type violation; this would not be the case for a counter of type integer.

Some computers support more than one kind of integer data format. Modula-2 implementations on such machines may define additional integer or cardinal data types (see Appendix 3).

4.1.2 Real

The *real* data type, denoted REAL in Modula-2, is again similar to the real data type in Pascal. The set of values is implementation dependent, and is normally determined by the floating-point format of the host computer. On nearly all machines, the internal representation of reals is as a pair of values, a *fraction* or *mantissa,* and an *exponent* or *scale factor.* Thus a real number such as 299,792,458 (speed of light in meters per second) could be written in Modula-2 as 299792458.0 or 2.99792458E8, but would be stored in the computer as two values that represent the fraction 0.299792458 and the exponent 9. Of course, not all computers are capable of storing real numbers this precisely; a typical small computer uses about 24 bits for storage of the fraction, giving a precision of approximately seven decimal digits.

The set of operations of the real data type includes addition, subtraction, multiplication, division, and negation, which are represented in Modula-2 by the following symbols:

Operation	Symbol
addition	$+$
subtraction	$-$
multiplication	$*$
division	$/$
negation	$-$

Each of these operations behaves according to the usual mathematical definition; but as for integers and cardinals, the programmer must avoid performing operations whose results are not in the value set of the real data type. Division by zero is again prohibited.

Some computers support more than one kind of real data format. Modula-2 implementations on such machines may define additional real data types (see Appendix 3).

4.1.3 Boolean

The *boolean* data type, denoted BOOLEAN in Modula-2, is again similar to that of Pascal. The set of values of this type is {FALSE, TRUE}, and the set of operations includes conjunction, disjunction, and negation. These operations are represented in Modula-2 by the symbols below (see also Appendix 3).

Operation	Symbol
conjunction	AND or &
disjunction	OR
negation	NOT

The Pascal programmer should note that the ampersand character may be used for the conjunction operation in Modula-2; this is not allowed in Pascal.

The definitions of these operations are based on the corresponding definitions from propositional logic. However, because of the nature of programming, an additional interpretation is necessary. It is possible for the value of an operand in an expression to be undefined or unevaluatable. For example, an operand that is a variable is always undefined at the beginning of a program and must be given a value before being used in an expression. An operand such as x/y, where x and y are real variables, and where the value of y is currently zero, is unevaluatable (erroneous), as is the value of the operand list[101], where list is an array variable with maximum subscript 100.

In general, expressions involving undefined or unevaluatable operands are themselves undefined. The boolean conjunction and disjunction operations, however, are defined in Modula-2 in a way that allows certain expressions to have values even though they contain undefined operands.

Compare the truth table definitions of conjunction and disjunction (Tables 4.1 and 4.2), first as defined in propositional logic and then as defined in Modula-2. The significance of these tables is that the two operands are evaluated *in*

TABLE 4.1   Truth Tables for Conjunction

Propositional Logic			Modula-2		
x	y	x and y	x	y	x and y
false	false	false	false	false	false
false	true	false	false	true	false
true	false	false	false	undefined	false
true	true	true	true	false	false
			true	true	true
			true	undefined	undefined
			undefined	false	undefined
			undefined	true	undefined
			undefined	undefined	undefined

the order in which they are written in the program. If the first operand is false, the conjunction operation does not evaluate the second operand; rather, it gives a false result immediately. If the first operand is true, the disjunction operation does not evaluate the second operand; rather, it gives a true result immediately.

This form of evaluation is sometimes called the *short-circuit* evaluation of boolean expressions. It has been a controversial topic in programming language design for some time. Pascal specifically prohibits it; that is, for an expression in Pascal to have a value, both operands must have values. Ada allows both forms, with x and y being the Pascal-like expression, and x and then y being the Modula-2-like expression (similarly in Ada: x or y, x or else y).

To illustrate the use of the short-circuit evaluation of boolean expressions, consider the common linear search algorithm. Assume the integer array A is declared to have subscripts ranging from 1 to 100, and that we wish to determine whether the value in the variable named key occurs in the array. If it does, the value of the variable named position should be the subscript where it first occurs; otherwise position should be set to 101. Although we have not yet

TABLE 4.2   Truth Tables for Disjunction

Propositional Logic			Modula-2		
x	y	x or y	x	y	x or y
false	false	false	false	false	false
false	true	true	false	true	true
true	false	true	false	undefined	undefined
true	true	true	true	false	true
			true	true	true
			true	undefined	true
			undefined	false	undefined
			undefined	true	undefined
			undefined	undefined	undefined

introduced the syntax of the statements in this example, the Pascal programmer should find it understandable.

Modula-2 Version: Linear Search

```
position := 1;
WHILE ( position <= 100 ) AND
        ( A[ position ] <> key ) DO
    position := position + 1
END;
```

Pascal Version: Linear Search

```
position := 1;
while ( position < 100 ) and
        ( A[ position ] <> key ) do
    position := position + 1;
if A[ position ] <> key then position := 101;
```

Notice that the algorithm used in the Modula-2 version would not work in Pascal, because the last time the while statement condition is evaluated, position is 101, and the reference to A[101] would give a subscript error. The Pascal version really gets out of the loop after 99 unsuccessful tests, and makes the hundredth test just after the loop. Experience has shown that most beginning programmers are more likely to try the algorithm used in the Modula-2 version above, only to have it fail in Pascal. If this algorithm is in fact more natural, the programming language should allow it with the intended meaning.

One other observation about the boolean data type: it may be considered to be an enumeration type (see Section 4.1.5), defined as

TYPE BOOLEAN = (FALSE, TRUE);

and therefore any of the Modula-2 functions and procedures defined for enumeration types may also be applied to the boolean type.

4.1.4 Character and String

The *character* data type, denoted CHAR in Modula-2, has a set of values that is implementation dependent. Most common is one of the International Standards Organization (ISO) character sets, such as the American Standard Code for Information Interchange (ASCII) character set. The ASCII set contains both *printable* characters, for which a graphical representation exists, and *control* characters, which effect some special action when used for communication (such as carriage return, backspace, and tab). The ASCII character set is shown in Table 4.3; the control characters are identified by mnemonics, while the printable characters are identified by their graphical representations.

As indicated in Table 4.3, the characters in the ASCII set appear in a specific order. The position of the character in the set, beginning with position 0, is called the *ordinal* value of the character. Clearly, there are mappings between the character set and the set of integers { 0, 1, . . . , 127 }. These

TABLE 4.3 ASCII Character Set

First Digits	Last Digit							
	0	1	2	3	4	5	6	7
00	nul	soh	stx	etx	eot	enq	ack	bel
01	bs	tab	lf	vt	ff	cr	so	si
02	dle	dc1	dc2	dc3	dc4	nak	syn	etb
03	can	em	sub	esc	fs	gs	rs	us
04		!	,,	#	$	%	&	'
05	(	)	*	+	,	−	.	/
06	0	1	2	3	4	5	6	7
07	8	9	:	;	<	=	>	?
10	@	A	B	C	D	E	F	G
11	H	I	J	K	L	M	N	O
12	P	Q	R	S	T	U	V	W
13	X	Y	Z	[	\	]	^	___
14	'	a	b	c	d	e	f	g
15	h	i	j	k	l	m	n	o
16	p	q	r	s	t	u	v	w
17	x	y	z	{	|	}	~	del

mappings are often useful in programming, and are discussed further in Section 4.4.4.

There are no operations defined on the character data type, although there are functions defined on characters, as discussed in Section 4.4.2.

Although there is not a formally defined *string* data type in Modula-2, sequences of characters are informally called strings. As described in Section 2.2, strings may be represented in programs as sequences of characters enclosed in apostrophes or quotation marks. The data type of such a string is actually an array, specifically, ARRAY [0..n − 1] OF CHAR, where n is the number of characters in the string. Arrays are discussed fully in Section 4.2.1.

4.1.5 Enumeration Types

In the early days of computing, almost all applications were numeric. Nearly all general-purpose programming languages reflect that fact by providing various numeric data types with a variety of associated operations. As the use of computers grew, more and more nonnumeric applications arose, and it became evident that programming languages would have to provide nonnumeric data types as well as numeric.

Modula-2 allows the definition of *enumeration* types, which are data types whose value sets are simply enumerated. The syntax of such a definition is shown in Figure 4.1. This kind of type declaration implies the declaration of constants, because each of the identifiers in the enumerated list is a constant of the data type. For the type of constant to be uniquely determined, not more than one enumeration type containing a particular identifier can be defined.

Like the character data type, the values of enumeration types appear in a

enumeration type

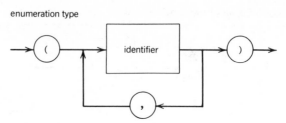

FIGURE 4.1 Syntax of an Enumeration Type

well-defined order, namely, the order shown in the declaration. This order defines the result of the relational operators (see Section 4.4.1) on values of enumeration types. The position of a particular value in the declaration determines its ordinal value, with the first value having ordinal value zero. Mappings exist between the set of values of an enumeration type and the set of integers $\{ 0, 1, \ldots, n - 1 \}$, where n is the number of values in the type. These mappings are discussed in detail in Section 4.4.4.

Uses of enumeration types are exemplified later in the book. As an introduction to these types, consider the following examples.

The months of the year are important data objects in many business applications, such as payroll, accounting, and inventory control. In Modula-2, a data type might be declared as:

TYPE months = (Jan, Feb, Mar, Apr, May, Jun,
                Jul, Aug, Sep, Oct, Nov, Dec);

In more primitive programming languages, the programmer would be tempted or forced to represent months with some other data type, such as integers 1 through 12. For most people, however, the enumeration type provides a much more understandable set of names for the months.

Enumeration types can be used to define a kind of multivalued logical type. For example, a comparison operation may be desired for a user-defined structured data type. A function subprogram is written to do the comparisons. If the possible outcomes of a comparison are "first object is less than the second object," "first object is equal to the second object," and "first object is greater than the second object," the value returned by the function might be of the enumeration type:

TYPE relationship = (lessthan, equal, greaterthan);

Again, in a more primitive programming language, the programmer might be tempted to have the function return integer values $-1, 0, 1$. In general, enumeration types allow Modula-2 programmers to express their ideas in a more natural way with terminology applicable to the problem at hand, rather than being cryptic and expressing everything as a number.

There are no operations defined on enumeration types, although there are some standard functions for manipulating objects of these types. These are discussed in Sections 4.4.2 and 4.4.4. As in Pascal, input and output for enumeration types is not predefined. A programmer wishing to do input and output must supply appropriate procedures.

4.1.6 Subrange Types

A *subrange* data type is a type whose value set is a contiguous subset of the value set of another data type, called the *base type*. A subrange type inherits its operation set from the base type. The base type must be a scalar type other than real; thus it may be integer, cardinal, boolean, character, or an enumeration type.

The syntax of the declaration of a subrange type in Modula-2 is different from Pascal, as shown in Figure 4.2 (see also Appendix 3).

Some examples of subrange declarations are:

```
TYPE
    digits  = [ 0..9 ];
    alpha   = [ 'A'..'Z' ];
    decade  = [ 1980..1989 ];
```

The major benefit of subrange types is that the programmer can express more precisely the values a variable might assume. Often a programming error can be detected at compilation time or at execution time when an attempt is made to give a variable an incorrect value. For example, if the programmer declares a subrange type:

```
TYPE years = [ 1965..1999 ];
```

and inadvertently allows the value of a variable of this type to go to 2000, the program will abort with an appropriate message. This alerts the programmer to look for the error and correct it. If the programmer had used the integer or cardinal data type, the same error would have gone undetected, possibly resulting in a program that apparently runs to completion normally, but in fact gives incorrect answers.

Because of this benefit, programmers are strongly urged to use subrange types whenever appropriate.

subrange type

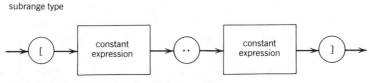

FIGURE 4.2 Syntax of a Subrange Type

4.2   Structured Data Types

The *structured data types* are those whose value sets contain objects that are themselves constructed of smaller, more primitive objects. These data types may be classified according to attributes in three categories: *size, homogeneity,* and *access method.*

   The size attributes are *fixed* and *varying.* Fixed size structured data types have value sets with objects that are always of the same size; that is, an object always occupies exactly the same amount of storage space. Normally, the declaration of such a data type includes an explicit specification of the size of the values of that type. The Pascal programmer will recognize arrays and records as examples. Varying size structured data types have value sets with objects that may vary in size as the execution of a program proceeds; the declaration of these data types does not specify a size. The Pascal file data type is an example.

   A structured data type is said to be *homogeneous* if its value set contains objects made up of individual components all of the same data type; otherwise the structured data type is *heterogeneous.* Arrays and files are examples of homogeneous data types, while records are heterogeneous.

   There are several access method attributes, but in this section we consider only two: *sequential* and *direct.* A structured data type is said to have sequential access if the components of an object of that type have an explicit or implicit order, and processing of those components always begins at the first component and proceeds sequentially through the others in order. Sequential files, such as the Pascal file type, are examples. A structured data type is said to have direct access if any component of an object of that type may be accessed for processing at any time, without regard for the component that is in the previous or next position for access. It does not matter whether there is an order to the components of an object. Thus arrays and records are examples of direct access structured data types. In Chapters 14 and 15 we will examine a variety of additional, user-defined data types introducing some other access methods.

   The programmer often finds, when facing a new problem, that the attributes of a new data type can be recognized. By knowing the classification of all the structured data types available in Modula-2, the programmer can easily choose the appropriate type for the new problem. It should be apparent that with three categories containing two attributes each, we have eight different classes of structured data types. The subsequent sections show how all eight classes can be used in Modula-2.

   Except for BITSET (described in Section 4.2.3), Modula-2 does not provide any specific predefined structured types, as it does for scalar types. Instead, like Pascal, it provides *type constructors,* which may be used to describe how the elements of the value set of a new data type may be constructed from simpler data objects. Therefore, in the discussions in this section, we do not consider operations on structured types (except BITSET). Combining structured values and operations will be considered in Part Two.

4.2.1 Arrays

An *array* is a fixed size, homogeneous, direct access structured data type. The concept of an array in Modula-2 is identical to that in Pascal, although the syntax of the declaration of an array type is somewhat different, as shown in Figure 4.3.

The elements of the array are all of the same data type, called the *base type*. This may be any data type at all, including another structured type. The *index type(s)* must be a simple data type, that is, boolean, character, enumeration, or subrange types. Each element of the array is distinguished from the other elements by its *index* or *subscript*.

The Pascal programmer should note that in Modula-2, the square brackets in a definition such as:

TYPE vector = ARRAY [1..100] OF REAL;

are part of the subrange definition (see Section 4.1.6), rather than part of the array definition. If the subrange had been previously declared as:

TYPE range = [1..100];

then the array declaration would appear as:

TYPE vector = ARRAY range OF REAL;

If the base type of an array is itself an array type, we call the structure an *array of arrays*. This is conceptually different from an array with two index types, which we call a *two-dimensional array*. Modula-2, like Pascal, provides different syntax for referring to objects of these two different types. Consider the following declarations.

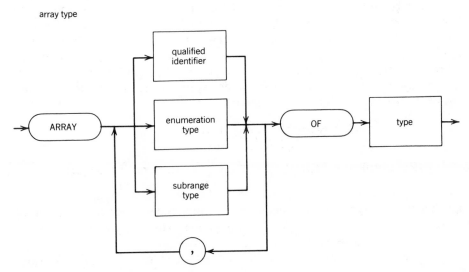

FIGURE 4.3 Syntax of an Array Type

```
CONST wordlength  = 12;
TYPE  word        = ARRAY [ 1..wordlength ] OF CHAR;
      wordlist    = ARRAY [ 1..1000 ] OF word;
      matrix      = ARRAY [1..10 ], [1..10 ] OF REAL;
VAR   dictionary  : wordlist;
      system      : matrix;
```

The tenth word in the variable named dictionary would be referenced by dictionary[10], and would be an object of type word. The second letter of the tenth word in dictionary would be referenced by dictionary[10][2], and would be an object of type character. References to elements of the variable named system would require two indices, which would be written inside a single set of square brackets, as in system[1, 2]. A reference to system with a single index is erroneous.

Modula-2, like Pascal, provides another interpretation of the declaration of multidimensional arrays. A definition such as:

ARRAY [1..10], [1..10] OF REAL

may be thought of as an abbreviation of the definition:

ARRAY [1..10] OF ARRAY [1..10] OF REAL

The notation in the example above, system[1, 2], is then considered to be an abbreviation of the notation system[1][2]. In Pascal, these two forms of notation are considered to be equivalent in all contexts, but in the original definition of Modula-2 by Wirth, this equivalence is not explicitly stated. We assume that most Modula-2 compilers will accept either notation in any context.

The programmer is urged, however, to use the notation that is consistent with the conceptual object being represented by an array data type. Thus when referencing a letter of a word in the dictionary variable example above, the form dictionary[wordnumber][letternumber] is always preferred, whereas when referencing an element of the system matrix above, the form system[i, j] is always preferred. Furthermore, because of the compatibility problems that often accompany the use of anonymous types (see Section 3.3 and Chapter 5), the programmer is urged always to use declarations such as that for wordlist above, rather than either of the following:

TYPE wordlist = ARRAY [1..1000] OF
                        ARRAY [1..wordlength] OF CHAR;

TYPE wordlist = ARRAY [1..1000], [1..wordlength] OF CHAR;

As indicated in the syntax chart in Figure 4.3, arrays may have any number of index types. Implementations may limit the number of dimensions of these multidimensional arrays. Comments similar to those above apply to index notation for such arrays.

In Section 2.2 we mentioned that strings are arrays of characters. More specifically, in Modula-2 we call an array a string if it has the following properties:

1. The base type of the array is CHAR.
2. The index type of the array is a subrange of CARDINAL, and the first value in that subrange is zero.

Pascal programmers should note that this definition differs from Pascal strings in two ways. First, Pascal strings must have an index type beginning at one, and second, Pascal strings must be packed. There is no counterpart in Modula-2 to packed structures. We will see in Chapter 13, however, that other features of Modula-2 provide capabilities comparable to packed structures.

Although the term "string" is commonly used for these arrays, the string abstract data type is substantially more versatile and more complicated. It is the object of detailed study in Sections 14.3 and 15.4. For the remainder of Part One, however, the term "string" denotes just an array of characters.

4.2.2 Record Types

A *record* is a fixed size, heterogeneous, direct access structured data type. The concept of a record in Modula-2 is identical to that in Pascal, although the syntax of the declaration of a record type can be somewhat different, as shown in Figures 4.4 and 4.5.

The following are examples of record type declarations.

```
TYPE
    point = RECORD
                x : REAL;
                y : REAL
            END;
    date  = RECORD
                day    : [ 1..31 ];
                month  : [ 1..12 ];
                year   : [ 1900..2050 ]
            END;
    event = RECORD
                name : ARRAY [ 0..31 ] OF CHAR;
                day    : date
            END;
```

The individual components of a record are known as *fields* and are referenced in program by their *field identifiers*. Because there may be several variables of the same record type, a special notation is needed to distinguish the same fields within different records. For example, consider the following declarations.

record type

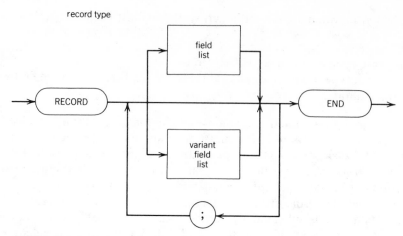

FIGURE 4.4   Syntax of a Record Type

field list

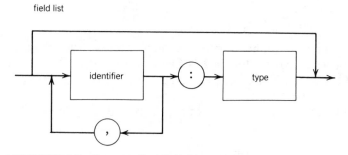

FIGURE 4.5   Syntax of a Field List

```
TYPE name       = RECORD
                    first    : ARRAY [ 0..15 ] OF CHAR;
                    middle : CHAR;
                    last     : ARRAY [ 0..15 ] OF CHAR
                  END;
     namelist   = ARRAY [ 1..500 ] OF name;
VAR  manager   : name;
     secretary  : name;
     customer  : namelist;
```

The last name of the manager is denoted manager.last, while the last name of
the secretary is denoted secretary.last. The last name of the third customer is
denoted customer[3].last.

There are clearly two very different notations for referencing components
of arrays and records, and there is a reason for this. An array is a homogeneous
data type that is used to represent a sequence of related values. Conceptually,

each component is just like all the others, but its position in the sequence distinguishes it. Hence the component is identified by its position or index. In a record, the components may be of different types, and the order in which they appear does not matter. Giving each component its own identifier (assuming they are well-chosen names) makes it easier for the programmer to remember the meaning or purpose of each component.

The record structure is very useful for organizing several conceptually related pieces of data into a single object. Sometimes it is desirable to allow variations from one such collection to another, but to think of them all as examples of a single data type. For example, in a personnel record for a business application, it may be necessary to store different salary information for hourly workers and exempt workers, or to store the names of the spouses of married workers. Modula-2 provides records with *variant* parts (also called *variant records*) for this purpose, as does Pascal; but Modula-2 allows any number of variant parts in a single record, whereas Pascal allows only one. The syntax of a record with a variant part is described in Figures 4.4 and 4.6 (see also Appendix 3).

A programmer familiar with Pascal should note especially the syntactic differences in Modula-2 variant records: the variant parts are separated by a stroke character, and variant field lists are not enclosed in parentheses, as in Pascal.

As examples of variant records, consider an analytic geometry application in which it is desired to represent points and lines in the x–y plane. A point data type was described above. A line may be represented by its slope and y-intercept (the y value where it crosses the y axis), except in the case of a vertical line. In this case, both slope and y-intercept are undefined, but the line may be specified by giving its x-intercept. Conceptually, both these cases are lines, and we want to allow both to be represented by our type definition. The following declarations will do this.

```
TYPE lineclass = ( vertical, nonvertical );
     line      = RECORD
                   CASE class : lineclass OF
                       nonvertical : slope      : REAL;
                                     yintercept : REAL |
                       vertical     : xintercept : REAL
                 END
               END;
```

The field named class in this example is called the *tag* field, and its purpose is to indicate which of the variants is currently defined. The tag field is a field in the record, accessed like any other. If its value is vertical, the remainder of the record contains the fields slope and yintercept, while if the tag field has the value nonvertical, the remainder of the record contains only the field xintercept.

Consider also the example below, which illustrates two variant parts within a single record.

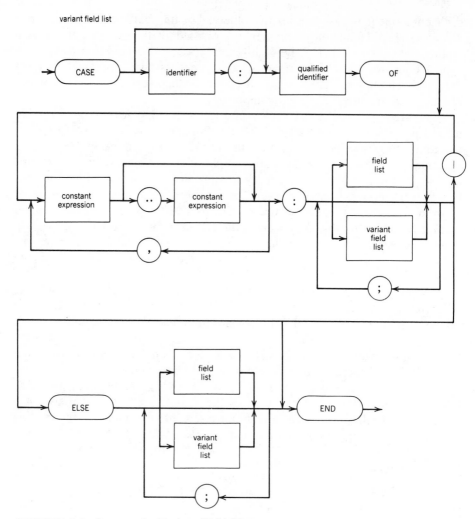

FIGURE 4.6 Syntax of a Variant Field List

```
TYPE salaryclass      = ( hourly, exempt );
     PersonnelRecord  = RECORD
        employee      : name; (* defined above *)
        CASE married  : BOOLEAN OF
           TRUE       : spouse : name |
           FALSE      :
        END;
        age           : CARDINAL;
        CASE category : salaryclass OF
           hourly     : hourlywage : REAL |
```

```
                exempt : monthlysalary : REAL;
                         rank : CARDINAL
         END;
         birthday      : date (* defined above *)
      END;
```

As is evident from the syntax chart for variant records, the tag field may be omitted from the definition, although a data type is still specified to make it clear what the variants may be. This feature has been quite controversial ever since it was invented for Pascal. For example, consider the Pascal declarations below, which show how a Pascal programmer might use a definition without a tag field.

```
type equivalence = record
                      case boolean of
                         true  : ( number : integer );
                         false : ( address : pointer )
               end;
```

Here we assume that the data type pointer has been previously declared in an appropriate manner, and it is indeed a pointer to another type. (Readers not familiar with pointer types in Pascal will want to reread this example after having studied Section 4.3.) For certain applications, it is desirable to do arithmetic on machine addresses (pointers), but Pascal does not allow this. Therefore the programmer declares the data type shown above and then tries the following code in the program.

```
         var eq : equivalence;
             p  : pointer;

         eq.address := p;
         eq.number := eq.number + 32;
         p := eq.address;
```

The intent of this code is to take advantage of the fact that the two variant parts of the record variable eq occupy the same storage locations, and by storing a pointer value in that location, and accessing it by its integer field name, arithmetic is actually being performed on pointers. This is an example of *type coercion,* or forcing a value of one data type to be interpreted as another data type. Type coercion is absolutely necessary in some applications, but this use of variant records is specifically prohibited in standard Pascal. Unfortunately, this use of variant records is also very difficult to catch, and most Pascal compilers will allow it.

Since there does not exist a formal standard for Modula-2, it is not possible to say that the corresponding technique in Modula-2 is specifically prohibited. We can say that it is considered to be bad programming practice (in any language), and that it is unnecessary in Modula-2. The same kind of type coercion can be accomplished cleanly in Modula-2 through *type transfer* functions, which are discussed in Section 4.4.4.

It is recommended that programmers adopt this interpretation of the code in the example above. Whenever an assignment is made to any field of a particular variant, all other variants immediately become undefined. Therefore, after the assignment to eq.address, the next statement should generate a program error, because it attempts to access an undefined value, namely, eq.number. It is further recommended that the programmer consider using an explicit tag field for each variant part of a record. Then in any part of the program where the variant currently defined may not be obvious, the tag field may be tested explicitly. Experience has shown that misuse of variant records can produce some of the most subtle program errors, and these recommendations will help the programmer avoid such problems.

4.2.3 Set Types

The *set* data types in Modula-2 are limited implementations of the corresponding concept from mathematics. A set is an unordered collection of elements chosen from a universe set; in Modula-2 the universe set must be the value set of a simple type, called the *base type* of the set. A set may then be considered to be a varying size, homogeneous, direct access data structure. It is of varying size in that its cardinality (the number of elements it contains) may change during program execution, although the representation of a set in computer memory is actually fixed size (described below). A set data object differs markedly from array and record objects in that its components are not accessed to examine or change their values, but rather to determine whether a particular component is present, or to insert a component or remove it from the set. Since these accesses may be made for any component at any time, the set is considered to have a kind of direct access.

The one predefined set type in Modula-2 is called BITSET. Its values are the power set (meaning the set of all possible subsets) of the universe set $\{0, 1, \ldots, w - 1\}$, where w is the number of bits in a memory word of the host computer system. Constants of this type are written using the familiar mathematical notation, such as:

{ }	the empty or null set
{ 0 }	the set containing only zero
{ 1, 2, 3 }	
{ 3, 2, 1 }	same as previous set; sets are unordered

In addition, to simplify the writing of larger set constants, the "`..`" notation of subranges is allowed, as in:

$$\{ 0..10, 12, 14 \}$$
$$\{ 0..3, 8..11, 15 \}$$

Other set types may be declared in Modula-2, with syntax as described in Figure 4.7.

The base type must be a simple type, that is, boolean, character, enumeration, or subrange. Furthermore, each implementation of Modula-2 will place

set type

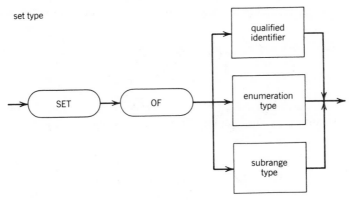

FIGURE 4.7   Syntax of a Set Type

restrictions on the cardinality of the base type; commonly this is limited to the number of bits in a memory word, or a small integer multiple of this value.

This limitation exists because sets are normally represented internally by a *bit vector,* which is a sequence of bits equal in length to the cardinality of the base type. A value of the set type may then be represented by a sequence of bits, where a zero bit indicates that the corresponding element *is not* in the set, and a one bit indicates that it *is* in the set. For example, with an implementation having a limit of 16 on the cardinality of the base type, the following representations are used.

Set	*Representation*
{ }	0000000000000000
{ 0, 1, 13, 15 }	1100000000000101
{ 1..7, 11 }	0111111100010000

On some computer systems it is customary to number the bits in a word from right to left, in which cases the representations above are reversed.

It is possible to declare several different set types with the same or intersecting base types. To distinguish constants of various set types, the type identifier of the set must precede the opening set bracket. For example:

$$\text{TYPE smallset} = \text{SET OF } [\ 0..3\ ];$$
$$\text{bigset}\quad = \text{SET OF } [\ 0..15\ ];$$

{ 0, 1 }	seems ambiguous; it could be a BITSET, smallset, or bigset
smallset { 0, 1 }	is of type smallset
bigset { 0, 1 }	is of type bigset
{ 0, 1 }	is of type BITSET, by convention

There are four binary (i.e., requiring two operands) operations on sets: union, intersection, difference, and symmetric difference.

Set union is denoted by the plus sign. The result of the operation is the set containing all elements that were in either operand set, or in both. For example:

$$\{\} + \{\} = \{\}$$
$$\{1, 2\} + \{\} = \{1, 2\}$$
$$\{1, 3, 5\} + \{2, 3, 4, \} = \{1, 2, 3, 4, 5\}$$

Set intersection is denoted by the asterisk. The result of the operation is the set containing only the elements that were in both operand sets. For example:

$$\{1, 3, 5\} * \{2, 3, 4\} = \{3\}$$
$$\{1..10, 12\} * \{8..15\} = \{8, 9, 10, 12\}$$
$$\{1, 2, 3\} * \{\} = \{\}$$

Set difference is denoted by the minus sign. The result of the operation is the set containing the elements of the first operand set that are *not* also in the second operand set. For example:

$$\{1, 3, 5\} - \{2, 3, 4\} = \{1, 5\}$$
$$\{1, 2, 3\} - \{\} = \{1, 2, 3\}$$
$$\{2, 3, 4, 6, 7, 8\} - \{1..10\} = \{\}$$

Symmetric set difference is denoted by the slash. The result of the operation is the set containing the elements that are in exactly one of the two operand sets. For example:

$$\{1, 3, 5\} / \{2, 3, 4\} = \{1, 2, 4, 5\}$$
$$\{1, 2, 3\} / \{\} = \{1, 2, 3\}$$
$$\{2, 4, 6\} / \{1..4, 7\} = \{1, 3, 6, 7\}$$

A common way of expressing these operations pictorially is through Venn diagrams. The rectangles in Figure 4.8 represent the universe set, the circles represent two sets A and B, and the shaded regions represent the results of the four operations on A and B.

Another important operation defined on sets is the elementhood or "element of" operation, denoted in mathematics by $\in$. This binary operation is represented in Modula-2 by the reserved word IN, and its first operand must be an expression of the base type of the set and its second operand a set. The result of the operation is a boolean value, true or false. For example:

$$3 \text{ IN } \{1, 3, 5\} = \text{TRUE}$$
$$4 \text{ IN } \{1, 3, 5\} = \text{FALSE}$$
$$(2 + 4) \text{ IN } \{1..10\} = \text{TRUE}$$

Two additional operations for sets that are implemented as procedures, namely, INCL and EXCL, are discussed in Section 4.4.2.

Set data types have several advantages for the programmer. First, they allow the representation of some mathematical algorithms in very straightforward notation. Second, they allow the testing of the validity of certain kinds of data in a very succinct manner. Third, because nearly all computers have

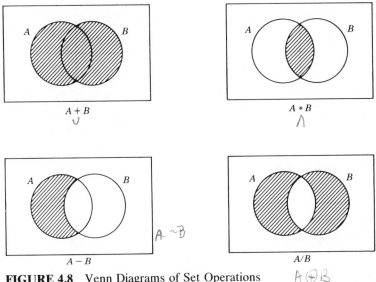

FIGURE 4.8   Venn Diagrams of Set Operations   A ⊕ B

machine instructions to do bitwise logical operations, and sets are represented by bit vectors, certain bit manipulations can be performed very rapidly and still be expressed in the program at a relatively high level of abstraction. The following examples illustrate these points.

Transitive closure of a graph or relation is an important operation with applicability in many areas of computer science. Briefly, we define a *graph* as a set of *vertices* and a set of *edges* from one vertex to another. We might think of the vertices as cities, and the edges as nonstop airline routes. For relations, we might think of the vertices as persons, and the edges as representing the "parent of" relation; an edge goes from each person to each of his or her children. The transitive closure of a graph contains the same vertices, but additional edges. For the cities/airline example, the additional edges represent paths from one city to another via a sequence of intermediate cities. For the parent/child example, the additional edges represent "ancestor of" relationships.

This operation is called "transitive closure" because it can be defined as the result of applying the transitive property repeatedly until no new edges result. At this point the graph is "closed." Figure 4.9 shows an example graph and its transitive closure.

Now consider the following declarations:

```
TYPE vertices      = [ 0..maxvertices ];
     neighborset   = SET OF vertices;
     graph         = ARRAY vertices OF neighborset;

VAR  vertex        : vertices;
     intermediate  : vertices;
     neighbors     : graph;
```

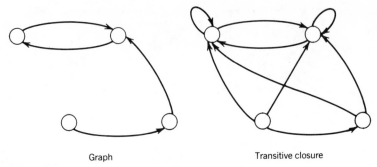

Graph   Transitive closure

FIGURE 4.9   Transitive Closure of a Graph

The transitive closure of a graph may then be computed by repeatedly adding to the neighbor set of a vertex the vertices that are themselves neighbors of a neighbor.

```
FOR intermediate := 0 TO maxvertices DO
    FOR vertex := 0 TO maxvertices DO
        IF intermediate IN neighbors[ vertex ]
            THEN neighbors[ vertex ] := neighbors[ vertex ] +
                                         neighbors[ intermediate ]
        END
    END
END
```

This alogrithm is attributed to Warshall (1962). It depends of course on the Modula-2 implementation allowing sets as large as the number of vertices in the graph.

Consider also a character that must be tested to determine whether it is alphabetic or whether it belongs to a particular set of characters. The latter case arises frequently in interactive applications where single-letter commands can be given to effect certain actions. Consider declarations such as:

```
TYPE characterset    = SET OF CHAR;

VAR   validcommands  : characterset;
      alphabetic     : BOOLEAN;
      command        : CHAR;
      character      : CHAR;
```

Then statements like the following could be used to achieve the desired results.

```
alphabetic := character IN characterset { 'A'..'Z', 'a'..'z' };

validcommands := characterset { 'A', 'I', 'D', 'N', 'S' };

IF command IN validcommands THEN . . .
```

Modula-2 implementations do not necessarily allow sets large enough to hold all characters. In Section 14.4 we will develop a way to represent arbitrarily large sets.

As a final example, suppose a computer system uses a byte (eight bits) to hold eight system status bits (sometimes called "flag" bits). A programmer could name and manipulate each bit individually with declarations and statements such as those shown below.

```
TYPE statusbitnames = ( overflow, carry, zero, negative,
                        link, interrupt, kernel, user );
     statusset      = SET OF statusbitnames;

VAR  statusbyte     = statusset;

(* to clear all the status bits *)
statusbyte := statusset { };

(* to determine if the carry bit is set *)
IF carry IN statusbyte THEN . . .

(* to set simultaneously the link and user bits *)
statusbyte := statusbyte + statusset { link, user };
```

4.2.4   File Types

Modula-2 does not have a file type constructor like that of Pascal. Instead, each implementation of Modula-2 will include a library module that provides file data types. Section 9.3 discusses a representative file library module, but readers are cautioned to examine the documentation of their own particular implementation to determine the file capabilities actually provided. It is not uncommon for an implementation to provide the equivalent of the sequential file structure of Pascal (a variable size, homogeneous, sequential access data structure), plus other file capabilities, such as indexed sequential or direct access files.

4.2.5   Summary of Structured Types

At the beginning of Section 4.2 we talked about the classification of structured data types by attributes in three categories. We have seen that Modula-2 provides data types with some of these combinations of attributes. For example, an array is a fixed size, homogeneous, direct access type, and a record is a fixed size, heterogeneous, direct access type.

The other six combinations of attributes characterize structured data types that are also usually available in Modula-2, although not as specific predefined types. To define the other six, we need to make some observations. First, although an array is a direct access data structure, it is possible for an algorithm to access an array sequentially. In practice, arrays are accessed sequentially more than half the time. Thus it is possible for the array structure to be used for an application that needs sequential access. Second, the variant record structure may be used to build heterogeneous structured types out of homogeneous types. For example, consider the following declarations.

```
TYPE
    variant   = ( cardtype, inttype, realtype );
    element   = RECORD
                    CASE elementtype : variant OF
                        cardtype : cvalue : CARDINAL |
                        inttype  : ivalue : INTEGER |
                        realtype : rvalue : REAL
                    END
                END;
    numbers  = ARRAY [ 1..100 ] OF element;
```

An array variable of the numbers type may be used to hold either a cardinal, an integer, or a real in each element, and thus may be considered to be a fixed size, heterogeneous, direct access structure.

All implementations of Modula-2 are expected to include a library module defining a file data type (see Section 9.3). Files provide varying size, sequential access structured types. If an implementation also provides a direct access file module, varying size, direct access structured types are available.

Table 4.4 summarizes the eight classes of structured data types.

4.3 Pointers and Dynamic Data Types

There are many programming situations in which the exact size or organization of a collection of data cannot be known in advance, since it may vary considerably from one execution of the program to the next. In such situations, arrays and records, which have fixed sizes and structures, are not sufficiently flexible to be useful.

A look at how arrays and records are normally stored in computer memory will help direct us to a new kind of data structure for these situations. Because arrays and records are fixed size, the compiler can determine exactly

TABLE 4.4   Structured Data Type Classes

Size	Homogeneity	Access	Modula-2 Structured Type
fixed	homogeneous	sequential	array, with algorithm that limits access
fixed	homogeneous	direct	array
fixed	heterogeneous	sequential	record or array of variant records, with algorithm that limits access
fixed	heterogeneous	direct	record of array of variant records
varying	homogeneous	sequential	sequential file
varying	homogeneous	direct	direct access file
varying	heterogeneous	sequential	sequential file of variant records
varying	heterogeneous	direct	direct access file of variant records

how much storage to allocate for a variable of such a type and can put the variable at a known memory location. Furthermore, since neither arrays nor records can grow during execution, the memory locations just before and just after may be allocated to other variables. The starting address of an array or record is known to the compiler, and the address of a single element or field can be determined by adding an offset to the starting address; the offset is a function of the subscript or field name. This address computation depends on the fact that all elements of the array or record are stored in consecutive locations in computer memory.

These facts make it nearly impossible to have arrays or records that might grow during execution, since such growth would require the relocation of the variables before or after it. However, if we relax the requirement that the elements be stored consecutively, growth can occur by adding storage locations wherever they may be available in memory. In doing this, we gain the flexibility of a data structure that can grow and shrink as needed, while giving up the capability to find a particular element of the structure via an address computation involving the starting address and offset. In somewhat oversimplified terms, we are replacing a fixed size, direct access data structure with a varying size, sequential access data structure.

To ensure finding all elements of the data structure, we require each element to include an indicator of where the next element is in memory. Thus each element consists of two parts: the data intended to be stored in that element, and the memory address of the next element. The concept of memory address is a very low level concept, and it differs from one computer to the next. Modula-2, like Pascal, provides a high level abstraction of this concept, called a *pointer*.

Actually, a pointer is not a single data type but rather a type constructor, as we have seen previously for arrays, records, and sets. Each pointer type is *bound* to another data type, called the *base type,* and the value set of a pointer type is the set of memory addresses of objects of the base type.

The declaration of a pointer type in Modula-2 differs from that in Pascal, as shown in Figure 4.10.

The base type of a pointer may be any data type that is already defined, including predefined types, or a type that is subsequently defined within the same block (defined in Chapter 8). This idea is discussed in more detail in Section 7.5. Note that this is the only place in Modula-2 where an entity may be referenced before it has been declared.

One predefined constant, named NIL, is a member of the value set of any

pointer type

FIGURE 4.10 Syntax of a Pointer Declaration

pointer type. This special value indicates that the pointer is not currently the address of any object of the base type. Note that this is different from a pointer variable being undefined.

The only operation defined on pointer types, called the *dereferencing operator,* is a unary postfix operator. That is, it operates on a single operand, and it appears after the operand; it is denoted by the upward pointing arrow or caret character (↑ or ˆ). The value of a dereferenced pointer is the value of the object to which the pointer points. It is an error to apply the dereferencing operator to a variable whose value is NIL, since that value indicates that the pointer does not point to an object.

For example, consider the following declarations.

TYPE integerpointer = POINTER TO INTEGER;

VAR ptr : integerpointer;

Suppose that the integer 25 is stored in memory location 1203, and that the pointer variable named ptr currently points to that location (which means that ptr has as a value the address 1203). We often diagram this relationship as shown in Figure 4.11, where the value of the pointer is represented by an arrow rather than an address that looks like an integer.

In this example, the variable named ptr is of type integerpointer and has as its value the address 1203. The dereferenced pointer ptrˆ, which is also a variable, is of type INTEGER and has as its value the integer 25. Because this integer variable is not declared with its own identifier, it is said to be an *anonymous* variable. It may be accessed only through the pointer.

Anonymous variables are not declared, so they must be created in another manner. Like Pascal, Modula-2 provides two predefined procedures for the creation and destruction of anonymous variables. The procedure NEW takes a single parameter of a pointer type, allocates storage of sufficient size to hold one element of the base type of that pointer type, and returns the pointer parameter with the value of the address of that allocated storage. The DISPOSE procedure takes a single parameter of a pointer type and deallocates the storage pointed to by that parameter. The parameter is returned undefined.

When allocating or deallocating storage for an anonymous variable of a record type with one or more variant parts, a second form of the NEW and DISPOSE procedures is available. In this form, additional parameters are supplied indicating the values of the tag fields that specify the variants desired. For example, consider the following declarations.

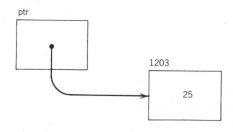

FIGURE 4.11   Pointer

```
TYPE
    classification = ( big, small, empty );
    box  = RECORD
                    length : REAL;
                    width  : REAL;
                    CASE class : classification OF
                        big     : name : ARRAY [ 1..100 ] OF CHAR;
                                    value : REAL I
                        small   : ident  : CHAR I
                        empty :
                    END
                END;
    ptr  = POINTER TO box;
VAR
    p : ptr;
```

A record of the *box* type may be allocated with the statement

$$\text{NEW (p)}$$

However, such a record can be of three different sizes, depending which of the three variants is to be used. In the absence of any knowledge of which variant is desired, the NEW procedure must allocate the maximum size. If we know that one of the smaller variants is needed, we can specify the allocation of a smaller block of storage by supplying the value of the tag field as a second parameter to NEW, such as:

$$\text{NEW (p, small)}$$

A subsequent invocation of DISPOSE must also specify a second parameter to indicate what size of block is being deallocated, such as:

$$\text{DISPOSE (p, small)}$$

When we deallocate a variant record, we must be careful to specify the same tag value used when we allocated it. If the record contains a tag field, as this example does, it is easy to remember the tag value. The allocation could be:

```
NEW ( p, small );
p^.class := small
```

and then the deallocation could be:

$$\text{DISPOSE (p, p^.class)}$$

Both Modula-2 and Pascal provide for allocating and deallocating variant records in which the last field in the last variant is itself a variant field. A third parameter for NEW and DISPOSE can specify the tag value of the inner variant field. Additional nested variant fields can be specified with additional parameters. We emphasize that only the tag value of a variant field that is the last field in another variant may be specified. This restriction allows the compiler to determine the offset of every field in the record, relative to the start of the record, without having to know which variants are active. This greatly simplifies the machine language instructions generated by the compiler for accessing record variables.

In Modula-2, the procedures NEW and DISPOSE are actually defined in terms of more primitive procedures ALLOCATE and DEALLOCATE, which themselves are *not* predefined. They must be supplied through a library module (see Section 10.2). All Modula-2 implementations include such a library module, and its design is discussed in detail in Section 15.6.

Variables of array and record types are said to be *static* because they exist in unchanging form throughout the lifetime of the procedure in which they are declared. In contrast, anonymous variables are said to be *dynamic,* since they can be created and destroyed at any time. If a dynamic variable is itself a record type that contains pointers, it is possible to build a chain of dynamic variables, each pointing to the next. Such a structure is commonly called a *linked list,* and is classified as a *dynamic data structure*. Such structures are examined in detail in Chapter 15.

4.4 Expressions

Most common programming languages, including Modula-2, have borrowed from mathematics the concept of an *expression*. In this section we look at the syntax and semantics of expressions, including some additional features of Modula-2 that are not present in Pascal. Most of the concepts in this section apply to most or all data types; hence they are collected here rather than being inserted in the preceding sections detailing the individual data types. Figures 4.12 through 4.17 show the syntax of expressions.

A *designator,* as described in Figure 4.16, represents either a variable or a function. In the latter case, it must be followed by an actual parameter list (see Section 7.4). Unlike Pascal, functions in Modula-2 must have an actual parameter list even if the function is defined with no parameters. In this case the actual parameter list is just a pair of parentheses. A designator may also include the dereference operator, array subscripts, or record selectors, as indicated in the syntax chart.

Like Pascal, Modula-2 provides a *with* statement to simplify references to

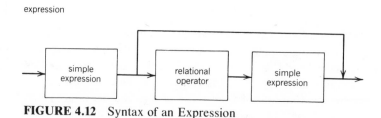

FIGURE 4.12 Syntax of an Expression

simple expression

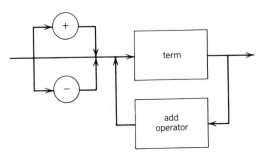

FIGURE 4.13   Syntax of a Simple Expression

term

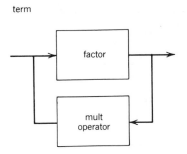

FIGURE 4.14   Syntax of a Term

many fields in the same record variable. The syntax of this statement is shown in Figure 4.18. To demonstrate its use, consider the declarations:

```
TYPE triangle = RECORD
                    x1, y1 : REAL;
                    x2, y2 : REAL;
                    x3, y3 : REAL
               END;

     VAR tri : triangle;
```

A statement that determines if the first two points in the triangle are equal might be written:

```
IF ( tri.x1 = tri.x2 ) AND ( tri.y1 = tri.y2 ) THEN . . .
```

The with statement allows us to specify expressions involving the fields of a record without writing the record identifier in every field reference. The statement above could therefore be written as follows:

```
WITH tri DO
    IF ( x1 = x2 ) AND ( y1 = y2 ) THEN . . .
END
```

factor

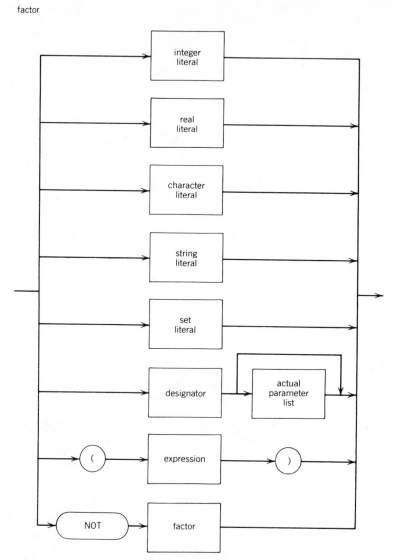

FIGURE 4.15 Syntax of a Factor

Within the body of the with statement, any occurrence of a field identifier is assumed to mean the field of the record specified in the with clause. While this statement does not provide any additional computational power to the language, it enhances the readability of programs that manipulate many record variables.

Because Modula-2 allows the definition of many different but related types, it is not possible to provide a separate set of operators for each type.

designator

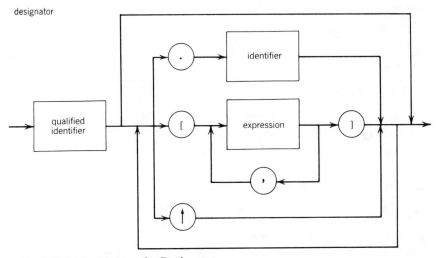

FIGURE 4.16 Syntax of a Designator

relational operator

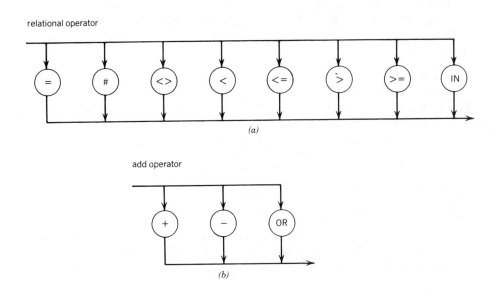

(a)

add operator

(b)

mult operator

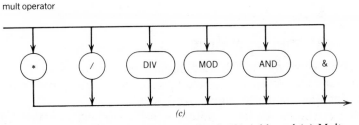

(c)

FIGURE 4.17 Syntax of Operators: (*a*) Relational; (*b*) Add, and (*c*) Mult

with statement

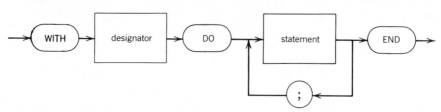

FIGURE 4.18   Syntax of a With Statement

Many of the common operators may be applied to operands of a variety of
types. For example, the addition operator, represented by the plus sign, may be
applied to integer, cardinal, real, and subrange types. In strongly typed languages like Modula-2, it is important for the compiler to be able to determine
that each operator is being applied to operands of appropriate types. For most
binary operators, the requirement that the operands be of the same type is too
strong; it would not allow, for example, the addition of an integer and a value of
an integer subrange type. Therefore we introduce the concept of *type compatibility,* and then require that operands be of compatible types. Two types T1 and
T2 are said to be *compatible* if and only if one of the following conditions is
true.

1. T1 and T2 are the same type. This means that both types are denoted by the
same type identifier.
2. T1 and T2 are defined to be equal types. This means that one of the following
declarations has been made:

TYPE T1 = T2;

TYPE T2 = T1;

3. T1 is a subrange of T2, or vice versa.
4. T1 and T2 are both subranges of the same base type.

For an expression to be semantically correct, the operands of most operators must be of compatible types. The exception is the IN operator, which
requires one operand of a set type and one operand of the base type of that set
type.

4.4.1   Relational Operators

Six *relational operators* are defined on all the scalar types (integer, cardinal,
real, boolean, character, enumeration, subrange). These operators and the
symbols denoting them are summarized below.

Each of the relational operators is a binary infix operator—that is, it
requires two operands and the symbol denoting the operator is written be-

Operator	Symbol
equal	=
not equal	<> or #
greater than	>
greater than or equal	>=
less than	<
less than or equal	<=

tween the operands. Each of the operators returns a boolean value, and the meanings of the operators are those of the corresponding mathematical operators. The Pascal programmer should note that Modula-2 provides an alternate symbol for inequality, the # character. This is the symbol closest in appearance to the mathematical symbol $\neq$ that we have on most computer terminals (see also Appendix 3).

The equality and inequality operators may also be applied to all pointer types, although both operands must be of the same type in any instance of these operators. Since dynamic variables may be anywhere in memory, their relative locations are unimportant; hence it is unnecessary to have the other four relational operators defined on pointer types.

Four of the relational operators are defined on set types. The equal and not equal operators have their usual meanings. The symbols <= and >= mean subset and superset, respectively. If A and B are sets, then in Modula-2 we would write A <= B and A >= B, where in mathematics we would write $A \subseteq B$ and $A \supseteq B$. Both these represent improper inclusion; proper inclusion would be represented in Modula-2 by (A <= B) AND (A <> B).

The relational operators are not defined on any other data types in Modula-2. The Pascal programmer should note that this includes arrays, hence includes strings, which are defined as ARRAY [0..n] OF CHAR in Modula-2. This is not as serious a limitation as it may seem, since Modula-2 provides much better capabilities than Pascal for defining new data types with associated operations. This is the subject of Chapter 12, and the string data type is treated in detail in Sections 14.3 and 15.4.

4.4.2 Predefined Functions and Procedures

Many of the commonly performed computations in Modula-2 are not represented by operator symbols but rather by functions and procedures. This is also the case in mathematics, where functions such as logarithm, exponential, sine, and cosine are seen frequently. Modula-2, like most common languages, has borrowed the notation of mathematics for functions, which is the function name followed by its arguments in parentheses, as seen in Figure 4.15. This notation will be familiar to Pascal programmers.

We will examine the predefined functions and procedures of Modula-2 in groups, based on the data type on which they are defined.

The absolute value function is defined for all numeric types, and is represented by ABS. It returns a value of the same type as its parameter.

Increment and decrement procedures, denoted INC and DEC, are defined for integer and cardinal types; each procedure has two forms. These procedures may be defined by equivalent assignment statements as shown below:

Procedure	*Definition*
INC (x)	x := x + 1
INC (x, n)	x := x + n
DEC (x)	x := x − 1
DEC (x, n)	x := x − n

The parity function ODD is defined on the cardinal type. It returns true if the parameter is an odd number, false otherwise. This function may also be defined as ODD (x) means x MOD 2 <> 0.

The increment and decrement procedures are also defined on the character data type and on enumerated types. In their simple forms, they return the next (successor) or previous (predecessor) value of the same data type. For example, INC ('A') = 'B' and DEC ('8') = '7'. If color is a variable of the enumeration type (red, orange, yellow, green, blue, violet), and currently has the value yellow, then INC (color) = green, and DEC (color) = orange. Note also that INC (violet) is undefined, as is DEC (red). In the two parameter forms, these functions are defined in the expected way: INC (x, n) is defined as INC (x) applied *n* times; similarly for DEC (x, n).

The uppercase or capitalization function, denoted CAP, is defined on the character data type and takes a single parameter: CAP (c) is defined to be c if the value of c is anything but a lowercase letter, and the corresponding uppercase letter when c is a lowercase letter. Thus CAP ('+') = '+', CAP ('B') = 'B', and CAP ('w') = 'W'. There is no corresponding lowercase function in Modula-2.

There are two procedures defined on set data types. The inclusion procedure, denoted INCL, is used to put a value into a set; the exclusion procedure, denoted EXCL, is used to remove a value from a set. Each takes two parameters. The first is a set variable, and the second is an *expression* of the base type of the set, the value of which is to be included in or excluded from that set variable. These functions may be defined by the following (syntactically incorrect) assignment statements.

Procedure	*Definition*
INCL (s, x)	s := s + { x }
DECL (s, x)	s := s − { x }

These assignment statements are incorrect because in Modula-2 the notation { ... } may be used only to express set *constants*, and each element listed inside the braces must be a constant expression of the base type of the set. Note that this is different from Pascal set expressions. The inclusion and exclusion procedures may be used to accomplish the addition or deletion of an element when that element is described by an expression rather than a constant (see, however, Appendix 3).

Modula-2 has several other predefined functions and procedures that are not classified as operations on data types. These are discussed in appropriate places later in the book.

4.4.3 Operator Precedence

The concept of *operator precedence* in programming language is derived from the corresponding concept in algebra. In expressions such as $2 + 3 * 4$, the multiplication operator takes precedence over (or has higher precedence than) the addition operator; that is, the multiplication must be done first, even though the addition operator is encountered first when reading from left to right. Thus this expression is evaluated as $2 + (3 * 4) = 14$, rather than $(2 + 3) * 4 = 20$.

In Modula-2, as in other programming languages that allow algebraic expressions, all operators are given a precedence that allows the unambiguous evaluation of expressions regardless of whether parentheses are present. The precedence of the operators in Table 4.5 is from highest to lowest; operators at the same level in the table have the same precedence.

The syntax of expressions, as seen at the beginning of Section 4.4, precludes consecutive operators except in expressions involving the dereferencing operator. For example, assume variables a and b are of the integer type, and p is a pointer to an integer. Then

a * −b	must be written a * (−b)
−b * a	is correct as written
pˆ + a	is correct as written

The operator precedence of Modula-2 is the same as that of Pascal. Experience has shown that many new programmers have problems because of the low precedence of the relational operators. For example, it is common to need to express a mathematical relation such as:

$$0 \le x \le 100$$

Both the following attempts to express this relation are incorrect.

$$0 <= x <= 100$$
$$0 <= x \text{ AND } x <= 100$$

The first is incorrect because the first operator produces a boolean result, and the second operator cannot be applied to one operand of type boolean and one of type integer. The second is incorrect because the AND operator has higher

TABLE 4.5 Operator Precedence

(dereferencing operator)
unary +, unary −, NOT
*(numeric), /(real), DIV, MOD, AND, &, *(sets), /(sets)
+(numeric), −(numeric), OR, +(sets), −(sets)
=, <>, #, <, <=, >, >=, IN, <=(sets), >=(sets)

precedence than the relational operators, implying that the first subexpression to be evaluated is x AND x, and the AND operator is not defined on integer operands. The correct form of this expression in Modula-2 is

$$(0 <= x) \text{ AND } (x <= 100)$$

4.4.4   Type Conversion and Type Transfer

In a strongly typed language like Modula-2, the data type of each constant, variable, and expression never changes. However, in some programming situations it is necessary to change the type of a value. Modula-2 provides a variety of functions for type conversion and type transfer.

At the lowest level, every data object is stored in the computer memory as a pattern of bits. An *interpretation* of such a pattern yields a *value* of a particular type. Many different interpretations may be applied to a given pattern, and we call these interpretations integer, real, character, bitset, and so on. At a higher level of abstraction, we can speak of values that are conceptually similar but are the results of applying different interpretations to different bit patterns. For example, the integer 1, the real 1.0, and the character '1' represent the same concept, but all are represented (on most computers) by different bit patterns.

We can then define type conversion and type transfer as follows:

Type conversion: changes a value from one type to another by changing the internal representation while maintaining the conceptual value.

Type transfer: changes a value from one type to another by maintaining the internal representation but changing the conceptual value.

Modula-2 provides two predefined type conversion functions. The truncation function, denoted TRUNC, is defined on the real data type and yields a value of the cardinal type. Conversion from cardinal to real is provided by the FLOAT function. The Pascal programmer should note three differences between Modula-2 and Pascal.

There is no conversion in Modula-2 that rounds rather than truncates. However, rounding may be accomplished by recognizing the relationship:

$$\text{round} (x) = \text{TRUNC} (x + 0.5)$$

for positive values of x.

The truncation function is defined only for nonnegative reals, since the result is a (nonnegative) cardinal value.

Conversion from integer to real is implicit in Pascal, but requires the FLOAT function in Modula-2. Furthermore, this function may be applied only to cardinal values, and hence not to negative integers.

Some implementations of Modula-2 may provide type conversion functions between real and integer types. When present, these functions may reside in the mathematical library module (see Section 10.1).

There are actually several other implicit type conversions in Modula-2 (and most other languages); these are found in the input and output procedures. For example, the cardinal value named "one hundred twenty-three" and the character string value "123" are the same conceptual value, but they have different internal representations. Input and output procedures normally convert between these two representations.

There are two groups of type transfer functions in Modula-2. The first group contains several functions that are similar to those of Pascal. Most familiar are the CHR and ORD functions. Assuming that the ASCII character set is being used, the CHR function maps the cardinals from 0 to 127 to the corresponding ASCII character, and the ORD function maps the ASCII characters to the cardinals 0 to 127.

As in Pascal, the ORD function is also defined on boolean, cardinal, integer, and all enumeration types. In all cases it yields a value that is the ordinal value (position in the value set of the type) of its parameter. For cardinal parameters it is the identity function. Its value on negative integer parameters is undefined.

Unlike Pascal, the inverse of the ordinal function is also defined on other types. The VAL function requires two parameters, the first being a type identifier, and the second the ordinal value to be transferred to that type. Consider the following declarations.

```
TYPE color = ( red, orange, yellow, green, blue, violet );

VAR  answer : BOOLEAN;
     paint  : color;
     letter : CHAR;
     number : CARDINAL;
```

The assignment statements below (see Chapter 5) will give the values to the variables as noted in the comments.

```
answer := VAL ( BOOLEAN, 0 ); (* answer gets FALSE *)
answer := TRUE;
number := ORD ( answer );      (* number gets 1    *)
paint  := VAL ( color, 4 );    (* paint gets blue  *)
paint  := DEC ( paint );       (* paint gets green *)
number := ORD ( paint );       (* number gets 3    *)
letter := VAL ( CHAR, 66 );    (* letter gets 'B'  *)
letter := CHR ( 66 );          (* letter gets 'B'  *)
letter := INC ( letter, 10 );  (* letter gets 'L'  *)
number := ORD ( letter );      (* number gets 76   *)
```

Since VAL and ORD are inverse functions, the following relationships hold for value x of type T and value n of type CARDINAL:

$$VAL (T, ORD (x)) = x$$

$$ORD (VAL (T, n)) = n$$

The second group of type transfer functions in Modula-2 have no counterparts in Pascal. The type identifier of any type may be used as a function identifier to transfer a value of any other type into that type. There is one important restriction on the use of this feature. Since a type transfer preserves the internal representation of the value, the two types involved must have internal representations of the same size. Thus the definition and behavior of these functions is completely implementation dependent.

This kind of transfer function is necessary to do arithmetic when one operand is integer and the other is cardinal. For example, if the variable int is an integer and card is a cardinal, the expression

int + card

is not valid, but both the following are valid.

int + INTEGER (card)

CARDINAL (int) + card

The first expression gives an integer sum, while the second gives a cardinal sum.

In some implementations, the same size restriction may be relaxed somewhat in that a value of a type with a smaller internal representation may be transferred to a type with a larger internal representation, with the understanding that the extra (leading) bits are all set to zero. Programmers are advised to investigate carefully the actual definitions of these type transfer functions on their own Modula-2 implementations.

On many computers, machine addresses and cardinal numbers occupy the same amount of storage (often two bytes = 16 bits, or four bytes = 32 bits). For system programming applications, it is often desirable to be able to do arithmetic on addresses. Consider the following definitions:

```
TYPE  address = POINTER TO block;
      block   = RECORD
                    ...
                END;

VAR   blockptr : address;
```

If it were necessary to increment the address in the variable named blockptr by 32, for example, we could write:

blockptr := address (CARDINAL (blockptr) + 32):

Here the type identifier CARDINAL is used as a function to transfer the value of blockptr to the cardinal type, to which we can then add 32. Then the type identifier **address** is used as a function to transfer the resulting value back to the address type. This is necessary because the target of the assignment, blockptr, is of the address type. Notice that this capability makes it unnecessary to do the unusual things with variant records described in Section 4.2.2. Another way of doing address arithmetic in Modula-2 is described in Section 13.1.2.

In nearly all cases, Modula-2 compilers do not generate any machine instructions for the type transfer functions. In the preceding example, only code to add 32 and store the result will be generated. The existence of type transfer functions allows programmers to state explicitly that they intend for a particular internal bit pattern to be interpreted differently from normal expectations. This explicit statement of intent has been seen to be extremely valuable, because it allows the compiler to recognize all unintended type transfers. Such unintended transfers have long been known to be a source of subtle and difficult-to-find errors in programs written in untyped or weakly type languages (like Fortran). If properly used, type transfer functions provide very powerful capabilities for the programmer, while still allowing the language to provide the enormous benefits of strong typing.

5

Assignment
Statement

The *assignment* statement is used to give a value to a variable. Its syntax is defined in Figure 5.1.

The symbol := is called the *assignment operator*. The designator on the left-hand side of the assignment operator must designate a variable, commonly called the *target* of the assignment. As shown in Figure 4.16, the designator may be a simple identifier, a qualified identifier, an array designator (such as list[i], when the target is an element of an array), a record field designator (such as box.length, when the target is a field of a record variable), or a dereferenced pointer (such as p^, when the target is an anonymous variable pointed to by pointer p). The target may also be a formal parameter of a procedure, as described in Section 7.4.

The expression on the right-hand side of an assignment may be any expression that satisfies the syntax described in Section 4.4. Nearly all "computations" specified in a program appear in the expression of an assignment statement. Thus this statement is the workhorse of programming. In the early days of programming, the assignment statement often accounted for as much as 70% of the statements in a program. That percentage is lower in modern languages, in which procedure invocations and control structures are more powerful and more numerous.

There is one semantic rule for assignment statements that is of critical importance in strongly typed languages such as Modula-2:

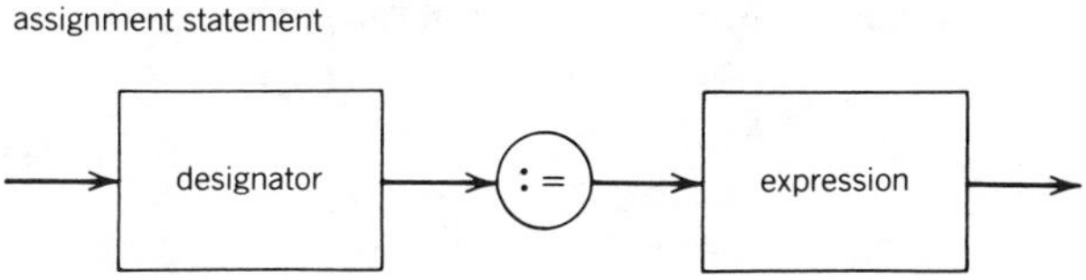

assignment statement

FIGURE 5.1 Syntax of an Assignment Statement

The data type of the target variable and the data type of the expression must be *assignment compatible*.

This rule guarantees that no unintentional type transfers will occur; the importance of this is discussed in Section 4.4.4.

Two data types T1 and T2 are said to be *assignment compatible* if and only if one of the following conditions is true.

1. T1 and T2 are the same type. This means that both types are denoted by the same type identifier.
2. T1 and T2 are defined to be equal types. This means that one of the following declarations has been made:

$$\text{TYPE T1} = \text{T2};$$

$$\text{TYPE T2} = \text{T1};$$

3. T1 is a subrange of T2, or vice versa.
4. T1 and T2 are both subranges of the same base type.
5. T1 is INTEGER or a subrange of INTEGER and T2 is CARDINAL or a subrange of CARDINAL, or vice versa. This is not a special case of rule 3, since on most computers the integer type includes negative values that are not of the cardinal type, and the cardinal type includes very large values that are not of the integer type.
6. T1 and T2 are both string types (ARRAY [0..upperlimit] OF CHAR), and the length of the target string is at least as great as the string on the right-hand side.

Assignment compatibility can be determined by the compiler by examining the definitions of the two types. An assignment statement involving assignment-compatible target variable and expression can nevertheless cause a program error if the value of the expression is not within the value set of the data type of the target. Such an error, in general, cannot be detected or anticipated by the compiler, since the values of the data objects in the expression, hence the value of the expression, are not known to the compiler.

The following examples illustrate the concept of assignment compatibility.

```
TYPE small     = [ 0..9 ];
     digit     = small;
     large     = [ 0..999 ];
```

```
VAR  number1   : INTEGER;
     number2   : INTEGER;
     number3   : small;
     number4   : digit;
     number5   : large;
     number6   : CARDINAL;
```

All the following assignments are correct, since the variables involved are of assignment-compatible types.

```
number1 := number2;   (* condition 1 *)
number3 := number4;   (* condition 2 *)
number1 := number3;   (* condition 3 *)
number3 := number1;   (* condition 3 *)
number4 := number5;   (* condition 4 *)
number6 := number2;   (* condition 5 *)
```

In the fourth, fifth, and sixth examples, however, it is possible for a program error to occur, since the variable on the right might have a value that is not in the value set of the type of the target variable (such as number1 = 100, and number2 = −1).

Consider also the following declarations.

```
TYPE list    = ARRAY [ 1..100 ] OF INTEGER;
     intlist = ARRAY [ 1..100 ] OF INTEGER;
     cardlist = ARRAY [ 1..100 ] OF CARDINAL;

VAR  list1   : list;
     list2   : intlist;
     list3   : cardlist;
     list4   : ARRAY [ 1..100 ] OF INTEGER;
     list5   : ARRAY [ 1..100 ] OF INTEGER;
```

All the following statements are incorrect, since the types of the variables in each statement are not assignment compatible.

```
list1 := list2;
list2 := list3;
list4 := list1;
list4 := list2;
list4 := list5;
```

The variables list4 and list5 are of *anonymous* types; that is, no type identifier has been defined for them. The use of anonymous types frequently leads to incompatibilities like those in the preceding examples, and therefore programmers are urged to avoid them.

When assigning a shorter string to a longer string variable, the target string is padded with the ASCII null character (0C).

In Modula-2, the assignment statement may be used with target variables of all data types. Pascal programmers will note that the same is not true in

Pascal; in that language assignment is not defined on file types. In both languages, programmers must be careful with data objects that are represented by dynamic data structures and accessed via a pointer. Assignment is defined on pointers, but a pointer assignment makes one pointer contain the same value as another pointer; it does not yield two distinct copies of the dynamic structure at the end of those pointers. In such cases, we will want to distinguish assignment from making a copy. This topic is considered in more detail in Chapter 15.

Because assignment is defined on all types in Modula-2, it is possible to copy values of arrays and records in a single statement. For example:

```
TYPE intlist    = ARRAY [ 1..100 ] OF INTEGER;
     cardlist   = ARRAY [ 1..100 ] OF CARDINAL;
     cell       = RECORD
                      list     : intlist;
                      average  : REAL;
                      symbol   : CHAR
                  END;

VAR  list1      :  intlist;
     list2      :  intlist;
     list3      :  cardlist;
     box1       :  cell;
     box2       :  cell;
```

To copy the value of list1 into list2, we need only write

```
list2 := list1;
```

Note that it is *not* necessary to use a loop to accomplish this task; we do not need something like:

```
FOR i := 1 TO 100 DO
    list2[ i ] := list1[ i ]
END
```

On the other hand, since intlist and cardlist are not assignment-compatible types, we *cannot* write:

```
list3 := list1;
```

In this case, we must use a loop such as:

```
FOR i := 1 TO 100 DO
    list3[ i ] := list1[ i ]
END
```

The assignment statement in the body of this loop is correct, because the integer and cardinal types are assignment compatible.

Similarly, to copy the value of box1 into box2, we need only write

```
box2 := box1;
```

Again, it is *not* necessary to write the three statements:

```
box2.list := box1.list;
box2.average := box1.average;
box2.symbol := box2.symbol;
```

A programmer new to strongly typed languages is urged to study the assignment-compatibility rules carefully before beginning to use Modula-2. A thorough understanding of these rules can prevent a large number of simple programming errors.

6

Control
Structures

In the early days of computing, programmers were more aware of and concerned with the various hardware components of the computer (addition unit, multiplication unit, comparison unit, etc.) because they had to program in machine language. The *control unit* was the part of the machine that interpreted an instruction and caused the appropriate actions to take place in the other units. The sequence of instructions passing through the control unit became known as the *flow of control*. Normally, instructions stored in consecutive memory cells were executed in order. However, certain instructions were devised that affected this normal order; these control instructions were one of the major differences between computers and earlier calculating machines.

As programming languages evolved from machine language through assembly languages to the high level procedural languages such as Fortran, PL/I, Pascal, and Modula-2, control instructions evolved into control statements. The revolution came in the late 1960s when it was realized that certain patterns of control flow appeared repeatedly in programs. Programs would be easier to write and more reliable if there were a programming language that included statements that represented the abstract ideas behind these patterns (decisions, loops, etc.) in precise and straightforward terms. These control abstractions, and the statements that implement them, have come to be known as *control structures*.

The control structures of most modern languages can be categorized in three groups, which we will call the *sequence* group, the *alternative* group, and the *iteration/recursion* group. Each group is defined and discussed in detail in the following sections.

Two other topics related to control structures must be mentioned before we discuss the major Modula-2 control structures. The first is the special predefined procedure named HALT. This procedure is introduced here because it has a very dramatic effect on the flow of control—it terminates it. The procedure may be invoked anywhere in a Modula-2 program, in the main program or in a subprogram, and it has the effect of terminating execution immediately. Of course, this normally means returning control to the operating system, rather than halting the computer entirely.

The HALT procedure is used only in very unusual circumstances, such as the detection by the program of an unexpected or error condition from which no meaningful recovery can be made. It is not necessary in a main program to invoke this procedure as the last statement, since, like Pascal, a Modula-2 program halts automatically after the execution of the last statement in the main program.

The second topic we want to examine here is a point of programming style: indentation. In free-format languages like Modula-2, the programmer can place statements or parts of statements anywhere on a line, or extend them over several lines. However, even though the syntax of the language does not require any particular formatting of statements and programs, experience has indicated that certain patterns are easier to read and understand than others. As the coming sections illustrate, nearly all the control structures consist of introductory or controlling phrases and a group of one or more controlled statements. Indentation of the controlled statements makes it visually obvious what the extent of a control structure is. In control structures containing several groups of controlled statements, a uniform indentation pattern again makes the extent of each group visually obvious.

The importance of indentation should not be underestimated. In at least one controlled experiment, it was shown that indentation is superior to comments for making the control flow of a program understandable.

There is no universally accepted indentation style for Modula-2 programs. We use examples of different styles throughout this book; the reader may decide to adopt still another style. There is general agreement on the following points, however.

1. Each level of indentation should begin two to four spaces to the right of the previous level. One space is not enough to make the indentation visually obvious, while more than four rapidly sends the program far to the right on the page or screen when nested control structures are used. Most programmers seem to prefer two spaces per level of indentation.
2. The style that is adopted should be used consistently. Readers of a program will rapidly adjust to any particular style if it is consistent, and they can more easily find and understand the parts of the various control structures.
3. The use of appropriate comments in programs is strongly encouraged, but the placement of comments should not disrupt the indentation patterns of control structures.

6.1   Sequence Control Structure

The sequence control structure is so common that it is implicit in most common programming languages. It can be defined as requiring that in the absence of any other control structures, the statements in a program be executed in the order in which they appear in the program. Not all programming languages have this control structure; in some obscure languages each statement must explicitly identify the next statement. A program written in such a language would run correctly if you punched it on computer cards and shuffled the cards!

As an implicit control structure, there are no statements in Modula-2 that must be written in a program to indicate sequence.

6.2   Alternative Control Structures

An *alternative* control structure provides a way for the programmer to indicate that the program is to select one statement or group of statements from among several alternatives for execution. Some special cases have other names. A selection between executing and not executing a statement is called *conditional execution*. A selection between two alternatives is often called a *branch* or a *two-way branch*. A selection among more than two alternatives is often called a *multiway branch*. Each of these is available in Modula-2.

6.2.1   The If Statement

The *if* statement in Modula-2 is the most versatile alternative control structure, providing each of the three special cases described above. The syntax of this statement is shown in Figure 6.1.

The semantics of the if statement is virtually the same as in other similar languages, including English. For example, the following description relies on the reader to know the meanings of the English words "if," "then," and "else."

The boolean expression between IF and THEN is evaluated. If it is true, then the statements of the then clause are executed; control then passes to the statement after the if statement. If the boolean expression is false and there is an else clause, then the statements of that clause are executed, and control passes to the statement after the if statement. If there is an elsif clause instead of an else clause, it is treated as a new if statement, and the semantics just described applies again.

The Pascal programmer should note one important difference between Modula-2 and Pascal. In Modula-2, the if statement is terminated by the reserved word END, which along with the reserved words THEN and ELSE provide unambiguous bracketing of the statements in the then clause and the else clause. There is no need for a construct like the compound statement of Pascal.

if statement

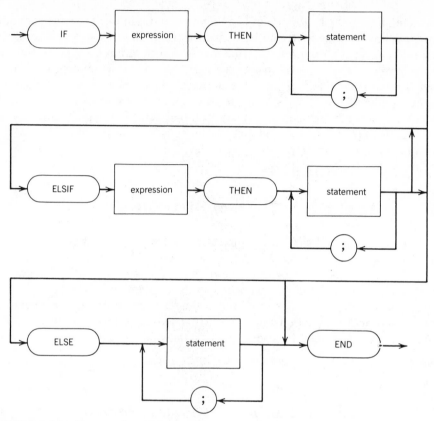

FIGURE 6.1   Syntax of an If Statement

In its simplest form, the if statement specifies conditional execution. For example, the statement

IF x < 0.0
        THEN x := −x
END

changes the value of x to its absolute value.

Some programmers will write so short an if statement on a single line:

IF x < 0.0 THEN x := − x END

A two-way branch is exhibited by the following example, which computes the real roots of the quadratic equation $y = ax^2 + bx + c$.

discriminant := b ∗ b − 4.0 ∗ a ∗ c;
IF discriminant < 0.0

```
    THEN ROOT1 := ( −b + SQRT ( discriminant ) ) / ( 2.0 ∗ a );
         ROOT2 := ( −b − SQRT ( discriminant ) ) / ( 2.0 ∗ a )
    ELSE WriteString ( "There are no real roots." )
END
```

In this example, SQRT is the square root function, and WriteString is a procedure to write a string (see Sections 10.1 and 9.2.1).

A multiway branch is shown in the following example, which is used to find the number of digits in the cardinal variable named number (assuming a computer with a 16-bit cardinal representation, so the largest possible cardinal is a 5-digit number).

```
IF      number < 10
    THEN digits := 1
ELSIF number < 100
    THEN digits := 2
ELSIF number < 1000
    THEN digits := 3
ELSIF number < 1000
    THEN digits := 4
    ELSE digits := 5
END
```

Two reminders are appropriate here. First, again notice the unusual spelling ELSIF. Second, remember that in this form of the if statement, as soon as one of the boolean expressions has been found to be true, and the subsequent then clause has been executed, the remainder of the if statement is ignored. This fact prevents us from having to write compound boolean expressions in the elsif clauses, such as:

```
IF      number < 10
    THEN digits := 1
ELSIF ( number >= 10 ) AND ( number < 100 )
    THEN digits := 2
ELSIF ( number >= 100 ) AND ( number < 1000 )
    THEN digits := 3
ELSIF ( number >= 1000 ) AND ( number < 10000 )
    THEN digits := 4
    ELSE digits := 5
END
```

The ELSIF feature of the Modula-2 if statement is not present in Pascal. The same result can be achieved without this feature, as shown in the examples below (taken from a binary search algorithm).

Usual Modula-2 Version
```
IF key = A[ middle ]
    THEN position := middle
```

```
        ELSIF key < A[ middle ]
           THEN high := middle − 1
           ELSE low  := middle + 1
        END
```

Pascal Version

```
if key = A[ middle ]
    then position := middle
    else if key < A[ middle ]
            then high := middle − 1
            else low  := middle + 1
```

Alternate Modula-2 Version

```
IF key = A[ middle ]
    THEN position := middle
    ELSE IF key < A[ middle ]
            THEN high := middle − 1
            ELSE low  := middle + 1
         END
    END
```

Notice that in Modula-2, which requires the terminator END for each if statement, a long sequence of nested if statements would finish with an equally long sequence of ENDs. Using the ELSIF form continues the same if statement rather than starting a new one, and eliminates all but one of the terminating ENDs.

6.2.2   The Case Statement

The *case* statement in Modula-2 provides another way to specify a multiway branch. The selection in an if statement is determined by the value of a boolean expression, and each of the two alternatives is associated with true or false, one of the possible values of that expression. The selection in a case statement is determined by the value of an expression of a scalar type (other than real), and each of the alternatives is associated with one of the possible values of that expression. The syntax of the case statement is defined in Figure 6.2.

The semantics of this statement is a natural extension of that for an if statement. The expression between CASE and OF is evaluated. If that value occurs in one of the case label lists, the corresponding statements are executed, and control passes to the statement after the case statement. If that value does not occur, and an else clause is present, the statements in the else clause are executed, and control passes to the statement after the case statement. If that value does not occur and no else clause is present, a program error occurs. Thus it is the programmer's responsibility to ensure that every possible value of the selector expression is considered, either explicitly in one of the case label lists, or through an else clause.

case statement

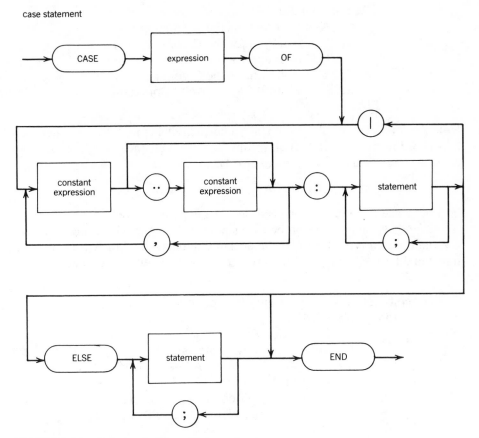

FIGURE 6.2   Syntax of a Case Statement

In addition to the else clause, the Pascal programmer should note two differences between Pascal and Modula-2 case statements. The first is Modula-2's use of the vertical stroke character to delimit the statements in each alternative. Pascal allows only one statement in each alternative, and thus at the end of that statement the compiler expects another case label list. Modula-2 allows any number of statements in an alternative, and thus requires some kind of indication that the alternative is finished and another case label list is beginning. In addition, Modula-2 allows ranges of case labels to be expressed with the subrange notation constant..constant, while Pascal requires that each value in such a range be written explicitly. Although this does not increase the power of the statement in Modula-2, it does increase its convenience.

As an example of the use of the case statement, consider an interactive program that expects one-letter commands and performs appropriate actions. A loop in the program might contain the following statement:

```
CASE command OF
    'a', 'A'  : (* action for the A command *) |
    'c', 'C'  : (* action for the C command *) |
    'i', 'I'  : (* action for the I  command *) |
    's', 'S'  : (* action for the S command *)
    ELSE      WriteString ( "Invalid Command" )
END
```

Note that commands will be recognized correctly whether they are entered in upper- or lowercase, and that all invalid command characters will produce an error message. This statement can also begin:

```
CASE CAP ( command ) OF
```

in which case the alternatives need only the uppercase labels.

Another common use of the case statement is in the processing of data of a variant record type. Consider the declaration below, and the case statement that could be used to print such a record value at the user's terminal.

```
TYPE
    symbolclass = ( string, number, code );
    symbol = RECORD
                id : INTEGER;
                CASE class : symbolclass OF
                    string  : name  : ARRAY [ 1..10 ] OF CHAR |
                    number : num   : REAL |
                    code    : codeletter   : CHAR;
                             codenumber : [ 0..9 ]
                END
             END;

VAR
    sym : symbol;

WITH sym DO
    WriteInt ( id, 8 );
    WriteLn;
    CASE class OF
        string  : WriteString ( name ) |
        number : WriteReal ( num, 12 ) |
        code    : Write ( codeletter );
                 WriteCard ( codenumber, 1 )
    END;
    WriteLn
END
```

In this example, the procedures WriteInt, WriteLn, WriteString, WriteCard, and Write perform terminal output (see Section 9.2).

The case statement may seem appropriate in some programming situations when in fact it is not. Many compilers will translate the case statement by creating a table of addresses of the compiled code for each of the alternatives; this table will be as long as the number of possible values of the selector expression. The example of the preceding section, which determined the number of digits in a cardinal number, could be written with a case statement as follows:

```
CASE number OF
    0..9        : digits := 1 |
    10..99      : digits := 2 |
    100..999    : digits := 3 |
    1000..9999  : digits := 4
    ELSE          digits := 5
END
```

Such a statement, while syntactically and semantically correct, may produce an address table of 10,000 entries. In such a situation it is much better to use the if statement as shown earlier.

6.3   Iterative Control Structures

The control structures in the iteration/recursion group allow the programmer to specify that a statement or group of statements be executed more than once even though written only once in the program. In this section we examine the iterative control structures of Modula-2, and in Section 6.4 we examine recursion.

An *iterative control structure* specifies a statement or group of statements to be executed more than once, and the conditions under which that repeated execution may occur. With such a control structure, each iteration or repeated execution of the group of statements must be completed before the next iteration begins; this requirement distinguishes iteration from recursion. An iterative control structure is commonly called a *loop,* and the repeated statements are called the *body* of the loop.

Modula-2 provides four different iterative control structures, three of which will be familiar to Pascal programmers. The next four sections discuss these control structures.

6.3.1   The While Statement

The syntax of the *while* statement is shown in Figure 6.3. The Pascal programmer should note that a while statement in Modula-2 is bracketed by the reserved words WHILE and END, and thus any number of statements may be in the body of the loop.

The semantics of this statement is identical to the while statement of Pascal. The boolean expression is evaluated; if the value is true, the body of the loop is executed, and the entire process repeated. If the value of the boolean expression is false, control passes to the statement after the while statement.

while statement

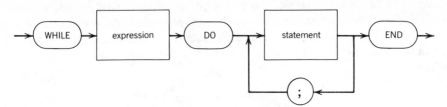

FIGURE 6.3   Syntax of a While Statement

Because the condition is tested first, this structure is sometimes called a *top-testing loop*. It is possible for the condition to be false the first time it is tested, in which case the body of the loop is not executed even once. This fact makes the while loop one of the most general iterative control structures; it is useful in many programming situations in which other loop structures may not be used.

We have seen an example of the while statement in Section 4.1.3, which discussed the linear search algorithm. That example is repeated below.

```
position := 1;
WHILE ( position <= 100 ) AND
          ( A[ position ] <> key ) DO
        position := position + 1
END;
```

This example illustrates succinctly a requirement of the proper use of a while loop: the body of the loop must in some way affect the value of the loop condition. In this case the loop condition depends on the value of the variable position, and the value of this variable is incremented inside the loop body. If this requirement is not met, the value of the boolean expression that controls the loop will never change. If that value is true, an infinite loop results.

As another example, consider the "Peasants' Multiplication Algorithm" below. This algorithm provides a way to multiply two cardinal numbers using only addition, doubling, and halving (ignoring any remainder); these operations are assumed to be known to the peasants.

```
(* Peasants' Multiplication Algorithm  *)
(*     Given values x and y, produces  *)
(*     the product p = xy.
p := 0;
WHILE x > 0 DO
        IF ODD ( x ) THEN p := p + y END;
        x := x DIV 2;
        y := y * 2
END;
```

This algorithm requires a top-testing loop. If the value of x is 0 initially, the body of the loop is never executed, and the value of p remains 0, which is the correct answer.

The reader will find it an interesting exercise to prove that this algorithm works. *Hint:* Represent the numbers in binary.

6.3.2   The Repeat Statement

The syntax of the *repeat* statement is shown in Figure 6.4. This statement is identical in syntax and semantics in Modula-2 and Pascal. The body of the loop is executed once before the boolean expression has been evaluated. If its value is true, control is passed to the next statement after the repeat statement; otherwise the loop body is entered again. Because the condition is tested last, this structure is sometimes called a *bottom-testing loop*. It is a less general control structure than the while loop, since it cannot handle programming situations that might call for the execution of the loop body zero times. However, each of these loops can do the job of the other, if additional statements are allowed, as illustrated in the following examples. In these examples we assume that the evaluation of the expression induces no side effects.

While Loop	*Equivalent Repeat Loop*
WHILE expr DO	REPEAT
statements	IF expr
END	THEN statements
	END
	UNTIL NOT (expr)

Repeat Loop	*Equivalent While Loop*
REPEAT	statements;
statements	WHILE NOT (expr) DO
UNTIL expr	statements
	END

The repeat statement is especially useful when the loop body must compute or input a value that is referenced in the loop condition. In such situations it is mandatory that the loop body be executed once before the first evaluation of the boolean expression. For example, the following loop will read in characters until a nonblank character is found.

repeat statement

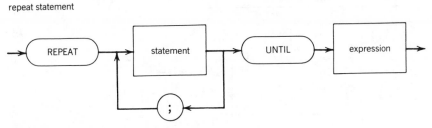

FIGURE 6.4   Syntax of a Repeat Statement

```
REPEAT
    Read ( character )
UNTIL character <> ' '
```

This kind of loop is common in applications with free-format interactive input. The loop is often followed by another loop that collects characters up to the next occurrence of a blank:

```
pos := 0;
REPEAT
    pos := pos + 1;
    string[ pos ] := character;
    Read ( character )
UNTIL character = ' '
```

Finally, the programmer should remember that in a while statement, a true loop condition means to stay in the loop, but in a repeat statement, a true loop condition means to get out of the loop.

6.3.3   The For Statement

The syntax of the *for* statement is shown in Figure 6.5. The variable after the reserved word FOR is called the *control variable,* and the whole loop is often called a *counter-controlled loop,* since the control variable "counts" through its range.

for statement

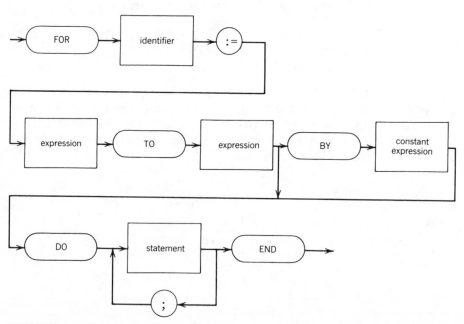

FIGURE 6.5   Syntax of a For Statement

The semantics of the Modula-2 for statement is similar to that of the Pascal for statement. The control variable takes on each of the values in the specified range, in the specified order, and for each such value the body of the loop is executed once. If there are no values in the specified range, the body of the loop is executed zero times. A for loop is therefore a top-testing loop.

The value of the control variable in a for statement may not be changed within the body of the loop. Upon exit from the loop, the control variable becomes undefined.

Like the while statement, the body of a for loop is bracketed by the for clause and the reserved word END, so any number of statements may be in the body. The Pascal programmer should note also two other differences from the Pascal for statement. First, Modula-2 allows the specification of an increment value (the constant after the reserved word BY) other than one; Pascal always assumes an increment of one. Second, if the control variable is to be decremented through a range, beginning at a larger value and ending at a smaller value, this is indicated by specifying a negative increment value; Pascal replaces the word to with downto to indicate a negative increment.

Notice also that the increment value must be a *constant*, while the beginning and ending values may be specified by expressions. This is necessary to ensure that the compiler is able to generate compact appropriate code for the loop exit test. In the case of a positive increment, the loop continues as long as the control variable is less than or equal to the ending value; for a negative increment, the control variable must be greater than or equal to the ending value. If the increment value were an expression, whose value were not known at compile time, the compiler would have to generate code for both tests, and code to determine which to execute.

The two forms of the for loop (positive and negative increment) can be defined in terms of the while loop as shown below. As in the previous section, we assume the evaluations of high and low induce no adverse side effects.

For Loop	*Equivalent While Loop*
FOR variable := low TO high BY	variable := low;
+increment DO	WHILE variable <= high DO
statements	statements;
END	INC (variable, increment)
	END

For Loop	*Equivalent While Loop*
FOR variable := high TO low BY	variable := high;
−increment DO	WHILE variable >= low DO
statements	statements;
END	DEC (variable, increment)
	END

The data type of the control variable and the starting and ending value expressions may be any scalar type except real; this includes integer, cardinal, character, boolean, enumeration, and subrange types. Although it is unusual to specify an increment (other than −1 when the control variable is to proceed downward through its range) for types other than integer and cardinal, it can be done. For example,

```
FOR character := 'A' TO 'Z' BY 4 DO
    Write ( character )
END
```

will produce the output AEIMQUY.

   The for loop is probably most often used to specify that a particular action is to be performed on each element of an array. Consider the following examples.

```
TYPE list      = ARRAY [ 1..100 ] OF CARDINAL;
     table     = ARRAY [ 'A'..'Z' ] OF CARDINAL;
     bigstring = ARRAY [ 0..1000 ] OF CHAR;

VAR  number   : list;
     counter  : table;
     string   : bigstring;
     position : [ 1..100 ];
     letter   : [ 'A'..'Z' ];
     sum      : CARDINAL;
     average  : REAL;

(* Read in the list named number *)
FOR position := 1 TO 100 DO
    ReadCard ( number[ position ] )
END;

(* Compute the average of the list *)
sum := 0;
FOR position := 1 TO 100 DO
    sum := sum + number[ position ]
END;
average := FLOAT ( sum ) / 100.0;

(* Count the occurrences of each letter in string *)
FOR letter := 'A' TO 'Z' DO
    counter[ letter ] := 0
END;

FOR position := 0 TO 1000 DO
    letter := CAP ( string[ position ] );
    IF ( 'A' <= letter ) AND ( letter >= 'Z' )
       THEN INC ( counter[ letter ] )
    END
END;
```

6.3.4 The Loop and Exit Statements

The *loop* statement, when used with the *exit* statement, provides the most general of the iterative control structures in Modula-2 (see Figures 6.6 and 6.7). The loop statement by itself provides an infinite loop—once it has been entered, the body of the loop is repeated indefinitely. When the exit statement, which provides a way out of the loop, has been executed, control passes immediately to the first statement after the loop statement. A loop statement without an exit *is* useful in some concurrent programming situations (see Chapter 16).

To illustrate that the loop statement is the most general, the examples below show how the while, repeat, and for statements can be implemented with loop and exit statements (plus some additional assignment and if statements).

While Statement
```
WHILE expression DO
    statements
END
```

Equivalent Loop Statement
```
LOOP
    IF NOT (expression) THEN EXIT END;
    statements
END
```

Repeat Statement
```
REPEAT
    statements
UNTIL expression
```

Equivalent Loop Statement
```
LOOP
    statements;
    IF expression THEN EXIT END
END
```

For Statement
```
FOR variable := low TO high
    BY increment DO
    statements
END
```

Equivalent Loop Statement
```
variable := low;
LOOP
    IF variable > high THEN EXIT END;
    statements;
    INC ( variable, increment )
END
```

loop statement

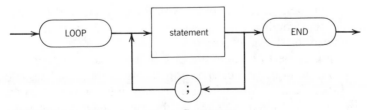

FIGURE 6.6 Syntax of a Loop Statement

exit statement

FIGURE 6.7 Syntax of an Exit Statement

In all three examples, the loop statement is not the preferred way of representing the loop. The while, repeat, and for statements exist because each one provides a more straightforward way of representing a particular control abstraction. The loop statement *is* valuable when the other three loops do not apply. The most common of these situations is called the *middle exit loop*. As the name implies, such a loop is neither a top-testing nor a bottom-testing loop, and it cannot be represented by any of the other three loop statements.

The middle exit loop is often used when it is desired to process a sequence of input values that is terminated by a special *sentinel* value. For example:

```
CONST sentinel = ...;

VAR     number  : INTEGER;
        result  : INTEGER;

LOOP
    ReadInt ( number );
    IF number = sentinel THEN EXIT END;
    result := (* expression involving number *);
    WriteInt ( result, 6 )
END
```

As will be seen in Sections 9.2.5 and 9.3, Modula-2 implementations usually provide a constant named EOL that is the character used to denote the end of a line of text. Reading and processing all the characters on an input line can be structured as follows:

```
LOOP
    Read ( character );
    IF character = EOL THEN EXIT END;
    (* process the character *)
END
```

6.3.5   Software Development Considerations

We assume that the reader is familiar with the usefulness of iterative control structures in programming. In this section we present some principles to guide a programmer in the design of loops.

If a loop is to perform a certain task in a program, each of the separate iterations of the loop body must perform a part of that task. Usually, as we design the loop, we think of each iteration contributing its part to the overall goal, and we rely on the knowledge that the preceding iterations have already prepared the way, in some sense, for the current iteration. For example, consider a summing loop such as:

```
item := 1;
sum := 0;
```

```
WHILE item <= 100 DO
    sum := sum + list[ item ];
    INC ( item )
END
```

Each time through the body of the loop we are confident that the variable named sum contains the sum of all the list items before the current one.

This idea of "what has been accomplished so far" in a loop can be formalized, as seen in the following definition.

Loop invariant condition (or **loop invariant** for short): an assertion (a statement of fact) about the values of the variables referenced in the loop, which must be true at the beginning of each iteration for the loop body to produce the correct result.

In the preceding example, the loop invariant is "the variable named item contains a value in the range 1 to 100, and the variable named sum contains the sum of list[1], list[2], . . . , list[item-1]." This loop invariant has two parts, and if either were false, it would not make sense to execute the loop body again. The first part guarantees that the value of item is within the proper range; if it were not, then we would not be able to access the value in list[item]. The second part guarantees that we have the proper sum so far; if the sum were incorrect, adding one more element to it would not help.

During the execution of the body of the loop, it is normally the case that the loop invariant becomes false temporarily. By the end of the loop body, however, we will *reestablish the loop invariant*. This is necessary to prepare for the next iteration, since we require the loop invariant to be true at the start of each iteration. In a correctly structured loop, the final iteration of the body does *not* reestablish the loop invariant, and we exit the loop. In the example above, the last iteration increments item to 101, violating the loop invariant and getting us out of the loop.

A programmer must be aware of the loop invariant for two very important reasons. The first has been discussed; namely, the programmer must rely on the loop invariant when designing the body of the loop. The second reason is more subtle. Since the loop invariant must be true at the beginning of each iteration, it must be true *at the beginning of the first iteration*. This requirement often forces the programmer to place one or more statements immediately before the loop to *establish the loop invariant*. In the example above, the two statements before the while loop are present for exactly this purpose. Because these statements are conceptually very closely related to the loop, it is a generally accepted rule of programming style that statements whose purpose is to establish a loop invariant are placed *immediately* before the loop.

A loop may reference many variables, but not all those variables will be mentioned in the loop invariant. In some loops the first thing done to a variable inside the loop is to give it a new value. In such a case, the variable may have any value whatsoever (including undefined) upon entry, and thus no assertion about its value need appear in the loop invariant. An example is the summing loop:

```
sum := 0;
LOOP
    ReadCard ( number );
    IF number = sentinel THEN EXIT END;
    sum := sum + number
END
```

For this loop, the loop invariant is "sum contains the sum of all numbers read so far." The statement before the loop establishes the loop invariant. The variable named number is not mentioned in the loop invariant, since its value may be anything at all and the loop is still correct. Notice also that after reading in a new value for number, the loop invariant is temporarily false, but the last statement in the loop reestablishes it.

In the first example above, the variable named list did not appear in the loop invariant. As long as it has a defined value, the loop remains correct. If we were being very precise, we might want to include a third part to the loop invariant, ". . . , and list is defined." This is seldom done, since programmers usually remember that any access of an undefined variable, whether inside a loop or not, is incorrect.

The concept of loop invariant is critical in advanced areas of computer science such as program verification. From the point of view of the practicing software developer, however, the loop invariant is a tool to help in the design of a correct loop, and to help identify the statements needed just before the loop to get the loop started correctly.

We finish this section with two additional examples of loops and loop invariants. Note in each case the statements preceding the loop that establish the loop invariants.

```
(* count positive and negative integers *)
poscounter := 0;
negcounter := 0;
LOOP
    ReadInt ( number );
    IF number = 0 THEN EXIT END;
    IF number < 0
        THEN INC ( negcounter )
        ELSE INC ( poscounter )
    END
END
```

The loop invariant is "poscounter contains the number of positive integers seen so far, and negcounter contains the number of negative integers seen so far."

(∗ set each element of an array to 1.0 ∗)

FOR position := 1 TO 100 DO
    A[position] := 1.0
END

The loop invariant is "position contains a value in the range 1 to 100, and the array elements A[1], A[2], . . . , A[position − 1] all contain 1.0." Notice in the case of a for statement, the assignment statement to establish the control variable part of the loop invariant is implicit in the for statement. We do not need to precede the loop with the statement position := 1;.

6.4   Recursion

The iteration/recursion group of control structures was defined in the preceding section to consist of the control structures that allow the programmer to specify that a statement or group of statements is to be executed more than once even though it is written only once in a program. The control structure specifies the statements to be repeated and the conditions under which the repeated execution may occur. We have seen that the distinguishing characteristic of iterative control structures is that each iteration of those statements must be completed before the next iteration begins.

A *recursive* control structure is a generalization of the iterative control structures. It relaxes the requirement that each iteration be completed before the next one is begun. Thus it is possible in a recursive control structure for a program to be only halfway through the first iteration when the second iteration is begun. After the second iteration is completed, the first iteration continues. In even more general cases, several separate iterations may interrupt the first one, or the third may interrupt the second, and so on.

6.4.1   Implementation of Recursion in Modula-2

The implementation of an iterative control structure (the machine language instructions generated by a compiler) is relatively simple. Since each iteration is completed before the next one begins, it is not necessary to remember anything about the status of an iteration before proceeding to the next. Simply test the loop exit condition, and transfer control to the top of the loop (the first statement in the body). For a recursive control structure, the problem is more difficult. First, the values of some or all of the variables referenced in the body of the control structure must be saved while the subsequent iteration is performed, and those values must be restored so that the original iteration can be completed. Second, the location of the interruption must be remembered, so that after completion of the subsequent iteration, control can be transferred back to the appropriate statement in the original iteration. A recursive control structure may produce a lengthy series of interruptions: the second iteration begins partway through the first, the third begins partway through the second, and so on. This requires a mechanism for remembering a series of values and locations, and restoring these in reverse order.

An experienced programmer will recognize these implementation requirements of a recursive control structure as the same requirements for subprogram linkage. Programming language designers and compiler designers have also recognized this fact. Instead of providing two different mechanisms that are implemented in the same way, they have combined the mechanisms into one. In Modula-2, as in most other common languages, recursion is implemented through procedure invocations. There is no separate recursive control structure in Modula-2 (although a few obscure languages have been designed that include a recur statement that provides the recursive control structure).

It is important to distinguish the definition of recursion from its implementation in a particular programming language. Although a procedure (subprogram) that invokes itself is usually called a *recursive procedure,* this is *not* the definition of recursion, but rather an example of one possible implementation of recursion. Chapter 1 introduced the idea of abstraction, of separating a general concept from any implementation of that concept. The overwhelming importance of this idea will become evident in Part Two of this book.

Just as for loops, it is the programmer's responsibility to avoid infinite repetition of the body of a recursive control structure (recursive procedure). This is accomplished by placing the recursive invocations of the procedure inside alternative control structures, so that under certain circumstances they will be executed, and under others they will not. The following examples illustrate this. (Pascal programmers should have no trouble understanding these examples; others, however, may want to skip first to Chapter 7, which discusses the syntax of procedures in Modula-2.)

First, consider the binary search algorithm. Assume the following declarations:

```
CONST tablemax   = 1000;

TYPE   tablerange = [ 1..tablemax ];
       table      = ARRAY tablerange OF CARDINAL;

VAR    partnum    : table;
       part       : CARDINAL;
       position   : 0..tablemax;
```

Assume that the variable partnum contains a list of part numbers, and the variable part contains one such part number. It is desired to find the position (subscript) in the partnum table where that part may be found, or to set position to zero if the part is not found. The procedure below implements a binary search, accessing the variables above as globals (see Section 7.5). The parameters of the procedure are the low and high subscripts of the segment of the array currently being searched. It is therefore invoked from the main program by the statement search (1, tablemax).

```
PROCEDURE search
    (       low  : tablerange;
            high : tablerange );

    VAR middle : tablerange;

BEGIN
   IF low <= high
      THEN middle := ( low + high ) DIV 2;
           IF key = partnum[ middle ]
              THEN position := middle
              ELSIF key < partnum[ middle ]
                      THEN search ( low, middle−1 )
                      ELSE search ( middle+1, high )
           END
      ELSE position := 0
   END
END search;
```

This binary search procedure has some important features. The two recursive invocations of the procedure occur in the two branches of an if statement, and therefore only one is executed each time through the procedure. Also, after that recursive invocation, there are no more statements to be executed; this implies that one invocation is completed before the next one begins. We recognize this as the characteristic of an iterative control structure. Two conclusions may be drawn. First, recursion can be used as a substitute for iteration, since it is possible to place the recursive invocation of the procedure last in the procedure. This confirms our earlier statement that recursion is a generalization of iteration. Second, this procedure may be rewritten using an iterative control structure. This is shown below.

```
PROCEDURE search;
        VAR low     : tablerange;
            high    : tablerange;
            middle  : tablerange;

        BEGIN
           low := 1;
           high := tablemax;
           position := 0;
           WHILE low <= high DO
              middle := ( low + high ) DIV 2;
              IF key = partnum[ middle ]
                 THEN position := middle
                 ELSIF key < partnum[ middle ]
                         THEN high := middle − 1
                         ELSE low  := middle + 1
              END
           END
        END search;
```

A more sophisticated use of recursion is found in the next example. We define a *partition of a positive integer n* as an expression of the form $a + b + c + \dots + k$ that is equal to n. We will consider expressions that can be derived from each other by rearranging the terms to be the same partition. Thus all the partitions of 6 are:

$$6$$
$$5 + 1$$
$$4 + 2$$
$$4 + 1 + 1$$
$$3 + 3$$
$$3 + 2 + 1$$
$$3 + 1 + 1 + 1$$
$$2 + 2 + 2$$
$$2 + 2 + 1 + 1$$
$$2 + 1 + 1 + 1 + 1$$
$$1 + 1 + 1 + 1 + 1 + 1$$

It is desired to determine how many partitions there are for the positive integer n. If we agree to write partitions in the form shown above, with terms decreasing from left to right, we can make an important observation. A partition of n that begins with the term k must have all other terms no greater than k, and the sum of all other terms must be $n - k$. Thus the number of partitions that begin with k is just the number of partitions of $n - k$ with largest term at most k. If we can compute this latter value for each possible $k = 1, 2, \dots, n$, the sum of these values is the solution to the original problem. We will adopt the convention that there is one partition of the number zero; this will make the observation above correct when $k = n$. We will also adopt the convention that there are zero partitions of a negative integer (rather than allowing this case to be undefined). If $n = 1$ or $k = 1$, there is only one partition possible; if $n = 1$ that partition is n, and if $k = 1$ that partition is $1 + 1 + \dots + 1$.

We will use a function subprogram (called a procedure in Modula-2; see Section 7.1) having two parameters: the number n to be partitioned, and the value k, which is the largest allowable first term. This subprogram will return the number of partitions.

```
PROCEDURE partitions
    (        n : INTEGER (* number to be partitioned *);
             k : INTEGER (* largest first term          *) )
    (* returns a value of type *) : INTEGER;
    VAR i      : INTEGER;
            count : INTEGER;
```

```
BEGIN
   IF n < 0
         THEN RETURN 0
         ELSIF ( n <= 1 ) OR ( k = 1 )
         THEN RETURN 1
         ELSE
            count := 0;
            FOR i := TO k DO
               count := count + partitions ( n−i, i )
            END;
            RETURN count
   END
END partitions;
```

A program that needs to use this procedure to find the number of partitions of the integer *n* will invoke the procedure in an expression containing

partitions (n, n)

6.4.2 Software Development Considerations

During the development of a particular piece of software, the programmer needs to recognize situations in which the use of recursion will provide a smaller, faster, and more straightforward algorithm. To examine this subject, we first introduce some terminology.

Consider a common problem from elementary geometry, determining the area of a rectangle given the length and width. A student might be asked to find the area of a rectangle with length 5 units and width 3 units; the correct solution is 15 square units. Similarly, the area of a rectangle with length 9 units and width 4 units is 36 square units. In each case the answer is numeric. A more general problem is to find a method of computing the area of any rectangle, given the length and width. The solution to this problem is an algorithm: multiply the length times the width.

We use the term *problem* to describe the general form of a problem such as the rectangle problem just described, and the term *instance of a problem* to describe the specific problem for which the values of all variables are given. We often call these given values the *inputs,* and we can define an instance of a problem as a pair: a problem and a particular set of inputs. The solution of a problem is an algorithm, while the solution of any instance of the problem will be a specific value (numeric or other). In software development, the programmer must provide the solution to the problem, and the computer then provides the solution to any instance of that problem.

The *size of a problem* is a numeric value associated with any instance of a problem, and is a measure of the amount or magnitude of the inputs of that instance. Notice that size is defined for an instance of a problem, not for the problem itself. One instance of a problem is said to be *smaller* than another if its size is smaller. The *smallest* instance of a problem is the one whose inputs are the smallest possible while still being meaningful. For the rectangle problem, we might measure the size as the maximum of the length and width. In the smallest instance both length and width would be zero, since the concepts of length and width are undefined for negative values.

A problem that lends itself to an efficient solution with recursion will exhibit two properties.

1. The solution of any instance of the problem (except the smallest) requires the solution of one or more smaller instances of the same problem.
2. The smallest instance of the problem may be solved directly, usually trivially.

We can see these two properties in the examples of the preceding section. In the case of the binary search, we can measure the problem size by the length of the segment of the table we are searching. As presented above, the size of the original instance of the problem was tablemax (= 1000). The solution of that instance required the solution of an instance of approximately half that size; specifically, it required searching either the upper half or the lower half of the table. The smallest instance is a table of size zero. This is directly (actually trivially) solvable, since the key can never be found in such a table, and the correct answer is always position = 0.

In the partitions of an integer problem, we can measure the problem size by the value of n, the integer to be partitioned. The solution of the original instance of the problem required the solution of several smaller instances; for example, when $n = 4$ the loop invokes the procedure four times, with respective values of $n = 3$, 2, 1, and 0. The smallest instances of this problem are solved directly; when n is negative the solution is always zero, and when n is zero or one, the answer is always one. Again the solutions to these smallest instances are trivial.

A programmer can learn to recognize the two properties that characterize a problem that is amenable to recursive solution. Sometimes it will take a little thinking to see how a solution depends on solutions to smaller instances of the same problem; but for inherently recursive problems, the rewards are significant. For such problems, a recursive solution, when coded in a modern programming language like Modula-2 and executed on a modern computer (including most microprocessor-based computer systems), will have fewer lines of code, require less storage, and execute faster than a nonrecursive solution of the same problem.

For problems that are not inherently recursive, it is still often possible to find a recursive solution. When the algorithm is designed, however, it is frequently the case that only a single recursive invocation is required, and it appears last in the algorithm. A programmer should recognize that in this situation an iterative solution will probably be better (smaller and faster).

For a more thorough discussion of recursion and the design of recursive algorithms, see Roberts (1985).

7

Procedures and Functions

There are three kinds of subprograms in Modula-2: procedures, function procedures, and modules. The first two, which are counterparts of procedures and functions in Pascal, are discussed in this chapter. Modules are the subject of Chapter 11.

7.1 Procedures and Function Procedures

Procedures and function procedures represent another important abstraction mechanism in Modula-2, commonly called *functional abstraction*. In a sense, they permit the programmer to extend the language, since arbitrarily complex computations may be defined and subsequently invoked by use of a single identifier.

As in Pascal, procedures consist of a *procedure heading,* which may include a *formal parameter list* (see Section 7.4), followed by a *block* (see Chapter 8), which consists of declarations and the program body. Figure 7.1 gives a more formal definition of the syntax of a procedure declaration.

By declaring a procedure, the programmer defines a new statement in the language, consisting of the procedure name followed by a parameter list (if needed). Such a statement is said to *invoke* the procedure, causing it to perform the specified computations.

A function procedure in Modula-2 corresponds to a function in Pascal.

procedure declaration

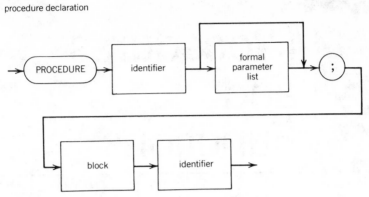

FIGURE 7.1 Syntax of a Procedure Declaration

The only difference is syntactic, in that Modula-2 uses the reserved word PROCEDURE instead of the word function, as shown in Figure 7.2.

As in Pascal, the type of value returned by the function is specified by the identifier after a colon at the end of the procedure heading. In Modula-2, this may be a qualified identifier, which has the form identifier.identifier, because the source of an identifier of that type might be another module (as described in Chapter 11). The original language definition allowed the value returned by a function to be of any data type, including structured types. It is not uncommon for an implementation of Modula-2 to require functions to return scalar types.

A function procedure is an abstraction of the mathematical concept of function and defines the computation of a value of the specified type. Therefore, a function procedure is invoked in syntactic constructs where values are expected, normally in expressions (see Section 4.4). A function procedure may not be invoked by using its name as a separate statement, as is the case for procedures.

function declaration

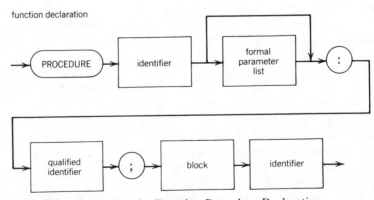

FIGURE 7.2 Syntax of a Function Procedure Declaration

7.2 The Return Statement

As in Pascal, exit from a procedure in Modula-2 occurs immediately after execution of the last statement in the body. In addition, Modula-2 provides an explicit *return* statement, which may be placed anywhere in the procedure body, to force an immediate return to the invoking program. The syntax of this statement is shown in Figure 7.3.

The optional expression in the return statement is used in a function procedure to specify the value that the function is to return. It is *not* possible in Modula-2 to use the function procedure identifier as a variable and assign the desired return value to it, as is done in Pascal. For example, the following function procedure determines the minimum of two cardinal values (see Section 7.4 for a discussion of parameters).

```
PROCEDURE mincard ( x, y : CARDINAL ) : CARDINAL;
BEGIN
   IF x < y
      THEN RETURN x
      ELSE RETURN y
   END
END mincard;
```

A return statement may be placed in the body of a main program, in which case it behaves as an invocation of the predefined procedure HALT.

7.3 Procedure Types

An experienced Pascal programmer is already familiar with the concept of data type, and with the declaration of both constants and variables of various types. For example, the declarations

CONST maximum = 99;

VAR value : CARDINAL;

define two objects of the cardinal data type. The object named maximum is a constant, and it *always* has the value 99. The object named value is a variable, and its value may vary during the execution of the program.

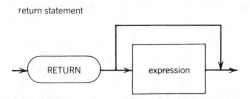

return statement

FIGURE 7.3 Syntax of a Return Statement

In Modula-2, we can also consider the class of all procedures to be the set of values of a data type; the set of operations includes assignment and equality test. In a normal procedure declaration, the name of the procedure is associated with a particular sequence of computations (the procedure body). That name *always* means that sequence; hence we may think of a procedure declaration as a declaration of a constant of the procedure type. It is only a small step up from Pascal to allow the declaration of variables of the procedure type.

Actually, we will want to be able to define many different procedure types, distinguished by the types of their parameters and, in the case of function procedures, by the type of the returned value. Figure 7.4 shows the syntax of a procedure type.

The following declarations and statements are then possible, assuming the functions sin and cos have been defined.

```
TYPE realfunc  =  PROCEDURE ( REAL ) : REAL;

VAR  trig        : realfunc;
      x           : REAL;
      y           : REAL;

trig := sin;
y := trig ( x );
trig := cos;
y := y + trig ( x );
```

7.4 Parameters

Parameters play the role for procedures that operands play for the common arithmetic operators; that is, they define the objects or values on which the procedure is to operate. To illustrate the importance of parameters, consider what programming would be without this capability for the arithmetic opera-

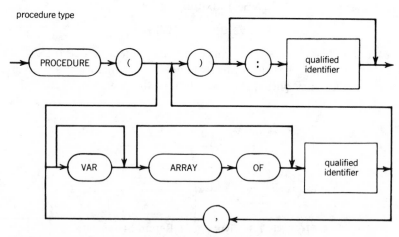

FIGURE 7.4   Syntax of a Procedure Type

tors. Suppose we define three variables x, y, and z, and require that all arithmetic be performed on x and y, with the result being placed in z. To do arithmetic on other operands, we would first have to copy the values of those operands into x and y, and then copy the result from z. Without operands, the operators can be represented by single symbols or words. Then the simple statement

$$e := (a + b) * (c - d)$$

would become

```
x := a;
y := b;
add;
temp1 := z;
x := c;
y := d;
subtract;
temp2 := z;
x := temp1;
y := temp2;
multiply;
e := z
```

For each of the arithmetic operators, we know that two numeric values are given, and that the result is a third numeric value (ignoring division by zero). For procedures, similar knowledge is needed by the programmer who intends to use those procedures. This is specified in the procedure heading in the *formal parameter list* (Figure 7.5). The syntax of the formal parameter list is similar to that of Pascal. The differences, procedure types and open array types, are discussed in subsequent sections.

A procedure is invoked in a program by a statement that consists of the

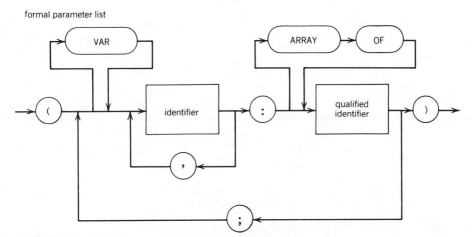

formal parameter list

FIGURE 7.5 Syntax of a Formal Parameter List

procedure name or *designator,* followed by the *actual parameter list,* if needed. The syntax of a procedure invocation statement is shown in Figure 7.6.

A designator is not always the declared name of the procedure. It may be a procedure variable whose current value is the desired procedure, or it may be a qualified identifier in the case of a procedure that is imported from another module (see Chapter 11). Since a procedure can be an element of an array or record, or an anonymous variable, the designator may include subscripts, record field name, or the dereferencing operator.

The actual parameter list syntax is shown in Figure 7.7. Notice that an actual parameter list always includes the parentheses, even if there are no parameters between them. Such an empty parameter list is necessary when invoking a function procedure that was defined with no parameters, but not for a procedure with no parameters. The relationship between the formal parameter list and the actual parameter list is described in the next section.

7.4.1 Parameter Mode and Parameter Binding

As indicated earlier, parameters provide a mechanism for communication of values between a procedure and an invoking program. This mechanism is valuable because it allows different invocations to specify different values on which the procedure must operate. There are of course two directions in which this communication can proceed: from the invoking program to the procedure, and from the procedure to the invoking program. The term *parameter mode* describes the direction of communication. Unfortunately, there are no univer-

procedure invocation

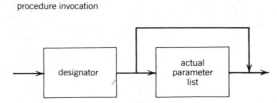

FIGURE 7.6 Syntax of a Procedure Invocation
Statement

actual parameter list

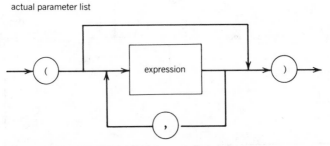

FIGURE 7.7 Syntax of an Actual Parameter List

sally accepted names for parameter modes. Two sets of names are relatively common, however, and it is suggested that programmers adopt the set they prefer.

The first mode describes a value that is sent into the procedure to be used but is not sent back to the invoking program. Such a parameter may be called an *in* or *input* mode parameter, or a *use* mode parameter. A value that is created in the procedure and communicated out of the procedure to the invoking program may be called an *out* or *output* mode parameter, or a *return* mode parameter. A value that is communicated in both directions may be called an *in/out* or *input/output* mode parameter, or an *update* mode parameter.

Clearly, the terms *in, out,* and *in/out* describe the communication from the point of view of the procedure. The terms *use, return,* and *update* describe what the procedure does with those parameters.

The Modula-2 language does not specify syntax for denoting parameter modes. It is therefore the prerogative of the programmer to provide this information via comments. In many of the examples that follow, the parameter mode appears as a comment in the formal parameter list.

When a procedure is invoked, the values of the parameter for that invocation are supplied in the actual parameter list. As we have seen, the formal parameters are specified by identifiers, while the actual parameters may in some cases be arbitrarily complicated expressions. What is actually being communicated, however, is a value, and we know that values may be represented by identifiers and by expressions. For a procedure to perform the task expected by the invoking program, it is necessary to *bind* the formal and actual parameters. After binding, a formal parameter identifier becomes an identifier of the actual parameter to which it is bound.

Several syntactic and semantic rules in Modula-2 govern binding. In addition, two binding mechanisms may be specified by the programmer. We will examine each of these.

A parameter may be bound *by value* or *by reference*. In the first case, only the value of the actual parameter is communicated to the procedure, often (but not always) by making a copy of that value, which is then stored in the local storage area of the procedure. The procedure is free to examine and to modify that value, but because it is only a copy of the original value, the original is not changed. This binding mechanism is appropriate for a parameter of the input or use mode. It is also the default binding mechanism in Modula-2; that is, it is used unless the programmer specifically asks for the other mechanism.

A parameter that is bound by reference requires that the original parameter be communicated to the procedure, often by making the parameter's physical memory address known to the procedure. Again, the procedure is free to examine and to modify the value of the parameter. In this case, however, the original can be changed, and thus the changed value is known to the invoking program. This binding mechanism is appropriate for a parameter of the output or return mode, or of the input/output or update mode. It is specified in Modula-2 as in Pascal, by preceding the identifier of a formal parameter with the reserved word **VAR**.

The binding mechanisms we call "by value" and "by reference" should be considered to be conceptual mechanisms. A compiler may actually use any of several other common binding mechanisms. For example, open array parameters may be bound *by descriptor,* in which a small block of storage containing the size and address of the actual parameter is communicated to the procedure. A small, in-mode parameter might have either a copy of its value or the address of a memory cell containing a copy of its value communicated to the procedure. In general, the binding mechanism used by a compiler is not known to programmers, nor is it under their direct and complete control.

In the common language of programmers, parameters bound by value are called *value parameters,* and parameters bound by reference are called *variable parameters.* Within the body of the procedure, a value parameter may be considered to be a *local* variable (see Section 7.5) that has already been given a value at the time the procedure begins executing.

For binding to be successful, several conditions must be met. First, the number of parameters in the formal and actual parameter lists must be the same. If this is true, there is a natural one-to-one relationship between the formal and actual parameters: the first actual parameter is bound to the first formal parameter, the second to the second, and so on. If the binding is by value, the types of the formal and actual parameter must be assignment compatible, as defined in Chapter 5. If the binding is by reference, the types of the formal and actual parameter must be identical.

7.4.2   Parameters of Procedure Types

In Modula-2, parameters of procedure types are specified in a manner different from Pascal. An experienced Pascal programmer will remember that in the original definition of Pascal (see Jensen and Wirth, 1975), a procedure heading with a procedure parameter might look like this:

```
procedure abc ( i : integer;
                procedure p;
                x : real );
```

When this procedure is invoked, the second actual parameter had to be the name of a procedure. In the body of procedure abc, this procedure could be invoked using the name p. However, it was soon recognized that there was no way for the compiler to determine if the parameters of procedure p specified at that invocation were suitable for the actual parameters. When Pascal was standardized, the ANSI standard required the declaration of a formal procedure parameter to include the parameter types and binding mechanisms. Thus the foregoing example might be changed to:

```
procedure abc ( i : integer;
                procedure p ( ch : char, var i : integer );
                x : real );
```

With this syntax, the compiler can make two different checks of parameter list congruity. First, it can check that within the body of the procedure abc, each invocation of procedure p has appropriate actual parameters (in this case a character expression and an integer variable). Second, it can check that in any program that invokes procedure abc, the second actual parameter is a procedure that was declared with a congruous formal parameter list, that is, one that matches in number, type, and binding mechanism of parameters.

Modula-2 solves the same problem in a much simpler way using procedure types. As we have seen, the definition of a procedure type requires a specification of parameter types and binding mechanisms. Once a procedure type has been defined, the same parameter compatibility rules apply as for other data types. In Modula-2, the example above might be written as follows:

```
TYPE xyz = PROCEDURE ( CHAR, VAR INTEGER );

PROCEDURE abc ( i : INTEGER;
                p : xyz;
                x : REAL );
```

As with other parameter types, procedure parameters may be bound by value or by reference.

The foregoing discussion applies also to function procedures. If the procedure named p in these examples is replaced by an integer function named f, then the (pre-ANSI) Pascal procedure heading:

```
procedure abc ( i : integer;
                function f : integer;
                x : real );
```

would be written in Modula-2 as follows:

```
TYPE xyz = PROCEDURE ( CHAR, INTEGER ) : INTEGER;

PROCEDURE abc ( i : INTEGER;
                f : xyz;
                x : real );
```

There is one predefined procedure type, denoted PROC. This type includes procedures with no parameters. The only operations available for procedure types are assignment and equality test. Chapter 16 introduces an important use of parameterless procedures.

A common use of procedure parameters is in mathematical applications. For example, consider a procedure that performs numerical integration of a function. Such a procedure can be given any real-valued function to integrate, plus the lower and upper limits of integration. Its heading might be:

```
TYPE realfunc = PROCEDURE ( REAL ) : REAL;

PROCEDURE integrate ( f : realfunc;
                      lower, upper : REAL ) : REAL;
```

A similar example is a procedure that plots the values of a function on a graphics plotter:

```
PROCEDURE plot ( f : realfunc; lower, upper : REAL );
```

7.4.3   Open Array Parameters

The second major difference between Modula-2 and Pascal formal parameter list syntax is in the definition of parameters of array types. Experienced Pascal programmers may again remember the discussions prior to the final adoption of the ANSI Pascal standard. In the original definition of Pascal a programmer who wished to perform similar operations on arrays of different lengths had to write two separate procedures. For example, consider a program with two different types of integer list, and the need to sort lists of both types. We might declare:

```
type shortlist = array [ 1..10 ] of integer;
     longlist = array [ 1..100 ] of integer;

procedure shortsort ( var list : shortlist );

procedure longsort  ( var list : longlist );
```

Because the formal parameter and actual parameter of such a sort procedure had to be of identical types, it would be impossible for a single procedure to be invoked once with a shortlist parameter and another time with a longlist parameter. This deficiency of Pascal was immediately and widely recognized, since it prevented the development of procedure libraries and reusable procedures.

The Pascal Standards Committees came very close to correcting this deficiency of Pascal when they proposed the concept of *conformant array parameters*. This concept was similar to the open array parameters of Modula-2, described below, and it survived the standardization process up to the final draft of the standard, when it was removed. Many implementations of Pascal provide this capability anyway, as an extension to the standard language.

Modula-2 uses a somewhat different approach to accomplish the same goal. As we have seen, the syntax of a formal parameter list allows the type of a parameter to be either a qualified identifier or an ARRAY OF qualified identifier. This latter case is called an *open array parameter*. It specifies that the formal parameter will be bound to an actual parameter that is a one-dimensional array of the specified type, but the index type of that array is not known. For the sorting example mentioned above, we might declare:

```
PROCEDURE SORT ( VAR list : ARRAY OF INTEGER );
```

It would then be possible to sort integer arrays of many different sizes, or more precisely, with many different index types. For example, each of the variables below could be the actual parameter in an invocation of the sort procedure.

```
VAR shortlist : ARRAY [ 1..10 ] OF INTEGER;
    longlist  : ARRAY [ 1..1000 ] OF INTEGER;
    letters   : ARRAY [ 'A'..'Z' ] OF INTEGER;
    colors    : ARRAY ( red, orange, yellow, green,
                        blue, violet ) OF INTEGER;
```

In the body of the sort procedure, it is not necessary to know the index type of the actual parameter, as long as there is a way to access each element of the array. Modula-2 provides this by adopting the rule that a formal parameter of an open array type is assumed to have an index type that is a subrange of the cardinal type, beginning at zero. The maximum subscript in that range is given by the predefined function HIGH, which takes the open array parameter as its parameter.

The example below demonstrates the use of an open array parameter and the HIGH function. The procedure prints an integer array, ten values per output line. The procedures WriteInt and WriteLn are used to print an integer and to start a new output line, respectively (see Chapter 9).

```
PROCEDURE print ( list : ARRAY OF INTEGER (* in mode *) );
    VAR pos : CARDINAL;
BEGIN
    FOR pos := 0 TO HIGH ( list ) DO
        WriteInt ( list[ pos ], 8 );
        IF pos MOD 10 = 9 THEN WriteLn END
    END;
    WriteLn
END print;
```

This procedure could be used to print any of the integer arrays in the variable declaration example above.

Modula-2 allows only one-dimensional open arrays. Chapter 15 demonstrates that a programmer can implement the equivalent of multidimensional open arrays.

7.5 Scope and Visibility

A procedure may declare entities (constants, types, variables, etc.) that are needed within that procedure. Each such declaration associates a meaning with an identifier. We define the *scope* of an identifier to be that section of a program in which the identifier maintains a particular associated meaning. In the early days of programming, the scope of an identifier was the entire program. It was soon recognized, however, that it was desirable to allow one identifier to have different meanings at different places in a program. This is particularly true within procedures, whose internal workings are usually of no importance to an invoking program. It would be an intolerable burden when developing large programs, particularly in a team programming environment, to ensure that no two procedures used the same identifier internally.

Algol 60, the grandfather of Modula-2, introduced a solution to this problem that has been used in nearly all major procedural languages since. Simply stated, the scope of an identifier was defined to be the block (see Chapter 8) in which the declaration of that identifier appeared, with one exception. If that same identifier was declared in a second procedure that was nested in the first,

the second procedure was excluded from the scope of the original identifier.
For example, consider the identifier x in the procedures p1, p2, and p3 below.

```
PROCEDURE p1;
    VAR x : CARDINAL;

    PROCEDURE p2;
        CONST x = 99;
        BEGIN
            (* body of p1 *)
        END p1;

    PROCEDURE p3;
    BEGIN
        (* body of p3 *)
    END p3;

BEGIN
    (* body of p1 *)
END p1;
```

The scope of the variable x declared in p1 is all of p1 except for procedure p2.
The scope therefore includes all of procedure p3. The scope of the constant x
declared in p2 is only the procedure p2.

An entity is said to be *visible* within the scope of its identifier. If an entity
is visible, it may be used in the usual ways for such an entity. In the example
above, the variable x may be referenced, such as in an assignment statement,
anywhere in the body of procedures p1 and p3, but not within procedure p2.
The constant x may be referenced, such as in a type declaration or assignment
statement, anywhere in procedure p2, but not within procedures p1 or p3.

The predefined identifiers in Modula-2 may be considered to be declared
in a procedure enclosing the main program. Thus the scope of a predefined
identifier includes the whole program, excluding any procedure in which that
identifier is redefined. An identifier declared in a main program is commonly
called *global,* and an identifier declared within any particular procedure is
commonly called *local* in the context of that procedure. An identifier visible in,
but not declared in, a procedure is called *nonlocal.* These concepts are informal, and some programmers use the term "global" for any nonlocal identifier.
In the main program, moreover, identifiers are simultaneously global and local.

The value of these rules for scope and visibility should not be underestimated. They allow each procedure to be written without having to know the
context in which the procedure will be placed. If there were no scope rules, in
large software development projects each programmer would have to consult
all the other team members whenever an identifier was to be declared, to make
sure that the identifier had not already been used. Even when programmers
work individually, these scope rules allow each of them to concentrate on one
procedure at a time, without cluttering their thinking with the internal details of
all the other procedures.

There is one bothersome detail regarding the scope rules; namely, there are two common but different interpretations of the meaning of those rules. Interpreted literally, the rule implies that the scope of an identifier begins with the first character after the procedure heading and ends with the semicolon at the end of the procedure. Consider the following example (the line numbers at the left are for reference; they are not part of the program).

```
1     PROCEDURE p1;
2         CONST c1 = 100;
3             (* other declarations *)
4
5         PROCEDURE p2;
6             CONST c2 = c1;
7                   c1 = 'A';
8             (* other declarations *)
9         BEGIN
10            (* body of p2 *)
11        END p2;
12
13    BEGIN
14        (* body of p1 *)
15    END p1;
```

Using the strict interpretation, the scope of the identifier c1 declared in line 2 includes lines 2 through 4 and lines 12 through 15. The scope of the identifier c1 declared in line 7 includes lines 6 through 11. Under this interpretation, the declaration of c2 in line 6 is in error, because the identifier c1 referred to in that declaration has not yet been defined.

The other interpretation of the scope rule allows the scope of one identifier to continue partway into an enclosed procedure, until a subsequent declaration of that identifier is encountered. This interpretation is often called the *one-pass scope rule,* since it facilitates the development of compilers that need only one pass through the source code. Under this interpretation, the scope of the identifier c1 declared in line 2 includes lines 2 through 6 and lines 12 through 15. The scope of the identifier c1 declared in line 7 includes only lines 7 through 11.

The one-pass scope rule would allow the example above to be compiled, while the strict scope rule would generate an error. But before we suggest that the one-pass scope rule is better, consider the following example involving the declaration of pointer and node types for construction of linked lists (see Section 15.1 for a discussion of linked lists).

```
1     PROCEDURE p1;
2         TYPE ptr  = POINTER TO node;
3              node = RECORD
4                         info : CARDINAL;
5                         next : ptr
6                     END;
```

```
7        (* additional declarations *)
8
9        PROCEDURE p2;
10         TYPE link   = POINTER TO node;
11             node = RECORD
12                         value : REAL;
13                         next  : link
14                       END;
15           (* additional declarations *)
16         BEGIN
17           (* body of p2 *)
18         END p2;
19
20     BEGIN
21        (* body of p1 *)
22     END p1;
```

In this example, either interpretation of the scope rule will allow correct compilation. With the strict interpretation, the node referred to in line 10 is the node defined in line 11; with the one-pass scope rule the node referred to in line 10 is the node defined in line 3. The reader will probably agree that the strict interpretation of the scope rule is more likely to be correct in this case. The examples above were tried on two Modula-2 compilers and two Pascal compilers, yielding different results. For the first example, one Modula-2 and one Pascal compiler compiled the programs successfully, using the one-pass scope rule. The other two compilers each gave different error messages; neither message clearly mentioned the scope problem. In compiling the second example, all four compilers interpreted the reference to node in line 10 as the node declared at line 11.

Until such time as the Modula-2 language is standardized, programmers may find either interpretation used. If the choice is not documented in the compiler manual, some experimentation may be necessary to determine which scope rule is being used.

This discussion of scope and visibility will be familiar to the experienced Pascal programmer. Modula-2 has some additional scope and visibility rules that are applicable in the context of modules rather than the context of procedures. These additional rules are discussed in Chapter 11.

7.6 Software Development Considerations

During the design of a software system, the developer is concerned with two components: data objects and actions to be performed on those objects. There are two design methodologies that are almost universally applicable and accepted, and these differ in their emphasis of the two software components in the early design stages. *Top-down design,* sometimes called *structured programming,* emphasizes actions. Using this methodology we concentrate, in very general terms, on the action to be performed first, the action to be performed second, and so on. Then, through a series of refinement steps, each of these actions is defined in more and more detail, until a level of detail is reached that can be translated directly into a programming language. The second methodology, commonly called *data abstraction* or *object-oriented design,* emphasizes data objects. We determine the types of data that are important and design new data types as needed. Inherent in a new data type is a set of operations on that type. Once the data types have been designed, it is usually a much simpler task to design the overall system, since much if not most of the work may be accomplished by performing the already defined operations on the new data types.

Procedures, including function procedures, are a fundamental building block in both these methodologies. Using top-down design, the very high level actions are expressed as phrases that eventually become names of procedures. The refinements of these actions become the design of the bodies of procedures. A main program can often be written directly from the highest level of design, taking the form of a series of procedure invocations. Each procedure performs a particular subtask, and its design may proceed in the same manner. Using data abstraction, the operations defined on each new data type are implemented as procedures. This process is described in more detail in Chapter 12, and is illustrated throughout the remainder of the book.

A procedure should do a single, well-defined task, and the name of the procedure should reflect that task. We should avoid the temptation to put two or more tasks into a single procedure just because it can be done. Consider, for example, a common class of problems in which a table of data is to be read in, printed, manipulated in some way, and then printed again. It may seem easier to have the output reflect the structure of the input if each piece of data is printed as it is read. This leads to a decomposition of the problem into three procedures:

read and print table

manipulate table

print table

A better approach is to recognize that reading, manipulating, and printing are all separate tasks, and each should be implemented by a separate procedure. The decomposition of the problem then involves three procedures, but four invocations.

read table

print table

manipulate table

print table

Procedures return answers to the invoking program primarily through parameters of output or input/output mode. Sometimes, a global or nonlocal variable may be changed to reflect the results of a procedure. Function procedures are quite different, in that they always return a single value. It is generally accepted practice among good programmers never to allow a function procedure to change the value of one of its parameters or to change the value of a nonlocal variable. Such actions are known as *side effects,* and they are discouraged because their occurrence is not often expected or apparent. Consider the statements:

$$\text{sum} := f(x, y) + x + y$$

$$\text{sum} := x + y + f(x, y)$$

Mathematically, we would expect the same result from each one, since addition is commutative. If, however, the function f were to change the values of either of its parameters, the resulting sum would depend very much on the order of the summands. It is therefore common practice to restrict function procedure parameters to input mode.

As we have seen, the mode of parameters must be known by a program that wishes to use a particular procedure. Programmers should develop a consistent way of making parameter mode obvious to someone reading a procedure.

Because of the scope and visibility rules described earlier, it is easy for a Modula-2 programmer to define local entities within a procedure that are used only by that procedure. These can and often should include subprocedures. This is valuable for the same reasons that local constants, types, and variables are valuable: the programmer does not need to know about identifiers used in surrounding contexts. Programmers should resist the temptation to place a subprocedure before a procedure rather than inside it.

The names of procedures should reflect their purpose. We have seen that variables represent data objects, and therefore their names are normally nouns. Procedures represent actions, and their names are normally verbs or verb phrases. The goal is an invocation statement that reads like an English imperative statement. Since function procedures represent values, their names are again usually nouns. An exception is a function that returns a boolean type, which is often given a name that is an adjective or participle describing the condition it represents.

Readers are urged to examine the procedures in the examples in this book, and in their own programs, to see how these recommendations have been applied.

8

Programs

The structure of a complete Modula-2 program is quite different from that of a Pascal program except in the case of very small programs. In Chapter 11 we will examine these differences in detail. In this section we look at the syntax of small programs, and discover that it is quite similar to Pascal.

A Modula-2 program consists of one or more *modules,* a feature that gives the language its name. Modules are classified as program, internal, definition, or implementation. Here we introduce only the program module, because it performs the same syntactic function as a Pascal program. The syntax of a program module is shown in Figure 8.1.

A Pascal programmer will note only small differences between a Modula-2 main module and a Pascal program. First, the first word is MODULE rather than program. Second, there is nothing comparable to Pascal's program parameters. Third, at the end of the module, the identifier that is the module's name is repeated. Examples below exhibit these differences.

The syntax of a *block* is shown in Figure 8.2. This entity is virtually identical in Modula-2 and Pascal.

All the syntactic entities of a block have been defined except for *statement.* The syntax of a statement is shown in Figure 8.3.

Notice that the statements that make up a block are *separated* by semicolons, not *terminated* by them. Programmers should discipline themselves to think and speak in terms of "the semicolon between statements" rather than "the semicolon at the end of a statement."

117

program module

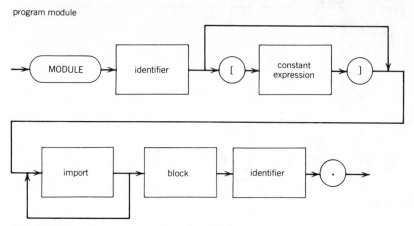

FIGURE 8.1   Syntax of a Program Module

   The semantics of a program module is like that of a program in Pascal. Execution begins with the first statement in the body, which is the first statement after the reserved word BEGIN. Execution continues until one of three things happens: the last statement in the body is executed, a HALT is executed anywhere in the program (including in a procedure), or a RETURN is executed in the body of the program module.

   We conclude this chapter with two very short examples of complete Modula-2 programs, Program 8.1 and Program 8.2. Actually, it is extremely rare for a program to consist of just a program module. These examples make use of the InOut module, described in Section 9.2, so strictly speaking they are not really complete.

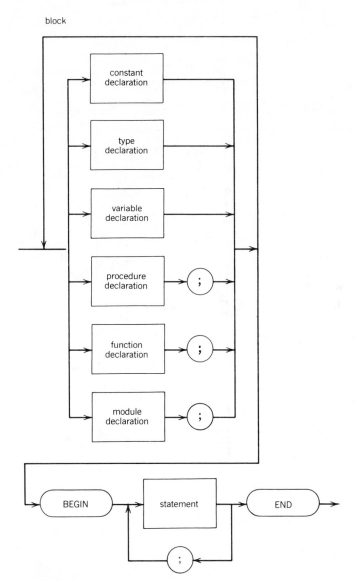

FIGURE 8.2 Syntax of a Block

statement

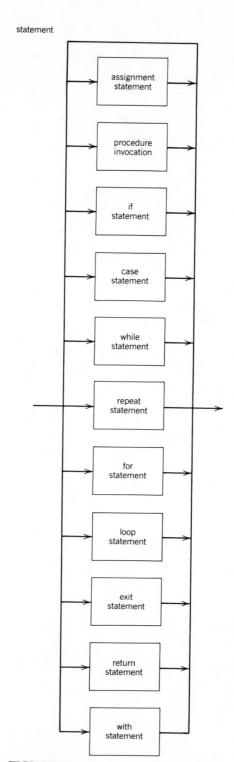

FIGURE 8.3 Syntax of a Statement

Program 8.1 Triangular Numbers

```
MODULE TriangularNumbers;

  (* This program computes and prints the first 25 triangular numbers. *)

FROM InOut IMPORT WriteCard, WriteLn;

VAR
  n  : CARDINAL;
  tri : CARDINAL;

BEGIN
  tri := 0;
  FOR n := 1 TO 25 DO
    tri := tri + n;
    WriteCard ( tri, 4 );
    WriteLn
  END
END TriangularNumbers.
```

Program 8.2 Character Counter

```
MODULE CharacterCounter;

  (* This program counts nonblank characters in an input line. *)

FROM InOut IMPORT
  (* const *) EOL,
  (* proc  *) Read, WriteString, WriteCard, WriteLn;

VAR count : CARDINAL;
    ch    : CHAR;

BEGIN
  count := 0;
  LOOP
    Read ( ch );
    IF ch = EOL THEN EXIT END;
    IF ch <> ' '
      THEN INC ( count )
    END
  END;
  WriteString ( 'Nonblank characters:' );
  WriteCard ( count, 5 );
  WriteLn
END CharacterCounter.
```

9

Input and Output

Input and output have long been a problem for programming language designers. In the early days of computing, a typical computer system had a card reader for input and a line printer or teletypewriter for output, plus maybe a tape drive for file input and output. Data transfers were fixed length records, and no interactive input and output was possible. Languages developed at that time provided straightforward input and output capabilities.

During the 1960s a variety of approaches to input and output were tried. The designers of Algol 60 recognized that I/O requirements differed from system to system, and provided no I/O capabilities in the language at all. Each implementation of the language was free to offer any facilities the implementors wanted. This simplified the definition of the language, but made programs virtually impossible to move from one system to another. Since one of the goals of Algol was to provide a standard language for all computer systems, the portability problem was serious.

The designers of PL/I provided an enormous number of input/output capabilities, since the language was intended to serve systems programmers, business applications programmers, and scientific applications programmers. The result was a relatively complicated language. Pascal offers a much simpler set of input/output capabilities, based on the sequential file model. Unfortunately, this model is not well suited to interactive input and output, nor does it serve the needs of users who require other file organizations.

Furthermore, in recent years input and output of data other than streams of characters have become increasingly important. Rather than printing terminals, most interactive computer users now use video terminals, which present a new set of requirements for input and output. Other forms of information, such as graphics, video, voice, and signals to or from other kinds of machinery have become a significant fraction of the input to and output from computers. It is almost impossible for a programming language to provide I/O capabilities for all these kinds of data.

Modula-2 tackles the input/output problem somewhat along the lines of Algol 60, in that there are no input or output *statements* in the language. Instead, a library module (see Section 11.4) containing input and output *procedures* may be provided. It is intended that each implementation of the language provide the same capabilities for input and output, although the actual implementation may differ substantially from one computer system to another.

This approach is similar to Pascal in that input and output are handled via procedures rather than statements, but it differs from Pascal in that the language definition does not say what these procedures must be. We will see that one set of procedures can be designed that provides capabilities almost identical to those of Pascal. A second set could provide the specialized input and output needed by a video terminal, a third set could provide sequential files, and a fourth set could provide direct access files. Any number of sets of procedures (library modules) can be supplied to serve the input/output needs of a very wide variety of users.

9.1 The Concept of Stream

Because the input and output devices attached to computer systems vary so greatly, it is necessary to find an abstraction or model on which to base the input and output procedures. This abstraction is called a *stream*. It may be viewed as a temporal or spatial sequence of data objects all of the same data type. Pascal programmers will recognize the Pascal file type as a stream.

The devices intended for input and output of human-readable data represent such data as patterns of characters. Even numeric data are represented as characters at the interface between the device and the human user. The translation between characters and internal representations of numeric data is hidden from the user as part of the input/output procedures. Thus the *character stream* is the model for legible input and output.

A character stream is not necessarily spatially linear. Most devices recognize certain control characters, such as the ASCII carriage return and line feed characters, causing the physical arrangement of the characters to be two-dimensional. Video display terminals may also recognize cursor control characters, allowing the displayed information to be placed anywhere on the screen at any time. Still, from the point of view of the programming language, the data sent to an output device are temporally linear.

Secondary storage devices such as tapes and disks may also be considered to be input and output devices. The data sent to these devices are not intended for human reading, and therefore do not need to be translated into characters. The same bit patterns that represent a data item in the main memory may be used on these devices. We therefore allow such things as a stream of integers, a stream of reals, or a stream of records to model the input and output on these devices.

A stream does not have a fixed length; it may be thought of as potentially infinite in length. The number of items in the stream at a given time is called the *length* of the stream. Access to the stream may occur at only one place, called the *current position*. Two kinds of access exist, corresponding to input and output operations. *Read* access allows input operations, and yields a copy of the value at the current position in the stream. A read access also advances the current position in the stream to the next item. *Write* access allows output operations, and appends a copy of a value to the end of the stream. When a stream is being used for output, the current position is always the position immediately after the current length of the stream. A write access fills this position and advances the position.

Before accessing a stream, we must *open* it. When we open a stream, we specify its *mode* as read or write. If the mode is read, the current position is set to the beginning of the stream. If the mode is write, the length of the stream is assumed to be zero, and the current position is set to the first position. After we have finished accessing a stream, we may *close* it. This allows subsequent reopening of the stream, if desired.

Modula-2 assumes two predefined character streams, which are abstractions of the default input and output devices for a particular user. In an interactive environment, these streams represent the input and output parts of the user's terminal. As the next section shows, it is possible to attach either or both of these streams to other devices, either temporarily or for the duration of a program execution. For the programmer to see the same interface to terminal streams and disk file streams, the InOut module described in the next section is built on two lower level abstractions, one for terminal input/output and one for disk input/output. Each of these provides similar primitive operations needed by the InOut module. Since these modules are very low level, they are implementation dependent. Examples of some typical features of these modules are described in Sections 9.3 and 9.4.

9.2   Human-Readable Input and Output

All implementations of Modula-2 may be expected to have a library module named InOut that provides input and output capabilities similar to those of Pascal for numeric and character data types. Typical implementations contain the procedures described below. For each procedure we give the procedure heading, including parameter type and mode, and a brief description of its purpose.

These procedures provide for input and output of a single data object. Programmers familiar with Pascal's read and write procedures, which may be given any number of parameters, may find Modula-2 input and output slightly cumbersome at first. However, by adhering to normal Modula-2 parameter rules, these procedures may be written in Modula-2, based on lower level input/output abstractions. This allows Modula-2 programmers to tailor the input and output module to their needs—a capability not present in Pascal.

9.2.1   Character and String Data

```
PROCEDURE Read
    ( VAR ch : CHAR (* out *) );
```

This procedure reads a single character from the current input stream (the user's terminal in an interactive environment), and returns that character in the parameter named ch.

```
PROCEDURE Write
    (      ch : CHAR (* in *) );
```

This procedure writes a single character to the current output stream (the user's terminal in an interactive environment); the character is supplied in the parameter named ch.

```
PROCEDURE ReadString
    ( VAR string : ARRAY OF CHAR (* out *) );
```

This procedure reads a sequence of characters from the current input stream. The reading is terminated either when the array is filled, or when one of an implementation-defined set of terminator characters is encountered. Those terminators normally include carriage return and new line characters. The parameter named string returns the data to the invoking program. The InOut module defines a character variable named termCH, which contains the terminator character. This variable may be accessed by a program if this character needs to be known.

```
PROCEDURE WriteString
    (      string : ARRAY OF CHAR (* in *) );
```

This procedure writes a sequence of characters to the current output stream. The parameter named string supplies the character string to be written, and may have any index type. The number of characters written will be HIGH(string) + 1.

9.2.2   Cardinal and Integer Data

```
PROCEDURE ReadCard
    ( VAR number : CARDINAL (* out *) );
```

This procedure reads characters from the current input stream, and converts them to a cardinal value. Leading blanks are ignored, and characters are read until a nondigit is encountered, or a value too large for the cardinal data type has been seen. The value is returned in the parameter named number.

```
PROCEDURE WriteCard
    (      number : CARDINAL (* in *);
           width   : CARDINAL (* in *) );
```

This procedure converts the cardinal value in the parameter named number into an appropriate string of characters, and then pads the string with leading blanks to achieve the number of characters specified by the parameter named width. If the number of characters needed to express the value exceeds width, no padding is done, nor is the character string truncated. The characters are then written to the current output stream.

```
PROCEDURE ReadOct
    ( VAR number : CARDINAL (* out *) );
```

This procedure is the same as ReadCard, except that the incoming characters are interpreted in octal rather than decimal notation.

```
PROCEDURE WriteOct
    (      number : CARDINAL (* in *);
           width   : CARDINAL (* in *) );
```

This procedure is the same as WriteCard, except that the number is expressed in octal rather than decimal notation.

```
PROCEDURE ReadHex
    ( VAR number : CARDINAL (* out *) );
```

This procedure is the same as ReadCard, except that the incoming characters are interpreted in hexadecimal rather than decimal notation.

```
PROCEDURE WriteHex
    (      number : CARDINAL (* in *);
           width   : CARDINAL (* in *) );
```

This procedure is the same as WriteCard, except that the number is expressed in hexadecimal rather than decimal notation.

```
PROCEDURE ReadInt
    ( VAR number : INTEGER (* out *) );
```

This procedure is the same as ReadCard, except that the parameter named number returns an integer value, and the sequence of digits read in may be preceded by a sign (plus or minus).

PROCEDURE WriteInt
 (number : INTEGER (∗ in ∗);
   width : CARDINAL (∗ in ∗));

This procedure is the same as WriteCard, except that the parameter named number is an integer. If the number is negative, the sequence of characters written begins with a minus sign. If the number is positive, a plus sign is not printed.

9.2.3 Real Data

In some implementations of Modula-2, the procedures below may be in a module named RealInOut, rather than in the module InOut. In addition, some implementations may provide more than one real data type, and therefore will provide additional input and output procedures (see Appendix 3).

PROCEDURE ReadReal
 (VAR number : REAL (∗ out ∗));

This procedure skips leading blanks and then reads a sequence of characters representing a real number. The representation must follow the rules for real constants (see Section 2.2). This includes two different forms, the first being the normal sequence of digits, decimal point, digits. The second is the exponential form, consisting of the following sequence: digits, decimal point, digits, letter E, sign, digits. Either form may be preceded by a sign character. The value represented by the characters is returned in the real parameter named number.

PROCEDURE WriteReal
 (number : REAL (∗ in ∗);
   width : CARDINAL (∗ in ∗));

This procedure converts the real value supplied in the parameter named number into a character string that represents that value. If the number of characters is less than the value supplied in the parameter named width, the string is padded with leading blanks to achieve this number of characters. If the string is already at least this long, no padding is done, nor is the string truncated. The string is then written to the current output stream.

9.2.4 Boolean Data

The original definition of the module InOut did not include procedures for input and output of boolean data. The following procedures may be added to that

module, or placed in a separate module. (See Section 9.2.6 for a definition of
the variable named Done.)

```
          PROCEDURE ReadBool
             ( VAR value : BOOLEAN (* out *) );
             VAR character : CHAR;

    BEGIN
       Read ( character );
       IF Done
          THEN IF ( character = 't' ) OR
                   ( character = 'T' )
                   THEN value := TRUE
                   ELSIF ( character = 'f' ) OR
                         ( character = 'F' )
                         THEN value := FALSE
                   END
          END
    END ReadBool;

    PROCEDURE WriteBool
          (      value : BOOLEAN (* in *);
                 width : CARDINAL (* in *));

          VAR spaces : CARDINAL;

    BEGIN
       FOR spaces := 1 TO width − 5 DO
          Write ( ' ' )
       END;
       IF value
          THEN WriteString ( 'true ' )
          ELSE WriteString ( 'false' )
       END
    END WriteBool;
```

These procedures are not as sophisticated as they might be. The Read-
Bool procedure cannot read the value written by WriteBool; this could be
remedied by having both procedures use single letters or by having both use
complete words. Also, the ReadBool procedure simply ignores invalid input.
A better version would take some action such as printing an error message.
These improvements are left as exercises.

9.2.5 Input and Output Line Control

Human-readable input/output is normally not completely linear, in that the
character streams are broken into lines. Modula-2 provides capabilities to begin
a new input or output line, and to recognize the end of an input line. These
capabilities are somewhat different from those of Pascal.

The InOut module defines an end-of-line character constant, named EOL, rather than an end-of-line boolean function like eoln in Pascal. After reading a character, the programmer must compare that character to EOL to determine if end of line has been reached. Although the practice is not recommended, it is also possible to write the EOL character to start a new line in the output stream (see the WriteLn procedure below.)

The following procedures are used to start a new input or output line; they are conceptually identical to their Pascal counterparts.

PROCEDURE ReadLn;

This procedure starts a new input line in the current input stream. This is done by skipping all characters in the stream up to and including the next occurrence of the EOL character. The current position of the stream becomes the position immediately after the EOL.

PROCEDURE WriteLn;

This procedure starts a new output line in the current output stream. It simply appends the EOL character to the stream.

The operating system under which a Modula-2 implementation runs may have specific formats for character streams or files. The most common difference from one operating system to another is the representation of end of line. Three common representations are a single line feed character (used, e.g., by the UNIX operating system), a single carriage return character, or the pair of characters carriage return/line feed (used, e.g., by several DEC PDP-11 operating systems). One of the merits of the Modula-2 approach to end-of-line representation is that the user does not need to know how the operating system represents end of line. The Modula-2 implementation translates what the operating system uses into the EOL character. This removes an implementation dependency from the language, making programs more portable.

9.2.6   Recognizing End of Input

Modula-2 provides the capability of recognizing the end of an input stream in a manner different from Pascal's eof function. The InOut module defines a boolean variable named Done that is set by the read procedures and the stream redirection procedures. After a read operation, Done is true if the read was successful, and false if the read failed because the end of the stream was encountered. After a redirection procedure (OpenInput or OpenOutput), Done is true if the new stream was successfully opened, and false otherwise.

Done may not be used to recognize invalid data. The effect of invalid data on program execution is implementation-dependent; on many implementations the program is aborted.

A program that reads and processes data until the end is reached will need a structure such as:

```
LOOP
    (* read an item *)
    IF NOT Done THEN EXIT END;
    (* process the item *)
END
```

The Pascal programmer should note that Modula-2's Done variable has the opposite value from Pascal's eof under similar circumstances. Some confusion is possible because it is easy to interpret the word "done" as meaning that all the input has been processed.

In implementations with separate InOut and RealInOut modules, there will be two different variables named Done. It is the programmer's responsibility to test the appropriate one. In such cases, a qualified identifier is required to distinguish one from the other; those identifiers are InOut.Done and RealInOut.Done. Qualified identifiers are discussed in more detail in Chapter 11.

9.2.7   Redirecting Input and Output

Unless otherwise specified, the procedures described above operate on the default input and output streams, normally the user's terminal. It is often desirable to read from or write to another stream, such as one attached to a disk device. The following procedures provide that capability.

```
PROCEDURE OpenInput
    (     name : ARRAY OF CHAR (* in *) );
```

This procedure closes the default input stream and opens the stream whose name is specified by the name parameter. This parameter is a character string, and its structure is defined by the implementation. Normally, it is the format required by the operating system for file names. If the procedure succeeds, subsequent input is read from this stream.

```
PROCEDURE OpenOutput
    (     name : ARRAY OF CHAR (* in *) );
```

This procedure closes the default output stream and opens the stream whose name is specified by the name parameter, as described for OpenInput above. If the procedure succeeds, subsequent output is written to this stream.

```
PROCEDURE CloseInput;
```

This procedure closes the current input stream and reopens the default input stream. No parameters are required.

```
PROCEDURE CloseOutput;
```

This procedure closes the current output stream and reopens the default output stream. No parameters are required.

9.3 File System Module

All Modula-2 implementations may be expected to include a module, often named FileSystem, that provides relatively low level access to the file system provided by the operating system. Such a module is implementation dependent, and we cannot provide a completely detailed description. However, the following general features may be expected.

First and foremost, the file system module will define a data type called FILE. The file procedures will operate on variables of this type. The module will also define a constant that is the end-of-line character used by the operating system.

Low level read and write procedures transfer basic units (bytes, words, blocks) of information to and from the file. The sizes of these units are implementation dependent.

Procedures to open and close files will be provided. The open procedure may be expected to allow the specification of the external file name (the name used by the operating system, not the Modula-2 file variable name) as a character string parameter. Procedures to create a new file (without writing anything to it yet), delete an old file, or rename a file may also be provided. These procedures manipulate the operating system's file directory and do not change the contents of the file.

If the operating system supports the indexed sequential file organization or the direct access file organization, additional capabilities may be present in the file system module, or perhaps in a separate module.

9.4 Low Level Terminal Input/Output Module

The input and output requirements of most terminals are relatively simple and straightforward. It is necessary to be able to read a character from the terminal keyboard, or write a character to the terminal printer or video display. Additional capabilities can usually be defined in terms of these two primitive operations, but for efficiency reasons, some may be provided directly. For example, most operating systems provide the ability to read or write a string of characters via a single input/output operation more efficiently than via several single character operations. Thus the following procedures are present in a typical Terminal module.

```
                PROCEDURE Read
                  ( VAR ch : CHAR (* out *) );
```

This procedure reads a single character from the terminal.

> PROCEDURE Write
> (ch : CHAR (∗ in ∗));

This procedure writes a single character to the terminal.

> PROCEDURE ReadString
> (VAR string : ARRAY OF CHAR (∗ out ∗));

This procedure reads a string of characters from the terminal. The read is terminated either when the string is filled, or a terminating character is read. Terminator characters are implementation defined, but usually include control characters and the space character. In some implementations leading spaces will be skipped before the read begins.

> PROCEDURE WriteString
> (string : ARRAY OF CHAR (∗ in ∗));

This procedure writes a string of characters to the terminal.

This module may also include ReadLn and WriteLn procedures, with the same definitions as described for the InOut module. One other procedure is usually available, a parameterless procedure named ReadAgain. Its purpose is to cause the next invocation of Read to reread the same character as the last invocation. Although at first this may seem to be an unusual procedure, it is actually very useful. In many of the higher level read procedures, such as ReadCard or ReadReal, it is not known in advance how many characters must be read to complete the value. The procedure therefore continues reading until it encounters a character that is not part of the value. That character may be part of the next value to be read; if the next read is a single character read operation, that character is the entire value. Thus it must be possible for the next read, whenever and wherever it occurs, to reread that character. The ReadAgain procedure makes this possible.

10

The "Standard" Modula-2 Library

There does not exist a recognized standard for the Modula-2 language, so we must be careful when using the word "standard" in describing any feature of the language. This is especially important when considering the library modules that may be expected to be present in any implementation. In this section we examine some typical modules, but readers should examine the actual modules present in their implementations. They are likely to be quite different.

10.1 Mathematical Library

In anticipation of the possibility of several specialized mathematical libraries, the original definition of Modula-2 included a library module named MathLib0. Each implementation of Modula-2 may be expected to have such a module, containing the function procedures described below. The parameters all are in mode, as is always the case for function procedures.

PROCEDURE sqrt (x : REAL) : REAL;

This function returns the square root of the parameter x, which must be non-negative.

PROCEDURE exp (x : REAL) : REAL;

This is the exponential function, and returns the value *e* raised to the power of parameter x.

PROCEDURE ln (x : REAL) : REAL;

This is the natural logarithm function, and returns the natural logarithm of the parameter x, which must be nonnegative.

PROCEDURE sin (x : REAL) : REAL;

This is the trigonometric sine function.

PROCEDURE cos (x : REAL) : REAL;

This is the trigonometric cosine function.

PROCEDURE arctan (x : REAL) : REAL;

This is the trigonometric inverse tangent, or arctangent, function.

PROCEDURE real (x : INTEGER) : REAL;

This is the type conversion function from integer values to real values.

PROCEDURE entier (x : REAL) : INTEGER;

This is the type conversion function from real values to integer values. "Entier" is the French word for "whole," meaning "integer" in numeric contexts. This function name was first used in Algol 60, a language developed in Europe.

Additional functions that may be present in the mathematical library module include common logarithms, additional trigonometric and inverse trigonometric functions, and hyperbolic and inverse hyperbolic trigonometric functions. In addition, an implementation may also include modules named MathLib1, MathLib2, and so on.

10.2 Storage Management

All Modula-2 implementations may be expected to include a module named Storage that provides dynamic storage allocation and deallocation capabilities. Two procedures are included in this module.

PROCEDURE ALLOCATE
  (VAR addr : ADDRESS (* out *);
        size : CARDINAL (* in *));

This procedure is given the size of the block of storage to be allocated, and returns the address of a block of (at least) that size. The size is measured in units equal to the size of a memory cell, which is machine dependent. The ADDRESS data type is discussed in Chapter 13.

```
        PROCEDURE DEALLOCATE
    (       addr : ADDRESS  (* in *);
            size : CARDINAL (* in *) );
```

This procedure is given the address and size of a block of storage that is to be deallocated. In general, the block must be one that was allocated by the ALLO-CATE procedure, and the value of the size parameter must be the same as at the time of allocation.

These procedures are often invisible to the programmer. Invocations of the predefined procedures NEW and DISPOSE (described in Section 4.3, and illustrated in Chapter 15) are translated by the Modula-2 compiler to invocations of ALLOCATE and DEALLOCATE. This module is considered in detail in Section 15.6.

10.3   Other Library Modules

Many other library modules may be provided with a Modula-2 implementation. Often these are inspired by the libraries provided by the operating system. Some relatively common modules are those that provide more sophisticated output capabilities for video display terminals. A line drawing module may be present to provide simple graphics capabilities. A window handling module may provide the capability to divide the display screen into several sections or windows, each of which may be used for output from a different part of a program.

One other common module provides for communication and synchronization among cooperating processes. This module is discussed in detail in Chapter 16.

Several examples in Part Two of this book refer to two general-purpose library modules available on the authors' implementations. These are described briefly here.

The module Arithmetic includes several simple operations on numbers. The functions mincard, maxcard, minint, maxint, minreal, and maxreal each take two parameters of the appropriate numeric type, and return the minimum or maximum of those values. Other functions include gcd (greatest common divisor) and lcm (least common multiple), both defined on pairs of cardinal numbers.

The module Utilities provides a variety of capabilities, including procedures for controlling the display of an intelligent video terminal. Among these are several cursor control procedures, such as ScGotoXY for direct cursor addressing and ScLeft, ScRight, ScUp, and ScDown for incremental cursor movement. The ScClrScreen procedure clears the screen. The ReadKey procedure reads characters from the keyboard until one of a specified set of characters is found, and that character is returned. The Yes procedure reads characters from the keyboard until either a 'y' or an 'n' (either case) is read; it returns true if the character was 'y', and false otherwise. The Spacebar procedure prints message "hit spacebar to continue" and waits for the user to hit the spacebar; it may be used to pause a program. The Printer procedure accepts a boolean parameter indicating whether a local printer attached to the terminal should be on or off.

There is an effort underway to define a "standard" set of Modula-2 library modules, similar to those described here. Until such a set is defined, users of Modula-2 should consult their system documentation to determine what additional library modules are present.

Exercises for Part 1

1. Determine whether your implementation has any restrictions on the length of identifiers, or on the number of significant characters in identifiers.

2. Determine whether your implementation allows both upper- and lowercase letters C, B, H, and E in numeric literal constants.

3. Some implementations restrict the form of constant expressions. Try the examples of constant declarations in Chapter 3 on your implementation.

4. Determine whether your implementation treats a tab character as a separator.

5. Determine the limitations imposed by your implementation on the size of set data types.

6. Determine the type transfer functions available on your implementation. Is it possible to perform a type transfer from a smaller object to a larger object?

7. What are the differences between the string types of Pascal and Modula-2?

8. Suppose a program is to read in the values a, b, and c, representing the coefficients of the quadratic equation $ax^2 + bx + c = 0$, and print the real roots of the equations. The program does this repeatedly until either the value of a is 0 or the equation has no real roots. Show how this loop can be structured with a while statement, and with loop and exit statements.

9. Determine the parameter binding mechanisms used by your implementation. Are these dictated by hardware or operating system conventions? How are open array parameters passed to a procedure?

10. Try the example of Section 7.5 on your implementation to determine how it interprets the scope rules.

11. Determine how your implementation provides input/output capabilities. Does it have separate InOut and RealInOut modules? Do the procedures differ from those described in Chapter 9? Are real numbers printed in the usual decimal form or the exponential form? Does the field width parameter of the WriteReal procedure affect the output form?

12. Rewrite the ReadBool and WriteBool procedures to correct the deficiencies mentioned at the end of Section 9.2.4.

13. Determine the capabilities of your implementation for file input and output. Are all the features described in Section 9.3 provided?

14. Determine the capabilities of your implementation for terminal input and output. Are all the features described in Section 9.4 provided?

15. Determine the mathematical library procedures offered by your implementation.

16. Implement the procedures of the Arithmetic module described in Section 10.3.

17. Implement the video terminal control procedures of the Utilities module described in Section 10.3.

18. **Standing Exercise:** In the programming examples throughout Part Two of this book, determine the loop invariant for each loop, and identify the statements prior to the loop that establish the loop invariant.

PART TWO

Software Development with Modula-2

The features of Modula-2 that are most different from Pascal were created to support the development of large, sophisticated software systems. In Part Two we examine these features and see how they may be used effectively.

The most import feature is the *module,* which is described in Chapter 11. Modules are the syntactic entities that allow us to express the data, functional, and process abstractions that are so important in modern software design.

Chapter 12 introduces the fundamentals of data abstraction, which is the basis for the object-oriented software design methodology. The related concepts of functional abstraction are also presented.

Chapter 13, 14, and 15 present a detailed look at the design and implementation of abstract data types. The Modula-2 features that support low level data manipulations are presented first, and then these features are used to demonstrate the implementation of static and dynamic data structures.

Chapter 16 introduces the important concepts of concurrent programming and develops the basic techniques for process synchronization and communication. Since concurrent software systems will be new to most readers, we discuss not only the language features that support concurrency, but also some approaches to the design of such systems.

Finally, Chapter 17 shows how all the features of Modula-2 can support the object-oriented software design methodology. Two case studies demonstrate how relatively complex software systems can be designed and developed in a highly structured way, using the Modula-2 language throughout.

11

Modules

Modules are perhaps the most important feature of Modula-2. There are four basic types: program modules, two types of library module, and internal modules.

Program modules are complete program units that may import software resources (constants, types, variables, procedures) from library modules. Program modules are discussed in Chapter 8.

Library modules have two parts that must be compiled separately: specification and body. A library module specification is called a *definition module*. A library module body is called an *implementation module*. Library modules are generally created with the intention of exporting reusable software components to other modules. We describe library modules in Section 11.3.

Internal modules may be defined within the body of either program modules or implementation modules. They are usually used to help control the scope and visibility of objects in the compilation unit in which they are defined. We discuss internal modules in Section 11.4.

In this chapter we introduce the basic modules. In later chapters we will show how these units support data abstraction, information hiding, and object-oriented software development.

11.1 Separate Compilation Versus Independent Compilation

A *compilation unit* is a compilable block of code in a programming language. In standard Pascal, the only compilation unit is a complete program. Independent compilation implies that program units may be compiled separately, and subsequently integrated to form a complete program or software system. The integration process is performed by a utility program called a linker or linkage editor. Without the facility of independent compilation, a language would be ill suited for large-scale software development.

Fortran has enjoyed widespread use in part because it supports independent compilation. Extensive precompiled Fortran subroutine libraries exist and form the environment for many software development projects. All the identifiers used in a Fortran subroutine either are formal parameters, are locally declared, or are explicitly declared in a common block, which specifies the variables that are defined outside the subroutine. If reference is made to other subroutines (from within a subroutine or main program), the compiler treats them as if they are externally declared and creates a list of external references to be resolved by the system linker. Because the programmer does not have to specify external references, the compiler assumes that all external references to common variables as well as to subroutines are correct.

Many Fortran programmers consider this a blessing. It is clear from the foregoing description that a Fortran compiler is very forgiving. A programmer can invent a subroutine call even if that subroutine doesn't exist. Top-down design! However, this may cause serious problems.

The Fortran compiler does not check whether a subroutine call has the correct number of parameters or the correct type of parameters, or whether the subroutine even exists. Unfortunately, the errors resulting from undefined external references or incorrect interfaces to external references are detected at link time or at run time, when errors are generally the most costly to rectify.

It is most desirable if a language supports both independent compilation and strong type checking across compilation boundaries. We have seen that Fortran lacks the feature of strong type checking across compilation boundaries (or even within compilation boundaries). Standard Pascal does not even support independent compilation.

The combination of independent compilation with strong type checking across compilation boundaries which is called *separate compilation,* allows software construction to be decentralized while preserving the benefits of strong typing. This type checking is performed at the time of compilation.

Modula-2 supports separate compilation. Program and library modules serve as the basic compilation units, as shown in Figure 11.1. Internal modules may be defined within program modules or within implementation modules. The compiler views the separate compilation units (library and program modules) as if they were part of one program for purposes of checking external references. Modula-2's support for separate compilation includes:

compilation unit

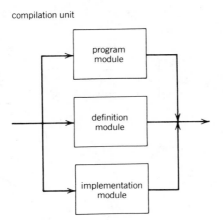

FIGURE 11.1 Syntax of a Compilation Unit

1. A check to ensure that all external references exist in precompiled form.
2. A check to ensure that the actual parameters in all external subprogram calls agree with the formal parameters of the subprogram in number, type, and binding mechanism.
3. A check to ensure that the version numbers for all implementation modules agree with the version numbers of the corresponding specification modules (this issue is examined in Section 11.3). This protects the system from the imposition of a change in a module specification without the necessary recompilation of all client modules (modules that import information from the specification module).

In the next section we describe how import and export lists in a compilation unit allow information to be passed from one compilation module to another and from one internal module to another.

11.2 The Concepts of Import and Export

Modules use import lists to control what outside software resources are available within the module and an export list to control what internal resources can be accessed outside the module.

Figures 11.2 and 11.3 show the syntax for import and export lists, respectively.

One may think of a module as a logical unit surrounded by a membrane. Information is passed through the membrane from inside to outside using the export list and from outside to inside using import list(s). Export or import lists are the only mechanism available in Modula-2 for transferring information through the membrane surrounding the modules.

Program modules can import software resources from library modules

import

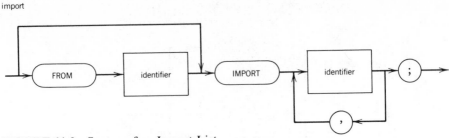

FIGURE 11.2   Syntax of an Import List

export

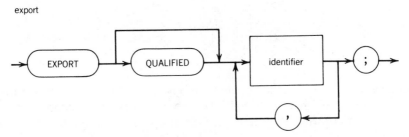

FIGURE 11.3   Syntax of an Export List

only. Internal modules, defined within a program module or implementation module, can export information to the surrounding logical unit as well as import resources from the surrounding logical unit. Library modules may export information to other library or program modules as well as import resources from other library modules.

Program modules typically import resources from the software library supplied with the system to support operations such as file and screen I/O, and mathematical functions. In addition, it is common for program modules to import resources from library modules that have been created for the particular application.

In program module ImportExport (Program 11.1), we display import and export lists using an internal module (see Section 11.4).

The main program module ImportExport brings the two input/output procedures WriteLn, and WriteString into the scope of the compilation unit with the simple import list IMPORT InOut. The import list

FROM InOut IMPORT WriteLn, WriteString;

in module Mod1, makes these procedures available inside Mod1. The export list

EXPORT
        (* type *) cartype,
        (* type *) fruittype,
        (* proc *) CarDescription;

Program 11.1 Illustration of Import and Export Lists

```
MODULE ImportExport;

IMPORT InOut;

  MODULE Mod1;

  FROM InOut IMPORT WriteLn, WriteString;

  EXPORT
    (* type *) cartype,
    (* type *) fruittype,
    (* proc *) CarDescription;

  TYPE fruittype = (apple, orange, banana);

  TYPE cartype = (Mazda, Subaru, Plymouth, Chevy);

  PROCEDURE CarDescription ( c : cartype);
  BEGIN
    CASE c OF
      Mazda    : WriteLn;
                 WriteString ("Uses a rotary engine.");  |
      Subaru   : WriteLn;
                 WriteString ("Excellent gas mileage.");  |
      Plymouth : WriteLn;
                 WriteString ("Front wheel drive.");       |
      Chevy    : WriteLn;
                 WriteString ("Low frequency of service problems.");
    END (* case *);
  END CarDescription;

END Mod1;

VAR
  car : cartype;

BEGIN
  car := Mazda;
  CarDescription (car);
END ImportExport.
```

makes the enumeration types cartype and fruittype and subprogram Car-Description visible in the main program module body below Mod1.

We discuss internal modules in more detail in Section 11.4.

11.3 Library Modules

Library modules are used to export software resources to other modules. These other modules may be part of a particular software system or may be modules in other separate software systems.

All Modula-2 systems include a set of library modules that support basic operations such as file I/O, screen I/O, mathematical routines, and storage management (see Chapter 10). At the time of writing there is a serious effort underway among the various Modula-2 vendors to standardize this set of modules. Library modules generally contain reusable software components that will serve in many applications.

There are two types of library module: *definition* and *implementation*. Associated with every definition module is an implementation module. We introduce each of these in the subsections that follow.

11.3.1 Definition Modules

Definition modules contain the interface to a set of software components. The definition module provides a set of specifications for the set of software components being exported to other modules.

Although it is possible and sometimes necessary to include an import list in a definition module, the main purpose of such a module is to export resources to other modules. The export list may contain constants, types, variables, and procedures (however, see Appendix 3).

Figure 11.4 shows the syntax of a definition module.

Following the export list in a definition module are a group of declarations. Constants are declared in the normal manner. A type may be declared to be *opaque* by specifying only the type identifier, not the representation, as in:

TYPE Stack;

The data structure (implementation details) of this opaque type must be supplied in the implementation module. If the opaque type Stack is included in the export list in the definition module, objects of type Stack may be declared in other modules that import this opaque type. The implementation details of Stack are invisible and, more important, inaccessible outside the implementation module that defines the data structure for Stack. In the next chapter we discuss the significance of this and underscore the importance of opaque types in supporting data abstraction.

Types may also be declared as *transparent*. In this case either a predefined data type or a programmer-defined data structure is used to define the type. If such a transparent type is included in the export list of the definition module, other modules that import this type may declare objects to be of the given type and may access the internal structure of these objects. As a consequence, if a record type or record variable is named in the export list, all the field names are also exported; they do not need to be listed separately in the export list.

Procedures are declared by providing only a procedure stub or heading containing the name of the procedure, its formal parameter list, and the type returned in the case of a function procedure.

As in the case of opaque types, the implementation details for each subprogram (procedure bodies) must be given in the implementation module. As

definition module

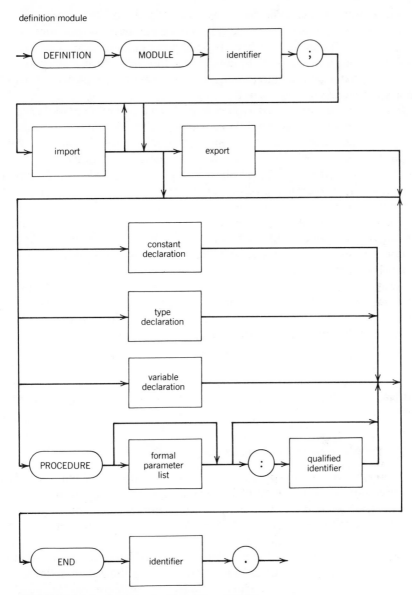

FIGURE 11.4 Syntax of a Definition Module

we will see in later chapters, Modula-2's ability to separate the specification of a software component from its implementation provides the underpinning for powerful software development techniques.

The definition module often is published, so that programmers who wish to use the exported software components can know what they are. However, the information required by the syntax of the language to be present in the definition module is not sufficient to explain fully the exported components. For example, the purposes of procedures and the modes of the parameters may not be apparent. Therefore, it is usually good programming style to include this kind of information in the form of comments. In a more formal programming environment, external documentation such as a users' manual would also be appropriate for each library module.

Software components that are exported from a definition module are cast into an unknown world of unpredictable names. The same name may be used in a definition module and in a client module. For example, a variable called position may be exported from a definition module to a module that already uses an identifier position. To avoid a name clash, the Modula-2 compiler requires that when referencing a component from a definition module, a qualified reference be made unless the dequalifier FROM is used in the import list of the client module. A qualified reference consists of the name of the module containing the component followed by a period character followed by the identifier representing the component. We illustrate this with a somewhat artificial example (Program 11.2).

Because of the qualified export, the identifiers increment and position may be used in the main program module even though they are used in the definition module ExportNames. It would not be possible, in Program 11.2, to use the dequalifier FROM and use an import list such as:

FROM ExportNames IMPORT increment, position;

If this were done, the identifiers increment and position in definition module ExportNames would clash with the corresponding identifiers in the MainProgramModule.

11.3.2 Implementation Modules

The implementation module provides the implementation details for the specifications given in the definition module. Opaque types declared in the definition module must be defined in the implementation module. The bodies (implementation details) of all procedures declared in the definition module must be given in the implementation module (Figure 11.5).

Except for the reserved word IMPLEMENTATION, an implementation module is exactly like a program module. It provides the actual definitions of opaque types and bodies of procedures promised in the definition module. As in program modules, each procedure includes a procedure heading, which must be identical to that given in the definition module.

If the interfaces given by the subprogram stubs in the definition module have been carefully designed, it should be possible to substitute one data structure for another in representing an opaque type, and one algorithm for another in implementing a subprogram, without requiring any coding changes or recompilation outside the implementation module. Good software engineering practice suggests the desirability of localizing changes in a complex software system to a few implementation modules.

Program 11.2 Qualified Export Example

```
DEFINITION MODULE ExportNames;

EXPORT  QUALIFIED
    (* var *) position,
    (* var *) increment;

    VAR
        position  : REAL;
        increment : REAL;

END ExportNames.
```

```
IMPLEMENTATION MODULE ExportNames;
(* No implementation details are required here *)
END ExportNames.
```

```
MODULE MainProgramModule;

IMPORT ExportNames; (* no dequalifier used *)

    PROCEDURE increment (r : REAL; x : REAL) : REAL;
    (* This procedure increments r by an amount x. *)

    BEGIN
        RETURN r + x;
    END increment;

    VAR
        r        : REAL;
        position : CARDINAL;

BEGIN
    ExportNames.increment := 5.0;
    ExportNames.position  := 2.0;
    r := increment (ExportNames.position, ExportNames.increment);
    position := 7;
                            (* other code ... *)

END MainProgramModule.
```

Software components that are imported into a definition module are not automatically imported into the associated implementation module. If duplicate resources are required in the implementation module, they must be imported separately.

An implementation module may contain constants, types, variables, and subprograms not declared in the definition module. These software components are invisible outside the implementation module and exist only to provide services to the subprograms whose interface is visible outside of the implementation module.

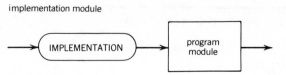

implementation module

FIGURE 11.5   Syntax of an Implementation Module

Program 11.3 presents a short illustration of an implementation module that determines the maximum and minimum positions of the elements in an array of real numbers.

Program 11.3   Determining the Maximum and Minimum Positions in an Array of Real Numbers

```
DEFINITION MODULE ArrayMaxAndMin;

EXPORT QUALIFIED
    (* type *) RealArray,
    (* proc *) MaxPos,
    (* proc *) MinPos;

  TYPE RealArray = ARRAY[1..1000] OF REAL;

  PROCEDURE MaxPos (a : RealArray) : CARDINAL;
  PROCEDURE MinPos (a : RealArray) : CARDINAL;

END ArrayMaxAndMin.
```

```
IMPLEMENTATION MODULE ArrayMaxAndMin;

  PROCEDURE MaxPos (a : RealArray) : CARDINAL;

  VAR
      index   : CARDINAL;
      max     : REAL;
      posmax  : CARDINAL;

  BEGIN
    max := a[1];
    posmax := 1;
    FOR index := 2 TO 1000 DO
      IF a[index] > max
      THEN
        max := a[index];
        posmax := index;
      END (* if then *);
    END (* for loop *);
    RETURN posmax;
  END MaxPos;
```

```
PROCEDURE MinPos (a : RealArray) : CARDINAL;

VAR
    index    : CARDINAL;
    min      : REAL;
    posmin : CARDINAL;
BEGIN
  min := a[1];
  posmin := 1;
  FOR index := 2 TO 1000 DO
    IF a[index] < min
    THEN
      min := a[index];
      posmin := index;
    END (* if then *);
  END (* for loop *);
  RETURN posmin;
  END MinPos;

END ArrayMaxAndMin.
```

The definition module ArrayMaxAndMin in Program 11.3 provides the interface to two procedures: one for finding the position of the maximum value in the array, and one for finding the position of the minimum value in the array. You are asked in Exercise 11.9 to rewrite module ArrayMaxAndMin using an open array parameter in each of the two subprograms. This will result in a much more general and powerful software resource.

11.3.3 Module Initialization

Implementation modules may contain initialization code. This code is executed only once before the code in the client module (a main program module or another library module). In the event that several library modules (implementation modules) contain initialization code, each block of initialization code is executed only once in the sequence given by the import list. As shown in Figure 11.4, an implementation module is structured exactly like a program module (except for the word IMPLEMENTATION). The initialization code of an implementation module corresponds to the body of a program module. This is illustrated in Program 11.4.

The output of Program 11.4 is shown below. Notice that the order of the messages is the same as the order of the modules in the import lists.

> In Library3.
> In Library1.
> In Library2.
> In main program module.

Initialization code may be very useful for establishing initial conditions for scalar or structured objects or to open files. The logo of a software company

Program 11.4   Initialization Code for Library Modules

```
DEFINITION MODULE Library1;
END Library1.
```

```
IMPLEMENTATION MODULE Library1;
FROM InOut IMPORT WriteLn, WriteString;
BEGIN
  WriteLn; WriteLn;
  WriteString("In Library1.");
END Library1.
```

```
DEFINITION MODULE Library2;
END Library2.
```

```
IMPLEMENTATION MODULE Library2;
FROM InOut IMPORT WriteLn, WriteString;
BEGIN
  WriteLn; WriteLn;
  WriteString("In Library2. ");
END Library2.
```

```
DEFINITION MODULE Library3;
END Library3.
```

```
IMPLEMENTATION MODULE Library3;
FROM InOut IMPORT WriteLn, WriteString;
BEGIN
  WriteLn; WriteLn;
  WriteString("In Library3.");
END Library3.
```

```
MODULE Main;
FROM InOut IMPORT WriteLn, WriteString;
IMPORT Library3;
IMPORT Library1;
IMPORT Library2;
BEGIN
  WriteLn; WriteLn;
  WriteString("In main program module.");
END Main.
```

or messages to the user may conveniently be embedded as initialization code in the custom utility library developed by a software company. If the library module containing this code is the first to be imported into the main program module, this logo will be displayed on the terminal before anything else.

11.3.4   The Order of Compilation

We have used the term "separate compilation" in describing the physical structure of Modula-2. It would be incorrect to characterize Modula-2's compilation structure as "independent compilation" because modules cannot be compiled independently.

The simple rule that defines a correct compilation sequence is:

Definition modules that export items to client modules must be compiled before their respective client modules.

Implementation modules may be compiled at any time after the following conditions have been met:

1. Their respective definition modules have been compiled.
2. The definition modules containing items imported by the implementation have been compiled.

For the compiler to verify that the interface to an external subprogram is correct, it must have access to the compiled version of the definition module containing the external subprogram. It follows that this definition module must be compiled before the client module containing the external subprogram reference.

There is typically more than one correct compilation sequence. In Program 11.5, we illustrate this point.

Program 11.5 may be compiled but not run until the implementation modules have been created and compiled. There are only two correct compilation sequences:

Library1, Library2, Library3, Main

Library1, Library3, Library2, Main

Note the use of the qualifiers Library1 and Library2 in calling PROC1 in the main program module to avoid a name clash in this identifier.

What happens if definition module Library1 is recompiled? What recompilation is required? Because modules Library2, Library3, and Main import Library1, all must be recompiled as a consequence of recompiling module Library1. If module Library2 or module Library3 is recompiled, only module Main needs to be recompiled.

Because the consequences associated with recompilation are the most severe when definition modules are recompiled, the software developer should exercise great care in constructing these modules. It is most desirable to limit software maintenance to changes in one or more of the implementation modules. When an implementation module is recompiled, there are no additional

Program 11.5 Compilation Sequence

```
DEFINITION MODULE Library1;

EXPORT QUALIFIED
  (* type *) type1,
  (* proc *) PROC1;

  TYPE type1;

  PROCEDURE PROC1;

END Library1.
```

```
DEFINITION MODULE Library2;

FROM Library1 IMPORT type1;

EXPORT QUALIFIED
  (* proc *) PROC1;

  PROCEDURE PROC1(VAR P : type1);

END Library2.
```

```
DEFINITION MODULE Library3;

FROM Library1 IMPORT type1;

EXPORT QUALIFIED
  (* proc *) PROC3;

  PROCEDURE PROC3(P : type1);

END Library3.
```

```
MODULE Main;

IMPORT Library1;

IMPORT Library2;

IMPORT Library3;

VAR j : Library1.type1;

BEGIN
  Library1.PROC1;
  Library2.PROC1(j);
  Library3.PROC3(j);
END Main.
```

modules to be recompiled. On some implementations, relinking may be necessary.

11.3.5   The Lifetime of Library Module Variables

A variable (other than a local variable within a procedure) declared in an implementation module has a lifetime equal to the life of the main program module that imports the library module. Because such a variable is invisible to modules outside the implementation module, we have the desirable situation of a variable that remains alive for the duration of the program but cannot be corrupted (have its value changed outside the module).

In Pascal, to keep a variable alive for the duration of a program, the variable must be declared global to the program. Such a global variable is accessible to the entire program and may be corrupted.

Modula-2 variables that remain alive for a program's duration are often called *static* variables. We show a practical application of a static variable in Program 11.6.

The static variable seed remains alive for the entire program and is invisible outside implementation module RandomNumberGenerator; hence it cannot be corrupted. The initial value of this variable is derived from the system clock time returned by the Time procedure. The static variable seed is essential because each new random number is dependent on the previous value of seed. These values must be remembered between calls of procedure Random.

Notice the existence of an empty formal parameter list for procedure

---

Program 11.6   A Random Number Generator and Static Variable

DEFINITION MODULE RandomNumberGenerator;

EXPORT QUALIFIED
  (* proc *) Random;

  PROCEDURE Random( ): REAL;
  (* Returns a uniformly distributed real number from 0.0 to 1.0 *)

END RandomNumberGenerator.

DEFINITION MODULE Utilities;

EXPORT QUALIFIED
  (* proc *) Time,
  (* proc *) Remainder;

  PROCEDURE Remainder(a, b : REAL) : REAL;
  (* Returns the remainder after dividing a by b *)

  PROCEDURE Time(VAR a, b : INTEGER);
  (* Returns two integers based on the internal clock time *)

END Utilities.

```
IMPLEMENTATION MODULE RandomNumberGenerator;

FROM Utilities IMPORT Remainder, Time;

   CONST modulus  =  65536.0;
         a1       =  25173.0;
         a2       =  13849.0;

   VAR seed : REAL;
       c    : INTEGER;
       d    : INTEGER;

   PROCEDURE Random( ): REAL;

   BEGIN
     seed := Remainder ( a1 * seed + a2, modulus );
     RETURN seed / modulus
   END Random;
BEGIN
   Time ( c, d );
   seed := FLOAT(d)
END RandomNumberGenerator.
```

Random. As noted in Chapter 7, this is necessary only for function procedures.

11.4 Internal Modules

An *internal* module is nested within another module or procedure and is contained within either an implementation module or a program module. Internal
modules may be used to create isolated environments for controlling the scope
and visibility of identifiers. The syntax of an internal module is shown in Figure
11.6.

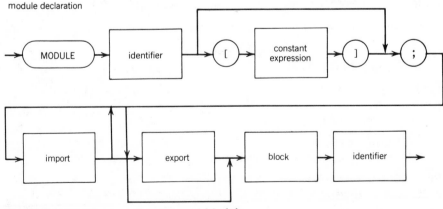

FIGURE 11.6 Syntax of an Internal Module

An internal module might be used to export a procedure that uses a variable that the programmer wishes to hide. Program 11.7 illustrates this situation.

Program 11.7   Internal Module Used to Hide Variables

```
MODULE HideVariables;

FROM InOut IMPORT WriteLn, WriteString, WriteInt;

  MODULE Internal;

    IMPORT WriteLn, WriteString, WriteInt;

    EXPORT
      (* proc *) setvalues,
      (* proc *) display;

  VAR
    a, b : INTEGER;
  (* These are the two variables that will be hidden *)

    PROCEDURE setvalues;
    BEGIN
      a := 15;
      b := 17;
    END setvalues;

    PROCEDURE display;
    BEGIN
      WriteLn;
      WriteString("The values in question are: ");
      WriteInt(a,1); WriteString(" ");
      WriteInt(b,1);
    END display;

  END Internal;

VAR
  a, b : REAL;

BEGIN (* HideVariables *)
  a := 3.5;
  b := 6.7;
  setvalues;
  display;
END HideVariables.
```

In Program 11.7, the internal module Internal creates a membrane around variables a and b and subprograms setvalues and display. Information can be passed through this membrane only by using an import list or export list. The output procedures WriteLn, WriteString, and WriteInt, which are imported in the main program module (from library module InOut), are not automatically visible within the internal module. They must be explicitly imported to get the information through the membrane. However, these procedures are now being imported from the outer module, not directly from InOut.

The information that is exported from the internal module, namely, subprograms setvalues and display, is passed out of the membrane using the export list.

Variables a and b inside module Internal are static variables. They remain alive as long as the module enclosing the internal module (the main program module) is alive. As we saw in the preceding section, static variables stay alive without necessarily being visible everywhere. In fact, variables a and b are not visible outside the internal module.

We note that the export statement used in module Internal is an unqualified export. This makes the identifiers on the export list immediately visible to the surrounding scope. If we were to substitute qualified export, the last two lines of the main program module would have to be changed to read:

Internal.setvalues;
Internal.display;

We would be motivated to do this if several internal modules used the same names for their identifiers.   ✦

We present another illustration of information passing through import and export lists, both qualified and unqualified, in Program 11.8. We also illustrate initialization code for internal modules.

In Program 11.8, the identifiers a and b are boolean at the global level, cardinal within module Internal1, and real and integer within module Internal2. There is no name conflict because of the isolation enjoyed by each inter-

---

Program 11.8   Information Passing for Internal Modules

```
MODULE InformationPassing;

IMPORT  InOut;

IMPORT  RealInOut;

  VAR
    a , b : BOOLEAN;

  PROCEDURE proc1;

    VAR
      a, b : CHAR;

  BEGIN
    InOut.WriteLn;
    InOut.WriteString("In proc1.");
    a := 'C';
    b := 'D';
  END proc1;
```

```
MODULE Internal1;

FROM InOut IMPORT WriteLn, WriteCard, WriteString;

EXPORT QUALIFIED
  (* var *) a,
  (* var *) b;

  VAR
    a : CARDINAL;
    b : CARDINAL;

BEGIN (* Initialization code *)
  WriteLn;
  WriteString("In internal module 1");
  a := 1;
  WriteLn;
  WriteCard(a,1);
  b := 1;
  WriteLn;
  WriteCard(b,1);
END Internal1;

MODULE Internal2;

IMPORT InOut;

IMPORT RealInOut;

EXPORT QUALIFIED
  (* var *) a,
  (* var *) b;

  VAR
    a : REAL;
    b : INTEGER;

BEGIN (* Initialization code *)
  InOut.WriteLn;
  InOut.WriteString("In internal module 2.");
  a := 2.0;
  InOut.WriteLn;
  RealInOut.WriteReal(a,1);
  b := 4;
  InOut.WriteLn;
  InOut.WriteInt(b,1);
END Internal2;

MODULE Internal3;

FROM Internal2 IMPORT a, b;

FROM InOut IMPORT WriteLn, WriteInt, WriteString;

FROM RealInOut IMPORT WriteReal;
```

```
BEGIN (* Initialization code *)
  WriteLn;
  WriteString("In internal module3.");
  a := a + 1.0;
  b := INTEGER( TRUNC(a) * TRUNC(a) );
  WriteLn;
  WriteReal(a,1);
  WriteLn;
  WriteInt(b,1);
END Internal3;

BEGIN (* Information Passing *)
  a := TRUE;
  b := FALSE;
  proc1;
  InOut.WriteLn;
  InOut.WriteCard(Internal1.a,1);;
  InOut.WriteLn;
  RealInOut.WriteReal(Internal2.a,1);
  InOut.WriteLn;
END InformationPassing.
```

nal module. Because modules Internal1 and Internal2 use a qualified export, the items on their respective export lists are protected from name clashes. Qualified access is required to use these items.

The initialization code is executed exactly once for each internal module in the order of appearance of the internal modules within the main program module. All the initialization code sequences will be executed before starting the main program module.

What will be the last number displayed? The answer is 3.0. This follows because the initialization code of module Internal3 increments the value of variable a in module Internal2.

The procedure proc1 and modules Internal1 and Internal2 create a local scope of definition for the identifiers a and b. What then is the difference between creating this local scope with a procedure and creating it with an internal module? Local variables a and b in procedure proc1 become activated (dynamically allocated) only when proc1 is called. These variables become deactivated (dynamically deallocated) when the procedure exists. This is in sharp contrast to variables a and b defined in modules Internal1 and Internal2. In these internal modules, variables a and b are static. They are alive as long as the internal modules are activated. They do not get created and then vanish, like variables a and b in procedure proc1.

Internal modules become activated when the logical unit enclosing them becomes activated. The enclosing logical unit may be a program module, an implementation module, another internal module, or a procedure. If an internal module is nested within a procedure, the internal module becomes activated when the enclosing procedure is called and deactivated when the enclosing procedure is terminated. These concepts are illustrated in Program 11.9.

Program 11.9   Internal Module Activation; Scope and Visibility of Procedures and Modules

```
MODULE ModuleActivation;

FROM InOut IMPORT WriteLn, WriteString, WriteCard;

FROM RealInOut IMPORT WriteReal;

IMPORT InOut;

IMPORT RealInOut;

  PROCEDURE EnclosingUnit;

  VAR
    a , b : CARDINAL;

    PROCEDURE NestedProcedure;

    VAR
      a, b : REAL;

    BEGIN
      a := 1.0;
      b := 2.0;
      WriteLn;
      WriteString("a = ");
      WriteReal(a,1);
      WriteLn;
      WriteLn;
      WriteString("b = ");
      WriteReal(b,1);
      WriteLn;
    END NestedProcedure;

    MODULE NestedModule;

    FROM InOut IMPORT WriteLn, WriteString, WriteCard;

    FROM RealInOut IMPORT WriteReal;

    EXPORT
      (* proc *) NestedInModule;

      PROCEDURE NestedInModule;

      VAR
        a, b : REAL;
```

```
    BEGIN
      a := 2.0;
      b := 3.0;
      WriteLn;
      WriteString("a = ");
      WriteReal(a,1);
      WriteLn;
      WriteLn;
      WriteString("b = ");
      WriteReal(b,1);
      WriteLn;
    END NestedInModule;


  BEGIN
    NestedInModule;
  END NestedModule;


  BEGIN (* EnclosingUnit *)
    a := 5;
    b := 6;
    NestedSubprogram;
    NestedInModule;
    WriteLn;
    WriteString("a = ");
    WriteCard(a,1);
    WriteLn;
    WriteLn;
    WriteString("b = ");
    WriteCard(b,1);
    WriteLn;
  END EnclosingUnit;


  VAR
    a, b : CARDINAL;


BEGIN (* ModuleActivation *)
  a := 7;
  b := 8;
  WriteLn;
  WriteString("a = ");
  WriteCard(a,1);
  WriteLn;
  WriteLn;
  WriteString("b = ");
  WriteCard(b,1);
  WriteLn;
  EnclosingUnit;
END ModuleActivation.
```

In Program 11.9, the identifiers a and b are used in four separate contexts (the main program module, the procedure EnclosingUnit, the procedure NestedProcedure, and the procedure NestedInModule). Let us walk through this program, focusing on module activation, and discuss scope and visibility issues.

When we begin execution of program module ModuleActivation, the only variables that are active are the two cardinal variables a and b associated with the main program. The first two lines of output are:

$$a = 7$$
$$b = 8$$

At the moment procedure EnclosingUnit is called, at the last line of the main program, local cardinal variables a and b, declared directly inside procedure EnclosingUnit, become activated (memory is dynamically allocated). The internal module nested within procedure EnclosingUnit, namely, module NestedModule, also becomes activated. Its initialization code is executed before the body of procedure EnclosingUnit is executed. Because the initialization code of NestedModule calls procedure NestedInModule, the two local real variables a and b declared in procedure NestedInModule become activated and the program outputs:

$$a = 2.0$$
$$b = 3.0$$

At this moment three sets of variables, each called a and b, coexist in memory. The first set is associated with the main program, the second set associated with procedure EnclosingUnit, and the third set associated with NestedInModule. As soon as the initialization code of internal module NestedModule is concluded, the two local real variables a and b of procedure NestedInModule are deactivated (dynamically deallocated).

The code sequence contained within the body of procedure EnclosingUnit is executed. The first statement in this body of code is a call to the procedure NestedProcedure. Its local real variables a and b become activated and the program outputs:

$$a = 1.0$$
$$b = 2.0$$

Upon the conclusion of this procedure, local variables a and b are deactivated. The next statement in the body of code for EnclosingUnit calls procedure NestedInModule, which is visible inside EnclosingUnit. Once again the real local variables a and b become activated and the program outputs:

$$a = 2.0$$
$$b = 3.0$$

After procedure NestedInModule concludes and real variables a and b become deactivated, cardinal variables a and b are assigned the values 5 and 6, and the program outputs:

$$a = 5$$
$$b = 6$$

When the procedure EnclosingUnit concludes, the local cardinal variables a and b associated with the procedure EnclosingUnit are deactivated, leaving only main program cardinal variables a and b active. Then the main program ends.

The procedure NestedInModule, exported from internal module Nested-Module, is invisible to the main program but visible only within EnclosingUnit after this procedure has been called.

Program 11.9 contains a student's dream: the coexistence of many As and Bs!

11.5 Summary

Modula-2 supports four types of module. Program modules are executable program units that may import software components (constants, types, variables, and procedures) from library modules.

Library modules have two parts, which must be separately compiled: definition and implementation. Library modules are generally created with the intention of exporting reusable software components to other modules in the software system or to other software systems. A definition module may import software components and export software components using a qualified export. A qualified export is required in a definition module to avoid clashes in identifier names with identifiers in client modules. An implementation module may import only software components. Software components that are imported into a definition module are not automatically imported into the associated implementation module. If duplicate resources are required in the implementation module, they must be imported into the implementation module.

Internal modules may be defined within the body of either a program module or an implementation module. They are usually used to control the scope and visibility of objects in the compilation unit in which they are defined.

Modules use import lists to control what outside software resources are available within the module and an export list (for definition modules and internal modules) to control what internal resources can be accessed outside the module.

11.6 Exercises

1. Rewrite Program 11.6 in Pascal. Discuss the differences between the static variable seed used in Program 11.6 and the variable seed used in your Pascal program.

2. Name and describe some programming languages that support independent compilation.

3. Discuss the difference between export and qualified export.

4. Explain whether the following statements are true or false.
   (a) When a data structure is changed in an implementation module, this generally requires recompilation of other modules in the system.
   (b) When an interface is changed to a subprogram in a definition module, this generally requires recompilation of other modules in the system.
   (c) An internal module always becomes activated when the program module surrounding it is activated.
   (d) Modules in Modula-2 may be compiled in any order.

5. What is the output of the following program?

```
MODULE WhatIsOutput;
    IMPORT InOut;
    MODULE m1;
        IMPORT InOut;
        EXPORT
            (* var *) a,
            (* var *) b,
            (* var *) c;
    MODULE M2;
        IMPORT InOut;
        EXPORT
            (* var *) d,
            (* var *) e,
            (* var *) f;
        VAR
            d, e, f : CHAR;
        BEGIN
            d := 'f';
            e := 'u';
            f := 'n';
            InOut.WriteLn; InOut.WriteLn;
            InOut.Write(d);
            InOut.Write(e);
            InOut.Write(f);
        END M2;
    VAR
        a, b, c : INTEGER;
    BEGIN
        a := 1;
        b := 2;
        c := 3;
        InOut.WriteLn; InOut.WriteLn;
```

```
        InOut.WriteInt(a,1);
        InOut.WriteInt(b,1);
        InOut.WriteInt(c,1);
     END M1;
     BEGIN
        InOut.WriteLn;
        InOut.WriteString("What is the output of this program? ");
     END WhatIsOutput.
```

6. What is the output of the following program?

```
        MODULE WhatIsOutput;
           IMPORT InOut;
           PROCEDURE Outer;
              MODULE M1;
                 IMPORT InOut;
                 EXPORT
                    (* var *) a,
                    (* var *) b,
                    (* var *) c;
                 MODULE M2;
                    IMPORT InOut;
                    EXPORT
                       (* var *) d,
                       (* var *) e,
                       (* var *) f;
                    VAR
                       d, e, f : CHAR;
                 BEGIN
                    d := 'f';
                    e := 'u';
                    f := 'n';
                    InOut.WriteLn; InOut.WriteLn;
                    InOut.Write(d);
                    InOut.Write(e);
                    InOut.Write(f);
                 END M2;
              VAR
                 a, b, c : INTEGER;
              BEGIN
                 a := 1;
                 b := 2;
                 c := 3;
                 InOut.WriteLn; InOut.WriteLn;
                 InOut.WriteInt(a,1);
```

```
            InOut.WriteInt(b,1);
            InOut.WriteInt(c,1);
        END M1;
    END outer;
BEGIN
    InOut.WriteLn;
    InOut.WriteString("Wonder what the output of this ");
    InOut.WriteString("program is? ");
END WhatIsOutput.
```

7. Describe the difference between separate compilation and independent compilation.

8. Describe the difference between program modules, library modules, and internal modules. Indicate how each might be used in software development.

9. Rewrite module ArrayMaxAndMin in Program 11.3, using an open array parameter in each of the two subprograms.

12

Data Abstraction

The process of abstraction may be described as identifying essential concepts while ignoring inessential details. It is one of our most powerful intellectual tools for dealing with complexity. As software developers, we use abstraction to help us design a complex system by first identifying major functional and data components of the system. This often requires the construction of a conceptual model of a system or subsystem and the subsequent representation of that model in a programming language.

We have already mentioned some abstractions that have found their way into programming languages: variables are abstractions of memory cells, decision and loop statements are control abstractions, and procedures are functional abstractions. In this chapter we look at *data abstraction,* which is one of the newest and most powerful abstractions. In Chapter 17 we will see how data abstraction supports the object-oriented software design methodology.

12.1 Data Types and Data Abstraction

In Chapter 4 we defined a data type to be a pair $<V, O>$, where

V is a set of values

O is a set of operations defined on those values

The Modula-2 language provides a variety of predefined data types. The sets of values of these types, particularly the numeric types, vary somewhat from one computer to the next, but the operation sets are the same. For example, the cardinal numbers always have addition, subtraction, multiplication, division, modulus, and negation operations. One of the important features of a strongly typed language like Modula-2 is that the compiler enforces the requirement that only the operations defined for a particular data type may be performed on values of that type.

The predefined data types may be considered to be low level data abstractions, in that they provide the essential concepts without forcing programmers to be concerned with inessential details, namely, the internal representations of those values and the hardware components that perform the operations. We will use these types, plus the structured type constructors, to build higher level data abstractions. Each of these also is a set of values and a set of operations, but they allow us to design software in terms closer to those of the problem domain and farther away from the computer.

An essential feature of data abstraction is the ability to define the essential concepts separately from the implementation details. We often use the term *data hiding* (or *information hiding*) to describe this ability. That is, the user of an abstraction is given information describing the set of values and the set of operations, but the implementation is hidden. This provides several important advantages for software developers.

First, we can use the data abstraction more easily, because we do not have to remember so many details. We are already used to this idea with the predefined data types. Imagine how difficult it would be to program if we did not have the real data type. For problems requiring real numbers, we would have to simulate reals, including all the operations, with some other data type. How many of us know the algorithm for division of real numbers? Even those who know would find it tedious to implement the algorithm every time they needed real division. The abstraction of real numbers greatly simplifies the solution of many problems.

Second, data hiding gives us the ability to guarantee the integrity of the values of an abstract data type. The user has no knowledge of the internal representation. Even though this representation may be something simple such as a record or an array, accessing the individual fields of a record or the elements of an array can be prohibited outside the abstraction. Only the operations defined for the abstract data type may be performed by users of that type, and we will assume that we have implemented these operations correctly.

Third, separation of the definition of a data type from its implementation gives us the option of changing the implementation. This is a great benefit in software prototyping, as discussed in Chapter 17. Also, if a new and better implementation is discovered, it is a simple matter to substitute it for the old implementation.

Fourth, data abstraction provides a way to put related software components together. This usually leads to cleaner software design, easier testing, and simplified maintenance.

Although the concept of data abstraction may be used to design software that will be implemented in any language, Modula-2 allows us to implement abstract data types so that the compiler can enforce data hiding. It may already be apparent that the definition and implementation modules introduced in Chapter 11 provide the vehicle for data abstraction. Particularly important is the concept of an opaque type, which provides complete and enforceable data hiding.

To illustrate abstract data types and the importance of the data hiding, we first consider a simple example as it might be implemented in both Pascal and Modula-2.

12.2 Example of Data Abstraction in Pascal and Modula-2

We want to demonstrate two important differences between Pascal and Modula-2 in the representation of an abstract data type. The first is structural. Without separate compilation, abstract data types in Pascal must be implemented with global declarations of constants, types, variables, and procedures. Since Modula-2 allows separate compilation, abstract data types may be structured as separate definition and implementation modules.

The second difference is the degree of data hiding allowed. As we will see, global declarations in Pascal programs make objects accessible everywhere in the program. Internal representations of data objects cannot be hidden, and manipulation of these objects cannot be limited to the defined operations of the data type. Only extreme discipline on the part of the programmer can allow the full benefits of the abstract data type to be realized, and such discipline is virtually impossible on all but the very smallest programs. In Modula-2, the export list and the use of opaque types can achieve complete data hiding, and the compiler will enforce the discipline needed on the part of the programmer.

To illustrate these points, consider a counter abstract data type. The values of this type are the nonnegative integers, but the only operations allowed are initialization (making the counter zero), increment, and decrement. A counter is therefore very different from the cardinal type because the two types have very different sets of operations. We would like to enforce the rule that only these three operations may be performed on a counter variable.

A Pascal implementation of a program using the counter abstract data type is shown in Program 12.1. The statements shown in the main program are typical of what might be done with a counter variable.

The intent in this example is to allow only the three operations to be performed on counters. Nevertheless, the main program could have contained statements such as:

count := count + 4;

count := 12 * count + 7;

Program 12.1   Counter Abstract Data Type in Pascal

```pascal
program CounterAbstraction ( input, output );

{ Pascal implementation of the counter abstract data type }

type counter = 0..maxint;

var
    index : integer;
    count : counter;

  procedure initialize    ( var c : (* out     *) counter );

  begin
    c := 0;
  end {initialize};

  procedure increment ( var c : (* in out *) counter );
  begin
    c := c + 1;
  end {increment};

  procedure decrement ( var c : (* in out *) counter );

  begin
    if c > 0 then c := c - 1
  end {decrement};

  procedure display     ( c      : (* in      *) counter );

  begin
    writeln (c);
  end {display};

begin {main program}
  initialize (count);
  for index := 1 to 10 do
    increment (count);
  for index := 10 downto 5 do
    decrement (count);
  writeln ('the value of the counter = ');
  display (count);
end.
```

Because these statements represent legitimate operations on integers, the Pascal compiler has no way to know that they should not be allowed on counters, since a counter is defined to be a subrange of the integers. We have to assume that these statements are in error, based on our knowledge of the counter abstract data type, but the compiler does not indicate an error.

In Modula-2 we can implement the counter abstract data type with a definition module, shown in Program 12.2, and an implementation module, shown in Program 12.3. We will declare the COUNTER type to be opaque, so that its actual representation cannot be known to any client module. Further-

Program 12.2   Counter Abstract Data Type Definition Module

DEFINITION MODULE Counter;

EXPORT QUALIFIED
  (* type *) COUNTER,
  (* proc *) Initialize,
  (* proc *) Display,
  (* proc *) Increment,
  (* proc *) Decrement;

  TYPE COUNTER;
  (* Opaque type *)

  PROCEDURE Initialize (VAR c : (* out *) COUNTER);
  (* Defines a counter and sets its initial value to zero. *)

  PROCEDURE Display (c : (* in *) COUNTER);
  (* Displays the value of a counter. *)

  PROCEDURE Increment (VAR c : (* in out *) COUNTER);
  (* Adds one to the current value of a counter. *)

  PROCEDURE Decrement (VAR c : (* in out *) COUNTER);
  (* Subtracts one from the current value of a counter if its value is
    positive, otherwise does nothing. *)

END Counter.

more, the compiler will allow only the three defined operations to be performed on counter variables. The counter type is not compatible with any numeric type in Modula-2 (the counter is actually a pointer), so any attempt to perform arithmetic on counters will be rejected by the compiler.

We have often mentioned the benefits of strong typing, which allows the compiler to find many common programming errors. In Modula-2, we can extend this idea to abstract data types to a very great degree, whereas in Pascal we are much more limited. Of course, in the Pascal example of Program 12.1, we could have defined the counter type as follows:

$$\text{type counterrange} = 0..\text{maxint};$$
$$\text{counter} \qquad = \text{\^{}counterrange};$$

This is the same idea as the opaque type in the Modula-2 version. This definition would allow the compiler to catch erroneous statements such as:

$$\text{count} := \text{count} + 4;$$

but it would not prevent a devious programmer from doing:

$$\text{count\^{}} := \text{count\^{}} + 4;$$

A similar statement could also be placed in a Modula-2 program that uses the counter abstract data type, but the compiler would reject it. Even though the

Program 12.3   Counter Abstract Data Type Implementation Module

```
IMPLEMENTATION MODULE Counter;

FROM InOut IMPORT WriteCard;

FROM Storage IMPORT ALLOCATE;

  TYPE COUNTER = POINTER TO CARDINAL;

  PROCEDURE Initialize ( VAR c : (* out *) COUNTER );

  BEGIN
    NEW ( c );
    c^ := 0;
  END Initialize;

  PROCEDURE Display ( c : (* in *) COUNTER );

  BEGIN
    WriteCard ( c^, 1 );
  END Display;

  PROCEDURE Increment ( VAR c : (* in out *) COUNTER );

  BEGIN
    INC ( c^ );
  END Increment;

  PROCEDURE Decrement ( VAR c : (* in out *) COUNTER );

  BEGIN
    IF c^ > 0
      THEN DEC ( c^ )
    END (* if then *);
  END Decrement;

END Counter.
```

count variable is a pointer to a cardinal, this fact is hidden and makes the statement shown above erroneous.

The real issue, then, is data hiding. How much can we prevent the user of an abstract data type from knowing? The less we know about the internal structure of a data type, the less likely we are to try to manipulate that internal structure. We consider this issue next.

12.3   Transparent and Opaque Abstract Data Types

In earlier programming languages like Pascal, it was typical for some of the early design decisions to be related to major data structures in the program. After agreeing on these structures, several programmers could work on parts of the program somewhat independently, with each part of the program manipulating those major data structures. Unfortunately, if software specification changes or discovery of a new and improved data structure necessitated replacing one of the major structures, every part of the program was likely to need changes. Thus this approach to program design usually leads to very costly maintenance.

If instead we can agree on the major data types instead of the major data structures, each programmer need know only the interface to those data types. The interface consists of the type name, which must be public to permit programmers to declare variables of that type, names of values of that type (if any) that may be used, and the names and operands of all the operations defined on that type. Not surprisingly, these are exactly the entities normally found in a Modula-2 definition module. The programmers can then proceed to produce their parts of the software without having seen any of the hidden implementation details of the data types. If a change in implementation (data structure) is needed, only the implementation of the data type is affected. This localization of the effects of specification or design changes can greatly simplify software maintenance.

Modula-2 provides both transparent and opaque types. Both may be used to define an abstract data type. We would like to present an example of the effects of choosing one over the other in the design of a new data type. That type is the complex number type, including a small set of typical operations.

Program 12.4, which shows the definition module for this data type, uses a transparent data type; that is, the actual data structure of the values of

---

Program 12.4 Transparent Complex Numbers Definition Module

```
DEFINITION MODULE TransparentComplexNumbers;

EXPORT QUALIFIED
    (* type *) ComplexNumber,
    (* proc *) Add,
    (* proc *) Divide,
    (* proc *) Multiply;

TYPE ComplexNumber = RECORD
                        RealPart : REAL;
                        ImagPart : REAL;
                     END (* record *);
(* Transparent data type - visible and accessible *)

PROCEDURE Add      (a, b  : ComplexNumber;
                    VAR c : ComplexNumber);

PROCEDURE Multiply (a, b  : ComplexNumber;
                    VAR c : ComplexNumber);

PROCEDURE Divide   (a, b  : ComplexNumber;
                \       VAR c : ComplexNumber);

END TransparentComplexNumbers.
```

this type is presented in the definition module. In this case, that data structure is a record; a complex number consists of a real part and an imaginary part. The rules of export in Modula-2 say that if we export a record type, we automatically export the names of the fields within that record. Therefore the identifiers RealPart and ImagPart are accessible by any client module

The implementation module is shown in Program 12.5. Notice that the type declaration is not repeated here, since it was complete in the definition module. The implementation uses the common rectangular coordinates form of complex numbers.

Now consider a program that uses the complex number data type, such as that shown in Program 12.6. This program accesses the internal structure of a complex number in two places. The main program uses assignment statements to give values to complex numbers, knowing that the two parts are each real numbers. The procedure Display again accesses the two parts in order to print

---

Program 12.5 Transparent Complex Numbers Implementation Module

```
IMPLEMENTATION MODULE TransparentComplexNumbers;

  PROCEDURE Add (a, b   : ComplexNumber;
                  VAR c :  ComplexNumber);

  BEGIN
    c.RealPart := a.RealPart  +  b.RealPart;
    c.ImagPart := a.ImagPart  +  b.ImagPart;
  END Add;

  PROCEDURE Multiply (a, b   : ComplexNumber;
                       VAR c : ComplexNumber);

  BEGIN
    c.RealPart := a.RealPart  *  b.RealPart -
                    a.ImagPart  *  b.ImagPart;
    c.ImagPart := a.RealPart  *  b.ImagPart  +
                    a.ImagPart  *  b.RealPart;

  END Multiply;

  PROCEDURE Divide (a, b   : ComplexNumber;
                     VAR c : ComplexNumber);

  BEGIN
    c.RealPart := (a.RealPart*b.RealPart  +
                    a.ImagPart*b.ImagPart)/
                    (b.RealPart*b.RealPart  +
                    b.ImagPart*b.ImagPart);
    c.ImagPart := (a.ImagPart*b.RealPart -
                    a.RealPart*b.ImagPart)/
                    (b.RealPart*b.RealPart  +
                    b.ImagPart*b.ImagPart);
  END Divide;

END TransparentComplexNumbers.
```

Program 12.6 Complex Number Application Program

```
MODULE MainDriverProgram;

FROM TransparentComplexNumbers
   IMPORT ComplexNumber, Add, Multiply, Divide;

FROM InOut IMPORT WriteLn, WriteString;

FROM RealInOut IMPORT WriteReal;

   VAR
      complex1, complex2, complex3 : ComplexNumber;

   PROCEDURE Display (complex : ComplexNumber);
   BEGIN
      WriteLn;
      WriteString ("Real part --> ");
      WriteReal (complex.RealPart, 30);
      WriteLn;
      WriteString ("Imag part --> ");
      WriteReal (complex.ImagPart, 30);
      WriteLn;
   END Display;

BEGIN (* MainDriverProgram *)
   (* We initialize complex numbers complex1 and complex2 and violate the
      principle of data abstraction. *)
   complex1.RealPart := 3.0;
   complex1.ImagPart := 4.0;
   complex2.RealPart := - 3.0;
   complex2.ImagPart := 4.0;
   Add (complex1, complex2, complex3);
   Display (complex3);
   Multiply (complex1, complex2, complex3);
   Display (complex3);
   Divide (complex1, complex2, complex3);
   Display (complex3);
END MainDriverProgram.
```

them. The compiler will not object to either of these accesses, although they are not made through the operations defined on the data type.

A programmer who writes a main program like Program 12.6 is tempted to access the internal structure of the data type for two reasons. First, it is transparent. Giving a programmer knowledge of the internal structure is an invitation to use that knowledge. Second, the abstract data type itself is incomplete. When we define a new data type, we must be sure that we have found all the operations on that type that will be needed. This data type needs at least two more operations (probably many more). It needs a way to give a constant value to a complex number variable. Since there are no literal constants of the complex type, we probably want to provide an operation that is given two real values and puts them into a complex number variable; those reals could be either literal constants or named objects (constants or variables). The complex number data type also needs a way to print a value. The absence of such an operation caused the writer of the main program to invent one, which then required accessing the internal structure of a complex number.

Now consider the problems encountered if the data structure were to be changed. Not only would the implementation module need to be rewritten, but all other parts of the program would have to be examined to find all references to the internal structure of the data type, which would then also need to be changed.

To avoid these difficult maintenance problems, we can implement the complex number data type as an opaque type. By hiding the internal structure of the type, the user of the type is no longer tempted to access that structure. Of course, we must be sure to supply a complete set of operations on the data type. If we omit an operation because of an oversight, the user of our data type will not be able to implement that operation. Instead, it is likely that we will be told of our error, which can be corrected by adding the desired operation.

To demonstrate how an opaque type can be used, and to demonstrate that it is not unusual to change the internal structure of the values of a data type without changing the definition, we present Programs 12.7, 12.8, and 12.9. Program 12.7 shows the definition module for a more complete complex number data type. In this version, we have decided to allow client modules to access the real and imaginary parts of the number, but not directly through the field names of the record data structure. Instead, we provide function procedures RealPart and ImagPart to retrieve those values. With these two functions, a procedure to write a complex number, such as the Display procedure in Program 12.6, can easily be written, but without needing knowledge of the structure of a complex number.

Program 12.7 Opaque Complex Number Definition Module

```
DEFINITION MODULE HiddenComplexNumbers;

EXPORT QUALIFIED
    (* type *) ComplexNumber,
    (* proc *) Initialize,
    (* proc *) PolarInitialize,
    (* proc *) Create,
    (* proc *) RealPart,
    (* proc *) ImagPart,
    (* proc *) Modulus,
    (* proc *) Angle,
    (* proc *) Add,
    (* proc *) Multiply,
    (* proc *) Divide;
    TYPE ComplexNumber;
```

```
PROCEDURE Create () : ComplexNumber;
(* Creates a complex number with zero real part and zero imaginary part. *)

PROCEDURE Initialize (realpart, imaginarypart : REAL) :
                      ComplexNumber;
(* Takes a real part and imaginary part, and returns a complex
   number. *)

PROCEDURE PolarInitialize (modulus, angle : REAL ) :
                      ComplexNumber;
(* Takes a modulus and angle and returns a complex number. *)

PROCEDURE RealPart ( n : ComplexNumber) : REAL;
(* Returns the real part of a complex number. *)

PROCEDURE ImagPart ( n : ComplexNumber) : REAL;
(* Returns the imaginary part of a complex number. *)

PROCEDURE Modulus (n : ComplexNumber) : REAL;
(* Returns the modulus of a complex number. *)

PROCEDURE Angle (n : ComplexNumber) : REAL;
(* Returns the angle of a complex number. *)

PROCEDURE Add (n1, n2 : ComplexNumber; VAR n3 : ComplexNumber);
(* Returns the sum of two complex numbers. *)

PROCEDURE Multiply (n1, n2   : ComplexNumber;
                    VAR n3 : ComplexNumber);
(* Returns the product of two complex numbers. *)

PROCEDURE Divide (n1, n2   : ComplexNumber;
                  VAR n3 : ComplexNumber);
(* Returns the quotient of two complex numbers. *)

END HiddenComplexNumbers.
```

The first implementation of this abstract data type (Program 12.8) again uses the familiar rectangular coordinates. The second implementation may be substituted for the first without changing the definition module, hence without requiring any changes in any client modules. This implementation (Program 12.9) uses polar coordinates, choosing the values modulus and angle to represent a complex number. Both values may be retrieved through the similarly named function procedures. Comparing the corresponding operations in the two implementations, we find them to be substantially different. However, they provide exactly the same abstract data type to the client modules. Changing from one implementation to the other not only does not require the client modules to be changed, it does not even require them to be recompiled.

In both implementations the complex number type is a pointer to a record, rather than a record, because Modula-2 requires that opaque types be represented by a one-word entity.

Program 12.8   Rectangular Coordinate Implementation of Complex
Numbers

```
IMPLEMENTATION MODULE HiddenComplexNumbers;
(* Rectangular coordinate implementation *)

FROM Storage IMPORT ALLOCATE;

FROM MathLib0 IMPORT sin, cos, sqrt, arctan;

  CONST pi = 3.1415192654;

  TYPE ComplexNumber = POINTER TO
                         RECORD
                           re : REAL;
                           im : REAL;
                           END (* record *);

  PROCEDURE Create () : ComplexNumber;

VAR
  c : ComplexNumber;

BEGIN
  NEW (c);
  c^.re := 0.0;
  c^.im := 0.0;
  RETURN c;
END Create;

PROCEDURE Initialize (realpart, imaginarypart : REAL) :
             ComplexNumber;

VAR
  c : ComplexNumber;

  BEGIN
  NEW (c);
  c^.re := realpart;
  c^.im := imaginarypart;
  RETURN c;
END Initialize;

PROCEDURE PolarInitialize (modulus, angle : REAL) :
             ComplexNumber;

VAR
  c : ComplexNumber;

BEGIN
  NEW (c);
  c^.re := modulus*cos (angle);
  c^.im := modulus*sin (angle);
  RETURN c;
END PolarInitialize;
```

```
PROCEDURE RealPart ( n : ComplexNumber) : REAL;
BEGIN
  RETURN n^.re;
END RealPart;


PROCEDURE ImagPart ( n : ComplexNumber) : REAL;
BEGIN
  RETURN n^.im;
END ImagPart;


PROCEDURE Modulus ( n : ComplexNumber) : REAL;
BEGIN
  RETURN sqrt (n^.re*n^.re + n^.im*n^.im);
END Modulus;


PROCEDURE Angle ( n : ComplexNumber) : REAL;

VAR
  a : REAL;

BEGIN
  a := arctan ( ABS(n^.im)/ABS(n^.re) );
  IF (n^.re >= 0.0) AND (n^.im >= 0.0)
  THEN (* first quadrant vector *)
    RETURN a;
  ELSIF (n^.re < 0.0) AND (n^.im >= 0.0)
  THEN (* second quadrant vector *)
    RETURN pi - a;
  ELSIF (n^.re < 0.0) AND (n^.im < 0.0)
  THEN (* third quadrant vector *)
    RETURN -pi + a;
  ELSE (* fourth quadrant vector *)
    RETURN -a;
  END (* if then elsif else *);
END Angle;


PROCEDURE Add (n1, n2 : ComplexNumber; VAR n3 : ComplexNumber);
BEGIN
  n3^.re := n1^.re + n2^.re;
  n3^.im := n1^.im + n2^.im;
END Add;

PROCEDURE Multiply (n1, n2   : ComplexNumber;
                       VAR n3 : ComplexNumber);

BEGIN
  n3^.re := n1^.re * n2^.re - n1^.im * n2^.im;
  n3^.im := n1^.re * n2^.im + n1^.im * n2^.re;
END Multiply;
```

```
PROCEDURE Divide (n1, n2 : ComplexNumber;
                        VAR n3 : ComplexNumber);
BEGIN
  n3^.re := (n1^.re*n2^.re  +  n1^.im*n2^.im)/
            (n2^.re*n2^.re  +  n2^.im*n2^.im);
  n3^.im := (n1^.im*n2^.re - n1^.re*n2^.im)/
            (n2^.re*n2^.re  +  n2^.im*n2^.im);
END Divide;

END HiddenComplexNumbers.
```

Program 12.9   Polar Coordinate Implementation of Complex Numbers

```
IMPLEMENTATION MODULE HiddenComplexNumbers;
(* Polar coordinate implementation *)

FROM Storage IMPORT ALLOCATE;

FROM MathLib0 IMPORT sqrt, sin, cos, arctan;

CONST pi = 3.1415192654;

TYPE ComplexNumber = POINTER TO
                        RECORD
                          modulus : REAL;
                          angle   : REAL;
                        END (* record *);

PROCEDURE Create () : ComplexNumber;

VAR
  c : ComplexNumber;

BEGIN
  NEW (c);
  c^.modulus := 0.0;
  c^.angle   := 0.0;
  RETURN c;
END Create;

PROCEDURE Initialize (realpart, imaginarypart : REAL) :
            ComplexNumber;

VAR
  c : ComplexNumber;
  a : REAL; (* angle used to compute actual angle *)

BEGIN
  a := arctan ( ABS(imaginarypart)/ABS(realpart) );
  NEW (c);
  c^.modulus := sqrt (realpart*realpart +
                        imaginarypart*imaginarypart);
```

```
  IF (realpart >= 0.0) AND (imaginarypart >= 0.0)
  THEN (* first quadrant vector *)
    c^.angle := a;
  ELSIF (realpart < 0.0) AND (imaginarypart >= 0.0)
  THEN (* second quadrant vector *)
    c^.angle := pi - a;
  ELSIF (realpart < 0.0) AND (imaginarypart < 0.0)
  THEN (* third quadrant vector *)
    c^.angle := -pi + a;
  ELSE (* fourth quadrant vector *)
    c^.angle := -a;
  END (* if then elsif else *);
  RETURN c;
END Initialize;

PROCEDURE PolarInitialize (modulus, angle : REAL) :
            ComplexNumber;

VAR
  c : ComplexNumber;

BEGIN
  NEW (c);
  c^.modulus := modulus;
  c^.angle   := angle;
  RETURN c;
END PolarInitialize;
(* The implementations of procedures RealPart, ImagPart, Modulus,
   Angle, Add, Multiply, and Divide are left as exercises. *)
END HiddenComplexNumbers.
```

12.4 Functional Abstraction

The implementation of an abstract data type includes a definition module that exports a type and one or more operations on that type. Two common variants of this idea are also very useful.

In some instances, we do not need to export a data type because we know that we need exactly one variable of that type. That variable may be declared in the abstraction rather than in a client module. We will see an example of this in the symboltable abstraction in Section 17.5. Sometimes we export this special variable, but more often it is hidden in the implementation module. This kind of abstraction is often called an *abstract data object* or *abstract variable*. Its implementation as a definition module and an implementation module provides all the benefits we have already seen for abstract data types.

On many occasions we need to provide a particular capability but do not need to define either a new data type or a new variable. Such a capability is often called a *functional abstraction*. We have already used this term to describe a single abstract operation or action without regard for the details of how that operation is accomplished. A procedure can be used to implement a single abstract operation, thereby hiding the details of how it works. Only the name of the procedure (and its parameter list, if any) is known outside the procedure.

We now want to extend this idea slightly to achieve a capability that has several functional components. The most important example of this idea is the input/output capability. We have seen that the module InOut provides a variety of input and output operations, but does not export any data type. These operations are all part of a single abstract capability, and so are all placed in the same module.

This kind of abstract capability is also exemplified by many of the other library modules discussed in Chapter 10. The Storage module provides the capability to allocate and deallocate storage. The mathematical library modules MathLib0 and Arithmetic provide packages of new operations for previously defined data types. Again, none of these provides an abstract data type or data object; they provide only an abstract capability.

In this section we look at an additional example of data abstraction and functional abstraction, motivated by a common problem in numerical computing: the solution of a system of linear equations. The usual method of solving such a system requires that it be represented as a matrix, which in turn is often represented in a programming language as a two-dimensional array.

Two levels of representation are necessary. At first it may appear that the lower level, a two-dimensional array, is trivial because it already exists in the Modula-2 language. If we attempt to define procedures for manipulating these arrays, we discover a problem. We would like such procedures to be able to work on arrays of different sizes, but the strong typing of Modula-2 forces us to define procedure parameters of a single type only, hence a single size. Remember that open array parameters must be one dimensional. Therefore we must create an abstract data type for a matrix that is not based on the built-in, two-dimensional array data structure. In effect, we provide two-dimensional open arrays.

The matrix abstract data type includes eight operations. Since it is a dynamically allocated data structure (to allow matrices of different sizes), it must have operations define (allocate) and destroy (deallocate). Matrices are often quite large, and not easy to type in or display on a terminal. Therefore we provide input and output operations to transfer a matrix to or from a disk file; these operations are called save and retrieve. Two other operations are the two-dimensional counterparts of the HIGH function for open arrays. The lower and upper functions return the lower and upper limits of the row and column indices of a matrix. Finally, we will provide operations access and assign to get an element from or put an element in the matrix. Program 12.10 shows the definition module for the matrix data type.

A discussion of the implementation of the matrix data type is postponed until Chapter 15, since it depends on some low level language features introduced in Chapter 13, and dynamic data structures techniques introduced in Chapter 15. The deferral of implementation details is common in software development, and is not a problem in Modula-2. We can continue to develop

Program 12.10   Matrix Data Type Definition Module

```
DEFINITION MODULE Matrix;
(* This is the definition of the dynamic matrix abstract data type. *)
FROM FileSystem IMPORT
  (* type *) File;

EXPORT QUALIFIED
  matrix,
  define, destroy, lower, upper, access, assign, save, retrieve;

TYPE
  matrix;
  range = ( row, column );

PROCEDURE define
  ( VAR m     : matrix              (* out    *);
        low1  : INTEGER             (* in     *);
        high1 : INTEGER             (* in     *);
        low2  : INTEGER             (* in     *);
        high2 : INTEGER             (* in     *) );

PROCEDURE destroy
  ( VAR m     : matrix              (* in/out *) );

PROCEDURE lower
  (     m     : matrix              (* in     *);
        index : range              (* in     *) ) : INTEGER;

PROCEDURE upper
  (     m     : matrix              (* in     *);
        index : range              (* in     *) ) : INTEGER;

PROCEDURE access
  (     m     : matrix              (* in     *);
        row   : INTEGER             (* in     *);
        col   : INTEGER             (* in     *) ) : REAL;

PROCEDURE assign
  (     m     : matrix              (* in/out *);
        row   : INTEGER             (* in     *);
        col   : INTEGER             (* in     *);
        value : REAL               (* in     *) );

PROCEDURE save
  (     f     : File               (* in/out *);
        m     : matrix              (* in     *);
        name : ARRAY OF CHAR (* in     *) );

PROCEDURE retrieve
  (     f     : File               (* in/out *);
    VAR m     : matrix              (* out    *);
        name : ARRAY OF CHAR (* in     *) );

END Matrix.
```

the modules that solve systems of linear equations once we have the definition module for the matrix type.

The capability to solve a system of linear equations is provided in definition and implementation modules named SimultaneousEquations (Programs 12.11 and 12.12, respectively). Notice that the definition module exports only two entities, the procedures LowerUpperFactor and Solve. No data type or data object is being defined, only a capability. Hence these modules are considered a functional abstraction.

We will not try to describe the mathematics of these modules. The interested reader may wish to consult a reference on numerical analysis (such as Cheney and Kincaid, 1980) for a discussion of the algorithms for lower–upper matrix decomposition and backtracking that are used in these modules.

This kind of packaged capability is common. Fortran subroutine libraries for numerical applications have existed for almost 30 years. Most programmers have used such libraries, and may have implemented similar libraries.

The major difference between a Fortran library and a Modula-2 library module is the type checking performed by the Modula-2 compiler when refer-

---

Program 12.11   Simultaneous Equations Definition Module

```
DEFINITION MODULE SimultaneousEquations;
(* NOTE: This package assumes that the matrix of coefficients is
          dimensioned from 1 to some upper limit for both rows and
          columns. *)

FROM Matrix IMPORT matrix;

EXPORT QUALIFIED
   (* proc *) LowerUpperFactor,
   (* proc *) Solve;

   VAR sub: ARRAY [ 1..200 ] OF INTEGER;
   (* An array of subscripts. *)

   PROCEDURE LowerUpperFactor ( VAR a : matrix );

(* Converts the input matrix "a" into an output matrix "a" factored into
   lower triangular form with the pivot factors stored in the upper
   triangle. *)

   PROCEDURE Solve
    ( VAR a : matrix;
      VAR c : ARRAY OF REAL;
      VAR x : ARRAY OF REAL );

(* Solves simultaneous linear equations in n unknowns. The coefficient
   matrix, "a", must already have been processed by PROCEDURE
   LowerUpperFactor and be in triangular form.  The vector "c"
   represents the forcing coefficients on one side of the equations. The
   vector "x" represents the solution vector to the problem. *)

END SimultaneousEquations.
```

Program 12.12   Simultaneous Equations Implementation Module

```
IMPLEMENTATION MODULE SimultaneousEquations;

FROM Matrix IMPORT matrix, upper, lower, access, assign;

FROM InOut IMPORT WriteLn, WriteString;

PROCEDURE LowerUpperFactor ( VAR a : matrix );


VAR
  size        : INTEGER;
  i, j, k, indx   : CARDINAL;
  pivot, max, b : REAL;
  r           : REAL;


BEGIN (* LowerUpperFactor *)
  size := upper (a, row);
  IF (lower (a, row) # 1) OR (lower (a, column) # 1) OR
    ( upper (a, row) # upper (a, column) )
  THEN
    WriteLn;
    WriteString ("Error in dimensioning matrix for factorization.");
    HALT;
  END (* if then *);
  FOR i := 1 TO size DO (* Initialize subscript array *)
    sub[i] := i;
  END (* for loop *);
  FOR k := 1 TO size -1 DO
    max := 0.0;
    FOR i := k TO size DO
      b := ABS ( access (a, sub[i], k) );
      IF b > max THEN
        max := b;
        indx := i;
      END (* if then *);
    END (* for loop *);
    IF max <= 1.0E-33 THEN
      WriteLn;
      WriteString ("Matrix of coefficients is near singular.");
      HALT
    END (* if then *);
    j := sub[k];
    sub[k] := sub[indx];
    sub[indx] := j;
    pivot := access (a, sub[k], k);
```

```
        FOR i := k + 1 TO size DO
          r := -access (a, sub[i], k) / pivot;
          assign (a, sub[i], k, r);
          FOR j := k + 1 TO size DO
            r := access (a, sub[i], j) + access (a, sub[i], k) *
                                            access (a, sub[k], j);
            assign (a, sub[i], j, r)
          END (* for loop *);
        END (* for loop *);
      END (* for loop *);
      FOR i := 1 TO size DO
        IF access (a, sub[i], i) = 0.0 THEN
          WriteLn;
          WriteString ("Matrix of coefficients is singular.");
          HALT
        END (* if then *);
      END (* for loop *);
    END LowerUpperFactor;

    PROCEDURE Solve
      ( VAR a : matrix;
        VAR c : ARRAY OF REAL;
        VAR x : ARRAY OF REAL );

    VAR
      size : INTEGER;
      i, k : INTEGER;

    BEGIN (* Solve *)
      size := upper (a, 1);
      IF size = 1
      THEN
        x[0] := c[0]/access (a, 1, 1);
        RETURN
      END (* if then *);
      x[0] := c[sub[1] - 1];
      FOR k := 2 TO size DO
        x[k-1] := c[sub[k] - 1];
        FOR i := 1 TO k-1 DO
          x[k-1] := x[k-1] + access (a, sub[k], i) * x[i-1];
        END (* for loop *);
      END (* for loop *);
      x[size-1] := x[size-1] / access (a, sub[size], size);
      FOR k := size -1 TO 1 BY -1 DO
        FOR i := k + 1 TO size DO
          x[k-1] := x[k-1] - access (a, sub[k], i) * x[i-1];
        END (* for loop *);
        x[k-1] := x[k-1] / access (a, sub[k], k);
      END (* for loop *);
    END Solve;
  END SimultaneousEquations.
```

ences are made to the library components. A Fortran compiler makes no such checks; in fact, the library is not even accessed until the program linking process. The information in all definition modules is available during the compilation of a Modula-2 program, so all procedure references can be checked to ensure that the parameters are correct with respect to number, order, type, and binding mechanism. This clearly allows detection of many common programming errors that would go undetected in a Fortran program.

12.5 Summary

Data abstraction in software development is the process of identifying data types (values and operations) that will be needed in a software system, without concentrating on the ways in which those types will be implemented. If these types can be defined during software design, implementation of the types and of the software components that use the types can proceed independently. Many common kinds of software maintenance will be much easier, because the changes will be localized in the implementations of the data types.

The extent of the data hiding (i.e., of separating the definition of a type from its implementation) determines to some degree the success of the data abstraction. Modula-2 offers transparent and opaque type definitions, with the latter providing complete data hiding. Transparent types are subject to abuse in some cases, since the programs that use them can manipulate their internal representations in ways other than those provided by the operations on the type.

Functional abstractions provide a software capability without providing a new data type or object. Functional and data abstractions are related concepts, and are implemented the same way in Modula-2: as a library (definition and implementation) module. Often a data abstraction is defined that provides a new data type and basic operations, and an associated functional abstraction is defined to provide a specialized capability or application for that new data type.

12.6 Exercises

1. Explain the terms "data abstraction," "functional abstraction," "abstract data type," "abstract variable," and "data hiding."

2. Describe how data hiding may be achieved in a Modula-2 implementation of an abstract data type.

3. Design and implement date and time abstract data types. Operations should include input and output, comparisons for before and after, and a subtraction operation that determines the period between two dates or two times.

4. Design and implement an abstraction that provides the capability to solve quadratic equations.

5. Design and implement an abstraction that provides the capability to determine the mean and the variance of a data set.

6. Design and implement a sorting abstraction for lists of up to 1000 real numbers. Provide at least two different implementation modules.

7. Demonstrate that a program module that uses the sorting modules of Problem 6 does not have to be recompiled after changing from one sorting implementation to another.

8. What other operations might be needed for the complex number abstract data type?

9. Implement the complex number operations that were omitted from Program 12.9.

10. Which operations on complex numbers might be better implemented as functions, thus allowing complicated expressions? Make the appropriate implementation changes in Programs 12.5 through 12.9.

13

Low Level
Abstractions

For many kinds of software systems, programmers need to know very low level details about the computer system on which the software will run. In systems applications, we might need to know the structure of the fields in a machine instruction word. For memory management, we need to manipulate blocks of memory identified by physical addresses. To develop type transfer functions for abstract data types, we need to know how data are represented internally. Many applications require the ability to manipulate bits within a single data word.

Modula-2 recognizes these low level needs and provides a set of abstractions to satisfy them. Although the details behind these abstractions are completely machine dependent, we can still develop low level software that is somewhat portable. In this chapter we examine these abstractions and see examples of how they may be used.

Because the low level features, especially those which defeat the strong typing rules, are easily abused and unlikely to be portable, they must be used with care. We recommend that their use be confined to modules that implement higher level abstractions.

13.1 The SYSTEM Module

Every implementation of Modula-2 includes a module called SYSTEM. This module exports several data types and procedures that are machine dependent.

These data types obey different compatibility rules, and the procedures obey parameter list compatibility rules different from those seen before. Therefore, SYSTEM is not a true library module insofar as it is not compiled separately and then made available to other modules. Because of the unique nature of the entities defined in this module, it must be built into the compiler.

We may think of the SYSTEM module as if it had been defined by the definition module shown in Program 13.1. The entities PROCESS, NEWPROCESS, and TRANSFER will be discussed in Chapter 16. All the other types and procedures are described in subsequent sections of this chapter.

Program 13.1   Definition Module SYSTEM

```
DEFINITION MODULE SYSTEM;

EXPORT QUALIFIED
   (* type *) BYTE, WORD, ADDRESS, PROCESS,
   (* proc *) ADR, SIZE, TSIZE, NEWPROCESS, TRANSFER;

TYPE BYTE;

TYPE WORD;

TYPE ADDRESS;

TYPE PROCESS;

PROCEDURE ADR
   (      object       : AnyType   (* in  *) ) : ADDRESS;

PROCEDURE SIZE
   (      object       : AnyType   (* in  *) ) : CARDINAL;

PROCEDURE TSIZE
   (      AnyType, ...             (* in  *) ) : CARDINAL;

PROCEDURE NEWPROCESS
   (      program   : PROC      (* in  *);
          workspace : ADDRESS   (* in  *);
          spacesize : CARDINAL  (* in  *);
     VAR  newproc   : PROCESS   (* out *) );

PROCEDURE TRANSFER
   ( VAR oldprocess  : PROCESS  (* out *);
     VAR newprocess  : PROCESS  (* in  *) );

END SYSTEM.
```

13.1.1   The BYTE and WORD Types

The values of the BYTE data type are those that occupy exactly one byte of memory; the values of the WORD data type are those that occupy exactly one word of memory. The only operation defined on these types is assignment. They are not compatible with any other data types; hence none of the arithmetic, relational, boolean, or bitset operations may be performed on objects of these types.

Not all computers have byte-addressable memory, and not all computers have the same memory word size. Therefore the BYTE data type may not be defined in some Modula-2 implementations, and the size of an object of the WORD type will vary from one machine to another. In addition, an implementation on a computer system with other memory organizations may provide other data types, such as HALFWORD or LONGWORD.

Type transfers may be used between the WORD type and any other type that occupies one machine word of storage. This constitutes a way to remove or provide an interpretation for a pattern of bits.

A formal parameter of a procedure that is declared to be of type ARRAY OF WORD or ARRAY OF BYTE may be bound to an actual parameter of any type and any size. This property makes these data types extremely useful for developing general procedures that can perform a particular task on any kind of data object. Many examples of this are given here and in subsequent chapters, including a way to create *generic* functional and data abstractions.

13.1.2   The ADDRESS Type and the ADR Procedure

The ADDRESS data type may be considered to have been defined as follows:

TYPE ADDRESS = POINTER TO WORD;

It is compatible and assignment compatible with all pointer types, and is also compatible with the cardinal data type. Therefore the operations that may be performed on addresses include pointer dereference, assignment, relational, and arithmetic operations.

The ADR procedure is a function procedure that returns the machine address of its parameter, which must be a variable.

Different computer systems may place restrictions on address manipulations. For example, on many byte-addressable machines, a word must begin at an address that is a multiple of two or four. For such machines, it would not make sense to add one to an address and still call it the address of a word (a pointer to a word). On such machines, if a character or boolean variable were stored at an odd address, the ADR function could not return a value of the ADDRESS type. A programmer using these features of Modula-2 must have a thorough knowledge of the addressing rules of the host computer system.

13.1.3   The SIZE and TSIZE Procedures

The SIZE procedure is a function procedure that returns the size of its parameter, which must be a variable. If it is a variable of a variant record type, the size is that which allows for the largest possible field in each variant part. The TSIZE procedure is a function procedure that takes a type identifier as a parameter and returns the size of objects of that type. If the type is a variant record type, additional parameters specifying the tag field values for the last variants may be specified, as described for the NEW procedure in Section 4.3. In fact, the compiler will translate the statement:

NEW (p, tag1, tag2, tag3)

into the statement:

ALLOCATE (p, TSIZE (rectype, tag1, tag2, tag3)

assuming that the variable p is a pointer to rectype.

Both these procedures measure the size of an object in memory storage units. On most computers this means the size is in bytes, although on some machines the size is measured in words.

13.2 Examples of Low Level Data Manipulation Techniques

Many software systems need to manipulate data as uninterpreted bit patterns, to manipulate bits within words, or to deal with physical addresses of objects. In this section we present some simple examples of such manipulations. We must warn the reader that these examples rely on the low level details of a particular Modula-2 implementation and will not necessarily work on other implementations. We attempt to point out these dependencies, to indicate to the reader what must be modified if the technique is used on another implementation.

We first consider a technique used frequently in applications such as the development of a file system. We want to be able to transfer data of any data type to and from disk files, but without writing a separate procedure for each data type. Because disk data are not human readable, there is no need to convert values to legible character strings when writing to disk, and so we just write uninterpreted bit patterns. The WORD data type can be used for this purpose.

Assume that we have a disk device that stores data in sectors of 256 words each, and a primitive operation WriteBlock that can transfer a block of data of this size to the disk. To simplify our example, we ignore the obvious need to specify a file or disk address for the transfer; instead we assume that the WriteBlock operation gets this information elsewhere. We declare a file buffer variable named block to hold the data until a full block is ready to be written to disk, and a cardinal variable named bpos that keeps track of how much of the block is filled.

Program 13.2 shows the needed declarations and the procedure put that puts data into the block. Notice that the parameter of put is an open array of words, which allows it to be bound to an actual parameter of any data type. The procedure copies the parameter, word by word, into the block. If the block becomes filled during the process, it is written to disk, and the copying continues. This allows the procedure to operate correctly on data objects either smaller than or larger than the disk sector size. Smaller objects are packed

---

Program 13.2 Disk File Output Example

```
CONST
  blocksize = 256;

VAR
  block : ARRAY [ 1..blocksize ] OF WORD;
  bpos  : CARDINAL;

PROCEDURE put
  ( item : ARRAY OF WORD (* in *) );

  VAR pos : CARDINAL;

BEGIN
  FOR pos := 0 TO HIGH ( item ) DO
    INC ( bpos );
    block[ bpos ] := item[ pos ];
    IF bpos = blocksize
      THEN WriteBlock ( block );
           bpos := 0

    END
  END
END put;
```

several to a sector, and larger objects are split over several sectors. We assume that the bpos variable is set to zero before this procedure is used.

A memory dump procedure is an example of an application that must access specific physical addresses in memory and print values without knowing the data types that may have been associated with those values in a user's program. Such a procedure can make use of Modula-2's address data type and type transfer functions. In this example we assume that an address and a cardinal value occupy exactly one memory word each. This is not the case on all computers, but it is not uncommon.

The dump procedure is given an address and a word count, and it must print that many words beginning at that address. We choose to print the values in hexadecimal notation, and thus we can use Modula-2's WriteHex procedure if the values are transferred to the cardinal type. We will print the values eight per line, with each line beginning with the address of the first value in the line. Again, if we transfer the address to the cardinal type, we know how to print it. Without these type transfers, neither addresses nor words could be printed.

Program 13.3 shows the dump procedure. Notice the two occurrences of the type transfer using the type identifier CARDINAL as a type transfer function identifier. This works on most implementations only if the two data types involved occupy the same amount of storage; hence the assumptions above. The variable loc is an address and thus a pointer, so we use the dereference operator to get the value at that address. Notice also that we can use the INC procedure on an address variable, since addresses are compatible with cardinals.

Program 13.3 Memory Dump Example

```
(* The following declarations are assumed to have been made in the
   module that contains this procedure. *)
FROM SYSTEM IMPORT
  (* type *) WORD, ADDRESS;

FROM InOut IMPORT
  (* proc *) Write, WriteHex, WriteLn;

PROCEDURE dump
  (     startaddr  : ADDRESS (* in *);
        wordcount : CARDINAL (* in *) );

  VAR loc    : ADDRESS;
      count : CARDINAL;
BEGIN
  loc := startaddr;
  FOR count := 1 TO wordcount DO
    IF count MOD 8 = 1
      THEN WriteLn;
              WriteHex ( CARDINAL ( loc ), 10 );
              Write ( ':' )
    END;
    WriteHex ( CARDINAL ( loc^ ), 10 );
    INC ( loc, TSIZE ( CARDINAL ) )
  END;
  WriteLn
END dump;
```

The data type BITSET in Modula-2 provides a way to name and access individual bits in a memory word. By using type transfers, we can transfer data of other types to the bitset type, and then access individual bits in values of those other types. We illustrate this with a procedure that prints the internal bit pattern, as strings of zeros and ones, of any data object. In this example, we assume that a bitset occupies one word of storage. We also assume that a constant named wordlength has been defined that contains the number of bits in a word.

The procedure showbits (Program 13.4) again uses an open array of words for the type of its formal parameter, so that the actual parameter may be of any data type. The procedure prints the parameter word by word, with each word being transferred to a bitset to gain access to the individual bits. This example was developed on a system that numbers the bits in a word from right to left, so the printing loop counts down through the bit numbers to achieve the normal left to right representation of the value.

In Chapter 4 we noted that Modula-2 does not provide packed data structures like those of Pascal. We would like to demonstrate that packed structures can be created and manipulated in Modula-2, using some of the low level features of the language.

Program 13.4 Bit Representation Example

```
PROCEDURE showbits
    (     item : ARRAY OF WORD (* in *) );

    VAR wordpos      : CARDINAL;
        bit          : CARDINAL;
        representation : BITSET;

BEGIN
    FOR wordpos := 0 TO HIGH ( item ) DO
        representation := BITSET ( item[ wordpos ] );
        FOR bit := wordlength-1 TO 0 BY -1 DO
            IF bit IN representation
                THEN Write ( '1' )
                ELSE Write ( '0' )
            END
        END;
        Write ( ' ' )
    END
END showbits;
```

Packed structures are manipulated at the machine language level by masking and shifting instructions (unless the computer has special instructions that operate on pieces of words, such as the byte instructions of the DEC PDP-10 computer system). In Modula-2, masking can be accomplished with bitset operations, and shifting with cardinal multiply and divide operations.

For this example, we define a packed record with fields a, b, c, and d, of 3, 9, 4, and 16 bits, respectively. We assume that this total of 32 bits fills one machine word. This example was again developed on a system that numbers bits in a word from right to left, so we place field a at the right-hand end of the word and field d at the left-hand end of the word, as shown in Figure 13.1.

We define two constants for each field in the record, a mask constant of the bitset type containing the numbers of the bits that constitute the field, and a shift constant that is the number by which we divide the word to shift the field to the right-hand end of the word. The shift constant is thus two raised to the power of the number of bits after the field. Those constants are:

```
CONST
    amask = { 0..2 };    ashift = 1;
    bmask = { 3..11 };   bshift = 8;
    cmask = { 12..15 };  cshift = 4096;
    dmask = { 16..31 };  dshift = 65536;
```

To retrieve the value from one of the fields, we perform the set intersection operation on the packed record and the appropriate mask to isolate just the desired field, and then divide by the shift constant to move the bits of that field to the right-hand end of the word. To store a new value into a field, we first

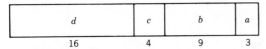

d	c	b	a
16	4	9	3

FIGURE 13.1   The Packed Record

perform the set intersection operation with the complement of the mask to clear the bits in the field. Then we multiply the new value by the shift constant to position the value, and add it to the packed record.

These operations are shown below. We assume that the packed record is stored in a variable named packedrec and that the value being stored or retrieved is named value.

To retrieve a value:

value := CARDINAL (BITSET (packedrec) ∗ mask)
            DIV shift

To store a value:

packedrec := WORD ((BITSET (packedrec) ∗
                ({ 0..31 } − mask)) +
                BITSET (value ∗ shift))

In each of these statements, the identifiers mask and shift must be replaced by the constants declared for the desired field.

Similar techniques can be used to develop packed records that occupy more than one word, and to develop packed arrays. The special case of a packed array of boolean data is essentially the same as a very large bitset; this data type is considered in detail in Section 14.4.

13.3   A Generic Sorting Module

A *generic* data abstraction may be defined as a data type for which the set of operations is specified, but not the set of values. For example, we might define a List data type with input, output, and sort operations, but without specifying either the length of the list or the type of objects in the list. A generic functional abstraction provides a capability that may be applied to many different data types.

Modula-2 does not support the formal declaration of generic abstractions, as does Ada, for example. It is nevertheless possible to provide a very similar functionality, using some of the low level features of the language.

Program 13.5 is an example of a generic functional abstraction. It provides two different sorting procedures, a simple exchange sort and the more efficient heap sort. (The reader may wish to consult a reference such as Reingold, Nievergelt, and Deo, 1977, for a discussion of these and other sorting algorithms.) Either of these procedures may be used to sort a list of objects, where the lists may be of any length and the objects of any data type.

Program 13.5 Generic Sorting Module

DEFINITION MODULE GenericSorting;

FROM SYSTEM IMPORT WORD;

EXPORT QUALIFIED
  (* proc *) GenericExchangeSort,
  (* proc *) GenericHeapSort;

  TYPE UserProc = PROCEDURE(ARRAY OF WORD, ARRAY OF WORD)
                        : BOOLEAN;
  (* The client program must supply a procedure that compares two
     objects for greater than of the type to be sorted. *)

  PROCEDURE GenericExchangeSort
    (VAR ObjectArray : ARRAY OF WORD;
      object1, object2 : ARRAY OF WORD;
      Gtr   : UserProc);

  (* GenericSort inputs an array of objects and returns the sorted array of
     objects. The purpose of object1 and object2 is to provide work space
     of the correct word size. The client program must supply Gtr. *)

  PROCEDURE GenericHeapSort
    (VAR ObjectArray : ARRAY OF WORD;
      object1, object2 : ARRAY OF WORD;
      Gtr   : UserProc);

  (* GenericHeapSort uses an efficient heapsort algorithm for performing
     in-place sorting of generic objects. *)

END GenericSorting.

IMPLEMENTATION MODULE GenericSorting;

FROM SYSTEM IMPORT WORD;

  VAR
    WordSizeOfObject : CARDINAL;
    NumberObjects   : CARDINAL;

  PROCEDURE GenericExchangeSort
    (VAR ObjectArray : ARRAY OF WORD;
      object1, object2 : ARRAY OF WORD;
      Gtr   : UserProc);

  VAR
    index : CARDINAL;
    pos   : CARDINAL;

  PROCEDURE interchange(index1, index2 : CARDINAL);

  VAR WordCount : CARDINAL;

```
BEGIN
  FOR WordCount := 1 TO WordSizeOfObject DO
    object1[WordCount-1] := ObjectArray[index1*
                    WordSizeOfObject + WordCount-1];
    object2[WordCount-1] := ObjectArray[index2*
                    WordSizeOfObject + WordCount-1];
  END (* for loop *);
  FOR WordCount := 1 TO WordSizeOfObject DO
    ObjectArray[index1*WordSizeOfObject + WordCount-1] :=
            object2[WordCount-1];
    ObjectArray[index2*WordSizeOfObject + WordCount-1] :=
            object1[WordCount-1];
  END (* for loop *);
END interchange;

PROCEDURE getobject( index       : CARDINAL;
                     VAR Object : ARRAY OF WORD );

VAR WordCount : CARDINAL;

BEGIN
  FOR WordCount := 1 TO WordSizeOfObject DO
    Object[WordCount-1] := ObjectArray[index*
                    WordSizeOfObject + WordCount-1];
  END (* for loop *);
END getobject;

PROCEDURE Maximum( UPPER    : CARDINAL;
                   VAR pos : CARDINAL );

VAR
  index       : CARDINAL;
  WordCount : CARDINAL;

BEGIN (* Maximum *)
  pos := 0;
  index := 0;
  getobject(index,object1);
  FOR index := 1 TO UPPER DO
    getobject(index,object2);
    IF Gtr(object2,object1)
    THEN
      FOR WordCount := 1 TO WordSizeOfObject DO
        object1[WordCount-1] := object2[WordCount-1];
      END (* for loop *);
      pos := index;
    END (* if then *)
  END (* for loop *)
END Maximum;
```

```
BEGIN (* GenericExchangeSort *)
  WordSizeOfObject := HIGH(object1) + 1;
  NumberObjects   := (HIGH(ObjectArray) + 1)
                         DIV WordSizeOfObject;
  index            := NumberObjects;
  REPEAT
    DEC(index);
    Maximum(index,pos);
    interchange(pos,index);
  UNTIL index = 0;

END GenericExchangeSort;

PROCEDURE GenericHeapSort( VAR ObjectArray : ARRAY OF WORD;
                           object1, object2  : ARRAY OF WORD;
                           Gtr               : UserProc           );

VAR i : CARDINAL;

  PROCEDURE interchange(index1, index2 : CARDINAL);

  VAR WordCount : CARDINAL;

  BEGIN
    FOR WordCount := 1 TO WordSizeOfObject DO
      object1[WordCount-1] := ObjectArray[(index1-1)*
                    WordSizeOfObject + WordCount-1];
      object2[WordCount-1] := ObjectArray[(index2-1)*
                    WordSizeOfObject + WordCount-1];
    END (* for loop *);
    FOR WordCount := 1 TO WordSizeOfObject DO
      ObjectArray[(index1-1)*WordSizeOfObject + WordCount-1] :=
                    object2[WordCount-1];
      ObjectArray[(index2-1)*WordSizeOfObject + WordCount-1] :=
                    object1[WordCount-1];
    END (* for loop *);
  END interchange;

  PROCEDURE getobject( index     : CARDINAL;
                       VAR Object : ARRAY OF WORD );

  VAR WordCount : CARDINAL;

  BEGIN
    FOR WordCount := 1 TO WordSizeOfObject DO
      Object[WordCount-1] := ObjectArray[(index-1)*
                    WordSizeOfObject + WordCount-1];
    END (* for loop *);
  END getobject;

  PROCEDURE createheap;
```

```
VAR
  node : CARDINAL;
  i    : CARDINAL;
  j    : CARDINAL;

BEGIN
  FOR node := 2 TO NumberObjects DO
    i := node;
    j := i DIV 2;
    IF j > 0
    THEN
      getobject(j,object1);
      getobject(i,object2);
    END (* if then *);
    WHILE (j > 0) AND ( Gtr(object2,object1) ) DO
      interchange(i,j);
      i := j;
      j := i DIV 2;
      IF j > 0
      THEN
        getobject(j,object1);
        getobject(i,object2);
      END (* if then *);
    END (* while loop *);
  END (* for loop *);
END createheap;


PROCEDURE adjust(k : CARDINAL);

VAR
    i : CARDINAL;
    j : CARDINAL;

BEGIN
    i := 1;
    j := 2;
    IF k >= 3
    THEN
      getobject(3,object1);
      getobject(2,object2);
    END (* if then *);
    IF (k >= 3) AND ( Gtr(object1,object2) )
    THEN
      j := 3
    END (* if then *);
    IF j <= k
    THEN
      getobject(j,object2);
      getobject(i,object1);
    END (* if then *);
```

```
    WHILE (j <= k ) AND ( Gtr(object2,object1) ) DO
      interchange(i,j);
      i := j;
      j := 2*i;
      IF j+1 <= k
      THEN
        getobject(j+1,object2);
        getobject(j,object1);
      END (* if then *);
      IF (j+1 <= k) AND ( Gtr(object2,object1) )
      THEN
        INC(j);
      END (* if then *);
      IF j <= k
      THEN
        getobject(j,object2);
        getobject(i,object1);
      END (* if then *);
    END (* while loop *);
  END adjust;
BEGIN(* GenericHeapSort *)
  WordSizeOfObject := HIGH(object1) + 1;
  NumberObjects    := (HIGH(ObjectArray) + 1)
                        DIV WordSizeOfObject;

  createheap;
  FOR i := NumberObjects TO 2 BY -1 DO
    interchange(1,i);
    adjust(i-1);
  END (* for loop *);
  END GenericHeapSort;

END GenericSorting.
```

The first parameter of each procedure is the list to be sorted. It is an in/out mode parameter, used both to send the list to the procedure and to return the sorted list. The next two parameters are sample objects of the data type of the objects in the list. The procedures use these for local temporary storage and for determining the size of an object.

The fourth parameter is a procedure parameter used by the sorting procedure to determine which of two objects is greater. Since the sorting procedure cannot know what type of data will be given, it cannot know how to compare objects. If the objects are of a user-defined record type, comparing them may be complex, involving several individual fields. A simple bit-by-bit comparison would not necessarily give the correct result. The actual parameter supplied by the client module must be a procedure with a matching parameter list. It must specify both parameters to be of type ARRAY OF WORD and must return a boolean value. For example, even though real numbers can be compared directly, a procedure such as the following would be necessary.

```
PROCEDURE RealGreater
  ( r1 : ARRAY OF WORD;
    r2 : ARRAY OF WORD ) : BOOLEAN;

  VAR p1, p2 : POINTER TO REAL;
BEGIN
  p1 := ADR ( r1 );
  p2 := ADR ( r2 );
  RETURN p1^ > p2^
END RealGreater;
```

The procedures getobject and interchange are slightly different for the two sorting procedures because of the index requirements of the different sorting algorithms.

The heap sort is significantly faster than the exchange sort. For example, in a test performed on a Sage IV computer using the Volition Systems Modula-2 compiler, the time to sort 3000 real numbers was 7 minutes; 17.92 seconds for the heap sort; and 3 hours, 54 minutes, 52.57 seconds for the exchange sort.

13.4 Summary

Modula-2 provides a variety of features for low level machine access. These features are exported from the module SYSTEM, a special module that is actually built into the compiler. These features are machine dependent, and their use greatly reduces the portability of software systems. Implementations are free to provide features not described in this chapter, so programmers should consult their language documentation carefully before attempting low level machine access.

The BYTE and WORD data types provide a way to define formal parameters that may be bound to actual parameters of any data type. This capability allows the development of generic data and functional abstractions. The ADDRESS data type and ADR procedure permit manipulation of machine memory addresses, facilitating the implementation of all kinds of dynamic data structures. The SIZE and TSIZE procedures provide a somewhat implementation-independent way of determining the size of data objects.

The use of these low level abstractions often allows the programmer to circumvent one of Modula-2's strong typing rules, and therefore opens the door to all kinds of subtle programming errors. The use of these features requires discipline on the part of the programmer. The best rule of thumb is that these features should be used only in the implementations of slightly higher level abstractions, and not in very high level modules or applications.

13.5 Exercises

1. Determine the differences between the SYSTEM module presented here and the one in your implementation.

2. Determine the sizes of objects of the word, cardinal, integer, real, and bitset data types in your implementation.

3. With what data types are WORD and ADDRESS compatible? What operations are defined on these data types?

4. In the packed record example in Section 13.2 we assumed that a word, a cardinal, and a bitset all occupied the same amount of storage. How could the technique be modified if these three data types were of different sizes? Remember that type transfers using type identifiers as functions requires that the types be the same size.

5. How could the generic sorting procedures of Section 13.3 be modified so that only a single parameter of the type being sorted would need to be supplied to the procedure?

6. If a character is smaller than a word in your implementation, and a single character is passed to a procedure with the formal parameter being of type ARRAY OF WORD, what value should the HIGH function procedure return for that parameter?

7. Develop a useful memory dump module, based on the techniques of Section 13.2.

14

Static Data Structures

We have seen that the concept of *data type* is central to the understanding of a programming language like Modula-2. In this chapter and the next we look at ways of representing a wide range of data types. In Chapter 17 we will see how a knowledge of data types leads to a very powerful technique of software design.

In Chapter 4 we defined a data type to be a pair, consisting of a set of values and a set of operations on those values; we also examined the predefined data types of Modula-2. In Chapter 12 we discussed the use of definition and implementation modules to define additional *abstract data types*. Of course, the term "abstract" is relative. As high level language programmers, we often consider data types such as integer and real to be concrete (not abstract), while a machine language programmer may consider these types to be abstract, especially on small computers that do not have hardware for real arithmetic. For our purposes, however, any data type not predefined in Modula-2 is considered to be abstract.

Before a new data type will do us any good, we must have a way to represent that type in our programming language. We must find two mappings, one from the conceptual set of values to values that can be represented in the language, and the other from the conceptual set of operations to operations that can be represented in the language. The first mapping, which may be defined using the various predefined types and type constructors of Modula-2, is called a *data structure*. The second mapping simply requires a way of implementing

205

functional abstractions, which we now know can be implemented as *proce-dures*. Thus a data type may be implemented as a data structure plus a set of procedures. We have already discussed procedures, so now we concentrate on data structures.

The two categories of attributes of data structures that concern us are *size* and *allocation*. In Section 4.2 we distinguished fixed size and varying size data structures according to how much storage was required to hold the structure at various times during execution of a program. Data structures of array and record types were seen to be fixed size, whereas data structures of file types were varying size. We also want to consider *static* and *dynamic* allocation of data structures. A statically allocated data structure uses the same amount of storage, at the same location, throughout the lifetime of the structure; a dynam-ically allocated data structure uses storage whose size or location (or both) may change during its lifetime. The size and allocation attributes of a data structure are independent. It is common for a fixed size structure to be either static or dynamic. A varying size structure is usually dynamic, but can be static under certain circumstances.

We must consider two kinds of dynamic allocation. In programming lan-guages like Modula-2, the storage available for data is divided into two concep-tual parts, commonly called the *stack* and the *heap*. The programming language itself determines when and how storage from the stack is allocated. This usu-ally consists of allocation of storage for parameters and local variables upon entering a procedure, and deallocating that storage upon exit. Because of the nesting of procedures, exits from procedures occur in the reverse order of the entries. The one-end-only access method of a stack (see Section 14.1) provides exactly the kind of allocation needed. Allocation on the stack is totally invisible to the programmer, and is often called *automatic* dynamic allocation. In most implementations of Modula-2, all storage is allocated from either the stack or the heap, so all storage is dynamic. Because the stack allocation is automatic and invisible, we often think of it as static. The programmer has no way to change the size or location of a data structure on the stack.

Storage on the heap is allocated and deallocated only upon specific re-quest from the programmer, and is often called *controlled* dynamic allocation. With this freedom of allocation come added responsibilities, as will be seen in the next chapter. In this chapter we consider statically allocated data struc-tures.

14.1 The Stack Data Type (Static Allocation)

Many problems exhibit a hierarchical structure of the data, and the processing requires similar operations at each level of the hierarchy. A program often must maintain certain values as it proceeds alternately up and down the hierar-chy, with those values being retrieved in the reverse order of their creation. A data structure that maintains a sequence of values, and allows new values to be added or old ones retrieved only from one end, is commonly called a *stack.* In this section we consider the design and implementation of a stack data type.

A stack may be classified as a varying size, homogeneous data structure, with a new kind of access method: one-end-only. A stack is a linear sequence of elements, and accesses may occur only at the specified end. Because of the similarity with physical stacks, such as the trays or plates at a cafeteria, the end at which accesses occur is called the *top* of the stack. A new element may be put in the sequence, by what is called a *push,* or the element currently at the top may be removed, by a *pop.* Other operations on stacks include the creation of an empty stack, which is a sequence with no elements, and testing the stack to determine whether it is empty.

Since a stack is a homogeneous linear sequence, it resembles an array, and we use an array data structure to hold the values of a stack. An array is a direct access structure, but we can limit the access to one-end-only by appropriate design of the procedures that implement the stack operations. We also need a variable to keep track of the top of the stack, which will be the subscript of the last element pushed on the stack. To combine the array and the top variable into a single data structure, we will use a record.

Figure 14.1 shows two stacks whose elements are integers. The first stack contains 10 and -2, and from the second we can see the result of a pop operation. Some elements of the array that holds the stack values are unknown or undefined; these are indicated by empty boxes. Notice that the array in the second stack has not changed, but the top variable has.

The definition and implementation modules for the stack data type are shown in Programs 14.1 and 14.2. We should note several things about these modules.

First, like an array, a stack is not a single data type but a type constructor. Different stack types may be defined for different element types. To make this example more general, we have not chosen a specific element type but have

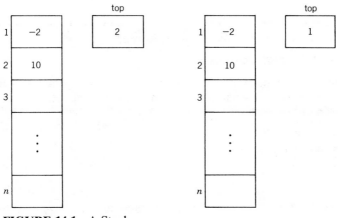

FIGURE 14.1 A Stack

Program 14.1   Stack Definition Module

```
DEFINITION MODULE stackadt;

   (* This module defines the public interface of the stack abstract data
      type. It imports the type "elementtype" which is the type of data
      objects to be stored in the stack. *)

FROM elements IMPORT
   (* type *) elementtype;

EXPORT QUALIFIED
   (* type *) stack,
   (* proc *) makeempty, empty, push, pop;

CONST
   stackmax = 100;      (* maximum number of items in a stack *)

TYPE
   stack    = RECORD
                space : ARRAY [ 1..stackmax ] OF elementtype;
                top    : [ 0..stackmax ]
              END;

PROCEDURE makeempty
   ( VAR s    : stack        (* out     *) );

PROCEDURE empty
   (     s    : stack        (* in      *) ) : BOOLEAN;

PROCEDURE push
   ( VAR s    : stack        (* in/out *);
         item : elementtype (* in      *) );

PROCEDURE pop
   ( VAR s    : stack        (* in/out *);
     VAR item : elementtype (* out     *) );

END stackadt.
```

Program 14.2   Stack Implementation Module

```
IMPLEMENTATION MODULE stackadt;

   (* This module is a static implementation of the stack abstract data type.
      It imports the type "elementtype" which is the type of data objects to
      be stored in the stack. *)

FROM elements IMPORT
   (* type *) elementtype;

PROCEDURE stackerror;

BEGIN
   (* error handling procedure: recovery, message, abort, etc. *)
END stackerror;
```

```
PROCEDURE makeempty
  ( VAR s    : stack         (* out    *) );
BEGIN
  s.top  := 0
END makeempty;

PROCEDURE empty
  (      s    : stack         (* in     *) ) : BOOLEAN;

BEGIN
  RETURN s.top = 0
END empty;

PROCEDURE stackfull
  (      s    : stack         (* in     *) ) : BOOLEAN;

BEGIN
  RETURN s.top = stackmax
END stackfull;

PROCEDURE push
  ( VAR s    : stack         (* in/out *);
        item : elementtype (* in     *) );
BEGIN
  IF NOT stackfull ( s )
    THEN INC ( s.top );
         s.space[ s.top ] := item
    ELSE stackerror
  END
END push;

PROCEDURE pop
  ( VAR s    : stack         (* in/out *);
    VAR item : elementtype (* out    *) );

BEGIN
  IF NOT empty ( s )
    THEN item := s.space[ s.top ];
         DEC ( s.top )
    ELSE stackerror
  END
END pop;

END stackadt.
```

assumed that some other module will provide that type. We have therefore imported the type elementtype from a module named elements.

Second, since we are using an array to hold the stack values, we have limited the maximum size of the stack to the declared size of the array. We can think of the stack as being of varying size as long as that size is no greater than the size of the array. At the implementation level, we might consider this stack to be of fixed size, but conceptually we will continue to classify a stack as a structure of varying size.

Third, not all stack operations are defined for all values. This is not an unusual situation; for example, division of numeric values is not defined when the divisor is zero. Undefined stack operations are attempting to pop an empty stack and attempting to push a full stack. Our implementation includes a stack error procedure whose action is undefined. Each program that uses the stack data type should supply an appropriate action, such as printing a message or aborting the program.

Fourth, the user of the stack data type is not aware of the implementation. The definition module defines a maximum stack size, but it does not export that constant (see, however, Appendix 3). The user thinks of the stack as capable of being arbitrarily large; hence the concept of a full stack does not exist. For this particular implementation, a full stack is a very real possibility. The implementation module supplies a function procedure to recognize a full stack, but this operation is not defined in the definition module. Such a *private* procedure or operation is common in the implementation module of an abstract data type. In Section 15.2 we develop another implementation of the stack data type that can never be full.

Fifth, the stack is implemented as a transparent type. This opens the door for potential abuse of the data structure by the programmer of a client module. Any access of the data structure other than through the exported procedures is conceptually prohibited, but the compiler cannot enforce this prohibition for a transparent type.

We have chosen a transparent stack type for two reasons. First, we wish to contrast transparent types implemented by static data structures in this chapter with opaque types implemented by dynamic data structures in the next chapter. Second, although this stack implementation is limited in size and offers potential for abuse, its simplicity makes it suitable for rapid software prototyping (see Section 17.3).

14.2   The Queue Data Type (Static Allocation)

The phrase "first come, first served" characterizes many real-life situations, and also the way data are processed in many programming applications. In such situations, values are produced at one point in a program, saved temporarily, and processed at another point in the program. To retrieve the values in the same order in which they were created, we need a data structure that maintains a sequence of values and allows new values to be added only at one end, and old values to be retrieved only at the other end. Such a data structure is called a *queue,* borrowing the term used for such real-life situations as queueing up at the ticket window of a theater. The term "queue" is more common in British English than in American English. However, the more common American usage "line" has other meanings as well, so "queue" is the preferred term.

A queue may be classified as a varying size, homogeneous data structure, with a new kind of access method: insert at one end, remove at the other end. A queue is a linear sequence of elements, and the two ends are called the *front* and the *rear*. A new element may be put in the sequence at the rear, or the front element may be removed from the sequence. Other operations on queues include the creation of an empty queue, which is a sequence with no elements, and testing the queue to determine whether it is empty.

The idea behind the implementation is virtually identical to that of the stack described in the preceding section. The major differences are the inclusion of both front and rear variables in the record, and the restriction of accesses to the appropriate end of the queue. Figure 14.2 shows two diagrams of a queue whose elements are integers. In the first, the queue contains the elements 5, 7, and 0; the second diagram shows the same queue after inserting the element 25. Note that the *front* variable always points to (contains the subscript of) the empty space just before the front element. This simplifies the recognition of full and empty queues.

One other point should be noted. As the insert and remove operations are performed, the portion of the array that contains queue elements migrates through the array. When that portion reaches the end of the array, we allow it to wrap around to the beginning of the array again; this is accomplished quite easily by incrementing the front and rear variables modulo the queue size.

Figure 14.3 shows a queue before and after an insertion that causes the full section of the array to wrap around.

A sequence of insertions might allow the rear variable to be incremented enough times to catch up to the front, while a sequence of removals might allow

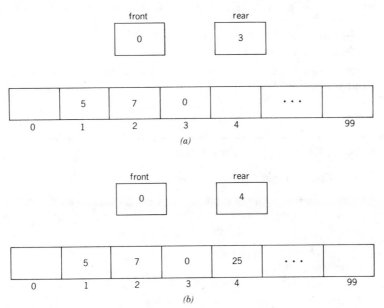

FIGURE 14.2   A Queue Before (*a*) and After (*b*) Insertion

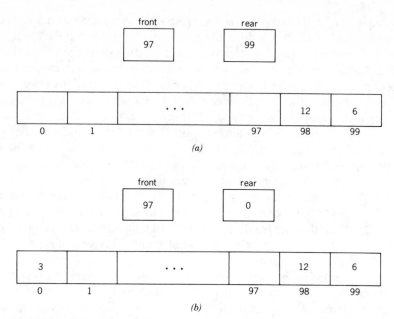

FIGURE 14.3 Wrap Around in a Queue Before (*a*) and After (*b*) Insertion

the front variable to catch up with the rear. To distinguish full and empty queues, we adopt the convention of stopping insertions one element short of rear catching up to front. Thus when front and rear are equal, we have an empty queue, and when front is one greater than rear, the queue is full (Figure 14.4).

The definition and implementation modules for the queue abstract data type are shown in Programs 14.3 and 14.4.

The queue data type has many applications in such areas as operating systems and simulation. We will see examples of queue applications in Chapters 16 and 17.

Program 14.3 Queue Definition Module

DEFINITION MODULE queueadt;

  (∗ This module defines the public interface of the queue abstract data
    type. It imports the type "elementtype" which is the type of data
    objects to be stored in the queue. ∗)

FROM elements IMPORT
  (∗ type ∗) elementtype;

EXPORT QUALIFIED
  (∗ type ∗) queue,
  (∗ proc ∗) makeempty, empty, insert, remove;

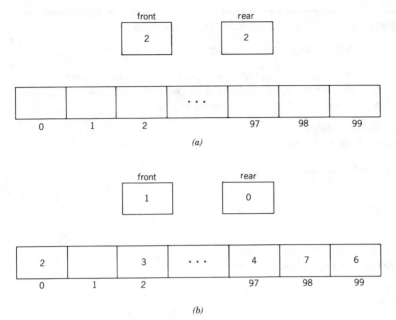

FIGURE 14.4 Empty (*a*) and Full (*b*) Queues

```
CONST
  queuesize   = 100;    (* maximum space in queue *)
  queuemax    = queuesize + 1;

TYPE
  queuerange  = [ 0..queuesize ];
  queue       = RECORD
                  space : ARRAY queuerange OF elementtype;
                  front : queuerange;
                  rear  : queuerange
                END;

PROCEDURE makeempty
  ( VAR q   : queue        (* out    *) );

PROCEDURE empty
  (     q   : queue        (* in     *) ) : BOOLEAN;

PROCEDURE insert
  ( VAR q   : queue        (* in/out *);
        item : elementtype (* in     *) );

PROCEDURE remove
  ( VAR q   : queue        (* in/out *);
    VAR item : elementtype (* out    *) );

END queueadt.
```

Program 14.4   Queue Implementation Module

```
IMPLEMENTATION MODULE queueadt;

  (* This module defines the implementation of the queue abstract data
     type. It imports the type "elementtype" which is the type of data
     objects to be stored in the queue. *)

FROM elements IMPORT
  (* type *) elementtype;

PROCEDURE queueerror;

BEGIN
  (* error handling procedure: recovery, message, abort, etc. *)
END queueerror;

PROCEDURE makeempty
  ( VAR q : queue (* out *) );

BEGIN
  q.front :=   0;
  q.rear  :=   0
END makeempty;

PROCEDURE empty
  (     q   : queue        (* in      *) ) : BOOLEAN;

BEGIN
  RETURN q.front = q.rear
END empty;

PROCEDURE full
  (     q   : queue        (* in      *) ) : BOOLEAN;

BEGIN
  RETURN q.front = ( q.rear + 1 ) MOD queuemax
END full;

PROCEDURE insert
  ( VAR q   : queue        (* in/out *);
        item : elementtype (* in      *) );

BEGIN
  IF NOT full ( q )
    THEN q.rear := ( q.rear + 1 ) MOD queuemax;
         q.space[ q.rear ] := item
    ELSE queueerror
  END
END insert;

PROCEDURE remove
  ( VAR q   : queue        (* in/out *);
    VAR item : elementtype (* out     *)  );
```

```
BEGIN
  IF NOT empty ( q )
    THEN q.front := ( q.front + 1 ) MOD queuemax;
         item := q.space[ q.front ]
    ELSE queueerror
  END
END remove;

END queueadt.
```

14.3 The String Data Type (Static Allocation)

The *character string* data type is one of the most often used structured data types, although many programs need only a very limited set of string operations. Many applications areas, however, call for a more complete string abstract data type. Text editing is a common example of such an application, but nearly all programs that process textual information can use this data type. This includes most programs that interact with a user at a terminal, since terminals can deal with character sequences only.

A string may be classified as a varying size, homogeneous data structure, in which all elements are characters. The access methods depend on the operations involved; but since some operations require direct access, we will so classify the string type.

The set of values of the string type is the set of sequences of zero or more characters. The set of operations is quite large, with different operations common for different applications. We consider here a representative set of operations.

Our implementation uses an array to hold the characters. The index type of the array is a cardinal subrange beginning at one; thus we number the character positions in a string beginning at one. To represent a varying length string in a fixed length array, we also keep a length variable with each string. The character array and the length are combined into a single entity by using a record.

Since Modula-2 provides a kind of string data type (an array of characters), it is desirable to be able to convert that kind of string into our kind. Two operations are provided to do this. The procedure convertarray converts an array of characters to a string, and the procedure convertliteral converts a Modula-2 literal string to our data structure.

Other simple operations are reading and writing strings, comparing strings for equality or inequality, and determining the current length of a string. The other string operations in this implementation include the following:

Concatenation: append one string to the end of a second, producing a new third string.
Search: search a given string for an occurrence of a second string, beginning

at or after a specified position; return the position of the start of that occurrence.

Delete: delete characters at a specified position in a string.

Insert: insert a copy of a string into another string at a specified position.

Extract: copy characters at a specified position in a string, producing another string.

The definition module for the string abstract data type is shown in Program 14.5. The purposes of the parameters are discussed in detail in the description of the implementation module.

Program 14.5   String Definition Module

```
DEFINITION MODULE string;

  (* This module defines a static string abstract data type. *)

FROM FileSystem IMPORT
  (* type *) File;

EXPORT QUALIFIED
  (* type *) string,
  (* proc *) concatenate, search, delete, insert, extract,
             length, equal, lessthan, readstring,
             writestring, convertarray, convertliteral;

  CONST stringsize = 100;

  TYPE    string    = RECORD
                        ch : ARRAY [ 1..stringsize ] OF CHAR;
                        len : [ 0..stringsize ]
                      END;

PROCEDURE concatenate
  (      str1     : string              (* in    *);
         str2     : string              (* in    *);
    VAR result    : string              (* out   *) );

PROCEDURE search
  (      str      : string              (* in    *);
         pattern  : string              (* in    *);
         start    : CARDINAL            (* in    *);
    VAR loc       : CARDINAL            (* out   *) );

PROCEDURE delete
  ( VAR str       : string              (* in/out *);
         start    : CARDINAL            (* in    *);
         count    : CARDINAL            (* in    *) );

PROCEDURE insert
  ( VAR str       : string              (* in/out *);
         substr   : string              (* in    *);
         start    : CARDINAL            (* in    *) );
```

```
PROCEDURE extract
    (       str        : string            (* in     *);
            start      : CARDINAL          (* in     *);
            count      : CARDINAL          (* in     *);
       VAR substr      : string            (* out    *) );

PROCEDURE length
    (       str        : string            (* in     *) ) : CARDINAL;

PROCEDURE equal
    (       str1       : string            (* in     *);
            str2       : string            (* in     *) ) : BOOLEAN;

PROCEDURE lessthan
    (       str1       : string            (* in     *);
            str2       : string            (* in     *) ) : BOOLEAN;

PROCEDURE readstring
    ( VAR infile       : File              (* in/out *);
      VAR str          : string            (* out    *);
          terminator : CHAR                (* in     *) );

PROCEDURE writestring
    ( VAR outfile      : File              (* in/out *);
          str          : string            (* in     *) );

PROCEDURE convertarray
    (       chars      : ARRAY OF CHAR (* in     *);
            count      : CARDINAL          (* in     *);
       VAR str         : string            (* out    *) );

PROCEDURE convertliteral
    (       chars      : ARRAY OF CHAR (* in     *);
       VAR str         : string            (* out    *) );
END string.
```

The skeleton of the string implementation module is shown in Program 14.6. The procedures that implement the string operations are displayed separately on the next several pages, along with explanations of their parameters and algorithms.

Program 14.6 String Implementation Module Skeleton

```
IMPLEMENTATION MODULE string;

    (* This module implements a static string abstract data type. *)

FROM FileSystem IMPORT
    (* type *) File,
    (* proc *) ReadChar, WriteChar, EOL, Eof;
FROM Arithmetic IMPORT
    (* proc *) mincard;

    (* string operations procedures *)

END string.
```

Program 14.7   String Concatenate Procedure

```
PROCEDURE concatenate
   (      str1   : string (* in   *);
          str2   : string (* in   *);
    VAR result : string (* out *)  );

   VAR temp : string;
       pos  : CARDINAL;
BEGIN
   temp := str1;
   pos  := 0;
   WHILE ( temp.len < stringsize ) AND ( pos < str2.len ) DO
      INC ( temp.len );
      INC ( pos );
      temp.ch[ temp.len ] := str2.ch[ pos ]
   END;
   result := temp
END concatenate;
```

The concatenate operation (Program 14.7) is given two strings, named str1 and str2, and produces a third string, named result, which contains a copy of str1 followed by a copy of str2. We must allow for the case in which the user of this procedure sends the same parameter for result as for either or both of the other strings. We do not want to destroy a string before all its characters have been copied. Therefore this procedure uses a local string variable named temp to hold the concatenated strings, and then copies the temp string to the result string.

It might be suggested that since str1 and str2 are value parameters, they have already been copied before the concatenation begins, and thus even if the result string is str1 or str2, the operation will proceed correctly. However, not all compilers will implement value parameters by copying the value. Furthermore, if execution speed is important, we might change the parameter binding mechanism for str1 and str2 to call-by-reference by preceding each with the symbol VAR in the formal parameter list. For many Modula-2 implementations, this would cause only the address to be passed to the procedure, not a copy of the entire string, and thus would be faster. Many programmers will do this as a matter of course for parameters that occupy a large block of storage. Note that the parameter modes of str1 and str2 remain *in*, even if we pass them by reference.

It is possible for the sum of the lengths of str1 and str2 to exceed the maximum string size (the constant stringsize). If this occurs, the extra characters are lost. This is an unfortunate situation, but it is inherent in data types that use static allocation. The problem is addressed and solved in Section 15.4.

The search operation (Program 14.8) attempts to match a pattern string within another string. The string to be searched is given in the parameter named str, and the string to be found is given in the parameter named pattern. To

Program 14.8   String Search Procedure

```
PROCEDURE search
   (      str      : string      (* in  *);
          pattern  : string      (* in  *);
          start    : CARDINAL (* in  *);
      VAR location : CARDINAL (* out *)  );

   VAR found : BOOLEAN;
       pos   : CARDINAL;
BEGIN
   found := FALSE;
   IF str.len >= pattern.len
      THEN location := start - 1;
         WHILE ( location <= str.len - pattern.len )
                 AND NOT found DO
            INC ( location );
            pos := 0;
            found := TRUE;
            WHILE found AND ( pos < pattern.len ) DO
               INC ( pos );
               found := str.ch[ location + pos - 1 ]
                      = pattern.ch[ pos ]
            END
         END
      END;
   IF NOT found THEN location := 0 END
END search;
```

facilitate a sequence of searches within the same string, a third parameter, named start, specifies the character position at which the search is to begin. The result of this operation is the position in str, greater than or equal to start, where the first occurrence of the pattern begins. If the search fails to find the pattern, the result is zero, by convention. The fourth parameter, named location, returns the result.

A sequence of searches may be made by specifying a value of one for the starting position for the first search and specifying each subsequent starting position to be the previous result location plus one. The searches may be terminated when the result location becomes zero.

The delete operation (Program 14.9) removes characters from a string. The string is given in the parameter named str, the starting position of the deletion is given in start, and the number of characters to be deleted is given in count. The characters after the deleted ones are moved to give a result string with no gaps.

The start position must be within the string, and all the characters to be deleted must be in the string. Thus if the start position plus the count exceeds the string length, it is considered to be an error, and no deletion occurs.

It may be desirable to delete a known substring from a string. This can be

Program 14.9 String Delete Procedure

```
PROCEDURE delete
  ( VAR str    : string      (* in/out *);
        start  : CARDINAL (* in    *);
        count : CARDINAL (* in    *) );

  VAR pos : CARDINAL;

BEGIN
  IF ( start >= 1 ) AND ( start + count - 1 <= str.len )
    THEN FOR pos := start TO str.len - count DO
            str.ch[ pos ] := str.ch[ pos + count ]
         END;
         DEC ( str.len, count )
  END
END delete;
```

accomplished by first searching for the substring using the search operation, and then using the delete operation beginning at the position returned by the search. The length function below may be used to specify how many characters to delete.

The insert operation (Program 14.10) puts a copy of a substring into another string. The string into which the insertion is made is given in the parameter named str. The inserted substring is given in substr, and the starting position of the insertion is given in start. After the insertion, the first character of the substring will be at position start in the new string. The original string is

Program 14.10 String Insert Procedure

```
PROCEDURE insert
  ( VAR str    : string     (* in/out *);
        substr : string     (* in    *);
        start  : CARDINAL (* in    *) );

  VAR pos : CARDINAL;

BEGIN
  IF ( start >= 1 ) AND ( start <= str.len + 1 )
    THEN FOR pos := mincard ( str.len, stringsize - substr.len )
                         TO start BY -1 DO
            str.ch[ pos + substr.len ] := str.ch[ pos ];
         END;
         FOR pos := 0 TO mincard ( substr.len,
                                   stringsize - start + 1 ) DO
            str.ch[ start + pos ] := substr.ch[ pos + 1 ]
         END
  END
END insert;
```

opened up to allow the insertion; that is, the characters at and after the start position are moved as many positions as the inserted substring is long.

The starting position must be within the given string. If the insertion causes the string to grow to a length greater than the maximum string size (the constant named stringsize), the extra characters are lost.

This procedure uses the function procedure named mincard, imported from the Arithmetic module, to determine the minimum value of two cardinal values. See Section 10.3 for additional information on the Arithmetic module.

The extract operation (Program 14.11) makes a copy of part of a string.

Program 14.11 String Extract Procedure

```
PROCEDURE extract
  (      str    : string    (* in  *);
         start  : CARDINAL (* in  *);
         count  : CARDINAL (* in  *);
    VAR substr : string      (* out *) );

  VAR pos : CARDINAL;

BEGIN
  IF ( start >= 1 ) AND ( start + count - 1 <= str.len )
    THEN FOR pos := 1 TO count DO
            substr.ch[ pos ] := str.ch[ start + pos - 1 ]
         END;
         substr.len := count
    ELSE substr.len := 0
  END
END extract;
```

The first three parameters are similar to those of the delete operation: the string from which the characters are to be extracted, the starting position of the extraction, and the number of characters to be extracted. The parameter mode of str is in, implying that the string is not changed in any way. Only a copy of the extracted characters is made, and that copy is returned in the parameter named substr.

The same error that is possible with delete can occur here if the start position plus the count exceeds the string length. In this case, the resulting value of substr is the empty string.

The length operation (Program 14.12) is a function procedure that returns

---

Program 14.12 String Length Procedure

```
PROCEDURE length
  ( str : string (* in *) ) : CARDINAL;

BEGIN
  RETURN str.len
END length;
```

the length of the string. This kind of function is common in an abstract data type, because in general, the user of the type is unaware of the internal structure of a value of that type. For this string implementation, we assume that the user does not know that a string is represented by a record, and that a field within that record contains the length. This kind of function is essential for opaque types, as will be seen in the next chapter.

The equal operation (Program 14.13) determines whether two given

---

Program 14.13   String Equal Procedure

```
PROCEDURE equal
  ( str1 : string (* in *);
    str2 : string (* in *) ) : BOOLEAN;

  VAR pos : CARDINAL;

BEGIN
  IF str1.len = str2.len
    THEN pos := 1;
      WHILE ( str1.ch[ pos ] = str2.ch[ pos ] ) AND
            ( pos < str1.len ) DO
        INC ( pos )
      END;
      RETURN str1.ch[ pos ] = str2.ch[ pos ]
    ELSE RETURN FALSE
  END
END equal;
```

---

strings are equal. Notice that it is not possible simply to compare two string variables with the Modula-2 equality operator, since the operator is not defined on records or arrays. Even if it were, it would yield incorrect results. Only part of the array field ch of a string contains valid characters; the rest of the array may contain unknown values. Two string variables of length five may have the first five characters in their respective arrays equal, but the remaining characters may not be equal.

The less than operation (Program 14.14) determines whether the first string is alphabetically less than the second string. For the reasons described for the equal operation, we cannot simply use the Modula-2 less than operator.

This procedure compares characters in the two strings, beginning in position one, until either the end of the shorter string is reached or two unequal characters are found. In the former case, by convention, we determine the shorter string to be less than the longer string.

The read string operation (Program 14.15) reads a string from a file. The first parameter, named infile, is the file from which the reading is done. This can be the predefined terminal file if the first actual parameter is the name of that file (in many implementations, its name is in or input). The second parameter is the string to be read. The third parameter, terminator, is the character that marks the end of a string. In many cases this may be the predefined

Program 14.14 String Less Than Procedure

```
PROCEDURE lessthan
  ( str1 : string (* in *);
    str2 : string (* in *) ) : BOOLEAN;

  VAR pos : CARDINAL;
      limit : CARDINAL;
BEGIN
  limit := mincard ( str1.len, str2.len );
  pos := 1;
  WHILE ( str1.ch[ pos ] = str2.ch[ pos ] ) AND
        ( pos < limit ) DO
    INC ( pos )
  END;
  IF str1.ch[ pos ] = str2.ch[ pos ]
    THEN RETURN str1.len < str2.len
    ELSE RETURN str1.ch[ pos ] < str2.ch[ pos ]
  END
END lessthan;
```

Program 14.15 Read String Procedure

```
PROCEDURE readstring
  ( VAR infile    : File    (* in/out *);
    VAR str       : string (* out    *);
        terminator : CHAR (* in      *) );

  VAR character : CHAR;
BEGIN
  WITH str DO
    len := 0;
    LOOP
      IF Eof ( infile ) THEN EXIT END;
      INC ( len );
      ReadChar ( infile, ch[ len ] );
      IF ch[ len ] = terminator
        THEN DEC ( len ); (* terminator not returned in string *)
             EXIT
      END;
      IF len = stringsize
        THEN LOOP
               IF Eof ( infile ) THEN EXIT END;
               ReadChar ( infile, character );
               IF character = terminator THEN EXIT END
             END;
             EXIT
      END
    END
  END
END readstring;
```

character EOL, which would cause an entire input line to be read as a single string. In other cases we might specify a blank as the terminator, which would cause only characters up to the next blank to be read. In any case, the terminator character is not placed in the string. The program that invokes this procedure knows what the terminator character is, since it supplied it.

The file parameter of this procedure is designated to be of the in/out mode. This is usually the case, since reading from a file does change the current file position.

The write string operation (Program 14.16) writes the string str to the file

---

Program 14.16 Write String Procedure

```
PROCEDURE writestring
  ( VAR outfile : File    (* in/out *);
        str      : string (* in      *) );

  VAR pos : CARDINAL;
BEGIN
  FOR pos := 1 TO str.len DO
    WriteChar ( outfile, str.ch[ pos ] )
  END
END writestring;
```

outfile. As for the read string operation, the predefined terminal file may be supplied as the actual parameter if terminal output is desired.

Note that it is not possible to use the procedure WriteString in the InOut module to write the characters, even if we want to write to the terminal. The statement WriteString (str.ch) is syntactically correct, but it will always write the entire array. In general, only part of the array contains meaningful characters, so we must use an explicit loop that writes only those characters.

The convert array operation (Program 14.17) may be thought of as a type conversion function, since it converts a character array to our string data structure. The first parameter is an array of characters, which may be of any size and may have any index type. Such an array is commonly called a string by Modula-2 programmers. This formal parameter is an open array type, which is always assumed to have cardinal subscripts beginning at zero. The second parameter specifies how many characters are to be copied from the array, and this value may not always be the size of the array. This makes it possible for a programmer to convert an array that is not completely filled. The resulting string is returned in the third parameter, str.

As in the other procedures that create strings, if too many characters are supplied, the extras are lost.

The convert literal operation (Program 14.18) is another type conversion function. It behaves like the convert array operation, except that no character count is provided. The entire array named chars is converted to our string data type. This operation is intended to be used primarily for converting string

Program 14.17   Convert Array Procedure

```
PROCEDURE convertarray
  (        chars : ARRAY OF CHAR (* in  *);
           count : CARDINAL        (* in  *);
     VAR str     : string          (* out *)  );

    VAR pos : CARDINAL;
BEGIN
  IF count < = stringsize
    THEN str.len := count
    ELSE str.len := stringsize
  END;
  FOR pos := 1 TO str.len DO
    str.ch[ pos ] := chars[ pos - 1 ]
  END
END convertarray;
```

Program 14.18   Convert Literal Procedure

```
PROCEDURE convertliteral
  (        chars : ARRAY OF CHAR (* in  *);
     VAR str     : string          (* out *)  );

BEGIN
  convertarray ( chars, HIGH ( chars ) + 1, str )
END convertliteral;
```

literals, but could also be used to convert array variables when the entire array is to be converted.

The body of this procedure is simply an invocation of the convertarray procedure above. The second parameter is determined using the predefined Modula-2 HIGH function, which returns the maximum subscript of a parameter of an open array type. Since the subscripts begin at zero, the length of the array is one greater than the maximum subscript.

14.4   The Character Set Data Type

The predefined set type BITSET and the other set types in most Modula-2 implementations severely limit the cardinality of sets, as described in Section 4.2.3. In many applications, larger sets are needed. In this section we demonstrate that the BITSET type can be used to construct a larger set abstract data type. For this example we choose the set of characters (assuming the ASCII character set) for the universe set from which sets will be constructed. Other applications may require even larger universe sets, but the same techniques may be used.

The operations on this abstract data type are taken directly from the operations defined in Modula-2 for the BITSET type. However, since we cannot attach new meanings to operator symbols, we will again use procedures and functions to implement the operations.

In the stack and queue data types described earlier in this chapter, we provided a procedure to give a special value, the empty stack or empty queue, to a variable. This kind of procedure is often needed, since it allows us to establish the loop invariant for a loop that uses a stack or queue to save values. We illustrate another approach to this idea in this character set data type.

Since a data type is a set of values and a set of operations, it is only reasonable that the definition and implementation modules provide some values as well as procedures for the operations. In all the examples we have seen so far, only procedures and types were exported. In this example we also export a value, the *null set*. Unfortunately, Modula-2 does not allow us to define constants of array and record types, but we can define a variable of such a type. If the value of the variable never changes, it may be thought of as a constant. We use appropriate comments in the definition module to inform the reader or user that the variable named nullset is to be considered a constant outside the module.

The implementation module includes statements to give the nullset variable the appropriate value. These statements appear in the module initialization section, and thus are performed automatically at the beginning of the execution of any program that uses this module. The user need not be aware of the existence of this code.

If we wish to give a character set variable the value of the null set, we simply use the assignment statement

setvariable := nullset;

We therefore do not need to supply a procedure to create this special value, as we did for stacks and queues. Note that this technique is subject to abuse, in that a client module could change the value of the nullset variable.

This technique may be used to supply other values that may be of particular importance to users of an abstract data type. In this example, we might also supply a full set or universe set containing all the characters. Other useful sets are suggested in the exercises. For the stack and queue types, we could have supplied empty stack and empty queue values, rather than the procedures that create these values.

We should note that this technique works only for data types for which assignment is defined. This normally excludes dynamically allocated types, such as most opaque types. We consider this problem further in the next chapter.

The idea behind the implementation is to use several small sets (bitsets) to implement a large set. To access a particular element of the large set, its value is converted to two values that identify the small set in which the element may be found, and tell where it will be in that set. The binary set operations may be performed by operating on the small sets independently.

The definition and implementation modules for the charset abstract data type are shown in Programs 14.19 and 14.20, respectively. For most of the operations, the parameters of the in mode could have been made reference rather than value parameters to increase speed on many implementations. The reader should verify that this will not present the problems described for the concatenate operation in Section 14.3, even when the result parameter is the same as one of the other parameters.

Program 14.19   Character Set Definition Module

```
DEFINITION MODULE characterset;

  (* This module defines the character set data type.  The universe set is
     the 128 character ASCII set. *)

EXPORT QUALIFIED
  (* const *) nullset,
  (* type  *) charset,
  (* proc  *) include, exclude, union, intersection,
                diff, symdiff, inset;

CONST
  piecesize  =   32; (* = TSIZE( BITSET ) *)
  setsize    =  128; (* size of universe set *)
  pieces     =    4; (* setsize DIV piecesize, rounded up *)
  maxpiece = pieces - 1;

TYPE
  piecerange = [ 0..maxpiece ];
  charset    = ARRAY piecerange OF BITSET;

VAR
  nullset              : charset; (* behaves like constant *)

PROCEDURE include
  ( VAR   chset    : charset (* in/out *);
          ch       : CHAR   (* in     *) );

PROCEDURE exclude
  ( VAR   chset    : charset (* in/out *);
          ch       : CHAR   (* in     *) );

PROCEDURE union
  (       chset1   : charset (* in  *);
          chset2   : charset (* in  *);
    VAR   result   : charset (* out *) );

PROCEDURE intersection
  (       chset1   : charset (* in  *);
          chset2   : charset (* in  *);
    VAR   result   : charset (* out *) );
```

```
PROCEDURE diff
  (         chset1    : charset (* in     *);
            chset2    : charset (* in     *);
    VAR     result    : charset (* out    *) );

PROCEDURE symdiff
  (         chset1    : charset (* in     *);
            chset2    : charset (* in     *);
    VAR     result    : charset (* out    *) );

PROCEDURE inset
  (         ch        : CHAR    (* in     *);
            chset     : charset (* in     *) ) : BOOLEAN;

END characterset.
```

Program 14.20 Character Set Implementation Module

```
IMPLEMENTATION MODULE characterset;

  (* This module implements the character set data type.  The universe set
     is the 128 character ASCII set. *)

VAR
  piece : piecerange;

PROCEDURE include
  ( VAR    chset    : charset (* in/out *);
           ch       : CHAR    (* in     *) );

BEGIN
  INCL ( chset[ ORD ( ch ) DIV piecesize ], ORD ( ch ) MOD piecesize )
END include;

PROCEDURE exclude
  ( VAR    chset    : charset (* in/out *);
           ch       : CHAR    (* in     *) );

BEGIN
  EXCL ( chset[ ORD ( ch ) DIV piecesize ], ORD ( ch ) MOD piecesize )
END exclude;

PROCEDURE union
  (         chset1    : charset (* in     *);
            chset2    : charset (* in     *);
    VAR     result    : charset (* out    *) );

  VAR piece : piecerange;

BEGIN
  FOR piece := 0 TO maxpiece DO
    result[ piece ] := chset1[ piece ] + chset2[ piece ]
  END
END union;
```

```
PROCEDURE intersection
  (          chset1    : charset (* in      *);
             chset2    : charset (* in      *);
      VAR    result    : charset (* out     *) );

    VAR piece : piecerange;

BEGIN
  FOR piece := 0 TO maxpiece DO
    result[ piece ] := chset1[ piece ] * chset2[ piece ]
  END
END intersection;

PROCEDURE diff
  (          chset1    : charset (* in      *);
             chset2    : charset (* in      *);
      VAR    result    : charset (* out     *) );

    VAR piece : piecerange;

BEGIN
  FOR piece := 0 TO maxpiece DO
    result[ piece ] := chset1[ piece ] - chset2[ piece ]
  END
END diff;

PROCEDURE symdiff
  (          chset1    : charset (* in      *);
             chset2    : charset (* in      *);
      VAR    result    : charset (* out     *) );

    VAR piece : piecerange;

BEGIN
  FOR piece := 0 TO maxpiece DO
    result[ piece ] := chset1[ piece ] / chset2[ piece ]
  END
END symdiff;

PROCEDURE inset
  (          ch        : CHAR    (* in      *);
             chset     : charset (* in      *) ) : BOOLEAN:

BEGIN
  RETURN ORD ( ch ) MOD piecesize IN chset[ ORD ( ch ) DIV piecesize ]
END inset;

BEGIN
  (* create the null set *)
  FOR piece := 0 TO maxpiece DO
    nullset[ piece ] := { }
  END
END characterset.
```

14.5   Summary

Allocation of storage for data in Modula-2 takes two forms: automatic allocation on the stack and controlled allocation on the heap. Since the programmer
has no control over the storage on the stack, objects stored there must be of
fixed size and location.

Data structures that remain the same size and at the same location
throughout their lifetimes are called static. The value sets of many useful abstract data types may be represented by static data structures and represented
in Modula-2 as library (definition and implementation) modules.

In many implementations of the language, static data structures may be
used only for transparent types, since opaque types are necessarily dynamic.
The use of transparent types makes it possible for client modules to abuse the
data type by accessing its internal representation directly, rather than through
the operations defined for that type. To prevent such abuse, programmers must
develop a disciplined approach to using transparent types.

14.6   Exercises

1. Add two more operations to the stack data type. One should return the
   value currently at the top of the stack, but without removing it from the
   stack. The other should return a boolean value indicating whether the stack
   is full.

2. Add two more operations to the queue data type. One should return the
   value currently at the front of the queue, but without removing it from the
   queue. The other should return a boolean value indicating whether the
   queue is full.

3. Is it better for the set data type to define a constant (actually a variable)
   for the null set, or a procedure that creates a null set each time the value is
   needed? Consider the potential for abuse.

4. What other string operations might be useful? Consider applications such
   as text editing.

5. How can single characters be manipulated in strings? Add string operations
   to change a single character in a string and to extract a single character
   from a string. Is it possible with the existing operations to convert a single
   character to the string data structure?

6. Confirm that the parameters of the binary set operations could be changed
   from value to reference parameters without affecting the behavior of the
   operations.

7. Add subset, superset, and set complement operations to the character set
   data type.

8. Add character set constants (actually variables) for the alphabet, the lowercase alphabet, the uppercase alphabet, and the digits.

9. Show how the techniques for large sets can be used to provide the equivalent of the Pascal structure packed array of boolean.

10. Develop abstract data types implemented with static data structures for a program that maintains a telephone directory. Data types such as name, address, and telephone number should be defined first, along with appropriate operations such as input, output, and comparison. Then develop a directory entry type, and finally a directory type. Provide an alphabetize operation for the directory type.

15

Dynamic Data Structures

In Chapter 14 we saw examples of data types that can vary considerably in size: stack, queue, string, and set. The static (fixed size) allocation methods developed there worked for only a limited range of values of those types; large values simply could not be represented. That is an inherent problem with statically allocated data structures. If we attempt to avoid the problem by defining excessively large static data structures, we find that most of the storage is unused most of the time.

The solution is to use a *dynamic data structure,* which allows the amount of storage allocated to a particular value to change as the size of that value changes. In this chapter we see two approaches to the design of dynamic data structures, discovering that with the versatility comes an increased burden on the programmer to be disciplined in the use of these structures.

The first approach is quite simple. When an operation produces a new value larger than the currently allocated space for that value, we allocate all new storage of sufficient size for the value, and deallocate the old storage. This approach works for data types of all kinds, but when the operations result in many very small changes in the size of a very large data structure, it can be relatively inefficient. The second approach is to build a large data structure from many small pieces. Small changes in size can be accommodated by allocating or deallocating only one or a few pieces, not the entire structure. This approach also works for data types of all kinds, but usually requires substantially more storage than the first approach. Thus we have the classic tradeoff of software design, speed versus storage.

Both approaches require the programming language to have a means of allocating and deallocating storage on the heap. Pascal provides this capability in a simple way, via the new and dispose procedures. In their simplest (one-parameter) form, these procedures are given a parameter of a pointer type. The new procedure allocates a block of storage of sufficient size to hold one object of the base type of that pointer type and returns the address of that block in the pointer. The dispose procedure deallocates a previously allocated block; that is, it returns the storage occupied by that block to the heap so that it may be subsequently reallocated.

With this method, the programmer has no direct control over the size of the block allocated; the size is always determined by the size of an object of the base type of the pointer parameter. Modula-2 implementations always provide a more versatile method of storage allocation that does allow direct control over the size of blocks. The library module named Storage defines two procedures, ALLOCATE and DEALLOCATE, as shown in the definition module in Program 15.1.

Program 15.1 The Storage Definition Module

```
DEFINITION MODULE Storage;

FROM SYSTEM IMPORT
  (* type *) ADDRESS;

EXPORT QUALIFIED
  (* proc *) ALLOCATE, DEALLOCATE;

PROCEDURE ALLOCATE
  ( VAR blockaddress : ADDRESS  (* out    *);
        blocksize    : CARDINAL (* in     *) );

PROCEDURE DEALLOCATE
  ( VAR blockaddress : ADDRESS  (* in/out *);
        blocksize    : CARDINAL (* in     *) );

END Storage.
```

Both the procedures exported from this module have two parameters. The first is the address and the second is the size, measured in machine storage units, of the block to be allocated or deallocated. Since an allocation request is not tied to a particular pointer type, we have much more freedom in allocating storage for a wide variety of data types. We demonstrate the full power of this freedom in Section 15.4.

Modula-2 also provides the procedures NEW and DISPOSE, which behave just like those of Pascal, described above. However, the Modula-2 compiler translates invocations of these procedures into invocations of ALLOCATE and DEALLOCATE. Consider the following declarations.

```
TYPE ptr  = POINTER TO box;
     box = RECORD
                  name : ARRAY [ 1..20 ] OF CHAR;
                  size  : CARDINAL;
                  next  : ptr
            END;
     VAR  p     : ptr;
```

In either Modula-2 or Pascal, we can allocate storage for a box variable (which will be an anonymous variable) with the statement:

NEW (p);

which returns the address of the allocated storage in the variable p. In Modula-2 we can accomplish the same thing with the statement:

ALLOCATE (p, TSIZE (box));

In fact, the Modula-2 compiler translates the first statement above into the second. Similarly, the compiler translates:

DISPOSE (p);

into:

DEALLOCATE (p, TSIZE (box));

This is why every module that uses either the NEW or the DISPOSE procedure must explicitly import the procedures ALLOCATE and DEALLOCATE either from the standard Storage module or from a user-supplied module. We examine the implementation of such a module in Section 15.5.

Dynamic data structures are so versatile that they are indispensable for all but the simplest software systems. However, they present problems for programmers that can be overcome only by adopting a very disciplined approach to their use. We introduce these problems and their solutions first, putting these solutions into practice in the examples later in the chapter.

To examine the first problem, we begin by reviewing the concept of opaque type. A definition module may declare a type identifier without defining the type, using a declaration such as:

TYPE string;

The compiler assumes that the string type will be defined in the implementation module, usually as a pointer type, and that the base type of that pointer type either will be imported by the implementation module or will be defined in that module (see also Appendix 3). The type is called opaque because the user of that type, who has seen only the definition module, cannot look inside the type to see or access its internal structure.

A variable of an opaque type is physically simply a pointer variable, but conceptually we think of the variable as holding a complicated, structured value. We can, of course, store such values by dynamically allocating a block of storage for a value, and having the pointer contain the address of the block. Thus a value is physically stored as two parts, a statically allocated pointer and a dynamically allocated block of additional storage.

The problem we must consider is the meaning of the assignment and equal (or not equal) operators on objects of opaque types. We have already seen that these operators are defined on all statically allocated types in Modula-2, including pointers. What do they mean for dynamically allocated data? Consider the following statements.

```
TYPE person;        (* opaque type *)

VAR  teacher : person;
     student : person;

teacher := student;

IF teacher <> student THEN ...
```

The assignment statement is syntactically and semantically correct. The student variable is a pointer to a dynamically allocated block of storage, and the assignment makes the teacher variable also point to that block. We then have one copy of that block, but two pointers to that block. This is different from having two complete copies of the value, residing in two separately allocated blocks. If we really want two copies, the assignment statement will not do it.

The if statement is also correct, but it compares two pointers, not the blocks to which they point. If we have allocated the teacher and student variables separately, and put identical data in each, the inequality test in the if statement will succeed. The two pointers are not equal, since they are the addresses of different blocks. If we really want to compare the contents of those blocks, the Modula-2 equality and inequality operators will not do it.

To solve this problem, the programmer must define new operations, corresponding to assignment and equality, for each dynamically allocated data type used in a program. A procedure named copy might be defined that actually makes a copy of a value by allocating new storage and copying the existing value into it. A boolean function procedure named equal might be defined that compares the values of two dynamically allocated variables, rather than comparing the pointers to those variables. Note that standard names for these operations can be adopted for all data types and names exported from all modules that define abstract data types. Modula-2's ability to use qualified identifiers will allow us to distinguish these operations from one type to another. The data types described in this chapter illustrate this solution.

The second problem with dynamically allocated data types appears when local variables of such types are declared in a procedure. Programmers are used to having local variables disappear upon exit from a procedure. This occurs because local variables are allocated on the stack, and deallocated automatically at the end of the procedure. The value of an opaque type or other dynamically allocated type is allocated on the heap and therefore requires explicit deallocation if that storage is to be recovered. The pointer to that storage, however, is on the stack. This presents the possibility of the following sequence of events.

1. Enter a procedure, allocating a pointer on the stack.
2. Allocate storage with NEW or ALLOCATE, using that pointer.
3. Process the value in that storage area.
4. Exit the procedure, deallocating the pointer on the stack.

At this point, the dynamically allocated storage still exists, but the pointer to it is gone. It is impossible to deallocate this storage, and it is lost forever. If a procedure that makes this error is invoked repeatedly, it is possible to allocate and then lose the entire heap, which ultimately results in a program failure.

To solve this problem, a programmer must exercise great care to be sure to dispose of or deallocate the storage for all dynamically allocated local variables in all procedures. This will be seen again in the examples later.

The third problem occurs when a dynamically allocated variable changes its value more than once, as might happen when such a variable is used repeatedly in a loop. If a new value requires a different amount of storage, the usual technique is to deallocate the old storage and allocate a new block of the correct size. However, the first time a value is given to the variable, there is no old storage to deallocate. Therefore it must be possible to determine whether a block of storage is currently associated with a variable. This may seem to be a very simple test. For example, for a variable of an opaque type, if the pointer part has a value, deallocate the storage identified by that pointer; otherwise, just allocate the storage for the new value. This works when the pointer has been defined; but remember that all variables are undefined at the beginning of the program or procedure in which they are declared, and there is no way in Modula-2 to determine whether a variable is defined.

The solution to this problem is for a programmer to define all dynamically allocated variables immediately upon entry to the program or procedure where they are declared. For variables of opaque types this is a simple task; the variable is set to NIL. However, since the type is opaque, the programmer does not know that it is really a pointer and that it can therefore be set to NIL. Instead, each opaque type or other dynamically allocated type should provide a procedure, perhaps named define, that gives an appropriate value to a variable.

We should ask whether any of these problems has a counterpart for statically allocated variables. Assignment and equality test are both defined for static types, so there is no counterpart to the first problem above. Variables of static types are always allocated on the stack at procedure entry and deallocated at procedure exit, so there is no counterpart to the second problem. Can a variable of a static type be given a new value, even if its current value is undefined? Yes. Since the values of such a variable always occupies the same amount of storage at the same address, the new value simply overwrites the old value, even an undefined value. No storage can be lost.

We can now summarize the disciplined approach to the use of dynamically allocated data types.

Be aware that assignments, equal test, and not-equal test are syntactically correct for dynamically allocated types, but they usually do not perform the desired task. If these operations are needed, they should be defined in and exported from the modules for an abstract data type.

Whenever a variable of a dynamically allocated type is declared in a procedure, its storage must be deallocated immediately before exiting the procedure.

A dynamically allocated abstract data type should define and export a procedure to change a variable from undefined to defined. That procedure should be invoked each time a variable of that type is declared in a procedure, so that it is possible later to determine whether storage must be deallocated before the variable is given a new value.

These three rules are illustrated repeatedly in the examples. A programmer who learns this disciplined approach and uses it carefully will find it relatively easy to take advantage of the great power of dynamic data structures.

15.1   Linked Lists

A *linked list* is a data structure for implementing varying size, homogeneous, sequential access data types. It uses the approach described earlier of storing a structured value in many small, separately allocated blocks of storage. We develop the fundamental techniques of linked lists in this section, and apply these techniques to the implementation of abstract data types in later sections.

The original motivation for linked lists came from some inherent problems of arrays as data structures. Arrays are normally implemented as contiguous blocks of storage, which allows a simple address computation to find an element, given its index in the array. The price we pay for easy, direct access is inability to insert or delete extra storage in the array. That is why we classified arrays as fixed size data type constructors.

If we do not require the storage to be contiguous but allow it to be scattered throughout the computer system memory, we lose the order of the elements implied by contiguous storage, but gain the freedom to insert or delete storage. To maintain the order of elements, we associate with each element the address of the next element. Each element will be structured as a record, to combine a value and an address into a single entity.

We represent linked lists with diagrams such as that in Figure 15.1. Since the exact addresses of the elements are not important, we represent addresses as arrows or pointers. The boxes in the diagram represent the elements of the list, and are commonly called *nodes*. Each node contains two fields, one for the value of the element and the other for the address of the next element. The box with the diagonal line represents the nil pointer.

One fundamental technique is the construction of a linked list, such as might be required in a procedure that reads a value of an abstract data type

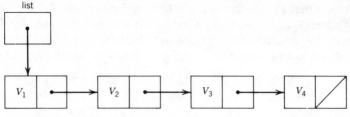

FIGURE 15.1   Linked List

Program 15.2   Constructing a Linked List

```
MODULE constructlist;

FROM InOut IMPORT
  (* proc *) ReadCard;

FROM Storage IMPORT
  (* proc *) ALLOCATE;

TYPE ptr   = POINTER TO node;
     node = RECORD
               info  :   CARDINAL;
               next  :   ptr
            END;
     list  = ptr;

VAR numlist  : list;
    number   : CARDINAL;
    last     : ptr;
    newnode  : ptr;

BEGIN
  ReadCard ( number );
  IF number < > 0 THEN
    NEW ( newnode ); (* construct first node *)
    newnode^.info := number;
    newnode^.next := NIL;
    numlist := newnode;
    last := newnode;
    LOOP
      ReadCard ( number );
      IF number = 0 THEN EXIT END;
      NEW ( newnode ); (* construct remaining nodes *)
      newnode^.info := number;
      newnode^.next := NIL;
      last^.next := newnode;
      last := newnode
    END
  END
END constructlist.
```

whose implementation is a linked list. Program 15.2, an example of this technique, constructs a list of cardinal numbers, taking those numbers from the terminal. A value of zero terminates the input; this value is not placed in the list.

A second fundamental algorithm is a linear search in a linked list. The procedure shown in Program 15.3 assumes the declarations of Program 15.2. It

---

Program 15.3   Linear Search in a Linked List

```
PROCEDURE search
   (       numbers : list           (* in  *) (* list to be searched    *);
           item      : CARDINAL (* in  *) (* item sought             *);
       VAR position  : ptr           (* out *) (* position where found *)  );

BEGIN
   position := numbers;
   WHILE ( position < > NIL ) AND
          ( position^.info < > item ) DO
      position := position^.next
   END
END search;
```

is given a list to be searched and a cardinal value to find, and returns a pointer to the first node containing that value. If the search is not successful, including the case where the list to be searched is empty, the result is a nil pointer. Notice that we take advantage of Modula-2's short-circuit evaluation of boolean expressions to simplify this linear search as we did in Section 4.1.3.

The ability to insert and delete elements easily, which was the prime motivation for linked lists, is considered in the next examples. A small problem appears in these operations, however. Suppose that we want to delete a value from the list, and we want to use the preceding search procedure to find that element before doing the actual deletion. Figure 15.2 shows a short linked list before and after deleting the element 12. The search procedure can easily find the node containing 12 and return a pointer to that node, but as the figure shows, it is the node before that node that actually changes its value. Unfortunately we have no easy way to get from the node found by the search back to the node to be changed.

One solution to this problem is to have the search procedure return two pointers, one to the node containing the value sought, and the other to the previous node (or nil if there is no previous node). The modified search procedure is shown in Program 15.4.

The delete procedure is shown in Program 15.5. Notice that we handle deletion of the first node in the list differently from deletion of later nodes.

Insertion of a new node in the list can take many forms. We might want all insertions to occur at the beginning or at the end of the list, or we might want to search for a particular value in the list and then insert the new node immediately before or immediately after the node containing that value. The proce-

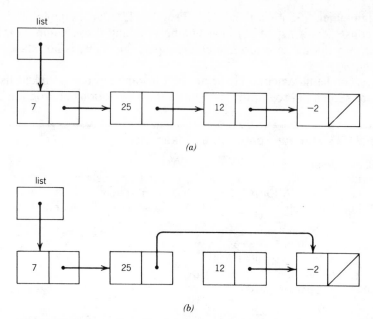

FIGURE 15.2   Linked List Deletion: (*a*) Before and (*b*) After

---

Program 15.4   Modified Search Procedure

```
PROCEDURE search
    (       numbers : list      (* in  *) (* list to be searched   *);
            item    : CARDINAL (* in  *) (* item sought            *);
      VAR position : ptr        (* out *) (* position where found *);
      VAR previous : ptr        (* out *) (* previous node          *)  );
BEGIN
   position := numbers;
   previous := NIL;

   WHILE ( position < > NIL ) AND
         ( position^.info < > item ) DO
     previous := position;
     position := position^.next
   END
END search;
```

dures shown in Programs 15.6 through 15.9 show each of the possibilities. In
each, the first parameter is the list into which the new node is inserted, and the
second parameter is the value to be placed in the new node. For the procedures
in Programs 15.8 and 15.9, a third parameter specifies the value before or after
which the insertion is to take place. If that value does not exist, no insertion is
done.

Program 15.5   Deletion in Linked List

```
PROCEDURE delete
   ( VAR numbers : list          (* in/out *) (* list to delete from *);
         item       : CARDINAL (* in      *) (* item to be deleted *) );

   VAR node      : ptr;
       prevnode : ptr;

BEGIN
   search ( numbers, item, node, prevnode );
   IF node < > NIL
     THEN (* the search was successful, delete the node *)
       IF prevnode < > NIL
         THEN (* node is not the first node in the list *)
               prevnode^.next := node^.next
         ELSE (* node is the first node in the list *)
               numbers := node^.next
       END;
       DISPOSE ( node )
   END
END delete;
```

Program 15.6   Insertion at the Front of a Linked List

```
PROCEDURE insertfront
   ( VAR numbers : list          (* in/out *) (* list to insert into    *);
         item       : CARDINAL (* in      *) (* item to be inserted *) );

   VAR node : ptr;

BEGIN
   NEW ( node );
   node^.info  := item;
   node^.next := numbers;
   numbers := node
END insertfront;
```

There are eight common variants of the linked list data structure, each of which has advantages in certain situations. We describe these variants briefly here and present some of them in applications later.

The problem of being unable to back up in a list has already been seen. We solved it for our simple cases above by modifying the search procedure. A more general solution is to place two pointers in each node, one pointing to the next node and the other pointing to the previous node. This structure is commonly called a *doubly linked* list, and our original structure is called a *singly linked* list. It is clear that we pay a small price with such a structure, in that each node is larger. However, the ability to move both ways in the list can greatly simplify many algorithms, saving both execution time and program storage space. Fig-

---

Program 15.7   Insertion at the Rear of a Linked List

```
PROCEDURE insertrear
  ( VAR numbers : list        (* in/out *) (* list to insert into   *);
          item    : CARDINAL (* in      *) (* item to be inserted *)  );

    VAR last  : ptr;
        node : ptr;

BEGIN
  NEW ( node );
  node^.info := item;
  node^.next := NIL;
  IF numbers <> NIL
    THEN last := numbers;
         WHILE last^.next <> NIL DO    (* find last node in list *)
           last := last^.next
         END;
         last^.next := node
    ELSE numbers := node                (* inserting first node *)
  END
END insertrear;
```

Program 15.8   Insertion Before a Given Node

```
PROCEDURE insertbefore
  ( VAR numbers : list        (* in/out *) (* list to insert into   *);
          item     : CARDINAL (* in      *) (* item to be inserted *);
          nextitem : CARDINAL (* in      *) (* item after insertion *)  );

    VAR node      : ptr;
        prevnode : ptr;
        newnode  : ptr;

BEGIN
  search ( numbers, item, node, prevnode );
  IF node <> NIL THEN
    NEW ( newnode )
    newnode^.info := item;
    newnode^.next := node;
    IF prevnode <> NIL
      THEN prevnode^.next := newnode
      ELSE numbers := newnode
    END
  END
END insertbefore;
```

Program 15.9   Insertion After a Given Node

```
PROCEDURE insertafter
  ( VAR numbers : list          (* in/out *) (* list to insert into    *);
        item      : CARDINAL (* in    *) (* item to be inserted   *);
        previtem : CARDINAL (* in    *) (* item before insertion *)

  VAR node      : ptr;
      prevnode : ptr;
      newnode : ptr;
BEGIN
  search ( numbers, item, node, prevnode );
  IF node < > NIL THEN
    NEW ( newnode );
    newnode^.info := item;
    newnode^.next := node^.next;
    node^.next := newnode
  END
END insertafter;
```

ure 15.3 shows such a list, and the declarations below show a possible implementation.

```
TYPE ptr    = POINTER TO node;
     node = RECORD
                  prev : ptr;
                  info : elementtype;
                  next : ptr
            END;
```

In some algorithms, the end of the list must be treated differently from the rest of the list because the last node does not point to another node. If we allow the last node to point back to the first node, we have a *circularly linked* list (Figure 15.4). Such a list may be either singly or doubly linked. The end of a circularly linked list may be recognized by finding a node that points to the same node as the list variable itself.

As we have seen already, an empty list is a special case that must often be treated separately in an algorithm. The use of a *header node* in a list can eliminate this special case. Such a node is always present, even in an empty

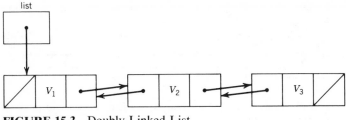

FIGURE 15.3 Doubly Linked List

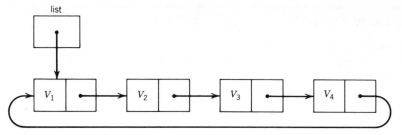

FIGURE 15.4   Circularly Linked List

list; its information field may be a special header value, or it may be undefined. As we will see below, it may also be useful in algorithms such as the search algorithm. Figure 15.5 shows two lists with header nodes, first the empty list and then a list with two elements. These lists are doubly linked and circularly linked. A shaded box represents the information field of a header node.

We have seen the common linear search algorithm several times (Sections 4.1.3 and 6.3.1; examples earlier in this section). In all these instances of this algorithm, the while loop required that two conditions be tested each time around the loop: that we have not yet found the item, and that we have not yet encountered the end of the list. A common method of speeding up the linear search algorithm is to remove the test for the end of the list by guaranteeing that the search will always be successful. This is done by placing a copy of the item being sought at the end of the list. If the search is successful, it will find the item somewhere before the end of the list, while an unsuccessful search will find the

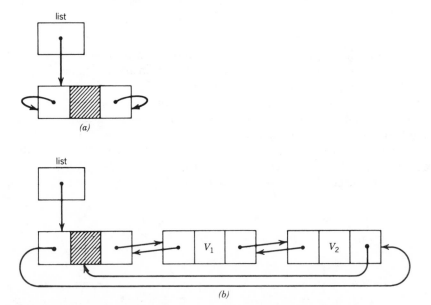

FIGURE 15.5   Lists with Header Nodes: (*a*) Empty List and (*b*) List with Two Elements

item at the end. We assume we can distinguish these two cases after exiting the loop.

If we have a circularly linked list with a header node, the header is conceptually at the end of the list (immediately after the last node). We can then use this technique for speeding up the linear search by placing the item sought in the header, and beginning the search with the node just after the header. The procedure in Program 15.10 demonstrates this technique.

Program 15.10   Improved Linear Search in a Linked List

```
PROCEDURE search
    (       numbers : list        (* in   *) (* list to be searched   *);
            item    : CARDINAL (* in   *) (* item sought            *);
        VAR position : ptr         (* out *) (* position where found *) );

BEGIN
    numbers^.info := item;
    position := numbers^.next;
    WHILE position^.info < > item DO
        position := position^.next
    END;
    IF position = numbers
        THEN position := NIL
    END
END search;
```

To illustrate how these variants of the basic linked list can be used to great advantage, compare the delete procedure in Program 15.5 with the one in Program 15.11. This new version uses a doubly linked, circularly linked list with a header. The search procedure is assumed to be the one in Program 15.10. Notice that this procedure does not consider deletion at the front of the list to be a special case, and the search procedure needs only to return a pointer to the node to be deleted.

Program 15.11   New Deletion Procedure

```
PROCEDURE delete
    ( VAR numbers : list        (* in/out *) (* list to delete from *);
            item    : CARDINAL (* in     *) (* item to be deleted *) );

    VAR node : ptr;

BEGIN
    search ( numbers, item, node );
    IF node < > NIL
        THEN node^.prev^.next := node^.next;
             node^.next^.prev := node^.prev;
             DISPOSE ( node )
    END
END delete;
```

When using a linked list with a header node, we can declare the list type in either of two ways. In the examples above, we have defined the list to be the same type as a pointer, and a list variable therefore consists of a pointer to the header node. We can also define a list to be the same type as a node, so a list variable is the header node. To illustrate the difference, consider the examples in Programs 15.12 and 15.13. Each procedure creates an empty list using the doubly linked, circularly linked structure. In the first, a list is a pointer to a header node; in the second, a list is the header node.

Program 15.12   Empty List with List as Pointer

```
TYPE ptr  = POINTER TO node;
     node = RECORD
                 info : CARDINAL;
                 prev : ptr;
                 next : ptr
            END;
     list = ptr;

PROCEDURE create
   ( VAR numbers : list (* out *) (* empty list to be created *) );

BEGIN
  NEW ( numbers );
  numbers^.prev := numbers;
  numbers^.next := numbers
END create;
```

Program 15.13   Empty List with List as Node

```
TYPE ptr   = POINTER TO node;
     node = RECORD
                 info : CARDINAL;
                 prev : ptr;
                 next : ptr
            END;
     list = node;

PROCEDURE create
   ( VAR numbers : list (* out *) (* empty list to be created *) );
BEGIN
  numbers.prev := ADR ( numbers );
  numbers.next := ADR ( numbers )
END create;
```

In summary, a linked list can be classified as either singly or doubly linked, linearly or circularly linked, and with or without a header node. These attributes are independent, thus giving eight different variants. A programmer can determine which one to use by examining the operations required on the list, and determining what special cases (empty list, end of list) are difficult to handle. Then the variant that makes the algorithms as simple as possible can be chosen.

15.2 The Stack Data Type (Dynamic Allocation)

The stack abstract data type, which was described in Section 14.1, can also be implemented as a dynamic data structure. We have seen that a stack is varying size and homogeneous, and has a special kind of sequential access. It is not surprising, then, that a linked list may be used to implement a stack.

Figure 15.6 shows a diagram of a stack containing three items. It is a singly linked list, but drawn vertically instead of horizontally so that the term "top" will have its normal meaning. Since access to the stack always occurs at the top, we need only a single pointer to the list to perform the stack operations. Thus the stack type may be declared to be equal to the pointer data type, as seen in the definition module in Program 15.14.

The four basic stack operations (makeempty, push, pop, and empty) are still needed, as are two new operations, define and destroy. These new procedures are necessary for the reasons discussed at the beginning of this chapter. We will leave it as an exercise to provide operations to copy a stack or to test two stacks for equality, since typical stack applications rarely call for these operations. The stack implementation in Section 14.1 provides a private procedure to test for a full stack, but such a procedure is not needed for dynamically allocated stack. The stack may grow arbitrarily large (within the limits imposed by the operating system or the physical memory size of the computer) by allocating new storage as necessary; hence the stack is never full.

In this example we will not use an opaque type. All the declarations of pointer and node types are made in the definition module, but not all are exported (see, however, Appendix 3). A program that uses this abstract data type need know only the type name and the operation names and parameters.

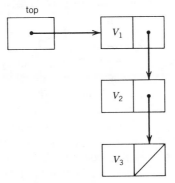

FIGURE 15.6 Linked Stack

Program 15.14 Linked Stack Definition Module

```
DEFINITION MODULE stackadt;

    (* This module defines the public interface of the stack abstract data
       type. It imports the type "elementtype" which is the type of data
       objects to be stored in the stack. *)

FROM elements IMPORT
    (* type *) elementtype;

EXPORT QUALIFIED
    (* type *) stack,
    (* proc *) makeempty, push, pop, empty, define, destroy;

TYPE
    stackptr   = POINTER TO stacknode;
    stacknode  = RECORD
                     contents :   elementtype;
                     next     :   stackptr
                 END;
    stack      = stackptr;

PROCEDURE makeempty
    ( VAR s    : stack       (* in/out *) );

PROCEDURE push
    ( VAR s    : stack       (* in/out *);
          item : elementtype (* in      *) );

PROCEDURE pop
    ( VAR s    : stack       (* in/out *);
      VAR item : elementtype (* out     *) );

PROCEDURE empty
    (     s    : stack       (* in      *) ) : BOOLEAN;

PROCEDURE define
    (     s    : stack       (* out     *) );

PROCEDURE destroy
    ( VAR s    : stack       (* in/out *) );

END stackadt.
```

As we have seen before, the use of a transparent type permits abuse of the values of the data type. Another approach is considered in Section 15.3.

Notice that the define operation is the only operation with a stack parameter of the out mode. All the other operations expect the stack parameter to be defined at the time the operation is begun. This is clearly necessary for the push, pop, and empty test operations, as was the case for the static stack in Section 14.1. The makeempty procedure is different here. It must be given a defined stack parameter so that it can determine whether the old storage associated with the stack must be deallocated before making the stack empty.

This definition module exports the same entities as the stack definition module of Section 14.1, plus the two new operations required for dynamic data structures. We should note especially that any program that uses either kind of stack will declare stack variables and invoke the four basic stack procedure in exactly the same way. This is one of the great advantages of designing software with abstract data types. If circumstances dictate a change in the implementation module of an abstract data type, it can often be made without changing the definition module, and without changing the program that uses the type. Even when we change from a static to a dynamic implementation, the changes to the using program are minor and predictable, as described at the beginning of this chapter.

The implementation module for the dynamic stack is shown in Program 15.15. Notice the similarity between the push procedure and the insertfront procedure in Program 15.6. Notice also the stackerror procedure. Even though we have eliminated the possibility of an error caused by trying to push a full stack, we still must consider the error caused by trying to pop an empty stack.

Program 15.15 Linked Stack Implementation Module

```
IMPLEMENTATION MODULE stackadt;

   (* This module is a dynamic implementation of the stack abstract data
      type. It imports the type "elementtype" which is the type of data
      objects to be stored in the stack. *)

FROM elements IMPORT
   (* type *) elementtype;

FROM Storage IMPORT
   (* proc *) ALLOCATE, DEALLOCATE;

PROCEDURE stackerror;

BEGIN
   (* error handling procedure: recovery, message, abort, etc. *)
END stackerror;

PROCEDURE makeempty
   ( VAR s       : stack      (* in/out *) );

BEGIN
   destroy ( s )
END makeempty;

PROCEDURE empty
   (     s       : stack      (* in     *) ) : BOOLEAN;

BEGIN
   RETURN s = NIL
END empty;
```

```
PROCEDURE push
  ( VAR s        : stack       (* in/out *);
        item     : elementtype (* in     *) );

  VAR newnode : stackptr;

BEGIN
  NEW ( newnode );
  newnode^.contents := item;
  newnode^.next := s;
  s := newnode
END push;

PROCEDURE pop
  ( VAR s        : stack       (* in/out *);
    VAR item     : elementtype (* out    *) );

  VAR oldnode  : stackptr;

BEGIN
  IF NOT empty ( s )
    THEN oldnode := s;
         item := s^.contents;
         s := s^.next;
         DISPOSE ( oldnode )
    ELSE stackerror
  END
END pop;

PROCEDURE define
  (     s        : stack       (* out    *) );

BEGIN
  s := NIL
END define;

PROCEDURE destroy
  ( VAR s        : stack       (* in/out *) );

  VAR node      : stackptr;

BEGIN
  WHILE s < > NIL DO
    node := s;
    s := s^.next;
    DISPOSE ( node )
  END
END destroy;

END stackadt.
```

The stack data type we have just seen has a value set containing sequences of objects of type elementtype, and an operation set containing the six common stack operations. We would now like to develop a generic stack data type. In Chapter 13 we defined a generic data type to be one for which the operations are specified but not the value set. Thus we want to implement a stack with the same six operations, in which any data type may be stored. Using some of the low level features of Modula-2, this is a relatively simple task.

The idea is to change the contents field of the stack nodes from a specific data type to the ADDRESS type. In that field we can then store the address of a dynamically allocated block of storage in which an object of any type may be stored. We also add a size field to each node so that a pop operation will know how big an item was previously pushed. The new type declaration is:

```
TYPE
    stacknode = RECORD
                    contents : ADDRESS;
                    size     : CARDINAL;
                    next     : stackptr
                END;
```

The implementations of three of the operations will need modification. The major change is that the formal parameters that represent objects to be pushed or popped are now open arrays of words, rather than a single specific type. As we have seen, such a formal parameter may be bound to an actual parameter of any type.

The push operation can no longer copy the item directly into the node. Instead, it must allocate a block of storage, and then copy the item into that block. Similarly, the pop operation cannot copy the item directly from the node. It must copy from the dynamically allocated block, and then dispose of that block. Finally, the destroy operation must not only dispose of the nodes in the linked list that constitutes the stack, but also deallocate all the blocks attached to these nodes. These three modified procedures are shown in Programs 15.16, 15.17, and 15.18.

Notice that the other stack operations (makeempty, empty, and define) do not need to be changed, since none of these operations deals with individual items in the stack. Notice also that although the definition of a stack implies that it is a homogeneous data structure, this generic stack implementation allows items of different types to be stored in the same stack. A program that uses this implementation must be designed so that the type of an item at the time it was pushed on the stack is the same as its type when it is popped. Otherwise an unintentional and probably erroneous type transfer would occur.

The techniques illustrated in this implementation of a generic stack may be used to implement generic data types of many kinds. The two salient features of such implementations are that the operation procedures use formal parameters that are open arrays of words and that storage for objects is allocated dynamically as it is needed. Another example of these techniques is presented in Section 15.5.

The advantage of using a generic stack is that several different stacks may be declared in a program, each containing a different data type; but only one

Program 15.16 Generic Stack Push Operation

```
PROCEDURE push
   ( VAR s    : stack               (* in/out *);
         item : ARRAY OF WORD (* in      *) );

   VAR newnode   : stackptr;
       wordcount : CARDINAL;
       location  : ADDRESS;

BEGIN
   NEW ( newnode );
   newnode^.size := ( HIGH ( item ) + 1 ) * TSIZE ( WORD );
   ALLOCATE ( newnode^.contents, newnode^.size );
   location := newnode^.contents;
   FOR wordcount := 0 TO HIGH ( item ) DO
      location^ := item[ wordcount ];
      INC ( location, TSIZE ( WORD ) )
   END;
   newnode^.next := s;
   s := newnode
END push;
```

Program 15.17 Generic Stack Pop Operation

```
PROCEDURE pop
   ( VAR s    : stack               (* in/out *);
     VAR item : ARRAY OF WORD (* out      *) );

   VAR oldnode   : stackptr;
       wordcount : CARDINAL;
       location  : ADDRESS;

BEGIN
   IF NOT empty ( s )
     THEN oldnode := s;
          location := s^.contents;
          FOR wordcount := 0 TO s^.size / TSIZE ( WORD ) - 1 DO
             item[ wordcount ] := location^;
             INC ( location, TSIZE ( WORD ) )
          END;
          DEALLOCATE ( s^.contents, s^.size );
          s := s^.next;
          DISPOSE ( oldnode )
     ELSE stackerror
   END
END pop;
```

Program 15.18   Generic Stack Destroy Operation

```
PROCEDURE destroy
  ( VAR  s : stack        (* in/out *) );

  VAR node : stackptr;

BEGIN
  WHILE s < > NIL DO
    node := s;
    DEALLOCATE ( node^.contents, node^.size );
    s := s^.next;
    DISPOSE ( node )
  END
END destroy;
```

copy of each procedure is needed. The disadvantage is that each push or pop operation requires an extra allocation or deallocation of a block of storage, thus making these operations a little slower.

15.3   The Queue Data Type (Dynamic Allocation)

We have seen that a stack may be implemented using an array (Section 14.1) or a linked list (Section 15.2). We have also seen that a queue may be implemented using an array (Section 14.2), with static allocation. In this section we present two additional implementations of the queue data type, but using dynamic allocation.

The four basic queue operations (makeempty, empty, insert, and remove) were defined in Section 14.2, and are present in our new implementations. We must also include operations to define a queue and to destroy a queue, since we are using dynamic allocation. As for stacks, operations to copy and compare queues are rarely needed and will be left as exercises.

In both implementations, the queue data type is declared as an opaque type. Only the type name appears in the definition module; the actual definition of the queue type appears in the implementation module. The first implementation (Programs 15.19 and 15.20) uses the same ideas as the queue of Section 14.2. We store the queue elements in a fixed length array, with the resulting possibility of an error when we try to insert an item into a full queue. In this implementation, however, the array is dynamically rather than statically allocated. Notice that the algorithms for the basic operations are identical to those seen before, although since a queue variable is a pointer, that pointer must be dereferenced everywhere we wish to access the queue.

Program 15.19 Dynamic Queue Definition Module

```
DEFINITION MODULE queueadt;

  (* This module defines the public interface of the queue abstract data
     type. It imports the type "elementtype" which is the type of data
     objects to be stored in the queue. Note that queue is an opaque type. *)

FROM elements IMPORT
  (* type *) elementtype;

EXPORT QUALIFIED
  (* type *) queue,
  (* proc *) makeempty, empty, insert, remove, define, destroy;

TYPE
  queue;

PROCEDURE makeempty
  ( VAR q    : queue      (* in/out *) );

PROCEDURE empty
  (     q    : queue      (* in     *) ) : BOOLEAN;

PROCEDURE insert
  ( VAR q    : queue      (* in/out *);
        item : elementtype (* in     *) );

PROCEDURE remove
  ( VAR q    : queue      (* in/out *);
    VAR item : elementtype (* out    *) );

PROCEDURE define
  ( VAR q    : queue      (* out    *) );

PROCEDURE destroy
  ( VAR q    : queue      (* in/out *) );

END queueadt.
```

Program 15.20 Dynamic Queue Implementation Module

```
IMPLEMENTATION MODULE queueadt;

  (* This module defines the implementation of the queue abstract data
     type. It imports the type "elementtype" which is the type of data
     objects to be stored in the queue. *)

FROM elements IMPORT
  (* type *) elementtype;

FROM Storage IMPORT
  (* proc *) ALLOCATE, DEALLOCATE;
```

```
CONST
  queuesize = 100;        (* maximum number of items in a queue *)
  queuemax = queuesize + 1;

TYPE
  queuerange = [ 0..queuesize ];
  queue      = POINTER TO RECORD
                  space : ARRAY queuerange OF elementtype;
                  front : queuerange;
                  rear  : queuerange
               END;

PROCEDURE queueerror;

BEGIN
  (* error handling procedure: recovery, message, abort, etc. *)
END queueerror;

PROCEDURE makeempty
  ( VAR q    : queue        (* in/out *) );

BEGIN
  IF q = NIL
    THEN NEW ( q )
  END;
  q^.front := 0;
  q^.rear := 0
END makeempty;

PROCEDURE empty
  (      q    : queue        (* in      *) ) : BOOLEAN;

BEGIN
  RETURN q^.front = q^.rear
END empty;

PROCEDURE full
  (      q    : queue        (* in      *) ) : BOOLEAN;

BEGIN
  RETURN q^.front = ( q^.rear + 1 ) MOD queuemax
END full;

PROCEDURE insert
  ( VAR q    : queue        (* in/out *);
        item : elementtype (* in      *) );

BEGIN
  IF NOT full ( q )
    THEN q^.rear := ( q^.rear + 1 ) MOD queuemax;
         q^.space[ q^.rear ] := item
    ELSE queueerror
  END
END insert;
```

```
PROCEDURE remove
  ( VAR    q    :  queue         (*  in/out  *);
    VAR    item :  elementtype   (*  out     *) );

BEGIN
  IF NOT empty ( q )
    THEN q^.front := ( q^.front + 1 ) MOD queuemax;
         item := q^.space[ q^.front ]
    ELSE queueerror
  END
END remove;

PROCEDURE define
  ( VAR    q    :  queue         (*  out     *) );

BEGIN
  q := NIL
END define;

PROCEDURE destroy
  ( VAR    q    :  queue         (*  in/out  *) );

BEGIN
  IF q < > NIL
    THEN DISPOSE ( q )
  END
END destroy;
END queueadt.
```

The second implementation of the queue abstract data type (Program 15.21) uses a linked list to hold the queue elements. This implementation, like that of the stack, is based on the linked list techniques developed in Section 15.1. A singly linked linear list without a header is used.

15.4   The String Data Type (Dynamic Allocation)

Early in this chapter we mentioned that there are two approaches to dynamic data structures. We have now seen several examples of one of these approaches, the linked list, which allocates storage for a large structure in small pieces that are linked together with pointers. The second approach is to allocate the storage for a large structure in one large block, reallocating storage whenever the size of the structure changes. As we saw earlier, this approach provides significant storage advantages because we do not need all the pointers. It does require reallocation when the size of the structure changes, but so does a linked list, and generally it is as easy to allocate a large block as it is to allocate a small node. The price we pay is that reallocation requires copying the values from the old block to the new block, assuming that some or most of the data in the block remains the same after reallocation.

Program 15.21   Linked Queue Implementation Module

IMPLEMENTATION MODULE queueadt;

   (* This module defines the implementation of the queue abstract data
      type. It imports the type "elementtype" which is the type of data
      objects to be stored in the queue. Note that queue is an opaque type. *)

FROM elements IMPORT
  (* type *) elementtype;

FROM Storage IMPORT
  (* proc *) ALLOCATE, DEALLOCATE;

TYPE
  queueptr   = POINTER TO queuenode;
  queuenode = RECORD
              contents : elementtype;
              next   : queueptr
           END;
  queue   = POINTER TO RECORD
              front   : queueptr;
              rear   : queueptr
           END;

PROCEDURE queueerror;

BEGIN
  (* error handling procedure: recovery, message, abort, etc. *)
END queueerror;

PROCEDURE makeempty
  (VAR   q   : queue   (* in/out *));

BEGIN
  destroy (q);
  NEW (q);
  q^.front := NIL;
  q^.rear := NIL
END makeempty;

PROCEDURE empty
  (q   : queue   (* in   *)) : BOOLEAN;

BEGIN
  RETURN q^.front = NIL
END empty;

PROCEDURE insert
  (VAR   q   : queue   (* in/out *);
         item   : elementtype (* in   *));

  VAR newnode : queueptr;

```
BEGIN
  NEW ( newnode );
  newnode^.contents := item;
  newnode^.next := NIL;
  IF empty ( q )
    THEN q^.front := newnode
    ELSE q^.rear^.next := newnode
  END;
  q^.rear := newnode
END insert;

PROCEDURE remove
    (        VAR q         : queue       (* in/out *);
             VAR item      : elementtype (* out     *) );

  VAR oldnode : queueptr;

BEGIN
  IF NOT empty ( q )
    THEN oldnode := q^.front;
         item := q^.front^.contents;
         q^.front := q^.front^.next;
         IF q^.front = NIL THEN q^.rear := NIL END;
         DISPOSE ( oldnode )
    ELSE queueerror
  END
END remove;

PROCEDURE define
    (        VAR q         : queue       (* out     *) );

BEGIN
  q := NIL
END define;

PROCEDURE destroy
    (        VAR q         : queue       (* in/out *) );

  VAR node : queueptr;

BEGIN
  IF q < > NIL THEN
    node := q^.front;
    WHILE node < > NIL DO
        q^.front := node^.next;
        DISPOSE ( node );
        node := q^.front
    END;
    DISPOSE ( q );
    q := NIL
  END
END destroy;

END queueadt.
```

This approach is especially useful for implementing a string data type, for two reasons. First, a linked list of characters is very wasteful of storage, since the pointers in a node occupy more storage than the character in a node. Second, the ability to increment an index variable through an array, or an address variable through a block of consecutive storage locations, provides an easy way to access the characters for most of the common string operations. We therefore use this approach in the implementation of the string data type presented in this section.

A string will be declared as an opaque type; hence it will be a pointer. What it points to is a block containing an array of characters (of whatever size is needed for a particular string), plus two cardinal fields. A length field keeps track of the current length of the string, and an allocation length field keeps track of how large the allocated block is. These two values will be the same when a string is first created, but some operations (such as delete) reduce the number of characters in the string. To save time, we will not reallocate storage after a deletion; we will keep the same block and leave some of it unused.

We will provide all the string operations discussed in Section 14.3, plus the new ones required for dynamically allocated data types: define and destroy. We will also provide a **createnull** operation, which creates an appropriately structured null string, and a **copy** operation, since assignment does not work for dynamically allocated data types. The definition module is shown in Program 15.22.

Program 15.22 Dynamic String Definition Module

```
DEFINITION MODULE string;

    (* This module defines a dynamic string abstract data type. *)

FROM FileSystem IMPORT
    (* type *) File;

EXPORT QUALIFIED
    (* type *) string,
    (* proc *) define, createnull, destroy, copy, concatenate, search,
               delete, insert, extract, length, equal, lessthan,
               readstring, writestring, convertarray, convertliteral;

TYPE string;

PROCEDURE define
    ( VAR      str   : string          (* out      *) ));

PROCEDURE createnull
    ( VAR      str   : string          (* in/out *) ));

PROCEDURE destroy
    ( VAR      str   : string          (* in/out *) ));

PROCEDURE copy
    (          str1  : string          (* in      *);
       VAR     str2  : string          (* in/out *) ));
```

```
PROCEDURE concatenate
    (      str1        : string            (* in     *);
           str2        : string            (* in     *);
     VAR result        : string            (* in/out *) );

PROCEDURE search
    (      str         : string            (* in     *);
           pattern     : string            (* in     *);
           start       : CARDINAL          (* in     *);
     VAR loc           : CARDINAL          (* out    *) );

PROCEDURE delete
    ( VAR str          : string            (* in/out *);
           start       : CARDINAL          (* in     *);
           count       : CARDINAL          (* in     *) );

PROCEDURE insert
    ( VAR str          : string            (* in/out *);
           substr      : string            (* in     *);
           start       : CARDINAL          (* in     *) );

PROCEDURE extract
    (      str         : string            (* in     *);
           start       : CARDINAL          (* in     *);
           count       : CARDINAL          (* in     *);
     VAR substr        : string            (* in/out *) );

PROCEDURE length
    (      str         : string            (* in     *) ) : CARDINAL;

PROCEDURE equal
    (      str1        : string            (* in     *);
           str2        : string            (* in     *) ) : BOOLEAN;

PROCEDURE lessthan
    (      str1        : string            (* in     *);
           str2        : string            (* in     *) ) : BOOLEAN;

PROCEDURE readstring
    ( VAR infile       : File              (* in/out *);
      VAR str          : string            (* in/out *);
          terminator : CHAR                (* in     *) );

PROCEDURE writestring
    ( VAR outfile      : File              (* in/out *);
          str          : string            (* in     *) );

PROCEDURE convertarray
    (      chars       : ARRAY OF CHAR (* in     *);
           count       : CARDINAL          (* in     *);
     VAR str           : string            (* in/out *) );

PROCEDURE convertliteral
    (      chars       : ARRAY OF CHAR (* in     *);
     VAR str           : string            (* in/out *) );

END string.
```

The implementation module provides an additional procedure, allocate-string. Its parameters are a string to be allocated and the number of characters desired. It then requests a block of storage with enough space for that many characters and the two cardinal fields, using the ALLOCATE procedure provided in the Storage module. The two length fields are given appropriate values: zero for the number of characters currently in the string, and the total block size for the allocated length. This procedure is invoked by several of the operation procedures whenever it is determined that a new, larger block of storage is needed for a string. The deallocation of a string is performed by the destroy operation.

Notice that the allocatestring and define operations are the only ones that have a string parameter of the out mode. Only these procedures may be given an undefined string variable as a parameter; all other procedures expect their string parameters to be defined at the time the procedure is entered. This is necessary to allow each procedure to determine whether to deallocate the existing storage for a string before giving it a new value. Correct use of these procedures requires discipline on the part of the programmer, as discussed at the beginning of this chapter.

The algorithms for the operations are all quite similar to those of the corresponding operations presented in Section 14.3. Most of the differences are due to the additional requirements of dynamically allocated data structures to deallocate old storage whenever possible. Program 15.23 presents the skeleton of the implementation module. The procedures that implement the string operations are presented and discussed separately.

In this implementation a string is the address of a block of storage (POINTER TO block) containing two length fields and an array of characters. Not all strings will be 65536 characters in length as the definition implies. This structure was chosen to allow the benefits of normal array subscripting into the string, even though different strings may be of different lengths. Compare this structure to that of the dynamic array in Section 15.5, which implements a similar object in another way.

The operations to allocate, define, and destroy strings, and the operation that creates the null string, are all straightforward (Program 15.24).

The copy procedure (Program 15.25) performs the same operation the assignment statement accomplishes for static data structures. We must remember to deallocate any existing storage for the target string before giving it a new value; hence the invocation of the destroy operation.

The concatenate operation (Program 15.26) must consider the possibility that two or all three of the parameters are the same string. If the result string is also one of the strings to concatenate, we must be careful to copy the old characters before destroying and reallocating storage for the result string. Thus a temporary string is created to hold the characters of the result string. After the characters have been copied from the first two parameters, we deallocate the storage currently allocated to the result string. If either of the concatenated strings is the same variable as the result string, its storage is of course simultaneously deallocated. Then we assign the temporary string pointer to the result

Program 15.23   Dynamic String Implementation Module Skeleton

```
IMPLEMENTATION MODULE string;

  (* This module implements a dynamic string abstract data type. *)

FROM SYSTEM IMPORT
  (* proc *) TSIZE;

FROM FileSystem IMPORT
  (* type *) File,
  (* proc *) ReadChar, WriteChar, Eof;

FROM Storage IMPORT
  (* proc *) ALLOCATE, DEALLOCATE;

FROM Arithmetic IMPORT
  (* proc *) mincard;

CONST
  stringmax = 65535;

TYPE
  block    = RECORD
                len     : CARDINAL;
                alloclen : CARDINAL;
                ch      : ARRAY [ 0..stringmax ] OF CHAR
             END;
  string   = POINTER TO block;

  (* string operation procedures *)

END string
```

Program 15.24   Dynamic String Basic Operations

```
PROCEDURE allocatestring
  ( VAR   str    :   string      (*   out    *);
          length :   CARDINAL  (*   in     *) );
BEGIN
  ALLOCATE ( str, 2 * TSIZE ( CARDINAL ) + length );
  str^.alloclen := length;
  str^.len := 0
END allocatestring;

PROCEDURE define
  ( VAR   str    :   string      (*   out    *) );
BEGIN
  str := NIL
END define;

PROCEDURE createnull
  ( VAR   str    :   string      (*   in/out  *) );
```

```
BEGIN
  destroy ( str );
  allocatestring ( str, 0 )
END createnull;

PROCEDURE destroy
  ( VAR  str      :  string         (*  in/out  *) );
BEGIN
  IF str < > NIL
    THEN DEALLOCATE ( str, str^.alloclen + 2 * TSIZE ( CARDINAL ) );
         str := NIL
  END
END destroy;
```

Program 15.25 Dynamic String Copy Procedure

```
PROCEDURE copy
  (       str1 : string (* in      *);
    VAR str2 : string (* in/out *) );

  VAR pos : CARDINAL;

BEGIN
  destroy ( str2 );
  allocatestring ( str2, str1^.len );
  FOR pos := 0 TO str1^.len - 1 DO
    str2^.ch[ pos ] := str1^.ch[ pos ]
  END;
  str2^.len := str1^.len
END copy;
```

Program 15.26 Dynamic String Concatenate Procedure

```
PROCEDURE concatenate
  (       str1   : string (* in      *);
          str2   : string (* in      *);
    VAR result : string (* in/out *) );

  VAR oldpos  : CARDINAL;
      newpos : CARDINAL;
      tempstr : string;

BEGIN
  allocatestring ( tempstr, str1^.len + str2^.len );
  newpos := 0;
  FOR oldpos := 0 TO str1^.len - 1 DO
    tempstr^.ch[ newpos ] := str1^.ch[ oldpos ];
    INC ( newpos )
  END;
```

```
FOR oldpos := 0 TO str2^.len - 1 DO
   tempstr^.ch[ newpos ] := str2^.ch[ oldpos ];
   INC ( newpos )
END;
tempstr^.len := str1^.len + str2^.len;
destroy ( result );
result := tempstr
END concatenate;
```

string. Notice we do not deallocate the temporary string; its storage has been given to the result string.

Some Modula-2 implementations will detect an error when concatenating a null string, since the limits of the for loop will be 0 and −1, and the control variable is of cardinal type. Using integer instead of cardinal type can correct this error.

The search procedure (Program 15.27) does not need any storage allocation or deallocation, and is similar to the search operation presented in Section 14.3.

The delete operation (Program 15.28) changes the length of a string, but we do not reallocate storage for the string. Instead, we change the length

---

Program 15.27 Dynamic String Search Procedure

```
PROCEDURE search
   (      str     : string    (* in  *);
          pattern : string    (* in  *);
          start   : CARDINAL  (* in  *);
     VAR location : CARDINAL  (* out *) );

   VAR found : BOOLEAN;
       pos   : CARDINAL;

BEGIN
   found := FALSE;
   IF str^.len >= pattern^.len
     THEN location := start - 1;
          WHILE ( location <= str^.len - pattern^.len ) AND
                  NOT found DO
            INC ( location );
            pos := 0;
            found := TRUE;
            WHILE found AND ( pos < pattern^.len ) DO
              found := str^.ch[ location - 1 + pos ] =
                          pattern^.ch[ pos ];
              INC ( pos )
            END
          END
   END;
   IF NOT found THEN location := 0 END
END search;
```

Program 15.28   Dynamic String Delete Procedure

```
PROCEDURE delete
  ( VAR str    : string      (* in/out *);
        start  : CARDINAL (* in      *);
        count : CARDINAL (* in      *) );

  VAR pos : CARDINAL;

BEGIN
  IF ( start >= 1 ) AND ( start + count - 1 <= str^.len )
    THEN FOR pos := start - 1 TO str^.len - count - 1 DO
            str^.ch[ pos ] := str^.ch[ pos + count ]
          END;
          str^.len := str^.len - count
  END
END delete;
```

field of the string storage block to reflect the new length. This approach saves us the time required for deallocation, reallocation, and copying the characters.

The insert operation (Program 15.29) takes advantage of the fact that the current length of a string may be less than the allocated length of its storage block. If there is enough space in the existing block for the insertion to be performed, no reallocation is performed. If not, a new temporary string is created, and the characters from the existing string are copied into it. In either case, some characters are moved to make room for the insertion, and the substring is copied into the vacated positions. Notice again that the temporary string is not deallocated; the original string is deallocated, and then the storage block of the temporary string is assigned to the original string.

Program 15.29   Dynamic String Insert Procedure

```
PROCEDURE insert
  ( VAR str    : string      (* in/out *);
        substr : string      (* in      *);
        start  : CARDINAL (* in      *) );

  VAR tempstr : string;
      pos     : CARDINAL;
BEGIN
  IF ( start >= 1 ) AND ( start <= str^.len + 1 )
    THEN IF str^.alloclen >= str^.len + substr^.len
            THEN (* insertion will fit in existing allocation *)
                 FOR pos := str^.len - 1 TO start - 1 BY -1 DO
                    str^.ch[ pos + substr^.len ] := str^.ch[ pos ]
                 END;
                 str^.len := str^.len + substr^.len
```

```
          ELSE (* new allocation is necessary *)
              allocatestring ( tempstr, str^.len + substr^.len );
              FOR pos := 0 TO start - 2 DO
                tempstr^.ch[ pos ] := str^.ch[ pos ]
              END;
              FOR pos := start - 1 TO str^.len - 1 DO
                tempstr^.ch[ pos + substr^.len ] := str^.ch[ pos ]
              END;
              tempstr^.len := str^.len + substr^.len;
              destroy ( str );
              str := tempstr
          END;
          (* now insert the substring *)
          FOR pos := 0 TO substr^.len - 1 DO
            str^.ch[ start - 1 + pos ] := substr^.ch[ pos ]
          END
  END
END insert;
```

The extract operation (Program 15.30) begins by destroying the existing storage block of the result substring. A new storage block of the appropriate size can then be allocated.

The length, equal, and less than operations (Program 15.31) require no allocation or deallocation, and are again essentially the same as those presented in Section 14.3.

The read string operation (Program 15.32) uses an algorithm very different from the one seen in Section 14.3. We do not know in advance how large the string will be, so we cannot allocate storage for it at the beginning of the

---

Program 15.30 Dynamic String Extract Operation

```
PROCEDURE extract
    (       str    : string      (* in    *);
            start  : CARDINAL (* in    *);
            count  : CARDINAL (* in    *);
      VAR substr : string       (* in/out *) );

  VAR pos : CARDINAL;

BEGIN
  destroy ( substr );
  IF ( start >= 1 ) AND ( start + count - 1 <= str^.len )
    THEN allocatestring ( substr, count );
         FOR pos := 0 TO count - 1 DO
           substr^.ch[ pos ] := str^.ch[ start - 1 + pos ]
         END;
         substr^.len := count
    ELSE allocatestring ( substr, 0 )
  END
END extract;
```

Program 15.31 Dynamic String Length, Equal, and Less Than Procedures

```
PROCEDURE length
  ( str   : string (* in *) ) : CARDINAL;
BEGIN
  RETURN str^.len
END length;

PROCEDURE equal
  ( str1 : string (* in *);
    str2 : string (* in *) ) : BOOLEAN;

  VAR pos : CARDINAL;
BEGIN
  IF str1^.len = str2^.len
    THEN pos := 0;
         WHILE ( str1^.ch[ pos ] = str2^.ch[ pos ] ) AND
                 ( pos < str1^.len - 1 ) DO
             INC ( pos )
         END;
         RETURN str1^.ch[ pos ] = str2^.ch[ pos ]
    ELSE RETURN FALSE
  END
END equal;

PROCEDURE lessthan
  ( str1 : string (* in *);
    str2 : string (* in *) ) : BOOLEAN;

  VAR pos : CARDINAL;
      limit : CARDINAL;
BEGIN
  limit := mincard ( str1^.len, str2^.len ) - 1;
  pos := 0;
  WHILE ( str1^.ch[ pos ] = str2^.ch[ pos ] ) AND ( pos < limit ) DO
    INC ( pos )
  END;
  IF str1^.ch[ pos ] = str2^.ch[ pos ]
    THEN RETURN str1^.len < str2^.len
    ELSE RETURN str1^.ch[ pos ] < str2^.ch[ pos ]
  END
END lessthan;
```

procedure. Instead, we declare a temporary string and allocate to it a small block of storage (here, 100 characters). The string parameter is destroyed and left empty. We then read characters into the temporary string. Each time this string is filled, we concatenate it to the string parameter. Thus the temporary

Program 15.32 Dynamic Read String Procedure

```
PROCEDURE readstring
  ( VAR infile     : File    (* in/out *);
    VAR str        : string  (* in/out *);
        terminator : CHAR (* in       *) );

  CONST tempsize = 100;

  VAR endfound : BOOLEAN;
      tempstr  : string;
BEGIN
  allocatestring ( tempstr, tempsize );
  destroy ( str );
  createnull ( str );
  endfound := Eof ( infile );
  WHILE NOT endfound DO
    WITH tempstr^ DO
      len := 0;
      LOOP
        IF Eof ( infile )
          THEN endfound := TRUE;
               EXIT
        END;
        INC ( len );
        ReadChar ( infile, ch[ len - 1 ] );
        IF ch[ len - 1 ] = terminator
          THEN DEC ( len ); (* terminator not put in string *)
               endfound := TRUE;
               EXIT
        END;
        IF len = tempsize THEN EXIT END
      END
    END;
    concatenate ( str, tempstr, str )
  END;
  destroy ( tempstr )
END readstring;
```

string is used repeatedly until the entire string has been read, after which it is destroyed.

The write string operation (Program 15.33) is again straightforward. Note that it may not be meaningful to try to write arbitrarily long strings to the terminal.

The convert array operation, like so many others, must deallocate the existing storage block of the string parameter before giving it its new value. Thus the procedure begins with an invocation of the destroy operation. The convert literal operation uses the convert operation, as described in Section 14.3. These operations are shown in Programs 15.34 and 15.35.

Program 15.33 Dynamic Write String Procedure

```
PROCEDURE writestring
  ( VAR outfile : File    (* in/out *);
        str     : string (* in      *) );

  VAR pos : CARDINAL;

BEGIN
  FOR pos := 0 TO str^.len - 1 DO
    WriteChar ( outfile, str^.ch[ pos ] )
  END
END writestring;
```

Program 15.34 Dynamic String Convert Procedure

```
PROCEDURE convertarray
  (       chars : ARRAY OF CHAR (* in      *);
          count : CARDINAL       (* in      *);
     VAR str    : string         (* in/out *) );

  VAR pos : CARDINAL;

BEGIN
  destroy ( str );
  allocatestring ( str, count );
  FOR pos := 0 TO count - 1 DO
    str^.ch[ pos ] := chars[ pos ]
  END;
  str^.len := count
END convertarray;
```

Program 15.35 Dynamic String Convert Literal Procedure

```
PROCEDURE convertliteral
  (       chars : ARRAY OF CHAR (* in      *);
     VAR str    : string         (* in/out *) );

BEGIN
  convertarray ( chars, HIGH ( chars ) + 1, str )
END convertliteral;
```

15.5 Implementation of the Dynamic Matrix Data Type

The definition module for the Matrix data type (Section 12.4) provides basic operations on matrices of all sizes and thus can be classified as a generic data type. The use of this type was illustrated with a software system for solving systems of linear equations. The reader may want to review Section 12.4 before studying the implementation that follows. We have postponed the implementation to this point because it makes use of several low level features of Modula-2, plus many dynamic data structure techniques.

The data structure for a matrix must, of course, include storage for the elements of the matrix, but it also must allow storage of the lower and upper limits of the row and column indices. This information is necessary to allow run-time checks of index values when the matrix is accessed. We therefore define the data structure as two pieces: a variable size piece that holds the matrix elements, and a fixed size piece that holds the index limits and the address of the other piece (Figure 15.7).

Because we are using a dynamic data structure, we provide operations to define and destroy a matrix. The define operation is given the four index limits, from which it can determine the total size of the matrix. The procedure then allocates storage for both parts of the data structure, although no values are stored in the matrix elements part. The destroy operations deallocates the storage for both parts.

The lower and upper operations permit a user program to determine the index limits of the matrix. Although these procedures are extremely simple, they are necessary when using an opaque type, since the user cannot access the index limit fields directly.

The block of storage that holds the matrix elements is organized in the common *row-major order* used to store two-dimensional arrays in high level programming languages. The first several locations hold the values of the first row of the matrix, followed by the values of the second row, and so on. The *offset* of a particular element, which is defined as the distance of that element past the beginning of the storage block, may be computed by the formula:

offset of element at row *i*, column *j* =
  ((*i* − minimum row index) ∗ row size +
  (*j* − minimum col index)) ∗ size of an element

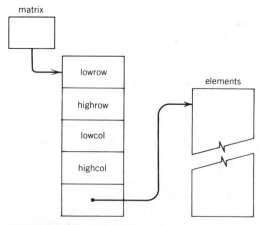

FIGURE 15.7 Matrix Data Structure

Adding this offset to the address of the storage block yields the address of the element.

Two private procedures are provided to support matrix accesses. The offset procedure implements the formula above, and the inrange function procedure checks that the indices provided for an access request are within the legal ranges. The access procedure returns the value of the specified element, and the assign procedure gives a new value to the specified element.

The private rangeerror procedure prints a message when an invalid index is given, and then halts. For some applications another form of error handling may be appropriate.

The save and retrieve operations are implementation dependent and are not given. They may be implemented easily if procedures for reading and writing the WORD data type are provided in an implementation. The save procedure simply opens the named file, and transfers the fixed size part and the variable size part of the matrix data structure to the file, word by word. The retrieve operation does the opposite. The fixed size part must be saved first, so when retrieving the matrix, the program can compute the size of the variable size part before reading it. In these procedures the parameter f is the Modula-2 file and the parameter name is a character string representing the operating system file name.

The implementation module for the dynamic matrix data type is shown in Program 15.36.

Program 15.36 Dynamic Matrix Implementation Module

```
IMPLEMENTATION MODULE Matrix;

   (* This is the implementation of the dynamic matrix abstract data type. *)

FROM SYSTEM IMPORT
   (* type *) ADDRESS,
   (* proc *) TSIZE;

FROM Storage IMPORT
   (* proc *) ALLOCATE, DEALLOCATE;

FROM FileSystem IMPORT
   (* type *) File
   (* proc *) (* implementation-dependent *);

FROM InOut IMPORT
   (* proc *) WriteString, WriteLn;

TYPE
   matrix = POINTER TO RECORD
               lowrow   : INTEGER;
               highrow  : INTEGER;
               lowcol   : INTEGER;
               highcol  : INTEGER;
               elements : ADDRESS
            END;
```

```
PROCEDURE define
  ( VAR m     : matrix        (* out *);
        low1  : INTEGER       (* in  *);
        high1 : INTEGER       (* in  *);
        low2  : INTEGER       (* in  *);
        high2 : INTEGER       (* in  *) );

BEGIN
  NEW ( m );
  WITH m^ DO
    lowrow  := low1;
    highrow := high1;
    lowcol  := low2;
    highcol := high2;
    ALLOCATE ( elements, TSIZE ( REAL ) *
             ( high1 - low1 + 1 ) * ( high2 - low2 + 1 ) )

  END
END define;

PROCEDURE destroy
  ( VAR   m     : matrix        (* in/out *) );

BEGIN
  WITH m^ DO
    DEALLOCATE ( elements, TSIZE ( REAL ) *
         ( highrow - lowrow + 1 ) * ( highcol - lowcol + 1 ) );
  END;
  DISPOSE ( m )
END destroy;

PROCEDURE rangeerror;

BEGIN
  WriteString ( "Matrix index out of range" );
  WriteLn;
  HALT
END rangeerror;

PROCEDURE inrange
  (       m   : matrix        (* in     *);
          row : INTEGER       (* in     *);
          col : INTEGER       (* in     *) ) : BOOLEAN;

BEGIN
  WITH m^ DO
    RETURN ( lowrow <= row ) AND ( row <= highrow ) AND
           ( lowcol <= col ) AND ( col <= highcol )
  END
END inrange;

PROCEDURE offset
  (       m   : matrix        (* in     *);
          row : INTEGER       (* in     *);
          col : INTEGER       (* in     *) ) : CARDINAL;
```

```
BEGIN
  WITH m^ DO
    RETURN CARDINAL ( ( row - lowrow ) * ( highrow - lowrow + 1 )
      * TSIZE ( REAL ) + ( col - lowcol ) * TSIZE ( REAL ) )
  END
END offset;

PROCEDURE lower
  (          m     :  matrix            (* in      *);
             index :  range             (* in      *) )   :  INTEGER;

BEGIN
  IF index = row
    THEN RETURN m^.lowrow
    ELSE RETURN m^.lowcol
  END
END lower;

PROCEDURE upper
  (          m     :  matrix            (* in      *);
             index :  range             (* in      *) )   :  INTEGER;

BEGIN
  IF index = row
    THEN RETURN m^.highrow
    ELSE RETURN m^.highcol
  END
END upper;

PROCEDURE access
  (          m     :  matrix            (* in      *);
             row   :  INTEGER           (* in      *);
             col   :  INTEGER           (* in      *) )   :  REAL;

  VAR addr : POINTER TO REAL;

BEGIN
  IF inrange ( m, row, col )
    THEN addr := m^.elements + offset ( m, row, col );
         RETURN addr^
    ELSE rangeerror
  END
END access;

PROCEDURE assign
  ( VAR     m     :  matrix            (* in/out *);
             row   :  INTEGER           (* in      *);
             col   :  INTEGER           (* in      *);
             value :  REAL              (* in      *) );

  VAR addr : POINTER TO REAL;
```

```
BEGIN
  IF inrange ( m, row, col )
    THEN addr := m^.elements + offset ( m, row, col );
         addr^ := value
    ELSE rangeerror
  END
END assign;

PROCEDURE save
  ( VAR    f      : File            (* in/out  *);
           m      : matrix          (* in      *);
           name   : ARRAY OF CHAR   (* in      *) );

BEGIN
  (* implementation-dependent *)
END save;

PROCEDURE retrieve
  ( VAR    f      : File            (* in/out  *);
    VAR    m      : matrix          (* out     *);
           name   : ARRAY OF CHAR   (* in      *) );

BEGIN
  (* implementation-dependent *)
END retrieve;

END Matrix.
```

To obtain the generality of the dynamic matrix data type, we must expect a performance penalty. A test comparing the access times of the dynamic matrix and a usual Modula-2 two-dimensional array indicate that the dynamic matrix was approximately eight times slower. The implementation shown in this section could be made faster by incorporating the range checks and offset computations in the access and assign procedures, thus eliminating the procedure invocation overhead.

15.6 Dynamic Storage Allocation

All Modula-2 implementations are expected to provide a storage allocation module that exports procedures to allocate and deallocate storage. In this section we look at two implementations of such a module. These examples show two very different approaches to storage allocation, which leads immediately to the question of which is "better."

Computer systems need dynamic storage allocation for a wide variety of applications. An operating system, for example, must allocate rather large blocks of memory (tens of thousands of bytes, typically) for program and data storage for users. These blocks are allocated and deallocated relatively infrequently, and they are so large that hardware considerations usually influence the allocation. A storage allocation scheme could be optimized for large blocks and infrequent allocation. However, a storage allocation scheme for small blocks that are frequently allocated and deallocated, such as for nodes of linked lists, would be optimized differently. It is virtually impossible to devise a storage allocation scheme that works well for allocation requests of all kinds.

For this reason, we sometimes want to provide different storage allocation modules for different applications. There are many different allocation schemes, but we will look only at two. Interested readers are directed to Knuth (1973) and Tremblay and Sorenson (1976) for a more detailed discussion of this topic.

The task of a storage allocation system is relatively simple to describe. The system must maintain a set or list of blocks of storage, some of which are free and some of which are currently allocated to a user. In response to an allocation request, it must locate a free block of sufficient size and allocate all or part of that block. In response to a deallocation request, it must recover the deallocated block. To maximize the probability of being able to satisfy a large allocation request, the system should be able to find adjacent free blocks and combine them into one larger block.

The definition module for the storage allocator (Program 15.37) exports procedures ALLOCATE and DEALLOCATE, through which a user program may access the capabilities of the allocator. Each has two parameters: the address and the size of the block to be allocated or deallocated. Remember that the ADDRESS data type is compatible with all pointer types, and with the type of the ADR function. This makes it possible to allocate and deallocate storage for variables identified by any pointer type and for these procedures to be compatible with the NEW and DISPOSE procedures.

Program 15.37   The Storage Definition Module

```
DEFINITION MODULE Storage;

FROM SYSTEM IMPORT
  (* type *) ADDRESS;

EXPORT QUALIFIED
  (* proc *) ALLOCATE, DEALLOCATE;

PROCEDURE ALLOCATE
  ( VAR blockaddress : ADDRESS (* out    *);
        blocksize    : CARDINAL (* in     *) );

PROCEDURE DEALLOCATE
  ( VAR blockaddress : ADDRESS (* in/out *);
        blocksize    : CARDINAL (* in     *) );

END Storage.
```

15.6.1   A First-Fit Storage Module

The implementation for a first-fit storage module (Program 15.38) is based on a very simple idea. The free blocks are linked together into a list, in no particu-

Program 15.38 First-Fit Storage Module

```
IMPLEMENTATION MODULE Storage;

    (* This module maintains a linked list of free blocks, and uses a first-fit
    allocation algorithm. Storage is allocated from a statically allocated
    first block. *)

FROM SYSTEM IMPORT
    (* type *) ADDRESS, BYTE,
    (* proc *) TSIZE, ADR;

CONST
    maxblocksize = 10000; (* size of first block *)

TYPE
    storageunit  = BYTE;      (* memory unit of host computer *)
    freeblockptr = POINTER TO freeblock;
    freeblock    = RECORD
                        blocksize : CARDINAL;
                        next      : freeblockptr
                    END;

VAR
    minblocksize : CARDINAL;
    freelist     : freeblockptr;
    firstblock   : ARRAY [ 1..maxblocksize ] OF storageunit;

PROCEDURE failure;

BEGIN
    (* allocation failure procedure: message, abort, etc. *)
END failure;

PROCEDURE insertblock
    (       block : freeblockptr (* in *) );

BEGIN
    block^.next := freelist;
    freelist := block
END insertblock;

PROCEDURE removeblockafter
    (       block : freeblockptr (* in *) );

BEGIN
    IF block < > NIL
        THEN (* block is not first in the free list *)
            block^.next := block^.next^.next
        ELSE (* block is first in the free list *)
            freelist := freelist^.next
    END
END removeblockafter;
```

```
PROCEDURE ALLOCATE
  ( VAR blockaddress : ADDRESS (* out *);
        blocksize      : CARDINAL (* in  *) );

    VAR
      actualsize  : CARDINAL;
      newblock    : freeblockptr;
      testblock   : freeblockptr;
      prevblock   : freeblockptr;
      blockfound  : BOOLEAN;

BEGIN
  actualsize := blocksize + TSIZE ( CARDINAL );
  IF actualsize < minblocksize
    THEN actualsize := minblocksize
    ELSIF ODD ( actualsize ) THEN INC ( actualsize )
  END;
  testblock    := freelist;
  prevblock    := NIL;
  blockfound := FALSE;
  WHILE NOT blockfound AND ( testblock < > NIL ) DO
    IF testblock^.blocksize > = actualsize
      THEN blockfound := TRUE;
            IF testblock^.blocksize - actualsize < minblocksize
              THEN (* allocate entire block *)
                    removeblockafter ( prevblock );
                    newblock := testblock
              ELSE (* allocate only a piece of the block *)
                    testblock^.blocksize := testblock^.blocksize
                                            - actualsize;
                    newblock := freeblockptr ( CARDINAL ( testblock ) +
                                            testblock^.blocksize );
                    newblock^.blocksize := actualsize
            END
      ELSE prevblock := testblock;
            testblock := testblock^.next
    END
  END;
  IF blockfound
    THEN blockaddress := freeblockptr ( CARDINAL ( newblock )
                            + TSIZE ( CARDINAL ) );
    ELSE failure
  END
END ALLOCATE;


PROCEDURE DEALLOCATE
  ( VAR blockaddress : ADDRESS (* in/out *);
        blocksize      : CARDINAL (* in      *) );
```

```
    VAR releasedblock     : freeblockptr;
        testblock         : freeblockptr;
        prevblock         : freeblockptr;
        combinedbefore : BOOLEAN;
        combinedafter    : BOOLEAN;


BEGIN
   releasedblock := freeblockptr ( CARDINAL ( blockaddress )
                        - TSIZE ( CARDINAL ) );
   testblock  := freelist;
   prevblock := NIL;
   combinedbefore := FALSE;
   combinedafter   := FALSE;
   WHILE NOT ( combinedbefore AND combinedafter )
         AND ( testblock < > NIL ) DO
     IF freeblockptr ( CARDINAL ( testblock ) +
            testblock^.blocksize ) = releasedblock
       THEN (* testblock is immediately before releasedblock *)
            removeblockafter ( prevblock );
            testblock^.blocksize := testblock^.blocksize +
                                    releasedblock^.blocksize;
            releasedblock := testblock;
            combinedbefore := TRUE
       ELSIF freeblockptr ( CARDINAL ( releasedblock ) +
               releasedblock^.blocksize ) = testblock
            THEN (* test block is immediately after released block *)
                 removeblockafter ( prevblock );
                 INC ( releasedblock^.blocksize,
                      testblock-.blocksize );
                 combinedafter := TRUE
            ELSE (* no combining possible, advance to next block *)
                 prevblock := testblock
     END;
     testblock := testblock^.next
   END;
   (* put the released block at the front of the free block list *)
   insertblock ( releasedblock )
END DEALLOCATE;


BEGIN
   minblocksize := TSIZE ( CARDINAL ) + TSIZE ( ADDRESS );
   (* put the static first block in the free list *)
   freelist := ADR ( firstblock );
   freelist^.blocksize := maxblocksize;
   freelist^.next := NIL
END Storage.
```

lar order. When an allocation request is received, the list is searched for the first block of sufficient size to satisfy the request; hence the name "first-fit." That block is removed from the list, and if it is larger than the request size, it is broken into two blocks. One is given to the requesting program, and the other is placed back on the free list.

To maintain the linked list of free blocks, we must have space for pointers. By definition, a free block contains storage not currently in use, so we simply put a pointer in each block. We also put the size of a block into each block. To access these two values, we define the freeblock data type and use a type transfer function to superimpose a record of this type on each free block.

We also choose to store the block size in each used block. This prevents each user program from having to put a size field in each dynamically allocated data structure, and thus eliminates the possibility that this field might be given an incorrect value. Since each block stores its own size, a deallocation request really must specify only the address of the block. We have kept the size parameter to be compatible with the DISPOSE procedure, which we know is translated by the compiler into a two-parameter deallocation request.

The allocation procedure first determines the minimum size of a block that can satisfy a request. The requested size must be increased by enough space to hold the block size field, and in this implementation we also increment the request if necessary to make it an even number. On some computer systems, storage blocks can be used more easily if they begin at addresses that are multiples of two or four; we assume two here. The procedure then performs a linear search of the free block list, looking for a block large enough to satisfy the request. It removes the first such block from the list and tries to break it into two blocks. One block goes to the user to satisfy the request, and the other is put back on the free list. If the leftover block is smaller than the minimum size of a free block, the user is given the entire block rather than just a piece. If no block of sufficient size is found, the system fails.

The deallocation procedure searches the list of free blocks to find adjacent blocks that can be combined. Two blocks are found to be adjacent if the address plus the size of one block equals the address of the other block. When a block is deallocated, if an adjacent free block exists, it is found, removed from the free block list, and combined with the deallocated block; then the larger block is placed back in the free block list. Since there can be at most one block before and one block after the deallocated block, if the procedure recognizes that two block combinings have been performed, it stops searching the list.

The procedures insertblock and removeblockafter are private procedures that manipulate the free block list for the other procedures. These procedures are based on techniques presented in Section 15.1.

For this example, we assume that we allocate from one very large statically allocated block. When this space is all allocated, the system will fail. A failure procedure is provided; but the body of this procedure should be added by the user, since there are several possible ways to attempt to recover, or to report the failure and abort the program.

The module initialization code determines the minimum size of a free block. Although this should be a constant, Modula-2 does not allow constant expressions to invoke the TSIZE procedure, and so a variable is used. Then the one large first block is placed on the free block list.

This implementation is relatively slow, primarily because both allocation and deallocation require searching a potentially very long list of free blocks. Also, it is subject to failure, since it uses the simple approach of beginning with one large statically allocated block. Nevertheless, it is simple to implement and illustrates all the concepts associated with dynamic storage allocation.

15.6.2 A Fibonacci Buddy System Storage Module

In this section we consider a way to speed up the storage allocation and deallocation process. The slowness of the first-fit storage module was a result of having to search the list of free blocks so often. A new approach can eliminate these searches almost entirely.

To eliminate searches during allocation, we need a way to find a free block quickly, once we know the desired size. Our approach will be to keep separate lists for each possible block size, organized as an array of lists indexed by block size. Since we will be given the size needed, we can access the appropriate list and remove the first block. Unfortunately, however, there can be an enormous number of block sizes. To avoid having a great many lists to manage, we will limit block sizes to a relatively small set of values. An allocation request that is not one of these values will be satisfied by allocating a larger block than requested. This results in some unused storage in most blocks, but it is a reasonable price to pay for the faster allocation that results.

To eliminate searches during deallocation, we need a way to locate any free block that is adjacent to the block being deallocated. Our approach will be to allocate and deallocate blocks in pairs, or "buddies," such that when a block is deallocated, its buddy can be located quickly. To accomplish this, we must have a way of determining for each block whether its buddy is before or after it in memory, and we must be able to find the size of its buddy.

Our approach is based on a Fibonacci number sequence, such as the sequence 1, 1, 2, 3, 5, 8, 13, 21, 34, 55, ... Each term in this sequence (except the first two) is the sum of the two preceding terms. We use such a number sequence to determine the block sizes we will allow. When a block can be split into smaller blocks during the allocation process, it will be split into blocks whose sizes are the next two smaller terms in the sequence.

A block will always be split with the larger piece being at the lower address, which is the same address as the block being split. The smaller piece will have a higher address. When a block is split, each of the pieces will be given a *split code* that records whether it is the lower or higher address piece. The code for the larger piece (the lower address piece) will be its parent block's code plus one. The code for the smaller piece (the higher address piece) will always be zero. Notice that this code allows us to find buddies. If the code is zero, the buddy is one size larger and has a lower address; if the code is not zero, the buddy is one size smaller and has a higher address. Since each block will also record its own size, we can easily compute the size and then the address of the buddy block. Figure 15.8 shows the sizes and split codes for a block, and the blocks into which it might be split.

The buddy system storage allocator is implemented in Program 15.39. Several points should be noted before reading this module. The Fibonacci sequence that determines the block sizes may start with two arbitrary values. The smallest block size, however, must be large enough to hold the information necessary in a free block. This includes a indicator of whether the block is free, its size, and its split code. Since the free blocks will be maintained with a doubly linked list, there must also be space for two pointers or addresses. In this implementation we have chosen 20 and 32 for the first two block sizes. Subsequent sizes are therefore 52, 84, 136, 220, 356, 576, and so on.

The size of a block is recorded as an index 0, 1, . . . , 10, rather than an actual block size in bytes. Since free blocks are kept in an array of lists according to their sizes, these indices are more useful than actual sizes. We also keep an array named lengtharray that contains the actual sizes, so we can convert a size index to an actual size when needed.

The free block lists are structured as an array of doubly linked lists with header nodes. The module initialization code makes each of the header nodes

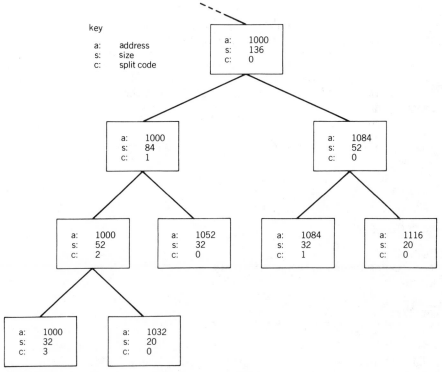

FIGURE 15.8 Hierarchy of Blocks and Buddies

Program 15.39   Fibonacci Buddy System Storage Module

IMPLEMENTATION MODULE Storage;

   (* This module implements a Fibonacci buddy system dynamic storage
   allocation system. *)

FROM SYSTEM IMPORT
   (* type   *)   ADDRESS,
   (* proc   *)   TSIZE, ADR;

FROM operatingsystem IMPORT
   (* proc   *)   opsysallocate;

CONST
   block0length   = 20;
   block1length   = 32;
   maxsizeindex   = 10;
   maxsplitcode   = maxsizeindex;

TYPE
   sizeindexrange   = [0..maxsizeindex];
   splitcoderange   = [0..maxsplitcode];
   freeblockptr   = POINTER TO freeblock;
   freeblock   = RECORD
                            free   : BOOLEAN;
                            sizeindex : sizeindexrange;
                            splitcode : splitcoderange;
                            next   : freeblockptr;
                            prev   : freeblockptr
                        END;
   headerarray   = ARRAY sizeindexrange OF freeblock;
   lengtharray   = ARRAY sizeindexrange OF CARDINAL;

VAR
   systemoverhead : CARDINAL; (* extra space in allocated blocks *)
   freelist   : headerarray;
   blocklength   : lengtharray;
   index   : sizeindexrange;
   block   : freeblockptr;

PROCEDURE failure;

BEGIN
   (* allocation failure: message, abort, etc. *)
END failure;

PROCEDURE emptylist
   (index : sizeindexrange (* in *)) : BOOLEAN;

BEGIN
   RETURN freelist[index].next = ADR (freelist[index])
END emptylist;

```
PROCEDURE insertblock
  (       block : freeblockptr      (* in *) );

BEGIN
  block^.free := TRUE;
  block^.next := freelist[ block^.sizeindex ].next;
  block^.prev := ADR ( freelist[ block^.sizeindex ] );
  freelist[ block^.sizeindex ].next^.prev := block;
  freelist[ block^.sizeindex ].next := block
END insertblock;

PROCEDURE removeblock
  (       block : freeblockptr (* in *) );

BEGIN
  block^.next^.prev := block^.prev;
  block^.prev^.next := block^.next
END removeblock;

PROCEDURE getfirstblock;

  VAR block : freeblockptr;

BEGIN
  opsysallocate ( block, blocklength[ maxsizeindex ] );
  block^.sizeindex := maxsizeindex;
  block^.splitcode := 0;
  insertblock ( block )
END getfirstblock;

PROCEDURE ALLOCATE
  ( VAR blockaddress : ADDRESS (* out *);
        blocksize    : CARDINAL (* in  *) );

  VAR
  block       : freeblockptr;
  buddy       : freeblockptr;
  requestsize : sizeindexrange;
  actualsize  : sizeindexrange;
  blockfound  : BOOLEAN;

BEGIN
  IF blocksize + systemoverhead <= blocklength[ maxsizeindex ]
    THEN (* request is feasible;
            determine minimum size index needed *)
         requestsize := 0;
         WHILE ( blocklength[ requestsize ] <
                  blocksize + systemoverhead )
              AND ( requestsize < maxsizeindex ) DO
           INC ( requestsize )
         END;
```

```
                    (* find the smallest free block of at least this size *)
                    actualsize := requestsize;
                    WHILE emptylist ( actualsize )
                            AND ( actualsize < maxsizeindex ) DO
                      INC ( actualsize )
                    END;
                    blockfound := NOT emptylist ( actualsize );
                    IF blockfound
                       THEN (* allocate all or part of this block *)
                               block := freelist[ actualsize ].next;
                               removeblock ( block );
                               (* split the block as many times as necessary *)
                               WHILE ( actualsize > requestsize ) AND
                                       ( actualsize >= 2 ) DO
                                 buddy := freeblockptr ( CARDINAL ( block ) +
                                             blocklength[ actualsize - 1 ] );
                                 buddy^.splitcode := 0;
                                 INC ( block^.splitcode );
                                 DEC ( block^.sizeindex );
                                 IF requestsize > actualsize - 2
                                    THEN (* allocate from larger piece,
                                            put smaller back *)
                                            buddy^.sizeindex := actualsize - 2;
                                            insertblock ( buddy );
                                            DEC ( actualsize )
                                       ELSE (* allocate from smaller piece,
                                              put larger back *)
                                            insertblock ( block );
                                            DEC ( actualsize, 2 );
                                            buddy^.sizeindex := actualsize;
                                            block := buddy
                                 END
                               END;
                               (* allocate the chosen block, hide the overhead *)
                               block^.free := FALSE;
                               blockaddress := freeblockptr ( CARDINAL ( block ) +
                                                   systemoverhead )
                          ELSE (* no block available,
                                  request more from operating system *)
                               getfirstblock;
                               ALLOCATE ( blockaddress, blocksize )
                       END
                  ELSE (* error: request is larger than maximum block size *)
                       failure
               END
            END ALLOCATE;

         PROCEDURE DEALLOCATE
           ( VAR blockaddress : ADDRESS  (* in/out *);
                 blocksize    : CARDINAL (* in      *) );
```

```
  VAR
     block      : freeblockptr;
     buddy      : freeblockptr;
     buddyfree : BOOLEAN;
BEGIN
  block := freeblockptr ( CARDINAL ( blockaddress ) -
                          systemoverhead );
  buddyfree := TRUE;
  WHILE buddyfree AND ( block^.sizeindex < maxsizeindex ) DO
     IF block^.splitcode > 0
        THEN (* block is low, buddy is at higher address *)
             buddy := freeblockptr ( CARDINAL ( block ) +
                           blocklength[ block^.sizeindex ] );
             buddyfree := buddy^.free AND ( buddy^.sizeindex =
                                                block^.sizeindex - 1 );
             IF buddyfree
                THEN (* combine the two blocks *)
                     DEC ( block^.splitcode );
                     INC ( block^.sizeindex );
                     removeblock ( buddy )
                ELSE (* combining not possible *)
                     insertblock ( block )
             END
        ELSE (* block is high, buddy is at lower address *)
             buddy := freeblockptr ( CARDINAL ( block ) -
                           blocklength[ block^.sizeindex + 1 ] );
             buddyfree := buddy^.free AND ( buddy^.sizeindex =
                                                block^.sizeindex + 1 );
             IF buddyfree
                THEN (* combine the two blocks *)
                     removeblock ( buddy );
                     block := buddy;
                     DEC ( block^.splitcode );
                     INC ( block^.sizeindex )
                ELSE (* combining not possible *)
                     insertblock ( block )
             END
     END
  END;
  IF block^.sizeindex = maxsizeindex
     THEN insertblock ( block ) (* no buddy possible *)
  END
END DEALLOCATE;

BEGIN
  (* determine systemoverhead; must be multiple of four *)
  systemoverhead := TSIZE ( freeblock ) - 2 * TSIZE ( freeblockptr );
  IF systemoverhead MOD 4 < > 0
     THEN systemoverhead := systemoverhead + 4 - systemoverhead MOD 4
  END;
```

```
(* create a table to convert size index to length in "bytes" *)
blocklength[ 0 ] := block0length;
blocklength[ 1 ] := block1length;
FOR index := 2 TO maxsizeindex DO
  blocklength[ index ] := blocklength[ index - 1 ] +
                          blocklength[ index - 2 ]
END;

(* create array of empty free block lists *)
FOR index := 0 TO maxsizeindex DO
  freelist[ index ].next := ADR ( freelist[ index ] );
  freelist[ index ].prev := ADR ( freelist[ index ] )
END;

(* get one block of the largest size from the operating system *)
getfirstblock
END Storage.
```

in the headerarray point to itself. The private procedures insertblock and removeblock manipulate these lists. The procedure emptylist is used to recognize an empty list.

The procedure getfirstblock is implementation dependent. It assumes that the operating system has a storage allocation capability (perhaps one optimized for very large blocks) that can supply the first block to be placed in the free block lists. If the allocation procedure ever fails, it will again request a very large block from the operating system so that it may continue. If this capability is not available from the operating system, the technique used in Section 15.6.1 may be used (i.e., allocating from a statically allocated block declared as a large array).

The allocate procedure first determines the minimum size block that can satisfy the request. This must include the requested space plus the space used for system overhead (block size, split code, and free indicator). It next searches the free block lists to find the first nonempty list with blocks at least this size. The first block in the list is removed. If it is sufficiently large, it will be split as many times as possible until a block of the appropriate size is created. All the buddy blocks created by these splits are returned to the free block lists. Finally, the address of the allocated block is incremented by the system overhead amount, so the user thinks the block starts just past the overhead space.

The deallocate procedure begins by decrementing the address it is given by the system overhead amount, thus recovering the true address of the block. It then enters a loop to try to combine this block with its buddy as many times as possible. It finds the buddy by examining the split code to determine whether the buddy is at a higher or lower address, and then computes the appropriate address. Next it examines the free field of the buddy block; if the buddy is free, the blocks may be combined. The buddy is removed from its free list and combined, and the loop is executed again. The loop terminates when a buddy is found that is not free, or when the maximum size block has been reconstructed. The resulting block is then put back in the appropriate free block list.

This storage allocation scheme is relatively fast, but it does allocate more storage than requested, since blocks come only in certain sizes. However, if the first two block sizes are appropriately chosen, the extra space will normally be in the range of 10–20% of the total space. Thus the speed is attained without paying a large penalty in wasted storage.

15.7 Summary

Dynamic data structures provide a very powerful and versatile way to implement abstract data types. Two approaches have been presented. With linked list implementations, large objects are built from many small, separately allocated pieces or nodes, which are linked together with pointers. Operations that change the size of an object require allocation or deallocation of small pieces, with most of the object remaining unchanged. The other approach allocates all the storage for an object in one large block. It has the advantage of requiring less storage, but may require more time to reallocate the entire object when performing an operation that changes its size. Both approaches are very useful, and the programmer should consider both when designing the implementation of an abstract data type.

We have also seen that the use of dynamically allocated data types requires programmer discipline. Each such data type needs to have operations to define and destroy objects of that type, and these operations must be used at appropriate points in programs. Usually, an object is represented internally with a pointer variable allocated on the stack and the remaining storage space allocated on the heap. We must be sure that the heap space has been deallocated explicitly before the pointer disappears from the stack. Otherwise, the heap space may be lost, which can result in a storage allocation failure.

Opaque types in Modula-2 are usually represented by dynamic structures. We have seen examples of the stack, queue, string, and matrix data types. We have also seen how generic data types may be implemented with dynamic data structures.

The techniques of this chapter are indispensable for all but the smallest software systems. However, the power that they provide must be exercised carefully, since experience has shown that misuse of pointers and dynamic structures is easy, and leads to very subtle program errors.

15.8 Exercises

1. Several additional operations were suggested for the stack, queue, and string data types in the exercises for Chapter 14. Add those same operations to these data types using the dynamic data structures of this chapter.

2. The string delete procedure did not reallocate storage. Modify the procedure so that if a relatively large number of characters are deleted, realloca-

tion takes place, but not for a relatively small number. What would be a reasonable dividing line between these large and small numbers?

3. Suppose a linked list were maintained in alphabetical or numerical order, depending on the items stored in it. Design a linear search algorithm for such a list that can terminate either by finding the item or by recognizing that all remaining items in the list are larger.

4. Comment on the suitability of a linked list of characters as a data structure for the string data type. Consider the amount of storage required, and the speed of the various string operations.

5. Comment on the suitability of using large single blocks instead of linked lists as data structures for the stack and queue data types. Consider the amount of storage required, and the speed of the various operations.

6. Consider a modification of the first-fit storage allocation system, in which the free block list is searched to find the block nearest in size to the request, rather than stopping at the first block that is large enough. Such a system might be called a "best-fit" system. Would this modification lead to better memory utilization?

7. If the free blocks in the first-fit storage allocation system were kept in increasing order by size, how would the first-fit and best-fit methods differ?

8. Suppose that over a period of time, all block sizes from one to the maximum size were requested equally often from the Fibonacci buddy system storage allocator. What would be the average amount of storage wasted, as a percentage of average request size?

16

Process
Abstraction

Throughout the brief history of computer programming, one of the best guides to software design has been to ask the question, "How would I do this if I were to do it myself with pencil and paper?" This question leads beginning programmers to such common algorithms as finding averages, linear search, and selection sort. In more advanced situations, the answer to this question might be, "I can do this part myself, but for this other part I would call a specialist." This answer too has its counterpart in programming; we can consider a procedure to be a specialist at solving a particular problem or class of problems.

We now challenge software developers, when approaching a new problem, to ask the slightly different question, "How would a team of people do this if they could work on it together?" In this chapter we will see how this question leads to a new, different, and extremely powerful software development methodology known as *concurrent programming*. To support this methodology, we need to develop a large group of concepts and techniques, which together we will call *process abstraction*.

To begin, let us consider two examples of teams working together to perform a task. The first is the team of carpenters, plumbers, electricians, masons, roofers, and others who collaborate to build a house. Each person is a specialist in a subset of the skills required. Some of the team members begin their work on the first day of construction; others start later. The members of a group of framing carpenters work together, but only in a loosely coordinated way. That is, most of the time they work as individuals, but from time to time they must perform a short, closely coordinated task, such as carrying the two ends of a plywood sheet, or having one person hold a piece of lumber while another cuts or nails it. After one of these periods of close coordination, the team members resume their independent work. Of course, to allow the periods of coordination, the workers must be able to communicate, both verbally and in the sense of passing materials from one to another. Similarly, they must be able to synchronize their actions, so that people do not try to start nailing before lumber has been cut to size, or begin framing the second story before the first has been framed.

Consider also the case of factory assembly line workers. They too work together on a large task, but the synchronization and communication among them is very highly structured. If they are assembling relatively small items, they may work at a conveyor belt. As a partially assembled item comes down the belt, a worker performs a very specific task, such as adding a few more parts to the item. The synchronization comes from the physical placement of the workers. The communication in the form of passing materials is handled by the conveyor belt.

From these examples we can abstract the important features of the team approach:

Each member of the team is skilled in and responsible for a relatively small part of the overall task.

Each person works independently most of the time.

Each individual's contribution is usually the repetition of one of a small set of tasks over and over. (A person does not do one thing and then go home for the day.)

The tasks performed by the team members are synchronized.

From time to time, the workers will communicate, either in the form of verbal messages or in the form of exchanging materials.

In the terminology of concurrent programming, we have just described the features of *cooperating sequential processes*. A sequential process is a sequence of actions performed repeatedly. Processes are said to cooperate if they can be synchronized and can communicate. For our purposes, we also require that the processes be *loosely coupled;* that is, the time spent in synchronization and communication can be only a very small part of the total time taken by a process. To design a concurrent program, we must develop the abstract concepts of process, process synchronization, and process communication. These concepts are the subjects of the next three sections.

Before looking at the details of process abstraction in Modula-2, let us consider two great advantages of this approach to software design. First, it is still another way of employing the *divide-and-conquer* approach to programming. In early programming languages, subprograms or procedures were provided to allow the software developer to break a big program into smaller pieces, and the value of this language feature is unquestioned. We have now seen that Modula-2 provides modules as another way of organizing the pieces of a program. The process abstraction concepts extend this set of programming tools, leading toward programs that are easier to design and more reliable in use.

The second advantage of concurrent programming is that loosely coupled processes can be run on separate processors, as long as there are ways for the processes to communicate and to be synchronized. With the advent of very low-cost microprocessors, it is reasonable to provide many processors in a single computer system. As such systems become more common, we will have a very real analogy to the human teams discussed earlier, and we will achieve the same goal: speed. If a fixed number of steps must be performed to accomplish a task, the more steps that can be performed simultaneously, the sooner the task will be completed.

The same software design ideas may be used regardless of the number of processors ultimately available for execution of that software. Most modern computer systems provide a *multiprogramming* or *multitasking* capability whereby several programs or tasks may be present in the computer at the same time. The operating system allows each to run for a few milliseconds and then switches to the next one. Because of the great speed of computers, this allows the appearance of simultaneous execution of all the programs. We call this kind of execution *quasi-concurrent* when we want to distinguish it from *concurrent* execution on several different processors. In informal discussions, however, we speak of the development of systems of cooperating sequential processes as concurrent programming regardless of the number of processors on which the system will be executed.

Although computer systems with a large number of separate identical processors are not yet common, most modern computer systems have several separate devices that can operate simultaneously. The terminals, printers, and disk and tape drives of most systems operate independently, except for brief periods of communication and synchronization. In fact, the design of software systems to control all these devices has provided most of the original motivation for concurrent programming. Only recently has it been recognized that concurrent programming concepts are important in all areas of application. We will look specifically at control of devices in Section 16.5.

When designing concurrent programs, we must consider two very important kinds of program correctness properties. The first kind, often called the *safety* properties, include the capacity of each process to perform correctly the parts of the process that are independent of others. We must also ensure that process communication is done in a manner that does not yield incorrect results because of synchronization problems, and that any communication sent by one process is eventually received by another. As an example of a violation of a safety property, consider the very simple case of two processes that share a counter variable. Each process increments that variable at appropriate times; this involves fetching the counter value from memory, adding one, and replacing that value in memory. If the processes are not carefully synchronized, both may try to increment the variable at almost the same time. Suppose the value of the counter is 25 when the two processes begin their respective incrementing steps. One process fetches the value 25, and while it is incrementing the value to 26, the second process also fetches the value 25. The first process replaces the value 26 in memory while the second increments its value 25. Then the second process also replaces the value 26 in memory. Two increments have resulted in the value stored in the counter variable going from 25 to 26. This error is classified as a violation of a safety property.

The steps in two processes that could cause violations of safety properties when executed at nearly the same time are called *critical sections*. To prevent such violations, we must be sure that no two processes are executing their critical sections at the same time. We achieve this by providing a way of ensuring *mutual exclusion* in concurrent programs. Simply stated, we require a process wishing to enter its critical section to wait if a second process is already in its critical section. When the second process leaves its critical section, the first process may resume execution and enter its own critical section.

The second kind of property to consider in the design of concurrent programs is often called a *liveness* property. We want each process to continue to make progress, regardless of what happens in another process. For example, if we have a process to control each device in a computer system, the failure of a tape drive would cause one process to be unable to perform useful work. However, we do not want the failure of this single process to cause all other processes to fail also. To satisfy the liveness properties, we require that any process wishing to enter its critical section eventually be allowed to do so.

All approaches to concurrent programming attempt to provide process synchronization and communication in ways that satisfy the safety and liveness properties. It is beyond the scope of this book to examine these several approaches in detail, and we concentrate instead on the features of Modula-2 that support process abstraction.

16.1 Processes in Modula-2

Modula-2 provides a small set of primitives for process abstraction. They are low-level features of the language and are defined in the module named SYS-TEM (see Section 13.1). In this section we look at three of these primitives: the PROCESS type and the procedures NEWPROCESS and TRANSFER. We then use these primitives to build modules that support much higher levels of process abstraction.

16.1.1 The Coroutine Concept

A procedure in Modula-2 is a subprogram, that is, a piece of a program, subordinate to a higher level of program. When a procedure is invoked, execution begins at the first statement and proceeds through to the end, unless a halt statement or a return statement is encountered. Upon exit, execution resumes in the invoking program. There is an explicit hierarchical relationship between the high level main program and the lower level subprogram.

Two procedures may also be defined with an equal relationship rather than a hierarchical one; these procedures are known as *coroutines*. Neither is the main program, and neither is the subprogram. They execute cooperatively, and either one is capable of relinquishing the processor for the other to use. This transfer of control may occur at any point in the code. Furthermore, when a coroutine resumes execution, it begins from where it left off, that is, where it previously relinquished control. This situation is like resuming a main program after a subprogram has executed, but each coroutine behaves this way. In a sense, they are both main programs that take turns using the processor. This is similar to the concept of cooperating sequential processes that we have just seen, and so coroutines may be used as a way of implementing processes.

Just as a main program must explicitly invoke a subprogram, a coroutine must explicitly relinquish control to another coroutine. It is therefore impossible for coroutines to satisfy the liveness property in all cases. If a coroutine encounters a fatal error condition before relinquishing control, all other coroutines are permanently prevented from executing. As we will see, concurrent programming is impossible in Modula-2 because this language provides only coroutines as a way of implementing processes. However, we will develop some process abstractions that are sufficiently close to concurrent programming to illustrate virtually all its techniques. In Section 16.6 we comment further on the possibility of doing real concurrent programing in Modula-2.

16.1.2 The PROCESS Type

In Modula-2, a *process* is a parameterless procedure declared at the highest level (not contained in any other procedure). Although technically a procedure, we do not invoke a process in the usual way, nor do we allow a process to exit, either by reaching its end or by executing a return statement. Many processes are structured as an infinite loop, using the loop statement without an exit statement. Of course, within the loop the process may temporarily relinquish control to another process (a coroutine).

The data type PROCESS, exported from module SYSTEM, provides the means of declaring processes in a program. A process will have associated with it some statements (the parameterless procedure) and some data storage space. Once these associations have been made (see Section 16.1.3), it is possible for the process to begin execution. Any number of process variables may be declared and started, with each relinquishing control to another from time to time. However, from the software designer's point of view, the processes are all executing simultaneously.

A process is a variable; hence is declared in the usual way. If a module imports the PROCESS type from SYSTEM, declarations like the following are valid.

```
var reader : PROCESS;
    printer : PROCESS;
```

16.1.3 The NEWPROCESS Procedure

The SYSTEM module exports the procedure NEWPROCESS to associate a procedure and some data space with a process. This procedure is defined as follows:

```
PROCEDURE NEWPROCESS
    (       program   : PROC        (* in  *):
            workspace : ADDRESS     (* in  *):
            spacesize : CARDINAL    (* in  *):
        VAR newproc   : PROCESS     (* out *) );
```

The first parameter is the parameterless procedure that will be the code of the process. Notice that it is of the predefined type PROC, which is the type of all parameterless procedures. The second parameter is the address of the workspace for the process, as described below; the third parameter is the size of this workspace. The fourth parameter is the process that is being created. After execution of NEWPROCESS, this process will have associated with it the program and the workspace and will be ready for execution.

Any program or procedure in Modula-2 must have storage space allocated for its stack, where its global data and the parameters and local data of its procedures are stored. A procedure is always given stack space that is part of the stack space of its parent program or procedure. However, since a process does not have a parent, it must be given stack space in a different way. The workspace for a process is allocated explicitly using the procedure AL-LOCATE.

The size of the workspace needed by a process is not always easy to determine. It must be large enough to hold all the global variables defined in the process, plus all the parameters and local variables of all the internal procedures that may be active at the same time. Remember that storage is required for a procedure only while it is active; if neither of two procedures invokes the other, they cannot be active at the same time. In addition to this variable space, the workspace must also include a few words of storage for procedure linkages at each level of procedure nesting. For small programs, such as the examples in this chapter, a workspace of 400 to 1000 storage units is typical. Processes containing large data structures may need considerably more.

16.1.4 The TRANSFER Procedure

Since a process is not invoked with a procedure invocation statement, there must be another method to get it started. This is supplied by the TRANSFER procedure, exported from the SYSTEM module, and defined as follows:

```
PROCEDURE TRANSFER
    ( VAR oldprocess  : PROCESS     (* out *);
      VAR newprocess  : PROCESS     (* in  *) );
```

The first parameter is the process that is relinquishing control; the second parameter is the process that is resuming control (or beginning). The current status (address to resume execution, hardware register contents, etc.) of the process that performs this transfer is saved in the parameter oldprocess. The status of the process gaining control is recovered from the parameter newprocess. Reversing the order of these parameters in a subsequent invocation of TRANSFER would resume execution of the original process at the point where it left off.

The NEWPROCESS procedure creates in a process variable the appropriate status for that process to begin. A subsequent transfer to that process allows it to begin execution at its first statement. Thereafter, each transfer to that process resumes where it relinquished control.

The TRANSFER procedure is implemented so that the current value of the second parameter is accessed before the new value of the first parameter is stored. Therefore it is possible for the same variable to be used as both actual parameters. This is a common practice when only two processes are present in a system, and a single process variable always holds the status of the process that is not currently active. In such a situation, the program will contain statements like the following.

```
VAR waitingprocess : PROCESS;
NEWPROCESS ( ..., waitingprocess );
TRANSFER ( waitingprocess, waitingprocess );
```

The same transfer would also appear in the body of the procedure that implements the other process.

16.2   Process Synchronization

The gradual development of methods of synchronizing processes is one of the more fascinating stories in the history of computer science. We will take advantage of the results of that development here, and develop rather easily a simple but powerful synchronization method, based on the concept of a *binary semaphore*. Later we will develop a more general process synchronization module, based on *general semaphores*. The references by Dijkstra (1968) and Ben-Ari (1982) present detailed discussions of these important concepts.

16.2.1   A Binary Semaphore Process Synchronization Module

We begin by developing a synchronization module that provides (exports) one data type and five procedures. The data type is called SIGNAL, and as the name implies, it provides a way for two processes to signal each other for synchronization purposes. A process may send a signal to indicate that a certain event has occurred, or it may wait for the receipt of a signal from another process before proceeding to do some action. This capability provides a method of mutual exclusion in critical sections. Each process sends a signal when leaving its own critical section, and each waits for such a signal from the other before entering its own critical section.

Since a signal is a data type, it has associated operations. Sending and waiting are two; a third is initialization. The fourth operation, which is a test to determine whether a process is currently waiting for a given signal, is implemented as a boolean function procedure. We do not need assignment or equality test for the signal type, even though it is implemented as a dynamic type.

The fifth procedure in our module is a higher level of abstraction of getting a process started. It combines the actions of the NEWPROCESS and TRANSFER procedures in a way compatible with the operations of the SIGNAL type.

The definition module for our simple process synchronization module is shown in Program 16.1. The relatively unusual choice of upper- and lowercase in the identifiers was chosen to match that of a similar module defined by Wirth (1982).

Program 16.1   Simple Process Synchronization Definition Module

```
DEFINITION MODULE Processes;

  (* This module provides a simple process synchronization abstraction
     based on binary semaphores. *)

EXPORT QUALIFIED
  (* type *) SIGNAL,
  (* proc *) Init, SEND, WAIT, Awaited, StartProcess;

TYPE
  SIGNAL;

PROCEDURE Init
  ( VAR s      : SIGNAL    (* out    *) );

PROCEDURE SEND
  ( VAR s      : SIGNAL    (* in/out *) );

PROCEDURE WAIT
  ( VAR s      : SIGNAL    (* in/out *) );

PROCEDURE Awaited
  (     s      : SIGNAL    (* in     *) ) : BOOLEAN;

PROCEDURE StartProcess
  (     p    : PROC       (* in    *);
        wssize : CARDINAL (* in    *) );

END Processes.
```

Let us describe in some detail the goals of this module before giving its implementation. Consider a software system containing several processes that conceptually are executing simultaneously. Two or more of them may share data in such a way that to satisfy the safety properties, only one process may work on the data at a time. We want to define a signal named "data free" for use in synchronizing access to these data. When a process wants to access the data, it performs the wait operation on the data free signal. The result is to suspend execution of this process until some other process sends that signal. If several processes are waiting for this signal, only one is allowed to resume execution upon receipt of it. After that process has finished using the data, it performs the send operation of the signal, allowing another process to resume.

At this level of abstraction, a process should not have to deal with explicit coroutine transfers. However, since a process is a coroutine in Modula-2, it must explicitly relinquish control to allow another process to execute. We solve this apparent problem by building the transfers into the implementation of the signal operations. Clearly, a wait operation should suspend the current process while it waits for the signal, and thus a transfer will appear in the implementation of the wait procedure. Conceptually, a send operation does not result in a transfer; the sending process keeps right on going. But the send operation is a voluntary operation on the part of a process, and we can take advantage of this gesture to let another process run for a while. Remember, our abstraction should allow each process to run often enough to satisfy the liveness properties and to give the appearance of simultaneous execution. After sending a signal, the current process is suspended, but it does not have to wait for a specific signal to resume. It must simply wait for its turn to run again.

The StartProcess procedure is another obvious place to do a transfer. As for the send operation, when we suspend the current process and start the new one, the suspended process is not waiting for a specific signal, but merely for its turn to use the processor.

When a send operation is performed, we need to be able to transfer to a process that is waiting for that signal. Since there may be an arbitrary number of processes waiting, we need a dynamic data structure to hold them. To be equitable, we should serve these processes on a first come, first served basis. Hence we need a dynamic queue for each signal variable.

When a process is suspended because of a wait operation, it is saved in the queue for the appropriate signal. When a process is suspended because of a send operation or the starting of a new process, it should be saved in a different queue, a queue of ready processes that are simply waiting their turns again.

One potential problem should be noted. If a process is waiting for a signal, another process sending that signal will result in an appropriate transfer of control. However, if one process sends a signal before another process has performed a wait operation, the signal can be lost. To prevent this, we associate with each signal a boolean variable named sent, which usually is false. If a signal is sent and no process is waiting, we set this variable to true to remember that the signal was sent. A subsequent wait operation can then detect that a signal has already been sent. A send operation that occurs after a wait will behave as described before; in this case the sent variable will remain false. This variable is related to a similar concept defined for semaphores (see Ben-Ari, 1982). The name *binary* semaphore is used because the variable can take on only two values.

We can now outline the implementation of this module. Since a signal is a queue plus a boolean variable, initializing a signal is the same as initializing the queue and the variable. The queue operation makeempty (see Section 15.3) may be used.

The send operation looks at the queue for the given signal to see whether any process is waiting for that signal. If so, the process at the front of the queue is removed, and the current process is placed on the queue of ready processes. A transfer is then made to the new process. If no process is waiting, the sent variable is set to true. If there are processes in the ready queue, a transfer is made to one of them. Otherwise, the current process is allowed to continue.

The wait operation inserts the current process in the queue for the given signal and transfers to the process at the front of the queue of ready processes. There is a possibility here for a gross violation of the liveness properties, because that queue might be empty. Such a situation, called *deadlock,* is clearly a fatal error. The wait procedure can recognize deadlock and can invoke a deadlock handler procedure. In our simple implementation, this procedure prints an error message and halts.

Programmers new to concurrent programming will find that deadlock occurs much more often than they expect. Remember that processes are supposed to cooperate. If one process waits for a signal, another process should eventually send that signal. If a programmer forgets to send that signal in a process, the effects in other processes can be disastrous.

The Awaited procedure determines whether any process is currently waiting for the named signal. This is easy to implement—we simply examine the queue for that signal to see if it is empty. This procedure may be useful when a process chooses not to send a signal if no other process is waiting for that signal.

The procedure to start a new process is given a procedure and the size of the workspace desired. The details of allocating the workspace, attaching the workspace and procedure to a process, and transferring control to that process are all hidden in the implementation. The PROCESS data type is not needed outside our module, since all the process variables are declared within the implementation module. The user program deals only with parameterless procedures.

A few other details should be mentioned before presenting the implementation module. We declare a variable in the module to hold the current process, and each transfer gives this variable a new value. We have a small problem when it becomes necessary to put the current process into a queue before transferring to another process. In our discussions of queues in Chapter 14 and 15, the values inserted in a queue were always copies of the original value (the queue insert procedure uses a value parameter). The transfer operation saves the status of the current process, and that is what should go in the queue. However, we cannot do the queue insert operation after the transfer, because the transfer gives control to another process. Nor can we do the queue insert operation before the transfer, because the status of the current procedure has not yet been saved.

The dilemma is expressed by our need to put a value into a queue before that value has been created. We want the transfer operation to store the status of the current process in the same variable that has already been put in the queue. This is a relatively common programming problem, in which the same value needs to be stored in several different places in such a way that changing any one of them changes them all. The solution is to store only one copy of the value, and let all the different places store pointers to the one original copy. As long as the original remains in the same location, it can be changed by means of an access through any of the pointers to the original.

For our implementation, our queues will contain pointers to processes, rather than the processes themselves. We can then insert a pointer to a process in a queue and still have the original process variable available for use in the transfer operation. We need to make only a small change to the queue definition and implementation modules of Section 15.3, namely, every occurrence of elementtype in those modules must be changed to ADDRESS. Since the address data type is compatible with all pointer types, this new queue implementation may be used unchanged for any application that needs a queue of pointers to some data type.

The implementation module for our abstraction is shown in Program 16.2. Study it carefully, since it forms the starting point for all later examples in this chapter.

Program 16.2 Simple Process Synchronization Implementation Module

```
IMPLEMENTATION MODULE Processes;

  (* This module provides a simple process synchronization abstraction
     based on binary semaphores. *)

FROM SYSTEM IMPORT
  (* type *) ADDRESS, PROCESS,
  (* proc *) TSIZE, NEWPROCESS, TRANSFER;

FROM Storage IMPORT
  (* proc *) ALLOCATE;

FROM queueadt IMPORT
  (* type *) queue,
  (* proc *) makeempty, empty, insert, remove, define, destroy;

FROM InOut IMPORT
  (* proc *) WriteString, WriteLn;

TYPE
  SIGNAL     = POINTER TO semaphore;
  semaphore = RECORD
                  sent  : BOOLEAN;
                  procs : queue
                END;
  processptr = POINTER TO PROCESS;
```

```
VAR
  currentprocess : processptr;
  readyqueue     : queue;

PROCEDURE deadlockhandler;

BEGIN
  WriteString ( 'Deadlock has occurred' );
  WriteLn;
  HALT
END deadlockhandler;

PROCEDURE Init
  ( VAR s      : SIGNAL (* out     *) );

BEGIN
  NEW ( s );
  s^.sent := FALSE;
  define ( s^.procs );
  makeempty ( s^.procs )
END Init;

PROCEDURE SEND
  ( VAR s      : SIGNAL (* in/out *) );

  VAR prevprocess : processptr;

BEGIN
  IF NOT empty ( s^.procs ) (* a process is waiting *)
    THEN insert ( readyqueue, currentprocess );
         prevprocess := currentprocess;
         remove ( s^.procs, currentprocess );
         TRANSFER ( prevprocess^, currentprocess^ )
    ELSE s^.sent := TRUE;
         IF NOT empty ( readyqueue )
           THEN insert ( readyqueue, currentprocess );
                prevprocess := currentprocess;
                remove ( readyqueue, currentprocess );
                TRANSFER ( prevprocess^, currentprocess^ )
         END
  END
END SEND;

PROCEDURE WAIT
  ( VAR s      : SIGNAL (* in/out *) );

  VAR prevprocess : processptr;
```

```
BEGIN
  IF sˆ.sent
    THEN sˆ.sent := FALSE
    ELSIF NOT empty ( readyqueue )
         THEN insert ( sˆ.procs, currentprocess );
              prevprocess := currentprocess;
              remove ( readyqueue, currentprocess );
              TRANSFER ( prevprocessˆ, currentprocessˆ )
         ELSE deadlockhandler
  END
END WAIT;

PROCEDURE Awaited
    (    s       : SIGNAL     (* in     *) ) : BOOLEAN;

BEGIN
  RETURN NOT empty ( sˆ.procs )
END Awaited;

PROCEDURE StartProcess
    (     p      : PROC       (* in     *);
          wssize : CARDINAL (* in     *) );

  VAR workspace  : ADDRESS;
       prevprocess : processptr;
BEGIN
  ALLOCATE ( workspace, wssize );
  insert ( readyqueue, currentprocess );
  prevprocess := currentprocess;
  NEW ( currentprocess );
  NEWPROCESS ( p, workspace, wssize, currentprocessˆ );
  TRANSFER ( prevprocessˆ, currentprocessˆ )
END StartProcess;

BEGIN (* module initialization *)
  define ( readyqueue );
  makeempty ( readyqueue );
  NEW ( currentprocess );
END Processes.
```

16.2.2 A General Semaphore Process Synchronization Module

In this section we develop a process synchronization module somewhat more general than that of the preceding section. The most important change is that we base our signal type on a general semaphore rather than a binary semaphore. Rather than developing the concept of a general semaphore in detail, we will discuss this change in terms of signals.

Remember that a signal is a way for one process to inform another process of the occurrence of an event. In general, it is possible for a process to send the same signal many times without another process knowing about it. It is the nature of concurrent programming that the relative speeds of two processes cannot be predicted. Thus in one situation, a process may send a signal before another process has executed a wait on that signal; in another situation the reverse may be true. If a process sends more than one signal before another process performs a wait, all signals but the first are lost. It is of course not possible for a process to perform more than one wait before another process sends a signal; the first wait suspends the process. This difference in behavior is undesirable in many applications, since the results of the program depend on process timing, and the programmer cannot control that timing. Notice also that this behavior is not inherent in the concept of a signal, but depends on our particular implementation.

To suggest a solution, we consider an example of a common concurrent programming situation known as a *producer-consumer problem.* One process, known as the *producer,* may read in data, perform some error checking or preprocessing, and send the value to the second process. This process, the *consumer,* performs additional processing on the value and prints an answer. Because it is anticipated that the two processes will not work at exactly the same speed on each item, we wish to provide a buffer. The producer inserts a value into the buffer whenever it has one to send; the consumer removes a value whenever it is ready to work on another one. To synchronize this communication, the producer sends a signal each time it puts a value in the buffer, and the consumer sends a different signal each time it removes one.

Now consider this possible sequence of events. The producer has a great burst of speed and puts several values in the buffer while the consumer continues to work on a single value. Because the consumer is not waiting, all but the first of the signals sent by the producer during this period are lost. Next, the producer runs out of data to read and stops producing values. No more signals are sent. Then the consumer finishes working on its value, and performs a wait operation. It finds that one signal has been sent, so it gets a value, processes it, and performs another wait. Because several signals have been lost, the consumer cannot proceed. Both processes sit idle, while the buffer contains several items that will never be consumed.

It might be suggested that the consumer be designed to keep consuming as long as the buffer is not empty (with the producer to keep producing as long as the buffer is not full, assuming a static buffer). This will not work, however, for the same reasons discussed in connection with the example of two processes sharing a counter. The buffer is a shared variable, and accessing it, including accesses to test for empty or full, must occur in critical sections of each process. To synchronize access to the buffer, the processes must send signals, and we are back to the same problem again.

The solution is to prevent signals from being lost. Since a particular signal does not carry any information with it other than the fact that it was sent, all occurrences of a given signal are identical. Thus to save signals, we simply need to count them. We associate a counter with each signal and start the counter at zero. When a signal is sent and a process is waiting for that signal, the waiting process may resume execution. If no process is waiting, however, we increment the counter for that signal.

When a wait is performed, if the counter is zero the process must wait. If the counter is greater than zero, at least one such signal has already been sent, so the process does not have to wait. In this case, it decrements the signal counter to indicate that one of the signals has been acknowledged or received.

With this new kind of signal, the problems described above disappear. The producer may send as many signals as it wants, each signal representing another item in the buffer. The consumer still performs a wait operation before trying to remove an item from the buffer; but if the signal counter is positive, the consumer may decrement the counter and proceed. Notice that the signal counter in this example also tells how many items are currently in the buffer.

The ability to remember how many send operations have been performed, rather than just whether one has been performed, distinguishes our new signal type from the preceding one. A similar concept for semaphores distinguishes general semaphores from binary semaphores.

In addition to associating a counter with each signal, we can add some other capabilities to our new process abstraction. First, remember that we have not allowed processes to halt. A Modula-2 coroutine that executes a halt statement will halt the entire program, whereas executing a return statement or reaching the end of the body of the process results in an error. In most situations, it is desirable for a process that has completed all it was required to do to terminate itself. This action should not halt any other process, but should just remove the terminated process from contention for use of the processor. We will add such an operation to our new module.

Second, it is common for a main program to be given the relatively simple chore of starting all the processes and "going to sleep" until all the processes have terminated. This is not possible with our current process abstraction operations, since the main program is one of the coroutines in Modula-2. What we need is a capability for the main program to perform a wait operation, waiting for a signal that all the processes have terminated. This is not quite as simple as it sounds, because we have no process that can send such a signal. Each process is aware of its own existence, and no more. Of course, each process expects to send and receive signals, and thus knows that there should be other processes out there somewhere, but no process can be aware of the status of other processes. Therefore we must provide this capability through our abstraction. We provide a new signal, named idle, to be sent by our abstraction when all processes have terminated.

Third, we might note that the procedure Awaited is probably unnecessary with our new kind of signal. The purpose of that procedure is to allow a process to avoid sending a signal if no other process is waiting for that signal, hence losing the signal. Now that we have prevented lost signals, this procedure is less useful. For compatibility with the preceding abstraction, however, we will keep it.

Fourth, we add another abstract data type, called processid. It is often useful for a process to be aware of its own identity, or for a program that serves several processes to know which process is currently requesting its services. The processid type provides these capabilities. The only operations needed are assignment and equality test, and our implementation will allow us to use the Modula-2 assignment operator. We provide a procedure for equality tests and also a constant named nullprocess, which is guaranteed not to be equal to any actual process and is useful for initializing variables of the processid type. Finally, we provide the variable currentprocess, which always contains the identity of the current process. Any process that accesses this variable therefore sees its own identity.

The definition module for our new process abstraction is shown in Program 16.3.

Program 16.3 Process Synchronization Definition Module

```
DEFINITION MODULE Processes;

  (* This module provides a process synchronization abstraction based on
     general (non-binary) semaphores. It also provides additional
     capabilities to support various process communication abstractions. *)

FROM SYSTEM IMPORT
  (* type  *) ADDRESS;

EXPORT QUALIFIED
  (* const *) nullprocess,
  (* type  *) SIGNAL, processid,
  (* var   *) idle, currentprocess,
  (* proc  *) Init, SEND, WAIT, Awaited,      (* for signals   *)
              StartProcess, Terminate, equal; (* for processes *)

TYPE
  SIGNAL;
  processid;

VAR
  nullprocess    : processid;
  idle           : SIGNAL;
  currentprocess : processid;

PROCEDURE Init
  ( VAR s     : SIGNAL   (* out    *)  );

PROCEDURE SEND
  ( VAR s     : SIGNAL   (* in/out *)  );

PROCEDURE WAIT
  ( VAR s     : SIGNAL   (* in/out *)  );

PROCEDURE Awaited
  (     s     : SIGNAL   (* in     *)  ) : BOOLEAN;
```

```
PROCEDURE StartProcess
    (    p      : PROC      (* in    *);
         wssize : CARDINAL  (* in    *) ) ;

PROCEDURE Terminate;

PROCEDURE equal
    (    p1     : processid  (* in    *);
         p2     : processid  (* in    *) )  : BOOLEAN;

END Processes.
```

The implementation of this abstraction has a few new features. To recognize when all processes have terminated, we maintain a counter of active processes named activeprocesses. This counter is set to zero during module initialization; it is incremented by the StartProcess procedure and decremented by the Terminate procedure.

We export a signal variable named idle, which is initialized in the module initialization. The main program can then perform a wait on this signal to put itself to sleep. Note that no other process should perform a wait on the idle signal; if it does, it can never terminate itself. This means that the process counter never would get to zero, and the idle signal never would be sent.

The Terminate procedure is responsible for recognizing when all processes have terminated. It first decrements the active process counter and then checks to see if it has become zero. If the counter has become zero, and if the main program is waiting for the idle signal, the terminate procedure moves the main program from the idle queue to the ready queue. Of course the ready queue must have been empty for this to happen, since all processes have now terminated. The procedure next performs a transfer to the next process in the ready queue, but without saving the current process (the one that invoked Terminate) in any queue. If no processes are in the ready queue, deadlock has occurred. Note that this is essentially a send (idle) operation, but without saving the current process.

The send operation always tries to do a transfer. If a process is waiting for the given signal, it resumes execution. Otherwise, if the ready queue is not empty, the process at the front of that queue resumes. Failing that, the current process continues.

For the processid data type, we use a pointer to the process created in the NEWPROCESS procedure. The null process can then be the nil pointer. We already have a variable to keep track of the current process.

In some implementations of Modula-2, assignment and equality tests may be defined on opaque types; in other implementations they may not be. We might therefore have to provide these operations as procedures. The implementation shown here was tested with a compiler that allows assignment of opaque types but not equality testing. Hence we provide the equal procedure.

The implementation module for our general semaphore process synchronization abstraction is shown in Program 16.4.

Program 16.4   Process Synchronization Implementation Module

```
IMPLEMENTATION MODULE Processes;

(* This module provides a process synchronization abstraction based on
   general (non-binary) semaphores. It also provides additional capabilities
   to support various process communication abstractions. *)

FROM SYSTEM IMPORT
   (* type *) ADDRESS, PROCESS,
   (* proc *) TSIZE, NEWPROCESS, TRANSFER;

FROM Storage IMPORT
   (* proc *) ALLOCATE;

FROM queueadt IMPORT
   (* type *) queue,
   (* proc *) makeempty, empty, insert, remove, define, destroy;

FROM InOut IMPORT
   (* proc *) WriteString, WriteLn;

TYPE
   SIGNAL    = POINTER TO semaphore;
   semaphore = RECORD
                   value :   CARDINAL;
                   procs :   queue
               END;
   processid = POINTER TO PROCESS;

VAR
   readyqueue      : queue;
   activeprocesses : CARDINAL;

PROCEDURE deadlockhandler;

BEGIN
   WriteString ( 'Deadlock has occurred' );
   WriteLn;
   HALT
END deadlockhandler;

PROCEDURE Init
   ( VAR s      : SIGNAL (* out    *) );

BEGIN
   NEW ( s );
   s^.value := 0;
   define ( s^.procs );
   makeempty ( s^.procs )
END Init;

PROCEDURE SEND
   ( VAR s      : SIGNAL (* in/out *) );
```

```
    VAR prevprocess : processid;

BEGIN
  IF NOT empty ( s^.procs ) (* a process is waiting *)
    THEN insert ( readyqueue, currentprocess );
         prevprocess := currentprocess;
         remove ( s^.procs, currentprocess );
         TRANSFER ( prevprocess^, currentprocess^ )
    ELSE INC ( s^.value );
         IF NOT empty ( readyqueue )
           THEN insert ( readyqueue, currentprocess );
                prevprocess := currentprocess;
                remove ( readyqueue, currentprocess );
                TRANSFER ( prevprocess^, currentprocess^ )
         END
  END
END SEND;

PROCEDURE WAIT
  ( VAR s      : SIGNAL (* in/out *) );

  VAR prevprocess : processid;

BEGIN
 IF s^.value > 0
   THEN DEC ( s^.value )
   ELSIF NOT empty ( readyqueue )
        THEN insert ( s^.procs, currentprocess );
             prevprocess := currentprocess;
             remove ( readyqueue, currentprocess );
             TRANSFER ( prevprocess^, currentprocess^ )
        ELSE deadlockhandler
  END
END WAIT;

PROCEDURE Awaited
  (      s : SIGNAL    (* in *) ) : BOOLEAN;

BEGIN
   RETURN NOT empty ( s^.procs )
END Awaited;

PROCEDURE StartProcess
  (      p     : PROC     (* in *);
         wssize : CARDINAL (* in *) );

  VAR workspace  : ADDRESS;
      prevprocess : processid;
```

```
BEGIN
  ALLOCATE ( workspace, wssize );
  INC ( activeprocesses );
  insert ( readyqueue, currentprocess );
  prevprocess := currentprocess;
  NEW ( currentprocess );
  NEWPROCESS ( p, workspace, wssize, currentprocess^ );
  TRANSFER ( prevprocess^, currentprocess^ )
END StartProcess;

PROCEDURE Terminate;

  VAR prevprocess : processid;

BEGIN
  DEC ( activeprocesses );
  IF ( activeprocesses = 0 ) AND NOT empty ( idle^.procs )
    THEN remove ( idle^.procs, prevprocess );
         insert ( readyqueue, prevprocess )
  END;
  IF NOT empty ( readyqueue )
    THEN prevprocess := currentprocess;
         remove ( readyqueue, currentprocess );
         TRANSFER ( prevprocess^, currentprocess^ )
    ELSE deadlockhandler
  END
END Terminate;

PROCEDURE equal
  (     p1    : processid (* in *);
        p2    : processid (* in *) ) : BOOLEAN;

BEGIN
  RETURN p1 = p2
END equal;

BEGIN (* module initialization *)
  Init ( idle );
  define ( readyqueue );
  makeempty ( readyqueue );
  nullprocess := NIL;
  NEW ( currentprocess );
  activeprocesses := 0;
END Processes.
```

16.3 Process Communication

There are many different ways for processes to communicate with each other, and all require some kind of synchronization to guarantee the safety properties. Since we now have two process synchronization abstractions, we can consider process communication. We look at three classes of communication, and show an implementation of each. These three classes are not really disjoint, and other classes exist. We choose these three because they illustrate some of the most common techniques for process communication. We urge the reader to look for other communications models that may be suggested by specific applications.

16.3.1 The Shared Variable Model

We have already talked about shared variables in our development of the synchronization abstraction. In summary, we note that the places where a process accesses a shared variable are critical sections, and processes must use signals to synchronize entry to and exit from these critical sections.

We demonstrate the use of shared variables by giving an implementation of the shared counter problem mentioned at the beginning of this chapter. Rather than trying to define why the processes are sharing the counter, we note that the statements in the two processes that increment the counter constitute critical sections. A signal named ok will be declared for controlling access to the critical sections. Each process performs a wait before entering its critical section and performs a send after leaving it.

If the two processes run at about the same speed, they will eventually become synchronized to the point of being able to alternate being in their critical sections. If, however, one process is much faster than the other, it can enter and leave its critical section many times in succession, with each send operation allowing itself to proceed through the next wait operation. Either behavior is correct; all that we need is mutual exclusion of access to the shared counter variable.

The simple (binary semaphore) process synchronization abstraction suffices for this example. Since that did not include the terminate operation and the idle signal, we must let the main program be one of the processes. It starts the second process and then sends the first signal to get things started. This first signal is appropriate because at the start of the program neither process is in its critical section, so it is "ok" for either process to enter its critical section.

Let us place some output statements in the two processes so that we can trace the execution behavior. The output of Program 16.5 is shown in Figure 16.1. Is the value of the counter unexpected?

Program 16.5 Shared Variable Communication

```
MODULE SharedVariable;

   (* This module demonstrates process communication via a shared
      variable; it uses the process synchronization module based on binary
      semaphores. *)

FROM Processes IMPORT
   (* type *) SIGNAL,
   (* proc *) Init, SEND, WAIT, StartProcess;
```

```
FROM InOut IMPORT
  (* proc *) WriteCard, WriteString, WriteLn;

VAR
  counter : CARDINAL; (* the shared variable        *)
  ok      : SIGNAL;   (* ok to enter critical section *)

PROCEDURE process2;

BEGIN
  WriteString ( 'Process 2 has started' );
  WriteLn;
  LOOP
    WAIT ( ok );
    WriteString ( 'Process 2 critical section' );
    WriteLn;
    INC ( counter );
    SEND ( ok );
    (* other processing *)
  END
END process2;

BEGIN (* main program is Process 1 *)
  WriteString ( 'Process 1 has started' );
  WriteLn;
  Init ( ok );
  counter := 0;
  StartProcess ( process2, 400 );
  SEND ( ok );
  LOOP
    WAIT ( ok );
    WriteString ( 'Process 1 critical section' );
    WriteLn;
    INC ( counter );
    IF counter > 10 THEN EXIT END;
    SEND ( ok );
    (* other processing *)
  END;
  WriteString ( 'counter =' );
  WriteCard ( counter, 3 );
  WriteLn;
  WriteString ( 'End of program' );
  WriteLn
END SharedVariable.
```

The shared variable model of process communication is the basis for all other models we will see. However, it is at a level of abstraction too low to be useful in the design of large software systems. We use it instead to develop higher level process communication abstractions.

Process 1 has started
Process 2 has started
Process 2 critical section
Process 1 critical section
Process 2 critical section
Process 1 critical section
Process 2 critical section
Process 1 critical section
Process 2 critical section
Process 1 critical section
Process 2 critical section
Process 1 critical section
Process 2 critical section
Process 1 critical section
counter = 12
End of program

FIGURE 16.1   Output from Program 16.5

16.3.2   The Buffer Model

In Section 16.2.2 we used as motivation for the general semaphore-based process synchronization abstraction the fact that one process may produce data faster than another process can accept it. In this section we implement a buffer to place between these two processes to hold the data.

The implementation of a buffer need not be known by the processes that use it. To hide the implementation, we organize the buffer as a definition and an implementation module. The processes do need to know how to put data into the buffer and how to get data out, and we provide this information as two exported procedures, called deposit and fetch.

The definition module for a buffer is quite simple, as shown in Program 16.6

Program 16.6   Buffer Definition Module

```
DEFINITION MODULE buffers;

    (* This module provides a process communication abstraction based on
      the buffer model. *)

EXPORT QUALIFIED
    (* proc *) deposit, fetch;

PROCEDURE deposit
    (        character : CHAR (* in   *) );

PROCEDURE fetch
    ( VAR character : CHAR (* out *) );

END buffers.
```

The most important aspect of this model is that the synchronization of accesses to the buffer also is hidden from the processes. The buffer is clearly a shared variable, and each access will create a critical section. Therefore we must bracket each access by appropriate wait and send operations, as we did in the example in Section 16.3.1. The waits and sends will be incorporated into the deposit and fetch procedures, and so will be hidden from the processes.

The buffer behaves like a queue. However, we need only two operations, corresponding to the insert and remove operations, but here called deposit and fetch. Initialization is done only once, in the module initialization, and thus does not appear as a separate procedure. We never will need the empty test, so it does not appear at all. For this example, we assume that the data being sent from one process to another are of the character type, and that only a relatively small buffer is needed.

We must borrow some ideas from the queue data type developed in Section 14.2. The buffer will be an array, with two variables to keep track of the front and rear of the filled part of the array. These variables will be incremented modulo the buffer size, as we previously did for queues.

Three important aspects of synchronization have been built into this module. First, we use the general signals developed in Section 16.2.2. Two signals are needed, one to indicate that a character has been placed in the buffer and one to indicate that a character has been removed (which is the same as an empty space being placed in the buffer). Hence the names charspresent and spacepresent are chosen. Both these signals are initialized in the module initialization.

Second, the send and wait operations are placed in the deposit and fetch procedures to bracket the statements that actually access the buffer. This guarantees mutual exclusion.

Third, because our signals incorporate counters, the signals themselves can keep track of how many characters and how many spaces are in the buffer at any time. To make this work, the module initialization sends the spacepresent signal as many times as the size of the buffer, in this case eight. This means that a process could deposit eight characters before the wait operation would actually suspend the process. Those eight deposits would also do eight waits, decrementing the spacepresent signal counter to zero, and eight sends, incrementing the charspresent signal counter to eight. We would then have the corresponding situation of a process that could do eight fetches before the wait operation would actually suspend the process. In practice, neither of these extreme situations occurs very often.

The implementation module for the buffer is shown in Program 16.7.

A shared variable that is encapsulated like our buffer is commonly called a *monitor*. We will look at monitors again in Section 16.5.

The buffer we have just described can be used by more than two processes. Any number of processes can deposit characters or fetch characters, in any order. In some situations this freedom is desirable, while in others a more disciplined communication between just two processes is desired. We consider this kind of communication in the next section.

Program 16.7 Buffer Implementation Module

```
IMPLEMENTATION MODULE buffers;

  (* This module provides a process communication abstraction based on
     the buffer model. *)

FROM Processes IMPORT
  (* type *) SIGNAL,
  (* proc *) Init, SEND, WAIT;

FROM InOut IMPORT
  (* proc *) Write, WriteString, WriteLn;

CONST
  buffersize = 8;

TYPE
  bufferrange = [ 0..buffersize - 1 ];

VAR
  buffer        : ARRAY bufferrange OF CHAR;
  charspresent  : SIGNAL;
  spacepresent  : SIGNAL;
  inpos         : bufferrange;
  outpos        : bufferrange;
  counter       : CARDINAL;

PROCEDURE deposit
  (       character : CHAR (* in *) );

BEGIN
  WAIT ( spacepresent );
  buffer[ inpos ] := character;
  inpos := ( inpos + 1 ) MOD buffersize;
  SEND ( charspresent )
END deposit;

PROCEDURE fetch
  ( VAR character : CHAR (* out *) );

BEGIN
  WAIT ( charspresent );
  character := buffer[ outpos ];
  outpos := ( outpos + 1 ) MOD buffersize;
  SEND ( spacepresent )
END fetch;

BEGIN
  inpos  := 0;
  outpos := 0;
  Init ( charspresent );
  Init ( spacepresent );
  FOR counter := 1 TO buffersize DO
    SEND ( spacepresent )
  END
END buffers.
```

16.3.3 The Channel Model

As we approach the day when computer systems have many processors, we must consider a very different kind of communications. Processes executing on different processors may not be able to access a shared variable, since each process stores its variables in the memory attached to its own processor. The two processors need to be connected by a communications medium, normally an electrical conductor. Information can be exchanged through this medium in much the same way that terminals and computer systems exchange data.

We would like to develop a process communication abstraction based on this idea, which we call the *channel* model. A channel has two properties. First, at any given time it is associated with only two processes, called the sender and the receiver. Second, a process may send only one piece of information through the channel at a time; an attempt to send a second piece will result in suspension of the sender process until the receiver has removed the first piece from the channel. The second property could be relaxed if we borrowed some of the buffer techniques from the preceding section. We leave that to the reader as an exercise.

Because a software system with many processes may need many channels, we develop a channel abstract data type, in contrast to the buffer abstract variable developed previously. Several operations are needed. First, we need an operation that defines or opens a channel. Such an operation is normally required for a dynamically allocated data type, as discussed in Chapter 15. Second, to satisfy the first property mentioned above, we must have two operations that attach a process to a channel. One process will be used to attach the sender process, the other to attach the receiver process. The obvious operations on channels are send and receive, which allow the transmission of information through the channel. Operations for detaching processes and closing a channel are considered in the exercises.

To make our channel as general as possible, we would like the ability to send any data type through it. To achieve this, we use the techniques of Chapter 13 for generic data structures. As we see in the definition module in Program 16.8, a message sent or received through a channel is considered to be an array of bytes. (We assume that the byte data type represents the smallest addressable unit of memory.)

The implementation of the channel type allows us to use all the features of the process synchronization abstraction developed in Section 16.2.2. In particular, we need to use the ability of a process to be aware of its own identity.

First, we must develop for a channel a data structure that has enough storage to hold any one data type. If we limit this to relatively simple data types or maybe even the predefined data types, a small number of bytes is sufficient. We have chosen 16 bytes in this implementation. The storage is to be shared by two processes, so we need two synchronization signals, just as we did for buffers. We call these signals idle and busy, indicating the current status of a channel. Before sending data, a process must wait for the idle signal, and after sending it must send the busy signal. The reverse is true for a receiving process.

Program 16.8 Channel Definition Module

```
DEFINITION MODULE channels;

  (* This module provides a process communication abstraction based on
     the channel model. *)

FROM SYSTEM IMPORT
  (* type *) BYTE;

EXPORT QUALIFIED
  (* type *) channel,
  (* proc *) open, attachsender, attachreceiver, send, receive;

TYPE
  channel;

PROCEDURE open
  ( VAR chan    : channel            (* out    *) );

PROCEDURE attachsender
  ( VAR chan    : channel            (* in/out *) );

PROCEDURE attachreceiver
  ( VAR chan    : channel            (* in/out *) );

PROCEDURE send
  ( VAR chan    : channel            (* in/out *);
        message : ARRAY OF BYTE (* in       *) );

PROCEDURE receive
  ( VAR chan    : channel            (* in/out *);
    VAR message : ARRAY OF BYTE (* out    *) );

END channels.
```

Note that the words "idle" and "send" are now being used in two contexts, processes and channels. There are many qualified identifiers in the implementation module to prevent ambiguities. Finally, we want each channel to know the identities of the associated sender and receiver processes, so two process identity variables are needed. We put all these pieces together in a record. Because of the similarity of one of these records to the buffer previously developed, we call these records "buffers." A channel is an opaque type, a pointer to a buffer.

The open procedure defines and initializes a channel. It must allocate space for the channel, and put appropriate values in the various fields. At the time a channel is opened, we do not know which processes to attach to it, so the sender and receiver fields are given the value of the null process. Each of the two signal fields must be initialized, using the operation exported from the process synchronization abstraction. Finally, to indicate that the channel starts empty, we send the idle signal.

The procedures attachsender and attachreceiver each attach a process to a channel. We allow a process to attach only itself to a channel, so these operations do not need a process parameter; each assumes it is to attach the current process. To avoid multiple, hence ambiguous, attachments, each of these processes checks that the currently attached process is actually the null process. If not, an error occurs.

The send and receive procedures are very similar to the deposit and fetch operations on buffers. The important difference is that these procedures ensure that only the attached processes are doing the sending and receiving. If any other process attempts either operation, an error occurs.

To handle the various errors that might occur, we provide a simple error procedure. We also define the errors enumeration type to use as error codes. A procedure that detects an error invokes this procedure with an appropriate error code parameter.

The implementation module for the channel data type is shown in Program 16.9. In the next section we develop a small software system that uses channels for process communication.

Program 16.9   Channel Implementation Module

```
IMPLEMENTATION MODULE channels;

   (* This module provides a process communication abstraction based on
      the channel model. *)

FROM SYSTEM IMPORT
   (* type *) BYTE,
   (* proc *) TSIZE;

FROM Storage IMPORT
   (* proc *) ALLOCATE;

IMPORT Processes;

FROM InOut IMPORT
   (* proc *) WriteString, WriteLn;

CONST
   channelsize = 16;
   channelmax = channelsize - 1;

TYPE
   channel = POINTER TO buffer;
   buffer  = RECORD
                    contents :   ARRAY [ 0..channelmax ] OF BYTE;
                    sender   :   Processes.processid;
                    receiver :   Processes.processid;
                    idle     :   Processes.SIGNAL;
                    busy     :   Processes.SIGNAL
                 END;
   errors  = ( senderconflict, receiverconflict,
                    senderror, receiveerror );
```

```
PROCEDURE error
    (      code    : errors            (* in      *) );
BEGIN
  WriteString ( 'Channel Error: ' );
  CASE code OF
    senderconflict :
      WriteString ( 'sender already attached' ) |
    receiverconflict :
      WriteString ( 'receiver already attached' ) |
    senderror :
      WriteString ( 'cannot send to this channel' ) |
    receiveerror :
      WriteString ( 'cannot receive from this channel' )
  END;
  WriteLn;
  HALT
END error;

PROCEDURE open
    ( VAR chan    : channel            (* out     *) );
BEGIN
  NEW ( chan );
  chan^.sender   := Processes.nullprocess;
  chan^.receiver := Processes.nullprocess;
  Processes.Int ( chan^.idle  );
  Processes.Int ( chan^.busy );
  Processes.SEND ( chan^.idle  )
END open;

PROCEDURE attachsender
    ( VAR chan    : channel            (* in/out *) );
BEGIN
  IF Processes.equal ( chan^.sender, Processes.nullprocess )
    THEN chan^.sender := Processes.currentprocess
    ELSE error ( senderconflict )
  END
END attachsender;

PROCEDURE attachreceiver
    ( VAR chan    : channel            (* in/out *) );
BEGIN
  IF Processes.equal ( chan^.receiver, Processes.nullprocess )
    THEN chan^.receiver := Processes.currentprocess
    ELSE error ( receiverconflict )
  END
END attachreceiver;

PROCEDURE send
    ( VAR chan    : channel            (* in/out *);
          message : ARRAY OF BYTE (* in      *) );
```

```
    VAR pos : CARDINAL;
BEGIN
  IF Processes.equal ( chan^.sender, Processes.currentprocess )
    THEN Processes.WAIT ( chan^.idle );
          FOR pos := 0 TO HIGH ( message ) DO
            chan^.contents[ pos ] := message[ pos ]
          END;
          Processes.SEND ( chan^.busy )
    ELSE error ( senderror )
  END
END send;

PROCEDURE receive
  ( VAR chan      : channel          (* in/out *);
    VAR message : ARRAY OF BYTE (* out      *) );

  VAR pos : CARDINAL;

BEGIN
  IF Processes.equal ( chan^.receiver, Processes.currentprocess )
    THEN Processes.WAIT ( chan^.busy );
          FOR pos := 0 TO HIGH ( message ) DO
            message[ pos ] := chan^.contents[ pos ]
          END;
          Processes.SEND ( chan^.idle )
    ELSE error ( receiveerror )
  END
END receive;

END channels.
```

16.4   Examples of Software Development with Processes

In this section we illustrate the use of the process abstractions of Sections 16.2 and 16.3 with two small example programs. Unfortunately, it is beyond the scope of this book to present a thorough discussion of concurrent program design. Our intent is rather to stimulate the reader to think about software design using the team analogy, and to develop and use appropriate abstractions in the design of software systems.

16.4.1   A Producer-Consumer Example

This example illustrates the use of the buffer abstraction in a simple producer-consumer problem. The producer process is named reader, and it reads characters and deposits them in the buffer. When an end-of-line character is encountered, the process terminates. The consumer process is named writer, and it fetches characters from the buffer and prints them with a tilde prefix (˜). After fetching and printing an end-of-line character, the process terminates.

The program is shown in Program 16.10. The main program starts the two

Program 16.10 A Producer-Consumer Example

```
MODULE BufferDemo;

  (* This program demonstrates process communication via a buffer. *)

FROM buffers IMPORT
  (* proc *) deposit, fetch;

FROM Processes IMPORT
  (* var   *) idle,
  (* proc  *) WAIT, StartProcess, Terminate;

FROM InOut IMPORT
  (* const *) EOL,
  (* proc  *) Read, Write, WriteString, WriteLn;

PROCEDURE reader;

  VAR character : CHAR;

BEGIN
  WriteString ( 'Process "reader" has started' );
  WriteLn;
  LOOP
    Read ( character );
    deposit ( character );
    IF character = EOL
      THEN Terminate
    END
  END
END reader;

PROCEDURE writer;

  VAR character : CHAR;

BEGIN
  WriteString ( 'Process "writer" has started' );
  WriteLn;
  LOOP
    fetch ( character );
    Write ( '~' );
    Write ( character );
    IF character = EOL
      THEN Terminate
    END
  END
END writer;

BEGIN
  WriteString ( 'BufferDemo has started' );
  WriteLn;
  WriteLn;
  StartProcess ( reader, 500 );
  StartProcess ( writer,  500 );
```

```
    WAIT ( idle );
    WriteLn;
    WriteString ( 'Restarting...' );
    WriteLn;
    WriteLn;
    StartProcess ( writer,  500 );
    StartProcess ( reader, 500 );
    WAIT ( idle );
    WriteLn;
    WriteString ( 'Main Program now terminating' );
    WriteLn
END BufferDemo.
```

processes and waits for them both to terminate. Then to demonstrate that the order in which the two processes are started is not important, the main program restarts both processes in the reverse order. After both have terminated again, the main program stops. Messages are printed at appropriate places to show how the program operates.

This program is not very useful. However, it demonstrates the ease of use of the abstractions we have developed. All the messy details of process synchronization and communication are hidden in those abstractions.

The output from this program as it would appear at the user's terminal is shown in Figure 16.2. The lines abc and xyz were typed by the user. All other lines are printed by the program.

16.4.2 A Channel Demonstration Example

Although the producer-consumer example had only two processes (excluding the main program), the buffer abstraction allows any number of processes to deposit and fetch characters. In a situation that requires a more private communication path from one process to another, we can use our channel abstraction. In this section we develop a small system with several processes and channels.

Again we must choose a somewhat artificial example to present the fundamental ideas without overwhelming the reader with lengthy specifications and lengthier code. The problem is to read in a line of characters, count the occurrences of uppercase letters, lowercase letters, and digits, and print these counts. We can solve this problem with four processes. The first reads in the characters and does the initial screening. Characters other than those to be counted are discarded; letters and digits are sent on. The second process receives the letters, distinguishes the uppercase from the lowercase, and counts them. The third process receives digits and counts them. The fourth process ultimately receives the counts and prints them. We will examine the design of each of these processes shortly. We also can recognize that four channels will be needed. The processes and channels are organized as shown in Figure 16.3.

Since this problem requires recognition of various classes of characters,

BufferDemo has started

Process "reader" has started
abc
Process "writer" has started
˜a˜b˜c˜

Restarting...

Process "writer" has started
Process "reader" has started

xyz
˜x˜y˜z˜

Main Program now terminating

FIGURE 16.2   Output from Program 16.10

we can make use of the character set abstract data type developed in Section 14.4. By assuming that the improvements to this data type suggested in the exercises have been made, we can very easily recognize letters and digits.

To demonstrate one of the advantages of software design with processes, we develop each process independently. The only coordination required is agreement on the names of the processes and channels shown in Figure 16.3. We no longer have to be concerned with deciding which program is a main program and which is a procedure. With a little practice, it becomes easy for a team of programmers to develop a team of processes.

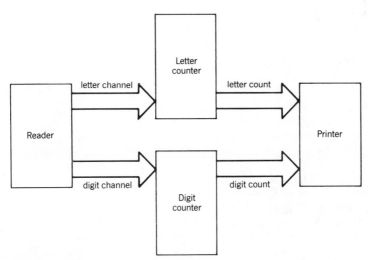

FIGURE 16.3   Organization of the Processes and Channels

The reader process (Program 16.11) must begin by attaching itself to two channels as sender, the letterchannel and the digitchannel. It is then free to send characters through those channels at appropriate times. Next, this process enters a loop to read and send characters. If the character is the end-of-line character, the process sends that character down both channels and terminates. If the character is a letter, it is sent through the letterchannel to the lettercounter process; if it is a digit, it is sent through the digitchannel to the digitcounter process. Any other character is ignored.

The lettercounter process (Program 16.12) must also attach itself to two channels, one as receiver and one as sender. It establishes its loop invariant by setting the two letter counters to zero and enters a loop. It receives a character from letterchannel and processes it. If the letter is really the end-of-line character, the process sends the two counts through the lettercount channel and terminates. Otherwise, the process distinguishes uppercase and lowercase letters and increments the appropriate counter.

The digitcounter process (Program 16.13) is very similar to lettercounter. It also attaches itself to two channels and loops to count digits. When it receives the end-of-line character, it sends the digit count through the digitcount channel and then terminates.

The printer process (Program 16.14) does not need a loop. It simply attaches itself to the two count channels, receives three values, and prints them. It does not matter which of the counter processes sends first; this process

---

Program 16.11   The Reader Process

```
PROCEDURE reader;

  VAR ch : CHAR;
BEGIN
  WriteString ( 'Process "reader" is beginning' );
  WriteLn;
  attachsender ( letterchannel );
  attachsender ( digitchannel );
  LOOP
    Read ( ch );
    IF ch = EOL THEN
      send ( letterchannel, EOL );
      send ( digitchannel, EOL );
      Terminate
    END;
    IF inset ( ch, alphabet ) THEN
      send ( letterchannel, ch )
    ELSIF inset ( ch, digits ) THEN
      send ( digitchannel, ch )
    END
  END
END reader;
```

Program 16.12 The Letter Counter Process

```
PROCEDURE lettercounter;

  VAR uppers : CARDINAL;
        lowers : CARDINAL;
        ch      : CHAR;

BEGIN
  WriteString ( 'Process "lettercounter" is beginning' );
  WriteLn;
  attachreceiver ( letterchannel );
  attachsender ( lettercount );
  uppers := 0;
  lowers := 0;
  LOOP
    receive ( letterchannel, ch );
    IF ch = EOL THEN
      send ( lettercount, uppers );
      send ( lettercount, lowers );
      Terminate
    END;
    IF inset ( ch, upperalpha )
      THEN INC ( uppers )
      ELSE INC ( lowers )
    END
  END
END lettercounter;
```

Program 16.13 The Digit Counter Process

```
PROCEDURE digitcounter;

  VAR count : CARDINAL;
        ch      : CHAR;

BEGIN
  WriteString ( 'Process "digitcounter" is beginning' );
  WriteLn;
  attachreceiver ( digitchannel );
  attachsender ( digitcount );
  count := 0;
  LOOP
    receive ( digitchannel, ch );
    IF ch = EOL THEN
      send ( digitcount, count );
      Terminate
    END;
    INC ( count )
  END
END digitcounter;
```

Program 16.14 The Printer Process

```
PROCEDURE printer;

   VAR result : CARDINAL;

BEGIN
   WriteString ( 'Process "printer" is beginning' );
   WriteLn;
   attachreceiver ( lettercount );
   attachreceiver ( digitcount  );
   WriteLn;
   WriteString ( 'Results:' );
   WriteLn;
   receive ( lettercount, result );
   WriteString ( ' Uppercase letters:' );
   WriteCard ( result, 4 );
   WriteLn;
   receive ( lettercount, result );
   WriteString ( ' Lowercase letters:' );
   WriteCard ( result, 4 );
   WriteLn;
   receive ( digitcount, result );
   WriteString ( ' Digits: ' );
   WriteCard ( result, 4 );
   WriteLn;
   Terminate
END printer;
```

waits to receive from lettercounter first. We assume that the designers of this process and lettercounter have agreed that the uppercase letter count will be sent first, then the lowercase letter count.

The main program does little more than get things started. It opens the four channels and starts the four processes, and then goes to sleep. When all four processes have terminated, the main program resumes, prints a message, and halts.

Notice that this system uses the same channel abstraction for two different types of data. The reader process sends characters through the letterchannel and digitchannel, while the lettercount and digitcount channels transmit cardinal values. We designed the channel type to have this capability, and now we can see it in use.

The skeleton of this system is shown in Program 16.15. We have added a few extra output statements in both the processes and the main program to clarify the sequence of execution.

An execution of this program produced the output in Figure 16.4. The line beginning with abc was typed by the user; all other lines were produced by the program. Notice that the four lines of output produced by the printer process are interrupted by an output line from the main program. This is normal in

Program 16.15 The Channel Demonstration Main Program

```
MODULE ChannelDemo;

   (* This module demonstrates the use of several processes that
      communicate via channels. *)

FROM Processes IMPORT
   (* var   *) idle,
   (* proc  *) StartProcess, Terminate, WAIT;

FROM channels IMPORT
   (* type  *) channel,
   (* proc  *) open, attachsender, attachreceiver, send, receive;

FROM InOut IMPORT
   (* const *) EOL,
   (* proc  *) Read, Write, WriteString, WriteCard, WriteLn;

FROM characterset IMPORT
   (* var   *) alphabet, upperalpha, digits,
   (* proc  *) inset;

VAR
   letterchannel : channel;
   digitchannel  : channel;
   lettercount   : channel;
   digitcount    : channel;

   (* processes are placed here *)

BEGIN
   WriteString ( 'Process Demo -- start of execution' );
   WriteLn;
   WriteLn;
   open ( letterchannel );
   open ( digitchannel );
   open ( lettercount );
   open ( digitcount );
   StartProcess ( reader, 500 );
   StartProcess ( lettercounter, 500 );
   StartProcess ( digitcounter, 500 );
   StartProcess ( printer, 500 );
   WriteString ( 'Main program now goes to sleep' );
   WriteLn;
   WAIT ( idle );
   WriteLn;
   WriteString ( 'Process Demo -- end of execution' );
   WriteLn
END ChannelDemo.
```

Process Demo -- start of execution

Process "reader" is beginning
abc 12345 (*) WXYZ -- 1 + 2 = 3 -- input data
Process "lettercounter" is beginning
Process "digitcounter" is beginning
Process "printer" is beginning

Results:
Main program now goes to sleep
   Uppercase letters: 4
   Lowercase letters: 12
   Digits: 8

Process Demo -- end of execution

FIGURE 16.4   Output from Program 16.15

software systems in which each of several processes writes to the terminal; if such interruption is undesirable, the system must be designed to prevent it.

This example again reveals the simplicity of the application program because the details of process synchronization and communication are hidden in the channel abstraction. To emphasize this fact, consider Figure 16.5, which shows the complete data structure of a channel, including the lower level data structures for signals, queues, and linked lists. By contrasting the complexity of this data structure with the simplicity of the open, send, and receive operations, we can again appreciate the power of abstraction in software design.

16.5 Device Handling and Interrupts

The first implementation of Modula-2 was for a DEC PDP-11 computer system. The language was supposed to be used to write an operating system for this machine. Therefore the original implementation included some very low level language features tailored to this goal for this machine. In particular, features were present to specify absolute memory addresses and to program hardware interrupt handlers.

Modula-2 is now available on a wide variety of computer systems, and for many of these systems it is not reasonable to supply PDP-11-specific features. Each implementation of the language is likely to supply features that can accomplish similar goals, but the form in which these features appear varies widely. In this section, therefore, we summarize the original PDP-11 features and try to make the reader aware of the motivation for them. Programmers should examine their own implementations to determine whether similar features are present.

The first feature is absolute memory addressing. In computer systems like the PDP-11, there are no machine instructions for input and output. Instead,

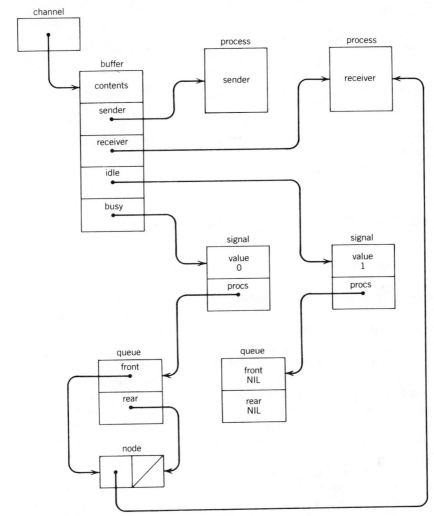

FIGURE 16.5   Data Structure of a Channel

each device is connected to the computer system memory bus at a specific address, and thus behaves as if it were a memory location. Any machine instruction that can send data to memory can send data to a device, and any instruction that can fetch data from memory can read data from a device. If we are developing input/output device handlers for an operating system, we must be able to specify the absolute memory addresses of devices. In a program, these addresses are referenced as normal variables, but the declaration of those variables must provide the absolute address to which those variables are assigned by the compiler. The syntax of such a declaration is shown in Figure 16.6.

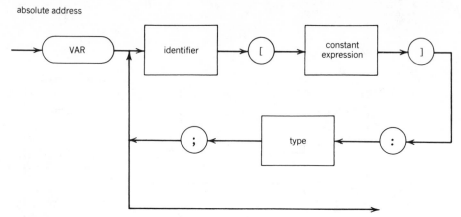

FIGURE 16.6   Syntax of an Absolute Address Specification

Many modern computers are designed so that each possible hardware interrupt causes a transfer of control to a fixed memory location, or to the address contained in a fixed memory location. To develop interrupt handlers in Modula-2, it must be possible to put the appropriate instruction or address into the specified memory location. The absolute addressing feature allows this to be done.

At a slightly higher level of abstraction, the original Modula-2 implementation provides another way of accessing interrupt handlers. The interrupt handler is viewed as a process, since it is not invoked explicitly from any program. When an interrupt occurs, the system should behave as if the currently executing user program had performed a process transfer to the interrupt handler. When the interrupt handler finishes its task, it transfers back to the user program.

The problem is that the user program cannot know when to do the transfer. Instead, an external signal, such as an input or output completion signal from a device, initiates the transfer. To make this possible, we must have a way of associating a process (a parameterless procedure) with a particular interrupt address, and a way to allow that process to transfer back to the user program after the interrupt has been handled. This capability is provided by the IOTRANSFER procedure. It is declared as follows:

```
PROCEDURE IOTRANSFER
  ( VAR handler  : PROCESS (* out *);
    VAR user     : PROCESS (* in  *);
        interrupt : ADDRESS (* in  *) );
```

The first two parameters are exactly like those of the TRANSFER procedure. The third parameter is the hardware interrupt vector address to be associated with this process.

To use this procedure, the main program (probably the operating system)

uses the NEWPROCESS procedure to create a process for the interrupt handler, and gets it started with a statement like:

TRANSFER (opsys, handler);

The interrupt handler then begins execution, doing whatever initialization it needs. It voluntarily relinquishes control back to the operating system with the statement:

IOTRANSFER (handler, opsys, interrupt);

This statement performs the transfer of control back to the operating system but also says that when the specified interrupt occurs, the handler is to regain control at the statement following the IOTRANSFER. Thus an interrupt behaves as if the statement:

TRANSFER (opsys, handler);

were suddenly executed in the operating system.

Using the concepts of our process abstraction of Section 16.2, we can think of the IOTRANSFER as performing a wait operation on a signal that can be sent only by an external device. That signal, an interrupt, resumes the execution of the interrupt handler. Only one handler may be waiting for a particular interrupt.

The fact that an interrupt can occur at unexpected times can cause problems for the processes in a software system. Remember that when a process is in its critical section, no other process may be in a corresponding critical section. This mutual exclusion was necessary to allow accesses of shared variables to satisfy the safety properties. With coroutines, it is easy to guarantee mutual exclusion. Each coroutine is designed not to relinquish control while it is in a critical section. Since coroutines are characterized by voluntary transfers, each coroutine has complete control over execution of its critical section.

An interrupt can occur when a process is in its critical section. If the interrupt handler shared a variable with the interrupted process, there is the possibility of violations of the safety property. Therefore we need a way for a process to prevent interrupts while it is in its critical section. To do this we need one new language feature, and we must adopt a programming convention, namely, that we will always encapsulate a shared variable in a module, as we did with the buffer in Section 16.3.2. All accesses of the shared variable will then be made through the exported procedures of that module, and thus all critical sections will be in the module. The new language feature is a way to assign a *priority* to the module, which will limit the kinds of interrupt that can occur while executing that module. A module with a priority is called a *monitor* and is declared as shown in Figure 16.7.

The meaning of a particular priority value is determined by the interrupt system of the particular computer. Some systems have only two levels, indicating that the interrupt system is either enabled or disabled. Other systems have several levels of priority. Interrupts caused by high speed devices such as disks have a high priority, since they must be handled quickly to allow the device to

monitor

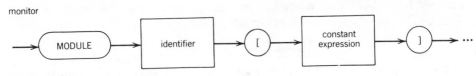

FIGURE 16.7   Syntax of a Monitor

operate at full speed. Interrupts from low speed devices like terminals have a lower priority. It is possible for a high priority interrupt to cause the suspension of a lower priority interrupt handler process, but not vice versa. The proper use of monitors therefore requires a detailed knowledge of the interrupt system of the host computer.

   The low level features described in this section are intended to provide the capabilities necessary to develop operating systems and other software for an essentially bare machine. A Modula-2 implementation that runs under an existing operating system is not likely to offer these features. In fact, on a multiuser system, it is desirable not to offer these features, since their use would almost certainly disrupt the programs of all other users. Instead, most such operating systems provide carefully controlled access to low level features of the computer. For example, the operating system will recognize and handle hardware interrupts but will inform a user program that an interrupt has occurred, if the user program has requested such notification. Again, readers are urged to examine carefully their own particular implementations of the language to determine what features are available.

   In Chapter 17 we will see an example of a software system that uses some of these very low level features of Modula-2.

16.6 Summary

The concept of cooperating sequential processes has been introduced as a way of thinking about and implementing software systems. Modula-2 provides coroutines as the basis for processes, plus some low level features for defining processes and controlling their execution. These features are at too low a level of abstraction to be easily used in the development of large software systems. We therefore developed some higher level abstractions.

   The first of these abstractions provided process synchronization. We were guided in the development of this abstraction by the safety properties and the liveness properties that should be satisfied in any multiprocess system. The abstraction provided a method for processes to send and receive signals from each other, and a way to get processes started. At the implementation level, sending and receiving signals resulted in coroutine transfers, but these transfers are hidden from the users of these signals.

   The second abstraction provided process communication. We examined three models for communication: shared variables, buffers, and channels. The latter two models are fairly high level abstractions, and hide virtually all the messy details of process communication. The design of software systems with many processes is simplified by building on these abstractions.

We have also seen that the coroutine model cannot always satisfy the liveness properties. We therefore concluded that Modula-2 does not support what is commonly called concurrent programming. However, it is quite possible for an implementation to supply addition modules that do provide better concurrent programming capabilities. If an operating system supports multiprogramming, and almost all but the simplest operating systems today do, it is likely that a Modula-2 implementation under that operating system will provide some kind of access to those capabilities. These may be relatively low level, and a programmer will need to develop higher level abstractions as we have seen in this chapter. We have kept this requirement in mind in presenting our abstractions, which were designed to deal with some of the problems of concurrent programming that just do not arise with coroutines.

We expect that for most readers, concurrent programming is a whole new world. We urge all programmers to begin thinking about software design in terms of processes and to use the abstractions presented here as a starting point for developing concurrent programs.

16.7 Exercises

1. Consider other models of human communication, such as putting notes on a bulletin board, advertising in a newspaper classified section, and radio broadcasting. How can these models lead to new process communication abstractions for software?

2. Modify the Terminate procedure in the synchronization abstraction so that it deallocates the workspace associated with the terminated process. *Hint:* Change the definition of a process pointer so that it points to a record containing a process and the workspace address.

3. Add a procedure to the synchronization abstraction that sends back the number of active processes in the system. Why would it be a bad idea simply to export the variable that contains this value?

4. Add procedures to the channel abstraction to detach the sender, detach the receiver, and close the channel. Each procedure should deallocate storage as necessary.

5. In a program that uses processes and channels, does it matter in what order the processes are started? Is it necessary to open a channel before starting a process that will use it, even though that process has not yet been attached to the channel? Can a process that uses a channel open it, or must the main program open the channel?

6. Modify the channel abstraction so that the size of a channel may vary. Change the open operation so that it specifies the size of the channel. *Hint:*

Let the contents field of the channel be a pointer to a dynamically allocated array, similar to the dynamic string data type.

7. Modify the channel abstraction so that a process can test whether the channel is busy. Is it possible to modify the printer process in Program 16.14 so that it receives first from the channel that sends first, rather than always receiving in a fixed order?

8. Add a delay operation to the synchronization abstraction. (This operation causes a process to put itself to sleep for a while by placing itself in the ready queue. The process resumes later when it reaches the front of the queue, rather than having to wait for a specific signal.) Now answer the question in Exercise 7 again.

9. What would happen if a process other than the main program were to perform a wait operation on the idle signal? A send operation? Would it be better to define a procedure to put the main program to sleep rather than exporting the idle variable? How could you ensure that only the main program invokes such a procedure?

10. We have allowed a procedure to terminate only itself. How could we also allow a process that starts another process to have the privilege of terminating that other process if it wants?

11. When errors occur in concurrent programs, it is desirable for the error message to include the name of the process causing the error. Modify the StartProcess procedure so that a third parameter may be given, which is a character string containing the name of the process being started. Then modify the channel abstraction so that the error routine prints the name of the offending process.

12. Modify the channel abstraction to allow several items to be in the channel at once, making it a buffer.

17

Object-Oriented
Software Design

In Chapter 1, in explaining the rationale for Modula-2, we introduced some general concepts associated with problem solving and the design and development of software systems. In this chapter we elaborate on these concepts, focus on object-oriented software development, and present two case studies.

In Table 17.1, we set the stage for this chapter by reproducing some key statements related to software development presented earlier in the book.

It is clear from Table 17.1 that abstraction and data hiding play a central role in engineering reliable and easily maintainable software systems.

In this chapter we explore the important methodology of object-oriented design that uses data abstraction as its centerpiece. We demonstrate the use of Modula-2 as a program design language with two case studies.

17.1　Data Abstraction in Object-Oriented Design

If a software system may be compared to a living organism, the principal goal of object-oriented design is to identify a set of data abstractions that form the major organs of the software system. A software bus, which accounts for the interdependencies among the modules, provides the arteries that connect the major organs. A modular design chart, introduced in Wiener and Sincovec (1984), may be used to represent the modular decomposition of a software system (i.e., the skeletal structure of the system).

333

TABLE 17.1 Observations on Software Development

For the past 15 years it has been recognized that the cost of developing software systems has been steadily increasing while the cost of hardware systems has been decreasing.

It is a rarity for large software systems to be delivered on time, within budget, and meeting all specifications.

The process of modification or extension of a software system (maintenance) is so difficult and expensive that many software organizations spend more than four-fifths of their budgets on software maintenance.

A principal goal of software engineering is the systematization of the software development process, to achieve lower cost software development and improved software reliability.

As the discipline of software engineering has matured, it has become apparent that languages and software tools must be created to enhance software reliability, streamline the process of software development, and promote more efficient software maintenance.

Decomposition is a process of reducing a large problem to a set of smaller, more manageable problems. Since software complexity appears to increase more than linearly with its size, it is much easier, in principle, to develop 20 programs of 2000 lines each than to develop a single program with 40,000 lines of code.

A major attribute of problem solving is abstraction. Abstraction involves model building. People manage complexity by means of abstraction. Abstractions provide a view of the essential components and processes that define a system. Because software development is a form of problem solving, abstraction plays a central role, particularly at the design level.

Our ability to separate the high level abstractions that we use to view a system from the implementation details (lower level abstractions) allows us to understand complex systems.

Data abstraction involves recognition of the data types (the values and operations) that are inherent in a software system.

Representation hiding for abstract data types assures consistency in the use of the type and lowers maintenance costs if the representation is later changed.

Object-oriented design may be described by the following steps.

1. Define an informal strategy (in words) for the problem solution. No software design methodology can replace basic human creativity; it can only harness it.
2. Identify the nouns (objects) used in the informal strategy. These nouns form the basis for the data abstractions used in the system.
3. Identify the verbs (operations) used in the informal strategy. These verbs form the basis for the functional abstractions used in the system.
4. Identify the concurrent processes present in the system.
5. Partition the software system into a set of modules, each specifying a data abstraction. A modular design chart may be used to represent graphically the software design.

6. Create a compilable modular design in Modula-2 that corresponds to the modular design chart.
7. Create a main program that mimics the informal strategy and uses all the abstractions specified in accordance with step 6.

When these seven steps have been performed, a compilable frame for the software system exists. To complete the software system, we write the implementation modules associated with each definition module. (This task typically is performed by a group of programmers, each assigned to write one or more implementation modules.)

High level system integration is assured because the modular design of step 6 and the main driver program of step 7 have been checked for interface compatibility by the compiler. In steps 6 and 7, Modula-2 is used as a program design language.

The object-oriented design, documented by modular design charts and design listings, embodies the interrelationship of concepts that underlies the software system. Because of the modular structure of an object-oriented design, later maintenance changes can be localized to the particular implementation modules in which they occur without requiring changes or recompilation elsewhere in the system.

The object-oriented design specifies a set of "conceptual sockets." Each conceptual socket consists of a definition module, usually containing the declaration of an abstract data type. Each socket embodies a concept or abstraction in the software system.

At the coding stage (implementation stage), it may be necessary to refine the software design and create additional functional abstractions for one or more definition modules. Thus, object-oriented design, like other design methodologies, is an iterative process.

17.2 Functional Components in a Software System

In designing software systems, it is quite common to identify a group of operations that must be performed in transforming the system inputs to the appropriate outputs. Graphical techniques for representing a software system, in terms of functional components, such as data flow diagrams (see Yourdon and Constantine, 1979; DeMarco, 1979; or Myers, 1978), have proved to be useful and popular. In such diagrams, bubbles represent the transformations or processes performed on data flowing through the system, and labeled arrows represent flow in and out of the transformation. Each bubble is a transducer that converts some data input to the appropriate output.

Figure 17.1 [reproduced from *Software Engineering with Modula-2 and Ada* (Wiener and Sincovec, 1984)] illustrates a data flow diagram for a spelling checker software system.

Functional decomposition is a process of identifying the operations re-

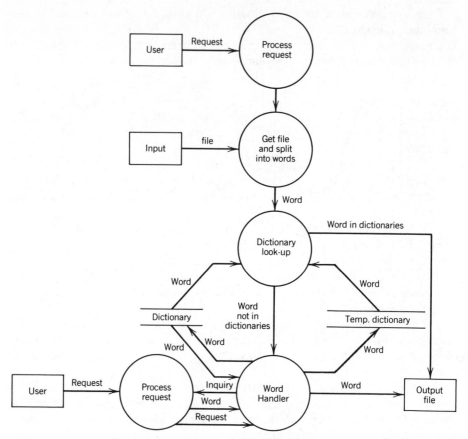

FIGURE 17.1 Data Flow Diagram for a Spelling Checker (*Software Engineering with Modula-2 and Ada,* Richard Wiener and Richard Sincovec. Copyright © 1984, John Wiley. Reprinted by permission.

quired of a software system as subprograms. Each operation is a functional component in the software system and may be mapped to a subprogram. The minor operations that must be performed to implement the major operations are often mapped into subprograms nested within the major subprograms. For example, the bubbles in a data flow diagram often map to the major subprograms. Each of these may contain several nested subprograms. This kind of top-down functional decomposition (structured programming) is familiar to Pascal programmers.

17.3 Rapid Prototyping

(Parts of this section are adapted, with permission, from Section 4.6 of *Software Engineering with Modula-2 and Ada,* Wiener and Sincovec, Wiley, 1984.)

In most branches of engineering, prototyping has long been an important part of the new product development process. A prototype is built to assess the system before committing the manufacturer to a final design. Various alternatives are tested using the prototype to determine whether both the functional and nonfunctional specifications for the system can be met. If not, the prototype is modified and reevaluated before hardware construction is permitted to commence. It is not necessary for the prototype to satisfy every requirement for the final system; it need include only the features that must be analyzed further before a final design can be decided. No engineer would consider beginning production without having thoroughly tested and refined a prototype.

Traditionally, however, software engineering has not considered prototyping to be a normal activity, mainly because there is no "production run" to produce a large number of product items. Indeed, in software engineering, the prototype *is* the production run. When multiple copies of software systems are needed, the time and cost required are insignificant compared to the development costs. This is certainly not the case in other branches of engineering, in which production costs may greatly exceed development costs. For such a mass-produced product the cost of a prototype represents a very small fraction of the final unit cost of the item. All too often software developers take the attitude that it is more economical to modify the finished system than to refine the needs before the system is constructed.

In many systems, requirements are incomplete or ill defined, resulting in somewhat arbitrary specification and design decisions. When several competing designs are possible, it is difficult to predict which ones will and will not meet performance specifications. When a user interface is part of the system, it is almost impossible to predict what will be perceived by the users as convenient, consistent, and user-friendly.

Software prototyping can address each of these problems. A prototype system can be used to clarify and elaborate requirements and specifications. The end users of the system and the developers may not be the same persons. In such cases, it is often difficult for the users to define their requirements in detail sufficient to allow the developers to proceed directly to the design and implementation of the ideal system. Experience shows that much of software maintenance is necessitated by changes or refinements in requirements and specifications. If it were possible to produce quickly a prototype version of a software system, the users could evaluate it and identify requirements that were incorrectly defined or misinterpreted by the developers. Several iterations of this process can lead to virtually complete and correct requirements and specifications.

Frequently in designing very complex software systems, a designer must choose among competing methods or algorithms. Each of these choices has an impact on the overall performance of the system, but it is nearly impossible to predict the ramifications of all these choices together. Again prototyping provides some help. If prototypes of subsystems can be rapidly produced, some performance measurements can be made during design. If performance problems are detected, the design can be modified. Iterations of this process can help guarantee that the final design will lead to an implementation that meets all performance specifications.

Modula-2 supports rapid prototyping because the specification of a module (subsystem) can be separated from its implementation. Several competing implementations (algorithms) may be substituted into the system without affecting the integrity or integration of the rest of the system.

The design of user interfaces is one of the most difficult aspects of software system design, partly because the evaluation of interfaces is very subjective and partly because even the users do not always know in advance what interface specifications are "desirable." Clearly, prototyping provides an important vehicle for iterated refinement of specifications for such interfaces.

The term "rapid prototyping" is often used in software engineering to reflect the differences between software prototyping and prototyping in other branches of engineering. Clearly, prototyping is useful in the areas just described only if it can be accomplished substantially faster than producing an entire finished system. To produce software prototypes rapidly, a variety of tools, techniques, and environments is evolving.

There are two major approaches to rapid prototyping: reusable code and executable specifications. There has been some success with each of these, and research in both areas continues. Both these approaches are closely tied to the development of integrated software development environments.

Modula-2 makes it much easier to reuse existing code than did previous languages. In Modula-2 it is possible to build extensive software libraries and to access individual packages or modules from a library whenever desired. A significant problem that remains to be solved is the development of a library cataloging system. How does a software developer know, given a particular requirement or specification, that there already exists in the library a piece of software that can satisfy that requirement?

A taxonomy of software components is beginning to emerge. Already it is possible to distinguish components such as abstract data types, mathematical routine packages, parsers, scanners, filters, and message channels, to name a few. As use of Ada and Modula-2 increases, libraries will grow and the need for improved classification systems will become increasingly apparent.

Software prototyping can be of great value, and as programming environments evolve, prototyping should have considerable influence on the traditional model of the software life cycle. Because it is such a new area of research, there is no consensus on the best approaches. The interested reader is directed to the working papers of the ACM SIGSOFT Rapid Prototyping Workshop (1982).

17.4   Editor–Spelling Checker Case Study

The subject of this case study is a toy editor–spelling checker. The code listing, not to speak of the explanation, that would be required if a commercial-grade editor–spelling checker were presented would more than fill this book. As the main purpose of the case study is to illustrate the methodology of object-oriented design, the use of data abstraction, and the use of process abstraction, this may best be done with a relatively simple software system.

The system presented in this section is implemented using the Volition Systems Modula-2 system on a Sage IV computer. Many of the low level coroutine procedures are not portable to other computers or Modula-2 implementations. Given the major purpose of this case study, however, the means are more important than the end.

The principal objective of the editor–spelling checker is to check up to 300 lines of text for spelling, as a cooperating process, while words are being typed in. The 300 lines of text must be kept in active memory during program execution. The dictionary for the spelling checker is to contain the 5000 most commonly used words in the English language. Only a create text (insert) option will be implemented for the editor.

The informal strategy for this system can now be developed.

1. Get the name of the text file to be edited.
2. Prompt the user to determine whether potentially misspelled words should be directed to the video terminal or to the printer.
3. Initialize a search table to empty. This search table will be used to maintain an alphabetized list of all potentially misspelled words.
4. Initialize a queue of lines to empty. This queue will be used to store all lines that have not been checked for spelling.
5. Initialize an interrupt status report process that prints the number of words checked for spelling after each line has been entered in the editor. The status report will be directed to the first line on the top of the video terminal. The interrupt that will trigger the status report process is a soft key interrupt (the return character).
6. Initialize a hardware keyboard interrupt process that takes control whenever any key on the keyboard is hit. When such a keyboard interrupt occurs, control transfers to the editor. The character that caused the interrupt is entered in the text buffer and printed on the video terminal.
7. Transfer control from the main program to the spelling checker process. Within this main process, lines of text are inserted in the queue whenever a "RETURN" is hit or whenever 78 characters have been entered in a line.
8. Halt the program, from the spelling checker process, if the escape key is hit.

As indicated in the informal strategy, three interrupt-driven processes—spelling checking, text editing, and status report—run together. Between keystrokes, the spelling checker fetches a line from the queue of unchecked lines, fetches words from the line, and checks each word for spelling. There is not a wasted moment using the given informal design strategy.

Code listings for all the implementation modules that comprise this system are not provided because this would take too much space. Besides, the object-oriented design, and the use of data and process abstractions, may be exhibited without concern about all the implementation details. We explore some of the implementation details in the exercises.

TABLE 17.2   Important Objects and Operations

1. Search Table and Word Type (base type for search table)
   Initialize search table to empty.
   Insert a word in the search table.
   Display the alphabetized list of words in the search table.
2. Queue
   Initialize the queue to empty.
   Test to see whether the queue is empty.
   Insert a line of text into the queue.
   Remove a line of text from the queue.
3. Dictionary
   Fetch a word from a line of text.
   Is word in dictionary?
4. Line: Line Type

In Table 17.2, we group the important nouns (objects) and verbs (operations) found in the informal strategy.

The software system is partitioned into five major specification modules (four modules representing the data abstractions given in Table 17.2 and an interrupt handling module) plus a main program.

The main program closely follows the eight steps presented in the informal strategy. It assumes that the functional abstractions (operations) associated with each abstract data type are available from the modules SearchTable, Dictionary, queueadt, Line, and IntHdlr. From definition module Search-Table, the main program uses the data type table and the operations CreateEmpty, Insert, and Display. From definition module IntHdlr, the main program uses the data type INTHDLR and the operations IntHdlrInit, KbdVector, and IntHdlrTerm. From definition module Line, the main program uses the transparent data type LineType. From definition module queueadt, the main program uses the data type queue and the operations makeempty, insert, remove, and empty. Finally, from definition module Dictionary the main program uses the hidden variable DICTIONARY and the operations InDictionary and FetchWord.

It is not important, at the design level, to be concerned about the implementation details (data structure and search algorithms) associated with the dictionary.

In Figure 17.2, we present a software organization chart that shows the partitioning of the software system into its component modules and the interrelationships among the modules. We display a design listing (Program 17.1) for the editor–spelling checker system containing the main program QuickSpell-Edit, followed by the five definition modules. We have provided extensive comments to explain some of the implementation-specific coroutine facilities used at the design level.

The six compilation units, separated by dashed lines, constitute the design architecture of the software system. The Modula-2 compiler verifies that

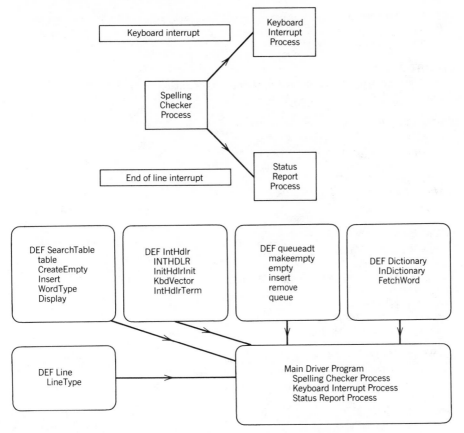

FIGURE 17.2 Software Organization for Editor–Spelling Checker

---

Program 17.1 Modular Design Listing for the Editor–Spelling Checker System

```
MODULE QuickSpellEdit;

FROM Utilities IMPORT
    (* type *) setofchar,
    (* proc *) ScClrScreen, ScGotoXY, ScClrLine, prompt, Printer,
               CenterMessage, Spacebar, ScLeft, ScRight, ReadKey,
               ScFindX, ScFindY;

FROM SYSTEM IMPORT
    (* type *) WORD, PROCESS,
    (* proc *) TRANSFER, NEWPROCESS, ADR;

FROM InOut IMPORT
    (* proc *) WriteLn, WriteString, WriteCard, Read, Write;
```

```
FROM Strings IMPORT
  (* type *) STRING,
  (* proc *) Length, Pos, Concat;

IMPORT Texts;
  (* Used to prevent overloading of the procedures WriteLn,
  and WriteString. *)

FROM Files IMPORT
  (* type *) FILE, FileState, FilePos,
  (* proc *) Open, Rename, Create, Close;

FROM Texts IMPORT
  (* type *) TEXT, TextState,
  (* proc *) Connect;

FROM SearchTable IMPORT
  (* type *) WordType,
  (* var *) table,
  (* proc *) CreateEmpty, Insert, Display;

FROM IntHdlr IMPORT
  (* var *) KbdVector,
  (* proc *) INTHDLR, IntHdlrInit, IntHdlrTerm;

FROM SYSTEM68 IMPORT
  (* proc *) Raise, ClearVector, Enable, Disable;
  (* Four Sage specific interrupt handling routines *)

FROM Line IMPORT
  (* type *) LineType;

FROM queueadt IMPORT
  (* type *) queue,
  (* proc *) makeempty, empty, insert, remove;

FROM Dictionary IMPORT
  (* proc *) InDictionary, FetchWord;

CONST
  statusvector = 13;

PROCEDURE getfile(VAR filename : STRING);
  (* Prompts the user to enter the name of the text file to be created and
     checked for spelling. *)

BEGIN
  prompt(5,15,"Text file name : ",filename,12,setofchar{'a'..'z'} +
       setofchar{'a'..'z'} + setofchar{'0'..'9'} +
       setofchar{'.'} + setofchar{' '} + setofchar{':'} +
       setofchar{''} + setofchar{'-'} + setofchar{'A'..'Z'});
  IF ( Pos(".TEXT",filename) = 81) AND
     (Pos(". text",filename)  = 81)
```

```
    THEN
    (* The suffix TEXT is not present in the file name. This suffix must be
        appended to the filename. *)
        Concat(filename,".TEXT",filename);
    END (* if then *);
END getfile;

VAR
    filename      : STRING;   (* Name of text file *)
    linenumber    : CARDINAL; (* Number in edit buffer *)
    searchtable   : table;    (* Used to store a list of

    EndsInS       : BOOLEAN;  (* Set to true if word ends in 's' *)
    ch            : CHAR;
    linepos       : CARDINAL; (* Line position in an edit buffer line *)
    endpos        : CARDINAL; (* Marks the position of the
                                 end of a word *)
    edit          : ARRAY[1..300] OF LineType; (* Edit buffer *)
    linequeue     : queue;    (* Holds lines of text for the
                                 spelling checker *)
    keyboard      : INTHDLR;  (* An interrupt driven process *)
    status        : INTHDLR;  (* An interrupt driven process *)
    spellprocess  : PROCESS;  (* The spelling checking process *)
    mainprocess   : PROCESS;  (* The main program *)
    buffer        : ARRAY[1..1000] OF WORD;
    (* Space for the system to track the spelling checker process *)
    currentpos    : CARDINAL; (* The line position in the edit
                                 buffer *)
    count         : CARDINAL; (* The number of words checked for
                                 spelling *)
    textfile      : FILE;
    t             : TEXT;
    fs            : FileState;
    ts            : TextState;
    fp            : FilePos;
    i             : CARDINAL;
    done          : BOOLEAN;  (* Used to signal termination
                                 of the program *)
    on            : BOOLEAN;  (* Used to signal whether output
                                 is directed to the printer *)
PROCEDURE StatusLine(dummy : CARDINAL);
    (* This procedure is attached to an software interrupt that is triggered
        whenever statusvector is raised. *)

VAR
    x, y : CARDINAL; (* The coordinates of the cursor position *)
    i    : CARDINAL;

BEGIN
    Disable(KbdVector);
    x := ScFindX();
```

```
    y := ScFindY( );
    ScClrLine(0);
    ScClrLine(1);
    ScGotoXY(0,0);
    WriteString(" Number of words checked for spelling -> ");
    WriteCard(count,1);
    WriteLn;
    (* Write dotted line to screen *)
    FOR i := 0 TO 79 DO
      Write('-');
    END (* for loop *);
    ScGotoXY(x,y);
    Enable(KbdVector);
END StatusLine;

PROCEDURE GetText(dummy : CARDINAL);
    (* This procedure is attached to a hardware interrupt that occurs every
      time a key is hit on the keyboard. *)

VAR
  ch : CHAR;

BEGIN
  Read(ch);
  edit[linenumber,currentpos] := ch;
  INC(currentpos);
  IF (currentpos = 78) OR (ch = CHR(13)) (* CHR(13) is RETURN *)
  THEN
    edit[linenumber,currentpos] := 0C;
    insert(linequeue, edit[linenumber]);
    INC(linenumber);
    currentpos := 0;
  END (* if then *);
  IF (ch = CHR(27)) (* CHR(27) is ESC *) OR (linenumber > 300)
  THEN
    WriteLn;
    Texts.WriteLn(Texts.output);
    Texts.WriteString(Texts.output," Possible misspelled words");
    Texts.WriteString(Texts.output," for ");
    Texts.WriteString(Texts.output,filename);
    Texts.WriteLn(Texts.output);
    Display(searchtable);
    WriteLn; WriteLn;
    WriteString("The number of words checked for spelling -> ");
    WriteCard(count,1);
    WriteLn; WriteLn;
    done := TRUE;
    IntHdlrTerm(keyboard);
    IntHdlrTerm(status);
  END (* if then *);
END GetText;
```

```
PROCEDURE CheckSpelling;
(* This is the spelling checking process *)

VAR
  line  : LineType;
  word : WordType;
  ln    : CARDINAL;

BEGIN
  LOOP
    REPEAT
    UNTIL (NOT empty(linequeue) ) OR done;
    IF NOT empty(linequeue)
    THEN
      REPEAT
        remove(linequeue, line);
        Raise(statusvector);
        linepos := 0;
        LOOP
          word := FetchWord(line, linepos);
          IF linepos = Length(line) + 1
          THEN
            EXIT;
          END (* if then *);
          endpos := Length(word) - 1;
          EndsInS := word[endpos] = 's';
          INC(count);
          IF NOT InDictionary(word)
          THEN
            IF NOT EndsInS
            THEN
              Insert(searchtable,word);
            ELSE
              word[endpos] := 0C;
              (* strips final 's' away *)
              IF NOT InDictionary(word)
              THEN
                word[endpos] := 's';
                (* puts final 's' back in *)
                Insert(searchtable,word);
              END (* if then *);
            END (* if then else *);
          END (* if then *);
        END (* loop *);
      UNTIL empty(linequeue);
    END (* if then *);
    IF done
    THEN
      FOR ln := 1 TO linenumber-1 DO
        Texts.WriteString(t,edit[ln]);
      END (* for loop *);
```

```
        HALT;
      END (* if then *);
      END (* loop *);
    END CheckSpelling;

BEGIN (* EditSpell *)
  done := FALSE;
  ScClrScreen;
  ScGotoXY(0,6);
  CenterMessage("Quick-Spell-Edit");
  Spacebar;
  ScClrScreen;
  WriteLn; WriteLn;
  getfile(filename);
  fs := Create(textfile,filename);
  fs := Close(textfile);
  fs := Open(textfile,filename);
  ts := Connect(t,textfile);
  WriteLn;
  CenterMessage("Display misspelled words on P(rinter, S(creen -> ");
  ch := ReadKey(setofchar{'p','s','P','S'});
  on := (ch = 'p') OR (ch = 'P');
  Printer(on);
  (* Initialize search table *)
  CreateEmpty(searchtable);
  count := 0;
  ScClrScreen;
  ScGotoXY(0,0);
  CenterMessage("Insert text below ...");
  ScGotoXY(0,1);
  FOR i := 0 TO 79 DO
    Write('-');
  END (* for loop *);
  ScGotoXY(0,2);
  linenumber := 1;
  linepos    := 0;
  currentpos := 0;
  makeempty(linequeue);
  ClearVector(NIL, NIL, statusvector);
  IntHdlrInit(status, statusvector (* soft key interrupt *),
            15(* higher priority than keyboard so that the
            keyboard cannot interrupt the status report *),
            1000 (* stack size for process *),
            StatusLine (* procedure attached to the interrupt *) );
  IntHdlrInit(keyboard, KbdVector (* hardware interrupt *),
            14(* priority *), 1000 (* stack size for process *),
            GetText (* procedure attached to the interrupt *) );
  NEWPROCESS(CheckSpelling (* name of the procedure that is the
            process *), ADR(buffer) (* space for the system to keep
            track of the CheckSpelling process *), 1000 (* size
```

of the buffer *), spellprocess (* name of the
process *));
  TRANSFER(mainprocess, spellprocess);
  (* TRANSFER triggers the spelling checker process *)
END QuickSpellEdit.

DEFINITION MODULE SearchTable;

EXPORT QUALIFIED
  table, WordType, CreateEmpty, IsEmpty, Delete, Insert,
  Deallocate, Display;

  TYPE WordType = ARRAY[0..19] OF CHAR;

  TYPE element   = WordType;

  TYPE table;
  (* A data abstraction for a search table. This table maintains an
    alphabetized list of potentially misspelled words. *)

  PROCEDURE CreateEmpty(VAR T : table);
  (* Creates an empty table. *)

  PROCEDURE IsEmpty(T : table) : BOOLEAN;
  (* Returns true if table T is empty, otherwise false. *)

  PROCEDURE Delete(VAR T : (* in out *) table; E : element);
  (* Removes the element E in table T, if it is present. *)

  PROCEDURE Insert(VAR T : (* in out *) table; E : element);
  (* Inserts the element E into table T. *)

  PROCEDURE Deallocate(VAR T : table);
  (* This procedure removes table T from memory. *)

  PROCEDURE Display(T : table);
  (* Displays the elements of the table. *)

END SearchTable.

DEFINITION MODULE IntHdlr;
(* Written by Volition Systems and used with their permission. *)

EXPORT QUALIFIED
  INTHDLR,   IntHdlrInit,   IntHdlrProc,   IntHdlrTerm,
  CrtVector,   RemOutVector, KbdVector,   RemInVector,
  ParallelVector, Clock1Vector, Clock2Vector, Clock3Vector,
  Clock4Vector, BreakVector,   ExecErrVector;

```
CONST
  (* --- SAGE Specific --- *)

    ParallelVector  =   1;
    CrtVector       =   2;
    RemOutVector    =   3;
    KbdVector       =   4;
    RemInVector     =   5;
    Clock4Vector    =   6;
    Clock3Vector    =   7;
    Clock2Vector    =   8;
    Clock1Vector    =   9;
    BreakVector     =  14;
    ExecErrVector   =  15;

TYPE
    INTHDLR;
    IntHdlrProc    = PROCEDURE (CARDINAL);

PROCEDURE IntHdlrInit ( VAR h : INTHDLR;
                            v : CARDINAL;    (* vector *)
                            p : CARDINAL;    (* priority *)
                            s : CARDINAL;    (* size in stg units *)
                            x : IntHdlrProc ); (* user handler *)
    (* Attaches the procedure x to the interrupt handler h *)

PROCEDURE IntHdlrTerm ( VAR h : INTHDLR );
    (* Terminates the interrupt handler h *)

END IntHdlr.
```

```
DEFINITION MODULE Line;

FROM SYSTEM IMPORT WORD;

EXPORT QUALIFIED
    (* type *) LineType;

  TYPE LineType = ARRAY[0..79] OF CHAR;

END Line.
```

```
DEFINITION MODULE queueadt;

  (* As in Chapter 14, with "elementtype" replaced by "LineType" *)

END queueadt.
```

```
DEFINITION MODULE Dictionary;

FROM Line IMPORT
    (* type *)   LineType;
```

```
FROM SearchTable IMPORT
  (* type *)   WordType;
EXPORT QUALIFIED
  InDictionary, FetchWord;
PROCEDURE InDictionary(w : WordType) : BOOLEAN;
  (* Returns true if word w is in the dictionary. *)
PROCEDURE FetchWord(line : LineType; VAR linepos (* in out *):
        CARDINAL) : WordType;
  (* Returns a word from a line starting at position linepos.  The
    lineposition (linepos) of the beginning of the word is updated. *)
END Dictionary.
```

high level system integration is correct (all external procedure calls from the main program use the correct interface) by performing type checking across compilation boundaries. All the abstractions that are required to solve the problem are present at the design level. The design code contains the framework within which the finished software product may be later implemented. The software will not run until five implementation modules have been written and tested.

Study the design listing carefully and examine the main program Quick-SpellEdit against the background of the steps outlined in the informal strategy.

To test quickly the design concepts represented in the modular design listing, it is desirable to use rapid prototyping. A quick and simple implementation of the dictionary and search table abstractions provides an initial working version of the system for testing. We assume that the modules queueadt and IntHdlr are available as preexisting software components.

For purposes of rapid prototyping, we may wish to implement a small dictionary using an array of, for example, 50 words. The important procedure InDictionary can be implemented using an inefficient linear search. Likewise, the SearchTable abstraction can be implemented as an array of 100 words (impractical for the final implementation, but easy to implement). The performance of the system using the rapid prototype implementations will be poor and will not meet the software requirements (i.e., a 5000-word dictionary). The spelling checker will lag the editor and the queue of text lines will quickly reach capacity. For this reason, the testing should be done using a relatively small text file. Once the process of testing has confirmed that the design organization is correct, it is appropriate to replace each of the simple implementations with better implementations that meet the requirements.

When changes are made in implementation modules Dictionary and SearchTable, only these modules need to be recompiled. The rest of the software system need not be modified or recompiled, although on most systems it will need to be linked again.

In actually testing the system, several dictionary structures and several search table structures were tested. The final search table implementation was constructed using a height-balanced binary search tree (see Kruse, 1984). This data structure provides for efficient maintenance of a list of alphabetized words.

After testing several dictionary structures, the final dictionary implementation was constructed using a hash table. This structure proved to be both memory and execution speed efficient.

We wish to underscore the sharp delineation and interplay between the design of the system and its implementation. The first major step in the object-oriented design was the development of an informal strategy. The informal strategy led to an identification of the processes and important data abstractions that constitute the system and the partitioning of the system into modules, each specifying an abstraction. Upon completing the object-oriented design, the first implementation step used rapid prototyping to develop a crude version of the final system. After verifying that the design concepts were correct, the crude implementations were replaced with a series of more refined implementations.

Thus far we have presented only the system design, even though we have displayed many lines of program design code. As indicated earlier, all the final implementation details are not shown because our main concern here is software design. In the exercises we ask you to experiment with some implementation details.

17.5 A Modula-2 Case Conversion Preprocessor

In Chapter 2 we mentioned that Modula-2 is unique among common programming languages in that it considers uppercase and lowercase letters in identifiers to be distinct. The reserved words must appear in uppercase, and many of the predefined identifiers are all uppercase or mixed case. These requirements make it more difficult for the programmer to enter a program, both because of the increased number of keystrokes required and because of the need to remember which cases are used where. To simplify the program entry process for the human programmer, we would like to let the computer do more of the work. In this section we develop a table-driven preprocessor program that converts a program written in mostly or all lowercase into a program with appropriate mixed case.

The design of this program illustrates two important points of software design. The first is the use of data abstraction to help in the design and in the prototype implementation. We have made this point many times before, but its importance cannot be overstated. The second point is the use of an algorithm based on the finite-state machine model. This model has many applications and is another technique that a software developer should know.

Let us start by examining at a very high level the idea for this program. A program file will be the input; this is a file of characters. The program reads these characters, and looks for sequences that constitute identifiers. Each identifier is looked up in a table containing the identifiers that should be converted to a particular pattern of mixed case or uppercase. If it is found, the identifier is converted; if not, it remains unchanged. The program produces an output file that is identical to the input except for the converted identifiers.

We can recognize quickly a data abstraction that will be needed, the symbol table. The only operation we will need is symbol conversion. This operation is given a symbol (an identifier), and returns it either converted as required, if it appears in the table, or intact if it is not in the table. Inherent in the concept of symbol or identifier is character string. We have already developed the string data type (Chapters 14 and 15), so it will be a relatively easy matter to select and use the operations needed. We can therefore write the definition module for the symbol table abstraction, as shown in Program 17.2.

To increase the flexibility of this table-driven program (in which all symbol conversions are based on values in a table), we will store the table in a file and read it in when the program needs it. Thus different users of this program are free to supply different files containing different symbols. We might assume that each such file would contain all the reserved words and standard procedures and functions, but each file might contain a different selection of symbols

---

Program 17.2 Symbol Table Definition Module

DEFINITION MODULE symboltable;

  (∗ This module provides a table of symbols that should be converted
    when encountered in a program. ∗)

FROM strings IMPORT
  (∗ type ∗) string;

EXPORT QUALIFIED
  (∗ proc ∗) convert;

PROCEDURE convert
  (VAR sym : string (∗ in/out ∗));

END symboltable.

---

from various library modules. With this approach, the module initialization code for the symbol table module must read in the appropriate file and store it in a suitable data structure.

There are many data structures and algorithms for tables that must be searched. Perhaps the simplest is an unordered array in which we do a linear search. More sophisticated structures include ordered arrays in which we could do a binary search, a binary search tree, and a hash table. Again, we do not need to make an irrevocable decision on a data structure at this point in the design. Instead, in our prototype we will choose one that seems simple and easy to implement. If performance requirements later dictate a faster search, we can simply replace the symbol table implementation module. Nothing else in the program will need to change.

With this in mind, let us choose a linear search. However, we will take one small step toward speed, namely, we will recognize that the set of symbols in the table is relatively small (probably between 100 and 200) and that the symbols are of various lengths. If we organize the table as an array and put all symbols of the same length together, we will need to search only a small segment of the table to find a symbol of a known length. For small tables, a linear search can be faster than one of the more sophisticated search techniques, and each segment of our table will be a small table. To facilitate the search, we will keep a second table that gives the lower and upper subscripts of the appropriate segment of the table for each symbol length. If the symbol data file is organized with all symbols of the same length appearing together, it will be simple enough to build this second table as the symbol table is read.

We note also that the frequency of appearance of symbols, such as reserved words, varies greatly. If we organize our data file such that within each group of symbols of the same length, the higher frequency symbols precede the lower frequency symbols, the linear search will be even faster. To do this, we might have the symbol table module count the number of times we look up each symbol. After running the program for several weeks, we would restructure the symbol file in the appropriate order.

The symbol table will contain entries that consist of two symbols. The raw symbol will always be all lowercase, while the actual symbol will be the uppercase or mixed case as supplied in the symbol file. When we look up a symbol, we simply try to match a raw symbol. A successful match causes us to convert the symbol to the actual symbol. This approach allows a programmer to override the conversion process by using a symbol with at least one uppercase letter. Such a symbol will not match a raw symbol, hence will not be converted.

We can now discuss the complete implementation module for the symbol table. The module initialization code must create the symbol table and the segment limit table. The major portion of this code is a loop that reads a symbol from the symbol file, stores it as an actual symbol, converts it to all lowercase, and stores it as a raw symbol. Since this involves both strings and characters, we can make use of some other data abstractions.

First, to read in the symbol, we declare an array of characters named symbol. After it has been read, we can use the string operation **convertarray** to convert it to the string data type; hence this operation is imported from the strings module. Second, to convert the letters in the symbol to lowercase, we import the procedure **lowercase** from the module named **Alpha**. This module is a collection of small procedures that manipulate alphabetic data; it is not a standard Modula-2 library module. The procedure we need is a function procedure that is the counterpart to the standard **CAP** function procedure. It is shown in Program 17.3.

The rest of the implementation module is straightforward. To simplify the process of reading in symbols, a procedure named **readsymbol** is present. The only other point we should mention is the construction of the segment limit table. A variable **prevlen** keeps track of the length of the previous symbol. When a symbol of a different length is read, it marks the end of one segment and the beginning of the next, so this information is recorded in the limit table.

Program 17.3 Lowercase Procedure

```
PROCEDURE lowercase
  ( character : CHAR (* in *) ) : CHAR;
BEGIN
  IF ( 'A' <= character ) AND ( character <= 'Z' )
    THEN RETURN CHAR ( ORD ( character ) + 32 )
    ELSE RETURN character
  END
END lowercase;
```

Remember that the data file is organized in groups of symbols having the same length.

The table file is terminated by an empty line, which the input procedure recognizes as a symbol of length zero. This gives the exit condition for the main loop in this module.

Program 17.4 is the implementation module for the symbol table abstraction. Since the operations on files differ from one Modula-2 implementation to another, readers should not worry about the open operation in this module being different from what they may have used before. Since the FileSystem module is always implementation dependent, we expect small portability problems with this module.

Program 17.4 Symbol Table Implementation Module

```
IMPLEMENTATION MODULE symboltable;

  (* This module provides a table of symbols that should be converted
     when encountered in a program. *)

FROM FileSystem IMPORT
  (* const *) EOL,
  (* type  *) File,
  (* proc  *) Open, Close, ReadChar;

FROM strings IMPORT
  (* type  *) string,
  (* proc  *) define, copy, equal, length, convertarray;

FROM Alpha IMPORT
  (* proc  *) lowercase;

CONST
  tablesize  = 200;
  maxlength  = 16;

TYPE
  symbolpair = RECORD
                 rawsym    : string;
                 actualsym : string
               END;
```

```
table       = ARRAY [ 1..tablesize ] OF symbolpair;
segment     = RECORD
                lower : CARDINAL;
                upper : CARDINAL
              END;
limittable  = ARRAY [ 1..maxlength ] OF segment;
chararray   = ARRAY [ 1..maxlength ] OF CHAR;

VAR
  symtable   :  table;
  tablelen   :  CARDINAL;
  limit      :  limittable;
  symfile    :  File;
  symbol     :  chararray;
  symlen     :  CARDINAL;
  endoffile  :  BOOLEAN;
  prevlen    :  CARDINAL;
  pos        :  CARDINAL;

PROCEDURE readsymbol
  ( VAR sym : chararray  (* out *);
    VAR len : CARDINAL (* out *) );

  VAR ch : CHAR;

BEGIN
  len := 0;
  LOOP
    ReadChar ( symfile, ch );
    IF ch = EOL THEN EXIT END;
    INC ( len );
    sym[ len ] := ch
  END
END readsymbol;


PROCEDURE convert
  ( VAR sym : string (* in/out *) );

  VAR pos : CARDINAL;
      len : CARDINAL;

BEGIN
  len := length ( sym );
  IF len <= maxlength
    THEN pos := limit[ len ].lower;
      LOOP
        IF pos > limit[ len ].upper THEN EXIT END;
        IF equal ( sym, symtable[ pos ].rawsym )
          THEN copy ( symtable[ pos ].actualsym, sym );
          EXIT
        END;
```

```
              INC ( pos )
          END
      END
  END convert;
BEGIN
    Open ( symfile, 'symbols', FALSE );
    (* make each table segment empty initially *)
    FOR symlen := 1 TO maxlength DO
      limit[ symlen ].lower := 1;
      limit[ symlen ].upper := 0
    END;
    tablelen  := 0;
    prevlen   := 0;
    endoffile := FALSE;
    LOOP
      readsymbol ( symbol, symlen );
      IF symlen = 0 THEN EXIT END; (* eof is blank line *)
      INC ( tablelen );
      define ( symtable[ tablelen ].actualsym );
      convertarray ( symbol, symlen, symtable[ tablelen ].actualsym );
      FOR pos := 1 TO symlen DO
        symbol[ pos ] := lowercase ( symbol[ pos ] )
      END;
      define ( symtable[ tablelen ].rawsym );
      convertarray ( symbol, symlen, symtable[ tablelen ].rawsym );
      limit[ symlen ].upper := tablelen;
      IF symlen < > prevlen
        THEN limit[ symlen ].lower := tablelen;
             prevlen := symlen
      END
    END;
    Close ( symfile )
END symboltable.
```

We can now design the main program for the case converter. The most difficult part of the design is determining how to recognize identifiers. It is not simply a search for sequences of letters and digits. We must be able to recognize comments and literal strings, each of which can contain sequences of characters that look like identifiers, but are not. Recognition of strings is relatively simple; we look for an apostrophe or quotation mark and treat every character up to the next occurrence of the same delimiter as a string. Comments are a little more difficult, since they may be nested. We will need to keep track of how many levels of nesting we have seen, to know when we are out of the comments and back in the program code. Finally, there may be character sequences inside comments that look like literal strings, and vice versa. Thus not every apostrophe begins a string, and not every left parenthesis–asterisk pair begins a comment.

The algorithm we use is based on the finite-state machine model. Such a machine is a very simple abstract computing device that can exist only in a finite number of states. We can think of a state as representing a summary of the input data so far. Each new piece of data (in this case each new character) can cause us to change states. Each such state transition can also cause us to produce some output.

For this program, we normally print each character as it is read. The exception consists of characters that make up identifiers; these are to be accumulated until the end of the identifier is found and converted as dictated by the symbol table. Therefore, the design of the program is directed toward recognizing symbols.

We define first a state called startstate. While in this state, each character read is printed immediately unless it is the first character of an identifier (in Modula-2 this means a letter). Once a letter has been found, we make a transition into a new state called insymbol, and we stay in this state as long as we continue to see characters that form an identifier (letters and digits). Any other character terminates the symbol, so we can convert it and output it.

An apostrophe or quotation mark will cause us to make a transition to a state called instring. We will stay in this state as long as we do not see a second apostrophe or quotation mark, which terminates the string and sends us back to startstate. Since strings do not require conversion, we output them as soon as we read them.

A left parenthesis might be the start of a comment. When we encounter one, we will go into a state called enteringcomment. If the next input character is an asterisk, we know we are beginning a comment, so we make a transition to the state called incomment; otherwise we will go back to startstate. A similar process occurs when we are processing a comment and encounter an asterisk. We make a transition to a state called exitingcomment. If the next character is a right parenthesis, we are out of the comment and back in startstate; otherwise we remain in the state incomment.

The preceding paragraph is valid if we ignore nested comments. To handle these, we must use a variable called commentlevel to count the level of comment nesting. Upon recognizing the left parenthesis–asterisk pair, we increment this variable, and upon recognizing the asterisk–right parenthesis pair we decrement it. Only if the decrement process makes it zero do we really get out of the comment and back to startstate; otherwise we stay in the state incomment.

All these transitions are summarized in Figure 17.3, which is called a *state transition* diagram. The circles represent states, and the arrows represent transitions. The characters that cause each transition are written next to the arrows.

The main program is relatively simple. After opening the files and doing some other initialization, it enters a loop that reads a character and performs a state transition. In the procedure performtransition, a large case statement determines what is done, depending on the current state. Within each part of the case, the current input character determines what is done. In most cases, we assign a new state and output the character. In the special cases discussed

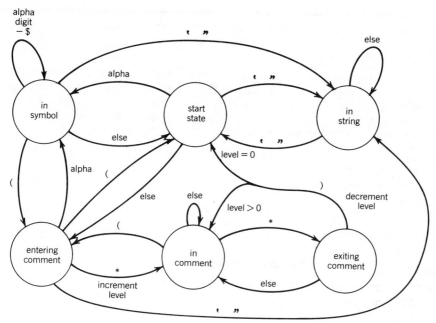

FIGURE 17.3 Case Converter State Transition Diagram

above, we do some additional actions, such as saving the character as part of the symbol, remembering the string delimiter, or changing the comment nesting level. The reader is urged to study this procedure to see that it corresponds to Figure 17.3.

Two other points can be mentioned. To accumulate characters of an identifier, we use a character array as we did in the symbol table abstraction. Then we transform it to a string before doing the case conversion. We have chosen to use the dynamic string abstraction, and therefore must define the symbol string before using it. Also, at one point in the program we must distinguish the characters that can be in an identifier from those that cannot. To simplify this operation, we use the character set data abstraction developed in Section 14.4. The variable identchars needs to contain all the letters (both cases) and all the digits. This program was developed using a Modula-2 implementation (the University of Hamburg compiler for the DEC VAX/VMS computer systems) that also allows the underscore and dollar sign characters in identifiers, so these were added to the set. The inset operation allows us to recognize all these characters quickly. Again we see that reusing previously developed modules aids in the rapid development of a software system.

The program module for the case conversion system is shown in Program 17.5.

The finite-state machine model can often be used to simplify the design of software. It is especially useful when, as here, an input sequence is to be scanned for a variety of special subsequences. This model is often used in the

Program 17.5 Case Conversion System Program Module

MODULE CaseConverter;

> (* This program accepts as input a Modula-2 program written primarily in
> lower case, and produces a copy of that program with reserved words
> and imported symbols converted to upper or mixed case as needed.
> The case of letters in strings and comments is left unchanged, as is
> the case of letters in identifiers not recognized as reserved words or
> imported symbols. *)

FROM FileSystem IMPORT
  (* const *) EOL,
  (* type *) File,
  (* proc *) Create, Open, Close, ReadChar, WriteChar, Eof;

FROM strings IMPORT
  (* type *) string,
  (* proc *) define, convertarray, writestring;

FROM symboltable IMPORT
  (* proc *) convert;

FROM characterset IMPORT
  (* const *) alphabet, digits,
  (* type *) charset,
  (* proc *) include, inset, union;

CONST
  buffersize = 80;

TYPE
  states   = (startstate, insymbol, instring, incomment,
                enteringcomment, exitingcomment);
  chararray = ARRAY [1..buffersize] OF CHAR;

VAR
  infile   : File;   (* input program file   *)
  outfile   : File;   (* output program file   *)
  currentstate : states;   (* state of the machine   *)
  character   : CHAR;   (* current input character *)
  buffer   : chararray; (* identifier being scanned *)
  bufferlen   : CARDINAL;   (* length of identifier   *)
  symbol   : string;   (* identifier as a string   *)
  delimiter   : CHAR;   (* string delimiter " or ' *)
  commentlevel : CARDINAL;   (* comment nesting level   *)
  identchars   : charset;   (* legal chars in identifiers *)

PROCEDURE openfiles;

BEGIN
  (* This procedure is system dependent *)
  Open (infile, 'input', FALSE);
  Create (outfile, 'output', TRUE, TRUE)
END openfiles;

```
PROCEDURE closefiles;

BEGIN
  (* This procedure is system dependent *)
  Close ( infile );
  Close ( outfile )
END closefiles;

PROCEDURE performtransition
  ( VAR state : states (* in/out *);
        ch    : CHAR (* in      *) );

BEGIN
  CASE state OF

    startstate :
      CASE ch OF
        'A'..'Z', 'a'..'z' : state := insymbol;
                             buffer[ 1 ] := ch;
                             bufferlen := 1 |
        '('                : state := enteringcomment;
                             WriteChar ( outfile, ch )    |
        '''', """"         : state := instring;
                             delimiter := ch;
                             WriteChar ( outfile, ch )
        ELSE                 WriteChar ( outfile, ch )
      END |

    insymbol :
      IF inset ( ch, identchars )
        THEN INC ( bufferlen );
             buffer[ bufferlen ] := ch
        ELSE convertarray ( buffer, bufferlen, symbol );
             convert ( symbol );
             writestring ( outfile, symbol );
             WriteChar ( outfile, ch );
             CASE ch OF
                 '('        : state := enteringcomment |
                 '''', """" : state := instring;
                             delimiter := ch
                 ELSE        state := startstate
             END
      END |

    instring :
      IF ch = delimiter
        THEN state := startstate
      END;
      WriteChar ( outfile, ch ) |
```

```
    enteringcomment :
      IF ( commentlevel = 0 ) OR ( ch = '*' )
        THEN CASE ch OF
            'A'..'Z', 'a'..'z' : state := insymbol;
                                 buffer[ 1 ] := ch;
                                 bufferlen := 1 |
            '*'                : state := incomment;
                                 INC ( commentlevel );
                                 WriteChar ( outfile, ch ) |
            '''', ''''''       : state := instring;
                                 delimiter := ch;
                                 WriteChar ( outfile, ch )
            ELSE               state := startstate;
                                 WriteChar ( outfile, ch )
          END
        ELSE state := incomment;
             WriteChar ( outfile, ch )
        END |

    incomment :
      IF ch = '(' THEN
        state := enteringcomment
      ELSIF ch = '*' THEN
        state := exitingcomment
      END;
      WriteChar ( outfile, ch ) |

    exitingcomment :
      IF ch = ')'
        THEN DEC ( commentlevel );
             IF commentlevel > 0
               THEN state := incomment
               ELSE state := startstate
             END
        ELSE state := incomment
      END;
      WriteChar ( outfile, ch )
  END
END performtransition;

BEGIN
  union ( alphabet, digits, identchars );
  include ( identchars, '_' );
  include ( identchars, '$' );
  currentstate := startstate;
  define ( symbol );
  openfiles;
  WHILE NOT Eof ( infile ) DO
    ReadChar ( infile, character );
    performtransition ( currentstate, character )
  END;
  closefiles
END CaseConverter.
```

first phase of a compiler, called a *scanner,* which breaks the program character sequence into *tokens.* These tokens include identifiers, numeric and string literals, reserved words, operators, delimiters, and comments. The tokens are then passed to the *parser* and the later phases of the compiler. A scanner for Modula-2 will have approximately 25 states, and its design is an interesting exercise for the reader.

17.6 Summary

Abstraction and data hiding play a central role in engineering reliable and easily maintainable software systems using object-oriented design. Because of the modular structure of an object-oriented design, later maintenance changes can be localized to the particular implementation modules in which they occur without requiring changes or recompilation elsewhere in the software system.

In object-oriented design, a set of "conceptual sockets" is specified. Each "conceptual socket" consists of a definition module, usually containing the declaration of an abstract data type.

Experience shows that much of software maintenance is necessitated by changes or refinements in requirements and specifications. If it were possible to produce quickly a prototype version of a software system, the users could evaluate it and identify where requirements were incorrectly defined or misinterpreted by the developers. Several iterations of this process can lead to software that meets requirements and specifications. Modula-2 supports rapid prototyping because of the separation that may be achieved between the specification of a module (subsystem) and its implementation.

17.7 Exercises

1. Design a tic-tac-toe game using object-oriented design. You may wish to treat the board, score, board lines (three horizontal, three vertical, and two diagonal), and moves as data abstractions. Display an informal strategy and a design listing.

2. Write two versions each of the remaining implementation modules for the editor–spelling checker given in Section 17.4.

3. Modify the editor–spelling checker to check 20,000 rather than 5000 words. Do you expect any changes in the data structure and algorithms required for dictionary lookup? Why?

4. List four software development projects that may be designed using the process abstraction. For each project, state an informal strategy, identify all the processes, and sketch an initial modular design chart.

5. Develop a scanner for the Modula-2 language, using the techniques described in Section 17.5.

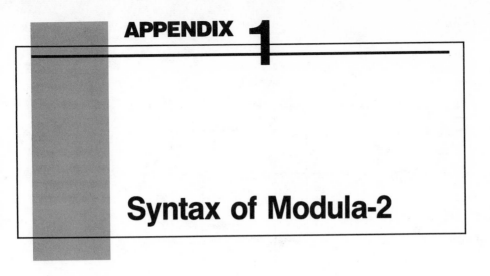

APPENDIX 1

Syntax of Modula-2

This appendix presents the collected syntax charts for Modula-2. A complete BNF description of the language may be found in Spector (1983).

compilation unit

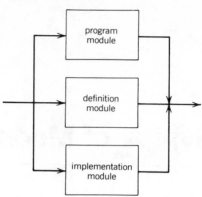

program module

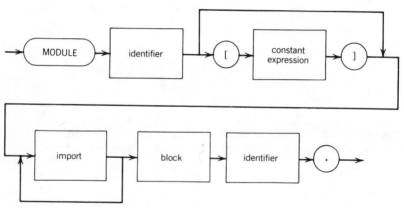

definition module

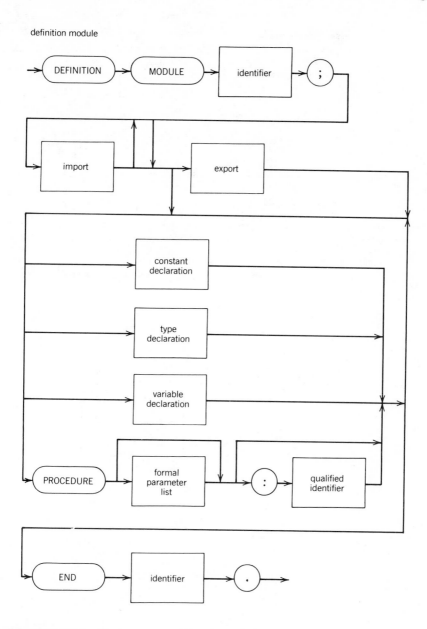

implementation module

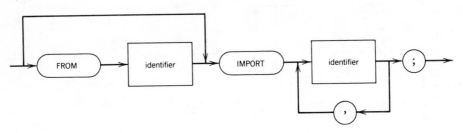

import

export

block

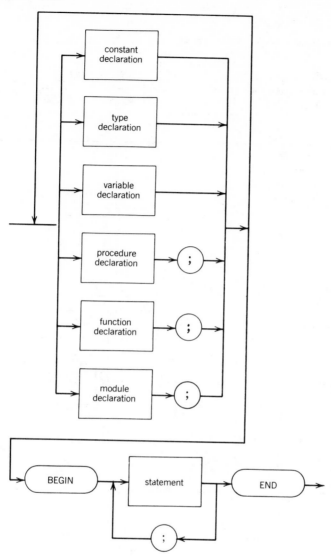

procedure declaration

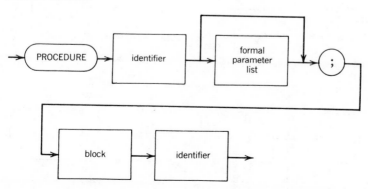

function declaration

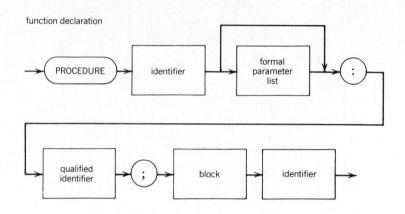

formal parameter list

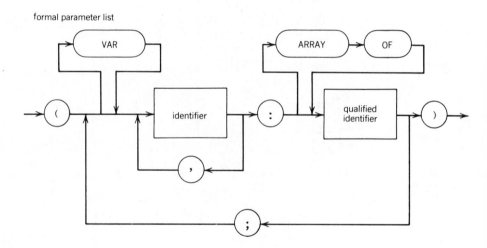

module declaration

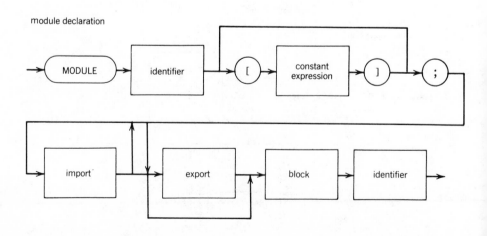

statement

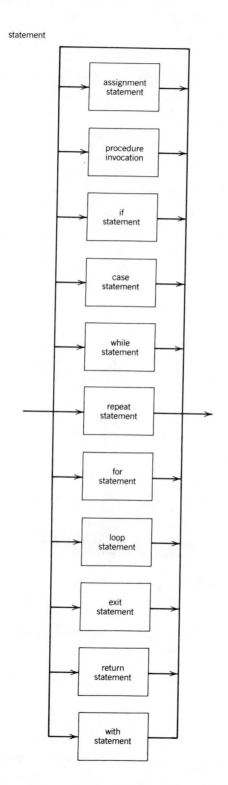

assignment statement

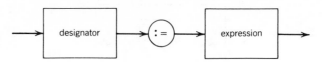

if statement

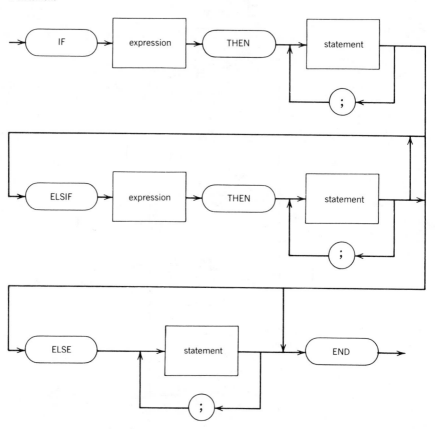

case statement

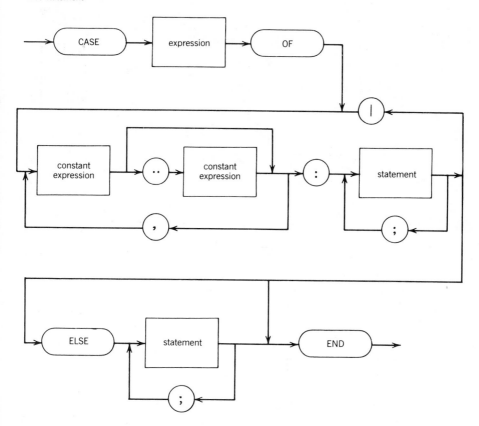

variable declaration

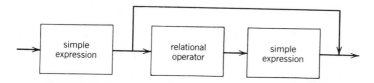

expression

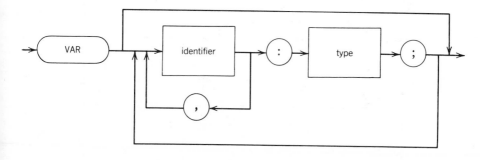

simple expression

term

factor

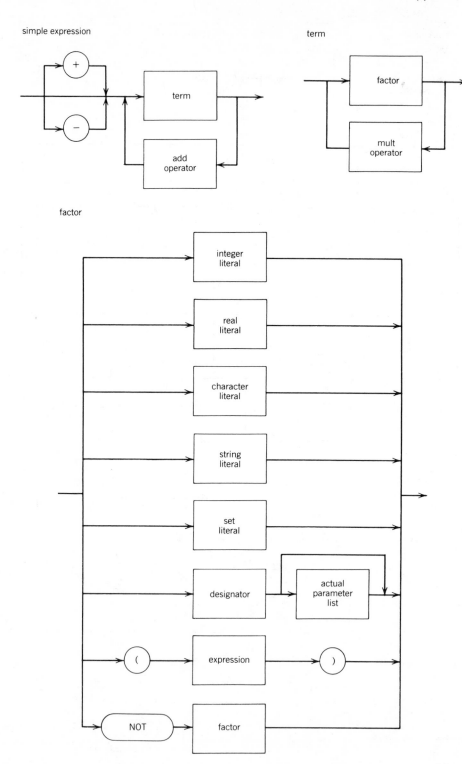

designator

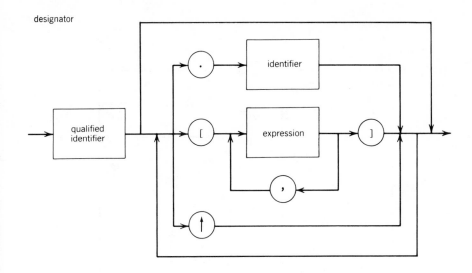

constant expression

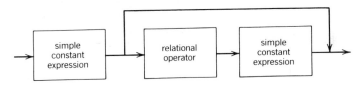

simple constant expression

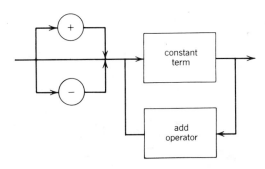

constant term

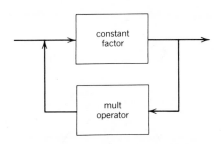

constant factor

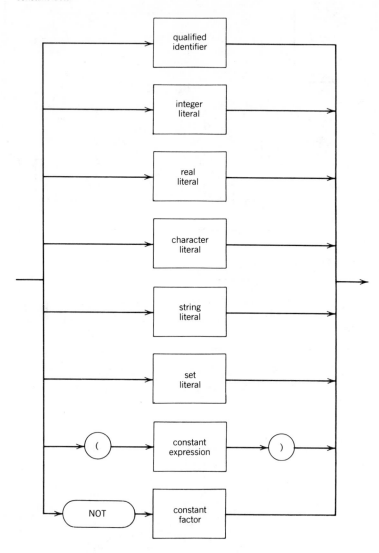

relational operator

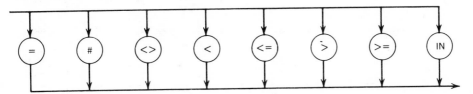

add operator

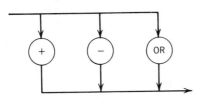

mult operator

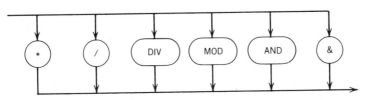

integer literal

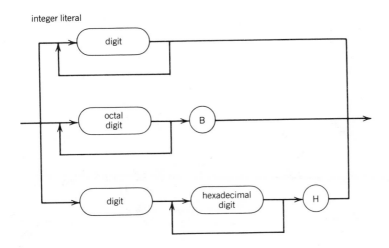

real literal

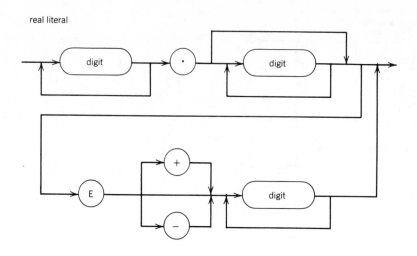

character literal

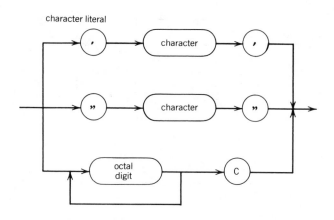

string literal

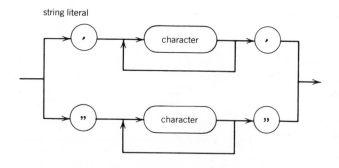

set literal

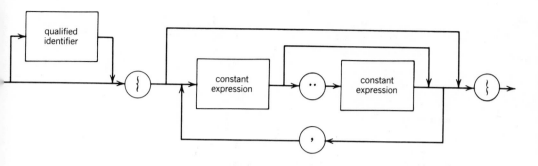

identifier

qualified identifier

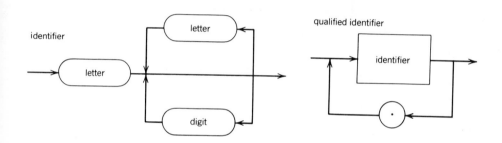

absolute address

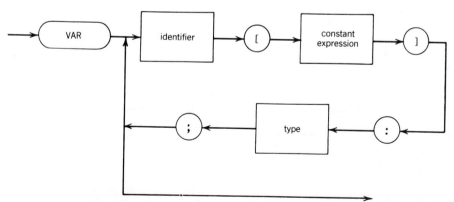

monitor

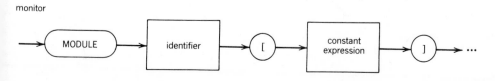

while statement

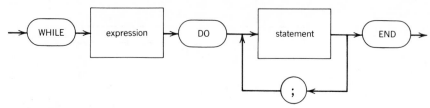

repeat statement

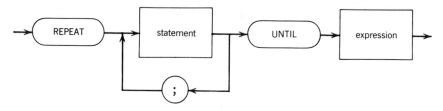

for statement

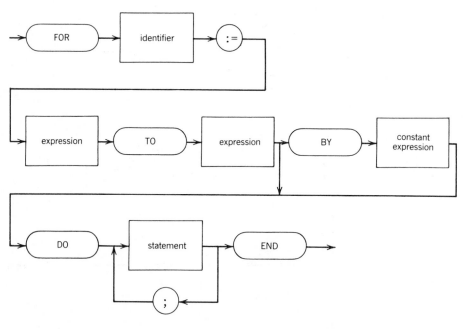

loop statement

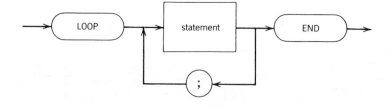

exit statement

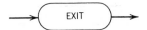

with statement

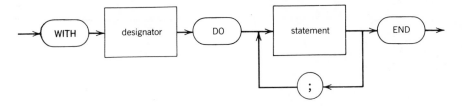

procedure invocation

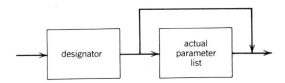

actual parameter list

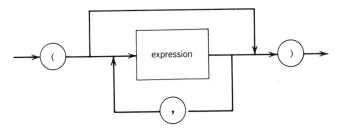

return statement

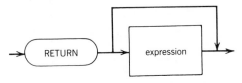

constant declaration

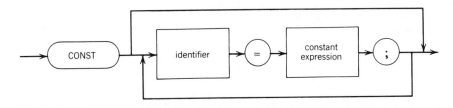

type declaration

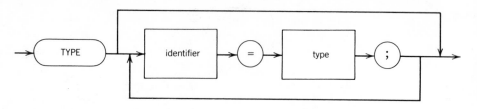

type

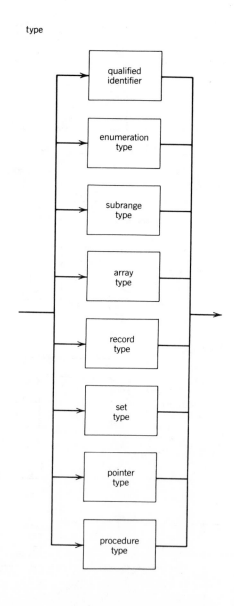

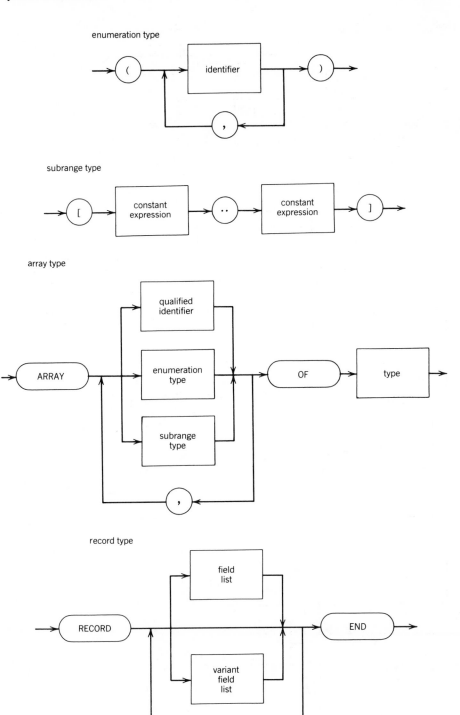

field list

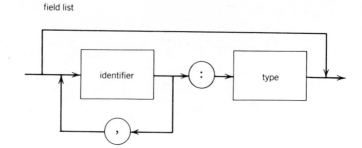

variant field list

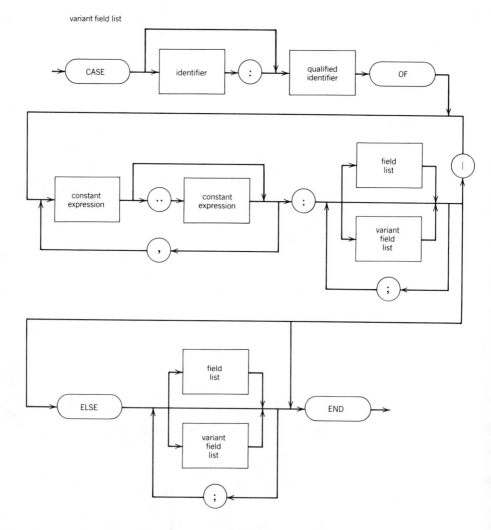

set type

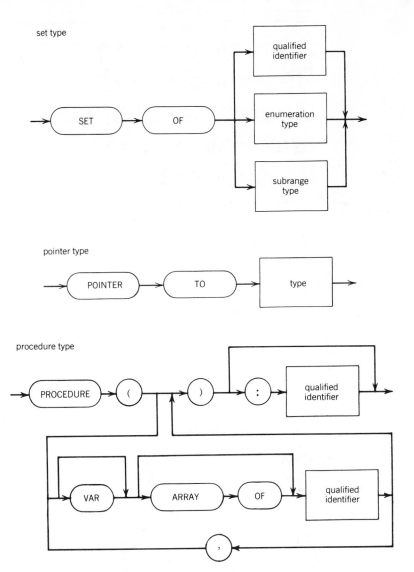

pointer type

procedure type

Summary of Modula-2 Reserved Words, Operators, Delimiters, and Predefined Procedures

Reserved Words in Modula-2

AND	LOOP
ARRAY	MOD
BEGIN	MODULE
BY	NOT
CASE	OF
CONST	OR
DEFINITION	POINTER
DIV	PROCEDURE
DO	QUALIFIED
ELSE	RECORD
ELSIF	REPEAT
END	RETURN
EXIT	SET
EXPORT	THEN
FOR	TO
FROM	TYPE
IF	UNTIL
IMPLEMENTATION	VAR
IMPORT	WHILE
IN	WITH

Operators and Delimiters in Modula-2

+	unary plus, addition, set union
−	unary minus, subtraction, set difference
*	multiplication, set intersection
/	real division, symmetric set difference
:=	assignment
&	boolean and
=	equal
<>	not equal
#	not equal
<	less than
>	greater than
<=	less than or equal to, subset
>=	greater than or equal to, superset
^	pointer dereference
( )	parentheses
[ ]	array index brackets
{ }	set braces
(* *)	comment delimiters
..	subrange delimiter
.	period
,	comma
;	semicolon
:	colon
|	alternative delimiter

Summary of Modula-2 Predefined Procedures

ABS (x)	absolute value function; x is numeric
ADR (v)	address function; v is a variable (exported from SYSTEM)
CAP (c)	capitalization function; c is a character
CHR (n)	character transfer function; n is a cardinal
DEC (x)	decrement procedure; x is a scalar value other than real,
DEC (x, n)	n is a cardinal
DISPOSE (p)	storage deallocation procedure; p is a pointer, optional
DISPOSE (p, ...)	parameters are variant record tags
EXCL (s, x)	exclude procedure; s is a set, x is an element of the base type of the set
FLOAT (n)	real conversion function; n is a cardinal
HALT	halt procedure
HIGH (a)	high index procedure; a is an open array, low index is assumed to be zero
INC (x)	increment procedure; x is a scalar value other than real,
INC (x, n)	n is a cardinal
INCL (s, x)	include procedure; s is a set, x is an element of the base type of the set

NEW (p)	storage allocation procedure; p is a pointer, optional
NEW (p, ...)	parameters are variant record tags
ODD (n)	odd function; n is an integer or a cardinal
ORD (s)	ordinal function; s is a scalar value other than real
SIZE (v)	size function; v is a variable (exported from SYSTEM)
TRUNC (r)	truncate function; r is a nonnegative real
TSIZE (t)	size function; t is a type identifier, optional parameters
TSIZE (t, ...)	are variant record tags (exported from SYSTEM)
VAL (t, n)	value transfer function; t is a type identifier, n is a cardinal

Recently Proposed Changes to Modula-2

This appendix summarizes the changes to the Modula-2 language that have been proposed by its designer, Niklaus Wirth. Each change is keyed to the section of the book in which the affected language feature is discussed. Programmers are urged to examine their own implementations carefully to determine which, if any, of these changes have been incorporated.

An implementation may include additional numeric data types. The identifiers LONGCARD, LONGINT, and LONGREAL are new predefined identifiers for these data types. (4.1.1, 4.1.2)

The boolean operator NOT may also be indicated by the tilde character ~. (4.1.3)

A character string of length one is assignment compatible with the CHAR data type. (4.1.4, 5)

The base type of a subrange of whole numbers is determined by the lower bound of the range. If that bound is signed, the base type is INTEGER; otherwise the base type is CARDINAL. (4.1.6)

A subrange definition may be preceded by the type identifier of the base type of the subrange, which therefore allows unambiguous specification of the base type. (4.1.6)

In a variant record definition with no tag field, the colon between the tag and the tag type must be present, as in the following example:

CASE : BOOLEAN OF

This simplifies the recognition of an identifier as a tag rather than a tag type. (4.2.2)

The unary minus may be used to denote the operation of set complement relative to the base type of the set. (4.2.3)

Elements of sets need not be constants. A constant set may contain constant expressions as elements; a set may contain expressions as elements. (4.2.3)

The symbol <> for the inequality relational operator is no longer allowed. Only the # symbol denotes that operator. (4.4.1)

Two new predefined functions MIN and MAX are defined. Each is given a single parameter that must be a type identifier of a scalar type other than real. They return the minimum and maximum values, respectively, of that type. (4.4.2)

The while and if statements may be defined in additional forms that allow more than one expression and body within a single statement. The syntax of these new forms is still to be specified. (6.2.1, 6.3.1)

A case statement may have a null or empty case, which contains no case labels and no statements. The effect of this change is to allow multiple case delimiter bars to appear consecutively. (6.2.2)

The loop control variable in a for statement must be compatible with the types of the value range expressions, not merely assignment compatible. (6.3.3)

A function procedure may return a value of any structured type, not just a scalar type. (7.1, 7.2)

Every entity declared in a definition module is exported. The export list is not needed. For compatibility with existing programs, an export list will be treated as a comment. (11.2, 11.3.1)

All import lists will begin with the reserved word FROM. Importing an entire module, previously written:

IMPORT modulename;

is now written:

FROM modulename IMPORT;

This change primarily benefits the implementor rather than the user of Modula-2. (11.2)

Assignment and equality (inequality) are defined on opaque types. An implementation may restrict the types that may be opaque, but such types will normally include pointers and any other one word types. (11.2, 12.3)

A procedure within a module defined with a priority may not invoke a procedure in a module with a lower priority. If a procedure within a module defined with a priority invokes a procedure in a module without a priority, the priority of the invoking procedure is maintained during the execution of the invoked procedure. (16.5)

References

ACM SIGSOFT Rapid Prototyping Workshop. 1982. *ACM Software Engineering News,* Vol. 7, No. 5, December.

Ben-Ari, M. 1982. *Principles of Concurrent Programming.* Englewood Cliffs, NJ: Prentice-Hall International.

Boehm, B. 1981. *Software Engineering Economics.* Englewood Cliffs, NJ: Prentice-Hall.

Cheney, W., and D. Kincaid. 1980. *Numerical Mathematics and Computing.* Monterey, CA: Brooks/Cole.

DeMarco, T. 1979. *Structured Analysis and System Specification.* Englewood Cliffs, NJ: Prentice-Hall.

Dijkstra, E. W. 1968. "Cooperating Sequential Processes," in F. Genuys (Ed.), *Programming Languages.* New York: Academic Press.

Downs, V. A., and S. J. Goldsack. 1982. *Programming Embedded Systems with Ada.* Englewood Cliffs, NJ: Prentice-Hall.

Jackson, M. A. 1975. *Principles of Program Design.* New York: Academic Press.

Jensen, K., and N. Wirth. 1974. *Pascal—User Manual and Report.* Heidelberg: Springer-Verlag.

Knuth, D. 1973. *The Art of Computer Programming,* Vol. 1: *Fundamental Algorithms.* Reading, MA: Addison-Wesley.

Kruse, R. L. 1984. Data Structures and Program Design. Englewood Cliffs, NJ: Prentice-Hall.

Myers, G. 1978. *Composite Structured Design.* New York: Van Nostrand.

Olsen, E. W., and S. B. Whitehill. 1983. *Ada for Programmers.* Reston, VA: Reston.

Reingold, E., J. Nievergelt, and N. Deo. 1977. *Combinatorial Algorithms: Theory and Practice*. Englewood Cliffs, NJ: Prentice-Hall.

Roberts, E. 1985. Thinking Recursively. New York: Wiley.

Sage Computer Technology, 4905 Energy Way, Reno, NV 89502.

Spector, D. 1983. "Lexing and Parsing Modula-2," *ACM SIGPLAN Notices*, Vol. 18, No. 10, pp. 25–32.

Tremblay, J. P., and P. G. Sorenson. 1976. *An Introduction to Data Structures with Applications*. New York: McGraw-Hill.

Volition Systems, P.O. Box 1236, Del Mar, CA 92014.

Warshall, S. 1962. "A Theorem on Boolean Matrices," *J. ACM,* Vol. 9, No. 1, pp. 11–12.

Wiener, R. 1984. "Generic Sorting in Modula-2," *J. Pascal Ada,* Vol. 3, No. 1, pp. 33–36.

Wiener, R., and R. Sincovec. 1983. *Programming in Ada*. New York: Wiley.

Wiener, R., and R. Sincovec. 1984. *Software Engineering with Modula-2 and Ada*. New York: Wiley.

Wirth, N. 1982. *Programming in Modula-2*. Heidelberg: Springer-Verlag.

Yourdan, E., and L. Constantine. 1979. *Structured Design*. Englewood Cliffs, NJ: Prentice-Hall.

INDEX